TEACHING YOUNG CHILDREN *in* MULTICULTURAL CLASSROOMS

ISSUES, CONCEPTS, AND STRATEGIES

4th Edition

Wilma Robles de Meléndez
Nova Southeastern University

Vesna Beck
Nova Southeastern University

WADSWORTH
CENGAGE Learning·

Australia • Brazil • Japan • Korea • Mexico • Singapore • Spain • United Kingdom • United States

WADSWORTH
CENGAGE Learning™

Teaching Young Children in Multicultural Classrooms: Issues, Concepts, and Strategies, Fourth Edition
Wilma Robles de Meléndez, Vesna Beck

Publisher/ Executive Editor: Linda Schreiber-Ganster

Acquisitions Editor: Mark Kerr

Assistant Editor: Joshua Taylor

Editorial Assistant: Greta Lindquist

Media Editor: Elizabeth Momb

Marketing Manager: Kara Kindstrom

Marketing Assistant: Klaudiya Markenzon

Marketing Communications Manager: Heather Baxley

Production Management and Composition: PreMediaGlobal

Manufacturing Planner: Rebecca Cross

Rights Acquisitions Specialist: Don Schlotman

Text Researcher: Isabel Saraiva

Cover Designer: Jeff Bane

Cover Image: Illustration by CMB design, Jeff Bane

For product information and technology assistance, contact us at
Cengage Learning Customer & Sales Support, 1-800-354-9706.

For permission to use material from this text or product, submit all requests online at **www.cengage.com/permissions.**
Further permissions questions can be e-mailed to
permissionrequest@cengage.com.

Library of Congress Control Number: 2011937657

ISBN-13: 978-1-111-83714-3

ISBN-10: 1-111-83714-7

Wadsworth
20 Davis Drive
Belmont, CA 94002-3098
USA

Cengage Learning is a leading provider of customized learning solutions with office locations around the globe, including Singapore, the United Kingdom, Australia, Mexico, Brazil, and Japan. Locate your local office at **www.cengage.com/global.**

Cengage Learning products are represented in Canada by Nelson Education, Ltd.

To learn more about Wadsworth, visit **www.cengage.com/Wadsworth**

Purchase any of our products at your local college store or at our preferred online store **www.cengagebrain.com.**

Printed in the United States of America
1 2 3 4 5 6 7 15 14 13 12 11

BRIEF CONTENTS

CONTENTS

PREFACE

As we complete the revision for the fourth edition, we reaffirm how proud we are of being Americans as we are of our own cultural heritages. We also feel proud when we hear and see that so many people still consider our country the bastion of freedom and hope. This pride is diminished, however, whenever we witness prejudice, discrimination, and unfairness against some members of our society. Instead of engaging in philosophical and theoretical discussions about such injustices, we, as educators, need to look for practical solutions that can effectively address the challenge of living in a pluralistic society. That solution is found in education. Our belief that people can learn to see the sameness in all has led us to write this book. Envisioning empowering classrooms where young children will find themselves and their cultures validated is the dream that sustains this work. Because we believe early childhood teachers are the cornerstones of educational success, we dedicate this work as a source of ideas that will allow them to create such classrooms for all children.

For us, writing this book is a personal and professional journey—personal because both of us came to the United States as immigrants and had the opportunity to witness firsthand the inadequacies of our educational system to provide for the needs of students from diverse backgrounds. Our professional experiences as professors of early childhood education at Nova Southeastern University inspired and guided us in selecting the content and creating the conceptual framework of this book.

PURPOSE OF THE BOOK

The primary purpose of the book is to serve as a text for teacher candidates who already have some theoretical background in child development and curriculum development. This includes undergraduate students who are getting ready to become early childhood educators as well as practicing teachers who want to gain new ideas. The book can be used as a primary text for courses in early childhood undergraduate and graduate programs.

The secondary purpose of the book is to be a resource for practicing early childhood professionals and anyone else interested in learning about diversity and multiculturalism. Many components of the book, such as chapter activities and recommended children's books, are intended to assist practitioners in creating more developmentally and culturally appropriate curricula and classroom environments conducive to young children's learning.

As we know, this book is not the only one of its kind. Many fine publications exist that address this topic very eloquently. Some works in the current market are very specialized and more narrowly focused than our book. For example, some books address only developmentally appropriate practice, whereas others are solely about the antibias curriculum. Although we recognize the value of the specialized approach, we wanted to create a book that is comprehensive in scope and presents diversity issues in a more complete context of our society. Diversity exists in sociological, historical, political, developmental, and instructional contexts. This book presents the multifaceted approach to diversity as it relates to the education of young children.

The selection of content and the conceptual scheme for the book came from our experiences with our very diverse undergraduate and graduate student populations. Many of our early childhood teacher candidates are bilingual and come from the United States as well as a multitude of countries ranging from Latin America, the Caribbean, Europe, Asia, and the Middle East. As future teachers, they have a special desire to facilitate tolerance and acceptance of cultural and ethnic differences among young children. The comprehensive approach of our book is also the result of our realization that, many times, early childhood professionals and teacher candidates who work in multicultural and diverse communities need ways to assist them in learning more how to meet the needs of children with culturally diverse backgrounds.

We believe that, whether white or "people of color," whether native-born or immigrants, early childhood educators need to have a knowledge base that promotes a more holistic understanding of diversity and the role it plays in the lives of young children and their families in our society. We believe that the comprehensive approach to the content we chose in our book achieves that goal.

ORGANIZATION OF THE BOOK

The book is organized in three parts. Part I deals with social foundations and theory of multicultural instruction. It contains the historical perspectives of multiculturalism, future trends, and the social and psychological developmental influences that affect young children. Part II explores the past and current issues and directions of multicultural education. It explores the historical background and different approaches to teaching diversity. Part III includes new content about English language learners and provides resources in the form of guidelines and ideas for classroom implementation. Several actual multicultural instruments, curriculum plans, and classroom techniques are presented.

CONCEPTUAL DEVELOPMENT

The book balances theory and practice, which makes it suitable for the several purposes mentioned earlier. The theoretical component is necessary for several reasons. First, we believe it is good practice to base the recommendations and conclusions on a sound scholarly knowledge base and proven practices. Second, teachers need to understand the principles and theories that underlie practices related to multicultural education in order to implement them properly. Third, the theoretical background provides a framework for multiculturalism that makes it fit into the larger context of teaching and learning. The practical aspect of the book is a consequence of our strong commitment to practitioners in the field of early childhood education and to the commitment of bonding theory and practice.

Four types of activities are provided throughout the book: "In Action . . . ," "Think and Reflect," "Focus on Classroom Practices," and "Making Connections . . ." They are intended to provide exercises, promote discussions, and present practical ideas. Each "In Action . . ." activity is accompanied by questions and other information related to the material discussed in the body of the chapter. "Think and Reflect" asks the reader to relate the ideas and concepts presented in the chapter to personal experiences, ideas, and values. "Focus on Classroom Practices" features examples of activities and suggestions for classroom application of the theoretical concepts discussed in each chapter. The activities at the end of the chapter, "Making Connections . . . ," provide additional practice for individuals and groups.

The activities in these special features of the book are intended for use with both pre-service and practicing teachers. We believe that most activities can be adapted to both groups.

NEW TO THIS EDITION

Some changes to the fourth edition were implemented as a result of the reviewers' suggestions, and other material was added and updated to make this edition more current. The major changes have occurred in three chapters. In this edition, we combined previous Chapters 7 and 8 to accommodate a new Chapter 8, about English language learners (ELL). One cannot discuss multicultural education without including the reality of ELL children. This group of young children and families comprise the core of the diverse population found in so many of our classrooms, early childhood centers, and in society at large. Data on demographics and other information related to the multicultural issues have also been updated. Children's books, Internet resources, and chapter summaries have been reviewed and updated as well.

Several new elements were added to this edition. New video cases found in most chapters link the reader to the Cengage video library. The videos, related materials, and activities provide excellent opportunities for reinforcement and enrichment. They provide glimpses about practices in diverse classrooms. Another new feature, *"Teachers Share,"* begins every chapter. These are vignettes the authors have observed or experienced through their students and colleagues over the years. These stories can be used as case studies by teachers to further discussions and critical thinking. Additional questions and activities for "Teachers Share" will be provided in the instructor's manual. *"Around the World"* are new vignettes related to cultural practices, experiences, and their influence on development and issues faced by young children and their families in the global community. The vignettes are intended to promote discussion and reflection on diversity issues faced in classrooms and communities both in United States and throughout the global village. They will also be reinforced through additional questions in the instructor's manual. The instructor's manual was revised and a new website for the book is available with additional resources including downloads.

Terminology

Throughout this book, we use the official terminology of the United States Bureau of Census when referring to various ethnic and cultural groups. The terms *white* and *black* are used, despite their social and political connotations. In some instances, race needs to be the predominant descriptor for both. This is particularly true of the term *black*, which cannot be interchangeable with *African American* in every instance.

Hispanic is the most widely used term to describe the various populations of Central and South America. We have decided to continue using it in this edition, but we also added the term *Latino*. Using both allows for more flexibility and respects the preferences of the members of this vastly diverse group.

The U.S. Bureau of Census does not have a classification for *Non-European Americans*. The term *other* is still used for groups that classify themselves as neither white nor black. We do not agree with that terminology and continue to use the term *Non-European Americans* to refer to all those born or descending from Non-Europeans. This group consists of Asian Americans, Hispanics, African Americans, Pacific Islanders, Native Hawaiians, Caribbean Islanders, Arabs, and Middle Easterners, as well as people of all native Indian nations and Alaskan natives.

Children's Books

Lists of children's books have been updated in every chapter with more recent publications. Some of the classic and important older publications remain because of their timeless value. Most children's literature resources are found in the "Literacy Connections . . ." boxes interspersed throughout each chapter. Some books are mentioned in more than one place in the book because they are appropriate for diverse topics and discussions. Lists of children's books have also been updated in Appendix A.

Video Case Call-outs

New video case call-outs that can be linked to the Cengage video library are a new feature to this edition. The videos were selected to support the content of the chapters. Many of them have additional exercises and supplemental materials that can be used for re-enforcement and enrichment.

Book Website

The Internet is an invaluable resource and research tool for most of us. We recognize that, as such, it needs to be linked to this book. The book companion website for this edition offers study tools for students including chapter quizzes, glossary flashcards, exercises, and additional website links. Among the resources are the instructor's manual, a sample syllabus, and a PowerPoint slide. New forms and surveys that can be downloaded have also been created for this edition. We invite all readers to visit the website as part of the journey through this book. To access the website, go to CengageBrain.com and click on any number of links that interest you.

Professional Standards Portfolio

The Standards Portfolio remains a part of this edition. It is a very important element of the book that has received much praise from students and teachers. The portfolio provides a unique experience because of its wide use in undergraduate and graduate programs as well as state and local agencies. As in the previous edition, we used the standards of the National Association of Education for Young Children (NAEYC) as the framework for the professional portfolio because they represent the most important and comprehensive guidelines for theoretical and practical aspects of the early childhood profession. The newest standards published in 2011 are used in this edition. We continue to correlate the NAEYC standards with widely known Interstate Teacher Assessment and Support Consortium (InTASC) standards to broaden the application of the portfolio. The InTASC standards are generic and appropriate for a very wide audience of professionals. The portfolio provides a special opportunity for teacher candidates and early childhood practitioners to gain valuable professional experiences through the process.

Chapters

All chapters have been revised to reflect the suggestions of the reviewers and as we thought appropriate. The specific changes in each chapter are listed here:

- Chapter 1: Updated demographic information.
- Chapter 2: Updated information about ethnicities.

- Chapter 3: Refined information about child development as it relates to the role of the family, family models, and the family's ways of socialization.
- Chapter 4: Added information about development, identity, and socialization of young children.
- Chapter 5: Revised and condensed some of the historical information and added information about equality, ELL children, and children with special needs. New children's books were added.
- Chapter 6: Provided more detail about specific curriculum models and developmentally appropriate practice (DAP).
- Chapter 7: The chapter provides an emphasis on planning with a focus on appropriate practices. Added information about children with special needs and ELL children.
- Chapter 8: This is a new chapter that addresses data and practices for young English language learners (ELL). Content provides ideas for responsive instructional planning.
- Chapter 9: Content was updated to include users of art and thematic teaching. New children's books were added.
- Chapter 10: Content was updated regarding family and community involvement, and new children's books were added.

Appendices

Appendix A has been updated with new children's books.

Illustrations

Some of the old pictures were removed at the recommendation of reviewers, and many new ones were added.

Instructor's Manual

The instructor's manual has a new format and is available online at www.CengageBrain.com. The purpose of the manual is to assist teachers in planning instruction based on this book. We have included what we believe are the essential elements that teachers require for planning. Each chapter is presented with purpose, objectives, key terms, and teaching strategies, as well as quizzes and further resources. A set of PowerPoint slides have also been created for classroom use and are available on the website.

ACKNOWLEDGMENTS

No work is ever accomplished without the support of family members, colleagues, and friends. We thank our families for their love, understanding, and support of this work. Thank you for staying at our side through many long hours, lost holidays, and working weekends. We are thankful to our students who generously continue to share their experiences and inspire us to continue our work in the field of multiculturalism and diversity. Their ideas and concerns have helped shape this work.

We wish to acknowledge the support of Joshua Taylor, assistant editor at Cengage, and particularly executive editor, Mark D. Kerr (¡Gracias, Mark!), for their guidance and patience.

We extend our most sincere appreciation to the reviewers enlisted through Cengage Learning for their constructive suggestions and encouragement: Bobbi Bartok, Kansas City Kansas Community College; Laureen Cate, St. Philip's College; Marissa Happ, Waubonsee Community College; Patty Kennedy, Ivy Tech Community College; Miranda Lin, Illinois State University.

A FINAL WORD FROM THE AUTHORS

As we completed this revision for our fourth edition, we reaffirmed our commitment to making this a better and fair place for every young child. We chose to write about education for diversity not only because we believe in its importance to education and to the future of our country, but also for very personal reasons. Like many others, we are both "newcomers" to the United States. We both have experienced, together and with our families, the tribulations and sometimes-painful adjustments of starting a new life in a strange new land. Many of the experiences we wrote about in the book have personal significance. We know firsthand what it is to be different. We have also experienced diversity as U.S. residents of other countries such as the U.S. Virgin Islands, Puerto Rico, Spain, Germany, India, and the former country of Yugoslavia. Our travels have taken us to many other interesting places as well. These experiences have enriched us and given us multicultural and global perspectives that we want to share through this book with our fellow educators and other readers. Join us in our journey!

Wilma Robles de Meléndez
Vesna Beck

PART I

Foundations for Multicultural Education in Today's Early Childhood Classrooms

Let us think of education as the means of developing our greatest abilities, because in each of us there is a private hope and dream which, fulfilled, can be translated into benefit for everyone and greater strength for our nation.

John F. Kennedy (1917–1963), 35th president of the United States

(1961–1963)

Living in Diversity: The Intricate Nature of Our Society

He met many people along the way. He shook hands with black men, with yellow men and red men.
—Allen Say (1994)

Wadsworth/Cengage Learning

STANDARDS: THE FOLLOWING STANDARDS ARE ADDRESSED IN THIS CHAPTER:

naeyc **Standard 1:** Promoting Child Development and Learning

naeyc **Standard 6:** Becoming a Professional

InTASC Standard 1: Learner Development

InTASC Standard 9: Professional Learning and Ethical Practice

TEACHERS SHARE: THE WORLD IN MY CLASSROOM

For Sally, a prekindergarten teacher, today was a special day. She had just started at the local preschool where she met her new group of four-year-olds. Getting ready to leave, she told one of her colleagues:

"Well, today I finally met my class. They are so vivacious! When I read their names, I never imagined I would find a mini-United Nations."

"Oh, I'm sure," responded Angela, a veteran toddler teacher. "That was actually what I had last year. This year, my new toddler class is also a mix of so many cultures. You see, this neighborhood has been changing. Since last year, we have seen more families from other countries moving here."

"That surely explains it," Sally said. "I have several children who are from Central America and the Caribbean, three who are Jamaican, one who is Haitian, two who just arrived from Puerto Rico, and one who is Bahamian. The rest are African American, like me. You see, I want to be their best teacher, but I don't think it will be easy. I still grapple with many issues related to diversity."

"I'm sure that this will be an interesting year for all of us. So much to learn!…" sighed the toddler teacher as she left the office.

CHAPTER OBJECTIVES

Upon reading this chapter and reflecting on its content, you will recognize the factors that define the nature of social diversity in our communities and their impact on young children and early childhood educators.

KEY CONCEPTS

- multicultural society
- cultural diversity
- immigration
- ethnic groups
- non-European Americans

WORKING IN TODAY'S DIVERSE CLASSROOMS

Like the teachers in the vignette, every day in classrooms across the country early childhood educators are greeted by the faces of children with diverse cultural and linguistic backgrounds. Although each has his or her own distinct ways and heritage, they all share similar developmental and educational needs. They are a reflection of the increased demographical diversity that defines the reality of life in a multicultural nation. Today, preparing ourselves to meet the needs of young children and their families with multicultural and diverse characteristics is a priority. For the early childhood educator, this is a continuous and everyday journey that begins by getting a sense of the culturally diverse nature of the country and community. In the sections that follow, we explore the elements and factors contributing to our increasing social diversity.

Wadsworth/Cengage Learning

Like this Eastern European family in Chicago (circa 1925), many Europeans migrated to the United States during the early part of the twentieth century. In search of a better life, they left behind their homelands to make this country their new home. Do you find any similarities between them and today's immigrant families?

THE UNITED STATES—A NATION OF CONTRASTS

Nothing in this world reflects diversity more than nature. The landscape of Earth is an intricate mix of shapes, forms, and colors, each with its own identity and spirit. They are separate and yet a piece of a whole. The land we live in probably best reflects this notion. The landscape of the United States, a quilt woven of dramatically different terrains, is populated by people equally unique and diverse. Glancing over the entire country from the Pacific to the Atlantic, you see many different environments coexisting: warm deserts, snow-capped mountains, golden plains, green valleys, lush marshlands, sandy beaches, and bustling cities. All are different yet of one country: the United States. No less than its geography, the people who inhabit the United States illustrate diversity. Much like its eclectic landscape, people of the United States mirror the diversity of the world. In small country towns and large cities alike, you will find numerous examples of world cultures. Whether they wear a sari, attend a mosque, or speak Tagalog, Hmong, or French Creole, members of different cultures have changed the semblance of our social landscape.

Throughout history, the presence of culturally diverse groups has brought people of the United States in contact with ways different from those established by the white European groups that founded this country (Baruth & Manning, 2008). Nowhere else is this more apparent than at the community level. This is where most people recognize to what extent pluralism permeates their world. Diversity makes itself known through the fascinating contrasts that bring a new vitality to our surroundings. For example, the variety of restaurants offering American food can be found beside those that serve flavorful sushi and spicy curry dishes; the Latin beat is heard on radio stations just as often as American rock and roll; sari-clad women shop next to women in jeans; and a Vietnamese-language newspaper can be found next to those in English at the neighborhood newsstand. School grounds echo with the different languages spoken by children and adults. Community centers all over the country are filled with newly arrived immigrants trying to learn the language of their adopted homeland.

Wadsworth/Cengage Learning

Through the entire history of our country, children of immigrants have learned about their new home culture through school. This group of first graders from 1928 shared many things in common, but one in particular characterized them: They were all born in different countries and spoke languages different from English. Can you imagine the challenges they faced?

SCHOOL—THE PLACE OF DIVERSITY AND ACTION

Today, educators at all levels are aware that there is diversity in schools. We recognize its effects on our way of thinking, and we know its impact through the new laws and regulations that mandate changes in the schools and society at large. On a more personal level, early childhood professionals know diversity through the joyous shouting of exotic words heard on the school playground and by witnessing the frustrations that accompany conquests of new knowledge.

It is well known that that the ethnographic composition of schools has changed dramatically in the last two decades. More and more schools are housing students with non-European cultural backgrounds (Hobbs & Stoops, 2002; Jarvis, 2003). The presence of non-European cultural groups varies from one geographical area to another. While Hispanics are found in greater numbers in Texas, South Florida, and California, cities such as Chicago and Seattle include large populations of Asian Indians and Vietnamese, while Alaska, Arizona, and New Mexico are home to large numbers of Native Americans. Even states such as North Dakota, Montana, Vermont, and Maine, traditionally known for being populated predominantly by European Americans, are inhabited by immigrants from other continents.

IN ACTION . . .

WHAT IS DIVERSITY?

You may not be fully aware of the diversity around you. To find out if diversity is a part of your community and your life, make a list of details about other cultural groups that you have observed in your community. Find out how much you know about individuals from other cultures, their backgrounds, their ways of life, traditions, and other distinctive characteristics. Then, consider:

- What roles do these individuals play in your life?
- How has their presence changed your community?
- What are some important things you learned from them?
- What do you think they know about you?

HOW DID WE BECOME A CULTURALLY DIVERSE SOCIETY?

Culture and diversity are terms that are part of today's educational jargon. Although this will be further explained in Chapter 2, here we will briefly explore what the terms signify. *Culture* is a very hard term to define because social scientists have not yet agreed on a single definition. Some define culture as a collection of beliefs, attitudes, habits, values, and practices that a human group uses to form a view of reality. This means that every cultural group, such as Filipinos, Koreans, and Jamaicans, for example, interprets life events (marriage, death, child rearing, and others) according to the established cultural frameworks it has formed over time. They represent the recognized and accepted frames of reference of a cultural group. Such frameworks are owned by every cultural group and are transmitted through generations. At the classroom level, this means that young children from different cultures view our world in very heterogeneous ways. This is especially true of children of newly arrived immigrants. This also implies that teachers may have different ways of interpreting life than the children they teach. This divergence of ideas is how you encounter diversity in the classroom. This is also what makes teaching today's young children exciting and challenging.

Young children in today's classrooms are a natural extension of the United States, where groups of many different ethnicities and extractions have come together to form a culturally diverse, pluralistic, or multicultural society (Baruth & Manning, 2008; Martorella, 2001).

Cultural diversity denotes contrasts, variations, or differences from the ways of the mainstream or majority culture. When diversity is used in reference to human beings, a multitude of elements are involved in the concept. These meanings will be explored in Chapter 2 when we focus on the connotation of the term *cultural origin* or *descent*.

Cultural diversity has not only transformed the composition of the U.S. population, but it has also enriched the character of life in the United States. The various

An elementary class of the 1950s resembles many of today's classrooms: More than half of these students were recent newcomers or children of first-generation immigrant parents. Is it true that history repeats itself?

groups have brought much knowledge about other parts of the world in forms of languages, traditions, customs, and folklore. This diversity is displayed in the classroom in countless ways: the various snacks children bring to school, the words and phrases they use, the ideas about families and social relationships they express, the special holidays they celebrate, and even the fashions they prefer. The classroom is a very polychromatic place that can be considered a microcosm of society. This polychromatic quality makes the United States exciting and special. This is also why U.S. society is described as culturally diverse. A culturally diverse society is one where different cultures exist, socially interact, and yet remain visible in their own context.

A Nation of Immigrants

The United States has traditionally been defined as a nation of immigrants. Looking at some of the historical events of the United States helps in answering how, why, and when the country acquired this multicultural personality. Nieto and Bode (2008) point out that immigration is an ongoing process of change and not a phenomenon of the past. In fact, it is an everyday experience as immigrants from all parts of the world make their way to our country in search of a better life for themselves and future generations.

THINK AND REFLECT...

THINKING ABOUT DIVERSITY

The first few pages of this chapter served to remind you of the nature of our very diverse society. Although we live among people of other cultures and ethnic origins, we seldom think in-depth about our relationship with them. As an early childhood professional, it is important to reflect and ask yourself questions in order to become cognizant of your own views regarding diversity. Working with young children includes learning and developing relationships with children and families from many different parts of the world. Ask yourself in what ways you are ready to support and work with children and families with diverse cultural and linguistic characteristics.

Wadsworth/Cengage Learning

FOCUS
ON CLASSROOM PRACTICES

LEARNING THAT WE ARE ALIKE AND DIFFERENT

Our present U.S. society has sometimes been described as a wonderful tossed salad. This same metaphor probably describes the children in most classrooms. As children begin to notice human diversity, it is just as important to guide them to discover how alike they are. You can begin with an activity such as paper plate self-portraits. You need a paper plate for each child, a set of cutouts of the different parts of the face, glue, and yarn for the hair and for hanging the portraits. To reflect differences among facial traits, cutouts should include a variety of facial features, such as different eye colors and different shapes of noses, mouths, and ears that resemble the traits of your students. Including face parts different from those of the children in the group can be a starter for later discussions. Distribute the materials, making sure that you have provided enough cutouts. Have children work on their portraits in pairs or in groups of four. This could be an introductory activity for a thematic unit, "Who We Are." After finishing their portraits, the children can follow up with a rhyme like the following:

Hello!

We are so alike!
> *(Have children face each other to point at face parts as they are named.)*

Eyes I have and so do you.

Both of us have noses, too.

Ears we both also have.

And mouths that say,

"Come be my friend!"

Wow! WOW! Wow!

We're alike and how! *(Showing surprise)*

You can also have them play "Simon Says." Here they would stand up as Simon asks: "Stand up if you have green eyes," ". . . if you have a long nose," and so on. You may want to include other body parts to further stress similarities. Teachers may want to share stories such as *All the Colors We Are* by Katie Kissinger (Redleaf Press, 1994) and *Black is Brown is Tan* by Arnold Adoff (Amistad, 2004).

The United States has also been described as a land where dreams for a better and more equitable life become a reality. Since the days of the first settlements, this part of North America has represented the pathways to liberty, justice, and opportunity. The journey that began with the seventeenth century Mayflower Pilgrims and still continues today helped establish the distinctive trait of this country: cultural plurality.

The Early Days: Immigrants of the 17th and 18th Centuries

European immigrants settled this country in the seventeenth and eighteenth centuries. Native Americans as well as Africans and people of the Caribbean brought over as slave laborers were the other significant population groups during that time. Historically, the beginning of today's U.S. multiculturalism is found in the social interaction patterns that emerged among these groups. Because these interactions were largely based on discriminatory distinctions among people based on their race and the color of their skin, the seeds of unfairness and inequality were planted in the early days of this nation. Long years of persecution of the African Americans, the systematic eradication of the Native Americans, and later the disenfranchisement of the large numbers of Mexican Americans hampered the efforts of unification among peoples destined to share this land.

The first settlers shaped the culture of this land in the early seventeenth century in unprecedented ways. In addition to many positive cultural trends, their values and social ethics defined a system of discrimination and persecution that still remains today. It first began with the early settlers' discrimination and systematic eradication of the East Coast Native American groups. This was the beginning of one of the longest, most tragic, and shameful chapters in U.S. history.

The beginning of slavery in the seventeenth century marked the start of violent persecution and segregation of African Americans that formally ended with the Emancipation Proclamation in 1864. The Civil War that ravaged the country ended slavery and preserved the union.

The Immigration Wave of the 19th Century

Economic, social, and political reforms following the post–Civil War years initiated a new era in America. This age also marked the beginning of a new kind of diversity that intensified the kaleidoscope nature of this country and presented new challenges.

The great waves of immigration in the nineteenth century began with the Irish as early as the 1850s. Most settled in the large cities, where they later made great strides in business and politics. On the West Coast, the Chinese were arriving at the same time. Some came as economic immigrants looking for a better life, whereas many more came to join the 49ers in their quest for California's gold. By 1870, over 60,000 Chinese were living mostly in California, the West, and the Southwest (Novas & Cao, 2004). The construction of the Central Pacific Railroad, completed in 1869, was largely a Chinese achievement.

IN ACTION . . .

DIVERSITY IN YOUR LIFE

Perhaps you have not yet discerned how diversity touches your life. To find out, you can do a personal inventory. You need a pad of self-stick notes, a pencil, and a piece of paper. Make five columns on the paper. Label the first four columns as *Things I Use, Wear, Eat,* and *Read*. Label the fifth column *Cultures*. Now, using the sticky notes, write names of things you consider a part of your world that come from cultures other than your own.

After you have finished your cultural search, place the sticky notes in the appropriate columns. Fill in the names of the cultures from which the items originate.

- What have you learned about diversity in your life?
- What are the implications of your findings?
- Can you draw some conclusions about diversity?

FOCUS
ON CLASSROOM PRACTICES

DISCOVERING DIVERSITY

At the core of diversity is the issue of human differences. Learning to live with diversity means helping children recognize its presence in their lives. To help children discover that we all hold distinctive traits, teachers can help them create a *Me Bag*. This could be a part of the activities conducted at the beginning of the school year. This activity is based on the belief that each person has unique characteristics. The *Me Bag* is intended to help children see differences as a typically descriptive element defining each individual. This activity starts by the teacher's preparation of his or her own *Me Bag* to be shared with the children. This activity helps in identifying your own diverse characteristics.

You will need one large brown bag for each child. Write the children's names on the bags and ask them to draw or paste their picture on the outside. Then, ask children to put inside the bag items, drawings, or words that are special to them. Invite children to share their bags and

have them talk about the things they selected. Lead children to identify the items that are common to everyone and those that are different. Use the following questions to engage children in a discussion of their findings.

- *What did we learn about our class? Tell me something you discovered about two of your friends.*
- *What things did we discover we have in common with our classmates? What things do we not have in common?*
- *In what ways are we all alike? Why?*
- *Tell me something that makes you special.*

Bags can be displayed and kept as an ongoing activity. Other details can be added throughout the year. Follow up by adding books to the literacy center to reinforce the characteristics of diversity found among the children in the group.

Presence of people of Hispanic descent traces back to the early sixteenth century explorers who first settled in Florida and then explored throughout the Southwest. During the nineteenth century, Mexicans came to build the Texas Mexican Railway. Earlier, many Mexicans worked in the gold mines in California and in the copper mines in Arizona. They were employed as general laborers and were always paid less than their white counterparts. Many of these laborers were migrants who never settled permanently in the states where they worked. Others found themselves strangers in their own land after the United States annexed Texas and California.

By the end of the nineteenth century, the United States had entered into an unprecedented age of industrialization and progress. This attracted new immigrants from European countries and the Balkans. Unfortunately, the newcomers inspired a new backlash that led to many discriminatory practices, some of which still exist today.

Search for Prosperity and Freedom: Immigrants of the 20th Century

The first great wave of immigrants during the twentieth century occurred between 1905 and 1915, when various economic and political events in Europe caused 10 million people to seek refuge in the United States (Novas & Cao, 2004). These were mostly economic immigrants, people who came to the United States primarily in search of

Ellis Island was the first glimpse of the "land of the free" for many immigrants in the beginning of the twentieth century.

a better life. These large **ethnic groups** were segments of larger societies whose members had a common origin, were of a specific race, and shared a common culture and often a common religion. Approximately 2 million Italians and 1.5 million Russians, many of them Jews avoiding persecution, came to the large cities on the East Coast. The new immigrants comprised 3 percent of the labor force. The majority of European immigrants came to the United States as common people. Settling in cities where there were jobs and where they could live with their own kind in places like little Italies, Bohemias, and Germantowns, they worked hard and struggled to make a living. Many women worked in sweatshops and earned even less than men. Most immigrants lived in slums in rundown tenements without heat and running water. Working conditions were just as deplorable. Hazardous working conditions caused many accidents in which many workers were maimed for life or even killed. Part of the new U.S. labor force consisted of children. They were largely children of the poor and of immigrant families who were not able to partake in the national prosperity experienced at the turn of the twentieth century.

IN ACTION . . .

PORTRAIT OF AMERICA

This is a description of New Rochelle, a suburb of New York City, in 1906 in E. L. Doctorow's *Ragtime*. This description eerily reaches into the present, whether or not we ride the trolley.

Teddy Roosevelt was President. The popularity customarily gathered in great numbers either out of doors for parades, public concerts, fish fries, political picnics, social outings, indoor meeting halls, vaudeville theaters, operas, or ballrooms. There seemed to be no end to entertainment that did not involve great swarms of people. Trains and steamers and trolleys moved them from one place to another. That was the style: that was the way

people lived. Women were stouter then. They visited the fleet carrying white parasols. Everyone wore white in summer. There was a lot of sexual fainting. There were no Negroes. There were no immigrants.

• What can you say about this United States?

• Are some corners of our country (or our minds) that are still like this?

• Write a paragraph about your community, emulating Doctorow's style.

Source: Doctorow, 1975.

IN ACTION . . .

AN INCREASINGLY MULTIRACIAL COUNTRY

For Mary, the birth of her first born was the most exciting experience in her life. Holding him for the first time as she welcomed him to the world was such a special time. When handed back the birth registration forms, the nurse quickly checked them and told Mary, "Oops, you forgot to complete the ethnic background. Could you please check the box?" Mary looked at her not knowing what to say. Finally, she replied, "But you see, I can't mark just one box, I have many cultures and my child now does, too."

Census Bureau (2010) provides a unique cultural and demographic portrait of the United States. The results showed that 3 in 10 people are members of ethnic minorities. Not only did the Census results confirm the growing multicultural character of the nation, they also exposed, for the first time, the existence of a new multiracial and multiethnic group

classified as "multicultural." The responses revealed the following:

- There were 6 million who identified their heritage as multiracial.
- Of people who defined themselves as multiracial, 93 percent stated having two races.
- Nearly 1 million children age 5 or younger were identified as having mixed racial origins.

What are the implications for the future? Projections tell us that by 2050, 22 percent of the population will be of mixed race origins. Given this trend, the number of young children with multiracial heritage in early childhood classrooms is expected to rise dramatically. For early childhood educators, learning about the needs of children and families with multiracial heritage is essential.

Source: U.S. Census Bureau, 2010.

Laws Limiting Immigration in the 20th Century

The first national limits on immigration in the form of a quota system, imposed in 1924, were known as the National Origins Act. The quotas limited the total number of immigrants per year to 150,000. Quotas for each nationality group were 2 percent of the total members of that nationality residing in the United States according to the 1890 Census. Western Europeans were exempt from the quota system because they were perceived as more desirable in terms of their education and the skills they possessed (Parillo, 2007). The main purpose of the quota system was to preserve the original racial and ethnic composition of the United States by preventing the poor and the illiterate from the Eastern, middle, and southern European countries; Russia; and Asia from coming in and becoming a social and economic burden to U.S. society. The system gave an enormous advantage to the British, the Germans, and other Western Europeans whose ancestors were among the pioneers who settled this country.

Immigration law was changed in 1952 with the passing of the McCarran–Walter Act that repealed the quota system and instead gave preference to skilled workers in fields that are experiencing shortages in the United States, reunification of families, and protection of the domestic labor force. This system was also biased in favor of the Western Europeans, whose immigration numbers continued to be unrestricted.

LITERACY CONNECTIONS...

TEACHING CHILDREN ABOUT IMMIGRANTS

Multicultural children's literature offers a rich and lively way to explore diversity concepts. Stories addressing topics related to cultural diversity are powerful learning sources for young children. The following titles will help you explore the very important topic of immigration.

- Anzaldua, G. (1993). *Friends from the other side.* San Francisco: Children's Press.
  Based on facts, the story tells about the experiences of Prietita, a girl who helps Joaquin and his mother when they come to live in the United States.

- Hoffman, M. (2002). *The color of home.* New York: Fogelman Press.
  The story tells the experiences of first grader Hassan, an immigrant boy from Somalia, as he goes to school in the United States for the first time. This is a powerful tale that conveys the feelings and emotions of a child who misses life in his country.

- Maestro, B. (1996). *Coming to America. The story of immigration.* New York: Scholastic.
  In a child-appropriate way, the story presents immigration as a shared reality that describes people in the United States.

- Pak, S. (2002). *A place to grow.* New York: Levine Books.
  In this story, an inquisitive child asks her father about the reasons he left his birthplace to come to a new country. This is a good starting point for families in sharing their own stories and reasons why they came to the United States.

- Recorvits, H. *My Name is Yoon.* (2003). 1st ed. New York: Ferrar, Straus and Giroux.
  The story is a moving account of the young Korean girl Yoon's adjustment to her new home in America.

- Sandin, J. (1986). *The long way to a new land.* New York: Scholastic.
  The story shares the struggles of nineteenth century Swedish immigrants as they come to the U.S. in search of a new life.

- Surat, M. (1989). *Angel child, dragon child.* New York: Scholastic.
  This story is about the experiences of an immigrant child from Vietnam as he begins to learn how to live in the United States.

In 1965, as a result of many political changes in the world, the increasing intensity of the Cold War, Castro's rise to power, and the Vietnam War, Congress passed an immigration law that was based on a humanitarian notion of "reunification of families." The law abolished the national origins system and the major restrictions against the Asiatic countries. The Western Hemisphere was also subject for the first time to an overall annual quota of 120,000. A seven-category system was created with preference given to reunification of families and to individuals with needed talents or skills.

Many immigrants who arrived in the 1960s and the early 1970s were political dissidents, artists, intellectuals, and entrepreneurs from the Eastern European communist countries, from Asia, and from Cuba. (It should be noted that this law was applied very selectively in the 1980s, granting immigrants from the communist countries legal entry whereas opponents to the right-wing dictatorships of countries such as Guatemala and El Salvador were forced to enter illegally.) Under the kinship system, newly arrived refugees did not need to have any job skills, education, or means of support.

YOUNG IMMIGRANTS

Etienne is a five year-old from Haiti. When the hurricane hit his island, he and his family came to Miami to live with relatives because their home was destroyed and his parents were not able to work. Since then, Etienne's family has been living with their uncle and aunt. His father and mother work in the nearby hotel and Etienne is going to school along with his brother and two sisters. He likes being in the United States, or *Amerique*, like his Mom says. There is enough food to eat and a school with a roof over it that is not so hot. Yesterday, his mother was crying and his father was arguing with a tall American man that came to the door. Etienne's' sister told him that they have to go back to Haiti because they were in Miami only "temporarily." What does that mean? asked the young boy.

Etienne is not the only child experiencing such challenges in his young life. Think about your own reactions to these experiences happening in communities around the country. Share your reflections on these events.

The "reunification" law brought 10 million newcomers to this country who were closely and distantly related to earlier immigrants. The second and third generations of those originally allowed into the United States are the ones changing the makeup of U.S. society.

According to the Census, the second-highest wave of people immigrated in the 1980s, when the Asians, Latin Americans, people from the Caribbean nations, and people from the countries of the Middle East arrived in the United States. Another amendment to the immigration law, which broadened the definition of "refugee," further increased the numbers of those admitted. Between 1985 and 1994, almost 10 million people came to the United States: 2.7 million came from Mexico, 1 million from the countries in the Caribbean, 1 million from Europe, and approximately 5 million came from other parts of the world. The current origins of the foreign-born population of the United Stated are reflected in Figure 1-1.

Immigration is a continuous reality in the United States. Data from the Migration Policy Institute (2008) show that 1,107,126 legal immigrants entered the United States in 2008. Their countries of origin are shown in Figure 1-2. It is not known how long, or

Figure 1-1   Region of Birth of Foreign Born

Europe	37,342,595
Asia	10,066,515
Africa	1,394,088
Oceania	203,721
Latin America	19,884,943
Northern America	841,350

Source: U.S. Census Bureau, 2005–2009. American Community Survey.

Figure 1-2 Inflow of Legal Immigrants (2009)

All countries	1,130,818
Africa	127,039
Americas and the Caribbean	487,108
Asia	413,311
Europe	105,386
Oceania including Australia and New Zealand	5,563

Source: Migration Policy Institute. (2009). Retrieved from http://www.migrationinformation.org/datahub/countrydata/files/DH_US_InflowLPRsbyCOB.xls

if, they will stay or return to their countries. The new arrivals, whether legal or illegal, have tended to settle in large cities where the job markets were believed to be better. The top four states with immigrant populations are California, Texas, New York, and Florida. The impact and educational implications of these demographics for services and programs for young children are very evident.

The U.S. Census Bureau (2010) projects that by the year 2050, there will be 439 million people in the United States. Projections indicate that Hispanics or Latinos will be the fastest growing population, rising from 13 percent to 23 percent. Census data estimates also indicate Asian Americans are the second-fastest growing ethnic group in the United States. Overall, the population will also be characterized by larger numbers of people under the ages of 5 and 18 (U.S. Census Bureau, 2005–2009, *American Survey*). This fact has direct implications in the planning of services for young children and their families. In particular, it calls for attention to programs that will best reflect the diverse cultural characteristics of the young.

IN ACTION . . .

HAVE YOU EVER WONDERED WHY PEOPLE IMMIGRATE?

If you know individuals who were born in another country, ask them what brought them to the United States. If you have parents or relatives who were born in another country, interview them to find out what brought them here. Write down their answers and reflect on their responses. What did you learn?

- What attracts people to this country?
- How do you feel about the people you interviewed?

- How do you feel about your country?
- What is the history of immigrants in your family?
- How are the stories of different immigrants you interviewed the same or different?
- Would you ever consider immigrating to another country? Why or why not?

THINK AND REFLECT...

A VIEW OF THE WORLD

When I came to catch my flight, I never thought that I would have such a remarkable experience. The hour and a half that I had to spend because of a flight delay showed me the real face of America. Everything started when I decided to have a second cup of coffee. I went to the coffee bar in one of the concourses where they serve the best *cortadito* (espresso with milk) and *pastelitos* (guava and cheese pastries). A smiling Cuban lady served me the aromatic coffee. While sipping it, I saw an airport employee greeting a friend just returning from his hometown in Nicaragua. At the same time, several Haitians chatted while also sipping coffee. Two Colombians joined the group in front of the coffee stand. I noticed two Indian ladies, who wore the prettiest saris, chatting about their children. I finally made the line to board my flight where I heard a father call his child in very distinct Arabic. As we flew out, a thought came to my mind: My country is not just a country, it's a world in itself, a world that I see in my classroom.

Source: Rosales, 1992.

Growing Cultural Diversity

The features of contemporary U.S. society have dramatically changed in recent years. A look at people in towns and cities across the country attests to that. No longer does one set of specific physical or ethnic characteristics make up a profile of a typical U.S. citizen. In fact, we have become a showcase of all possible human traits.

The findings of Census 2010 show a quickly evolving demographic picture. The population of European descent is losing its predominance due to the rapid growth of groups of non-European origin (Hobbs & Stoops, 2002). In essence, non-European Americans account for the growing cultural diversity now found in the United States. The term non-European Americans defines people with ethnic roots in continents other than Europe. Findings from the Census show that U.S. society is affected by the rapid growth of six main groups of non-European Americans (see Figure 1-3). In the section that follows, some of the relevant characteristics of

Figure 1-3
Largest Minority Groups Based on Race Alone with One or More Races

African American	39,643,472
American Indian and Alaska Natives	4, 587,931
Asian	14,930,099
Hispanic or Latino	45,476,938*
Arabs	3,500,000**
Native Hawaiian and Other Pacific Islanders	852,179

* *Latin Americans were not itemized by country and were selected by region of birth.*

** *Arabic population was not itemized by country and was only approximated.*

Source: U.S. Census Bureau, 2005–2009. American Community Survey.

Figure 1-4
Main Cultural Groups

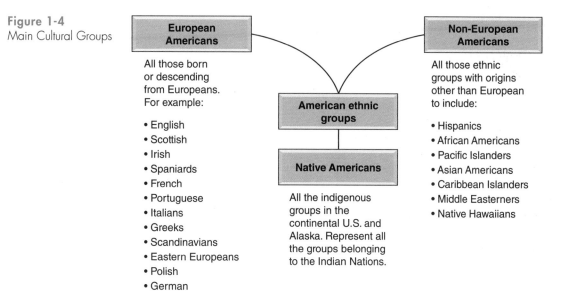

We all belong to the United States!

each of these groups will be discussed. While they represent major cultural groups, they are not heterogeneous. Within each, there are very distinct groups that must also be recognized for their uniqueness and contributions to U.S. society.

Asian-Americans

According to the classifications of the U.S. Census Bureau, Asian Indian, Chinese, Filipino, Japanese, Korean, Vietnamese, Cambodian, Hmong, Thai, and Laotian are the major groups that comprise Asian Americans (U.S. Census, 2010). There is also a category of "others" that includes much smaller numbers of people of Bangladeshi, Burmese, Indonesian, Pakistani, Malaysian, Nepalese, Singaporean, and Sri Lankan origin. Together, Asian Americans number approximately 10 million (U. S. Census, 2010). In the last two decades of the twentieth century and through the present, all the subgroups grew (except for Japanese Americans) to the point that they inhabit every state and the District of Columbia (Novas & Cao, 2004). Half of the Asian American population mainly resides in three states: California, New York, and Hawaii while New York City, Los Angeles, and Chicago have the largest concentrations of Asian Americans. Los Angeles County is the only county that has more than one million Asian Americans living in it. One of the most significant facts regarding Asian Americans is that 86 percent of them have earned a high school diploma.

The Chinese, and later other Asians, had different reasons for immigrating to the United States, which resulted in very distinct immigration experiences (Campbell, 2009). Chinese Americans began coming to California mostly for economic reasons in the first part of the nineteenth century. By the time California was annexed to the United States in 1848, the Chinese population provided basic labor on the railroads and services in laundry and

Multiracial children are increasingly found in classroom and communities throughout the U.S.

cooking establishments. In the second half of the nineteenth century, the Chinese became targets of hate and oppression, which resulted in the first antiracial law, the 1882 Chinese Exclusion Act. The law encouraged white immigration from Europe and made Chinese immigration illegal.

The Chinese who came to the United States in the nineteenth century and until World War II were largely poor and illiterate people from the vast rural areas of China. In contrast, the more recent immigrants from China, Hong Kong, and Taiwan are well-educated professionals and skilled blue-collar workers. Many came with their families in tow and their possessions intact. Some even had jobs waiting for them in the U.S. This new group of Chinese Americans has changed the nature of the Chinese communities across the country. During the past two decades, Chinese Americans have entered professions and moved to the suburbs. Yet, they maintain their roots and traditions.

FOCUS
ON CLASSROOM PRACTICES

TEACHING CHILDREN ABOUT IMMIGRATION

For most young children, immigration is a difficult concept to understand. Even for many who are immigrants themselves, the term will not be familiar. Others, either because of first-hand experiences or from comments by adults, might have a negative perception of immigration. However, as we move into developmentally responsive teaching, this concept becomes a part of what we want children to learn. The option here is to transform the topic into concepts familiar to children. Brainstorming what immigration means would probably yield the following words: movement of people, moving from one country to another, coming from another part of the world, and so on. We find that *moving* is a term that young children of immigrants recognize readily. Teachers can build a thematic unit based on the idea of moving. There are many possibilities in terms of how to develop it with your class.

For example, one kindergarten teacher developed her thematic unit after her group was moved into another part of the school building. Through the story of Su Lin, a character created by the teacher, who had left behind everything she had when her family came to the United States, the class began talking about what it means to move. Asking who knew what moving was like led to an interesting conversation. The children shared how they felt and why they felt sad or happy after moving. A list titled "We can move to . . ." included items like: "a bigger house," "another bedroom," "an apartment," "our grandparents' house," "another development," "a new city," and, of course, "a different classroom." The activity led the class to prepare a big book they titled "Places We Move To."

As a culminating activity, the class decided to prepare a welcome plan for children and adults. Needless to say, with new students arriving frequently, the plan was used almost immediately.

The Japanese and Filipino immigrants first came to Hawaii to work in the sugarcane industry. Many of them eventually migrated to the West Coast of the United States and settled in states from Alaska to California. The Japanese worked hard, saved their money, and bought farms. The success of the Japanese Americans was met with suspicion and prejudice. The worst offenses against them were committed during World War II, when Japanese Americans were incarcerated and their property confiscated by the U.S. government.

In the decades following World War II, both the Japanese and Japanese Americans experienced unprecedented growth and prosperity. In the 1980s and 1990s, the formidable Japanese economy surpassed the growth rate of the U.S. economy. Efforts to compete had severe repercussions in the U.S. labor force, not the least of which were reduced salaries, loss of jobs, smaller profits, and cuts in benefits. Japan's economic prosperity contributed to the latest wave of resentment of the Japanese in this country at the close of the twentieth century (Novas & Cao, 2004).

Filipinos were not subject to the immigration restrictions in the first half of the twentieth century because the Philippines became U.S. territories in 1898. Although they were not classified as aliens, Filipinos did not have citizenship. This was changed in 1946 when they became an independent nation. The economic and political events in the Philippines during the last two decades of the twentieth century facilitated steady streams of Filipino immigrants to the United States. Statistics show that in the past decade, unlike in earlier times, many of the recent immigrants are white-collar professionals in the medical and health-care professions.

Asian-Indian Americans began coming in significant numbers from the subcontinent of India in the first decade of the twentieth century. In spite of persecution and exploitation during most of the twentieth century, Asian Indians managed to prosper in agriculture and related services. It was not until 1965 that significant numbers of highly educated and well-trained professionals began to enter the United States (McLemore and Romo, 2005). This phenomenon is known as the "brain drain" from India. Asian Indians continue to be the highest educated group among Asian Americans. They have put their entrepreneurial skills to work in a variety of business enterprises as well as in the professional fields (Novas & Cao, 2004).

Korean Americans were subject to the same hardships as their fellow Asian immigrants. Like the Filipinos and the Chinese, many came first to the Hawaiian Islands at the turn of the twentieth century to work in the sugarcane fields. Before long, the desire for a better life lured them to the West Coast of the United States. Like other Asians, they suffered discrimination and struggled doing menial labor for minimum wages. During World War II, even though Korea was occupied by Japan, Koreans were considered Japanese

Wadsworth/Cengage Learning

Census data for 2006 shows that Asian Americans are the second-largest-growing ethnic group in the U.S.

citizens and were treated as enemies of the United States. In spite of that, Korean Americans fought in World War II alongside American GIs, bought war bonds, and joined the National Guard. After the Korean War, an immigration wave, mainly made up of war brides, took place. Adoptions of Korean children in the years following the Korean War also increased the numbers of this ethnic group (Novas & Cao, 2004).

The majority of Vietnamese Americans came to this country in four waves in the aftermath of the Vietnam War. The first large wave was transported by the U.S. military in 1975 for resettlement in the United States. They were well-educated and skilled technicians from the middle and upper-middle classes of South Vietnamese society. The second wave consisted of 40,000 to 60,000 South Vietnamese who, after they could not be transported by U.S. warships and planes, started a boat evacuation themselves within the first few weeks of the communist victory (Novas & Cao, 2004). Many "boat people" never made it to the United States, having either perished or landed in other safe havens in Southeast Asia. The third wave of Vietnamese immigrants consisted of "boat people" who continued to leave the Socialist Republic of Vietnam from 1979 into the early 1980s (McLemore & Romo, 2005; Novas & Cao, 2004). Their journeys on the South Seas were also perilous and deadly. The fourth wave was comprised of Amerasian children. *Amerasian* is a term used to describe individuals born of Vietnamese mothers and U.S. service members stationed in Vietnam during the Vietnam War. In 1987, Congress passed the Amerasian Homecoming Act to facilitate the transfer of Amerasian children born between 1962 and 1977 to the United States (Novas & Cao, 2004). This allowed nearly 75,000 Amerasians and their family members to come to the United States.

AROUND **THE WORLD**

RULES OF OUR GLOBAL COMMUNITY

As a teacher of young children with diverse backgrounds who interacts with parents and community members, it is useful to become familiar with some cultural do's and don'ts. Each group has its own etiquette that is just as important as our own ways. Here are some examples, with more to come.

- Never touch the head of a Thai child or adult. That is where the "guarding angel" dwells.

- Always ask an adult from another culture what he or she wishes to be called instead of using first names. In many cultures, addressing someone you just met by their first names is considered as disrespectful.

- Remember that every culture has its own special celebrations and holidays. Learn and acknowledge the ones that pertain to the children you teach and to their families.

- Avoid using American slang expressions with those who are not proficient in English. They may not be able to understand the meaning. Using appropriate and academic language benefits children who are learning English.

- Do not expect every child from another culture to "look you straight in the eye." In many cultures, this is considered disrespectful.

Source: Lynch and Hanson (2008); Axtel (1993).

LITERACY CONNECTIONS...

RECOMMENDED BOOKS ABOUT ASIAN AMERICANS

Asian Americans are a very diverse and culturally distinct group. Sharing their stories engages children in exploring and becoming familiar with their rich heritage of customs, legends, and traditions.

- Cheung, H. (2008). *K is for Korea*. CA: Children's Books.
- Khrisnawami, U. (2001). *Chajaji's cup*. CA: Children's Book Press.
- Lee, C. (1989). *Toad is the uncle of heaven*. NY: Holt.
- Lee-Tai, A. (2006). *A place where sunflowers grow*. New York: Children's Book Press.
- Mochizuki, K. (1995). *Baseball saved us*. New York: Lee and Low.

- Noguchi, R. (2002). *Flowers from Mariko*. New York: Lee and Low.
- Park, L. (2009). *The firekeeper's son*. California: Sandpiper.
- Say, A. (2008). *Grandfather's journey*. New York: Houghton Mifflin.
- Say, A. (1999). *Tea with milk*. New York: Houghton Mifflin.
- Tsai, I. (2008). *The frog in the well*. New York: CE Bilingual Books.
- Uchida, Y. (1996). *The bracelet*. New York: Paperstar.
- Yip, M. (2005). *Chinese Children's Favorite Stories*. NY: Tuttle Publisher.

Hispanic Americans

The terms *Hispanic* and *Latino* encompass an enormous range of people and cultures of Spanish and Portuguese origin. During 1980 to 2000, the Hispanic (Latino) population in the United States doubled (Hobbs & Stoops, 2002). From the 1990s to the present, the Hispanic population increased to 45.5 million, making it the largest minority group, surpassing African Americans by approximately 5 million people. Latinos represent about 15 percent of the population. Considering that they have the highest birth rate of any ethnic or racial group in the country, they are projected to grow in the future at a much faster rate than any other group. Hispanics are the largest ethnic group in states such as California, Texas, New Mexico, and Florida (U.S. Census Bureau, 2010).

Wadsworth/Cengage Learning

Hispanics are currently the fastest-growing group of non-European Americans.

LITERACY CONNECTIONS...

RECOMMENDED BOOKS ABOUT HISPANICS

Children's literature is one way to learn about Hispanic cultural traditions. It also provides an excellent source for young children to learn about the unique characteristics of the various Hispanic ethnic groups.

- Ada, A. (2001). *Gathering the sun. An alphabet in Spanish and English.* NY: Rayo.
- Blanco, A. (1998). *Angel's kite/La estrella de angel.* CA: Childrens Book Press.
- Castañeda, E.(1995). *Abuela's weave.* NY: Lee and Low.
- Delacre, L. (1993). *Vejigante.* NY: Scholastic.
- Dole, M.(2003). *Drum, Chavi, drum!/¡Toca, Chavi, toca!* CA: Childrens Book Press.
- Gonzalez, R. (2002). *My first book of proverbs.* CA: Childrens Book Press.
- Lazaro, G. (2004). *El flamboyán Amarillo.* NY: Lectorum.

Mexicans comprise two-thirds of the total Hispanic population in the U.S. The largest concentration, of approximately 13 million, is found in California, Texas, and the Southwest. Many are agricultural seasonal workers or employees of service industries. Mexicans are often exploited by business owners and farmers who pay them subsistence wages and offer no employment benefits. Lack of physical borders between United States and Mexico has made it possible for this group to have a higher number of illegal aliens than all other groups combined. The seriousness of this situation has caused the question of illegal aliens to be moved to the forefront of the political agenda in the United States. Ongoing discussions about borders between Mexico and the Unites States as well as the issue of illegal immigrants continue to dominate the daily media.

The latest census indicates that about 3 percent of the total Hispanic population are Cuban Americans (U.S. Census, 2010). There are, however, great social and economic differences even within this group. The early immigrants who fled Castro's regime and arrived in Florida in the 1960s represented Cuba's social, economic, and intellectual elite. They are largely responsible for making Miami an important commercial center and a "Gateway to South America." A second group of Cuban Americans arrived in the 1980 Mariel boatlift. More recently, the Cuban rafters who continue to arrive on the Florida coasts constitute the newest group of immigrants from this Caribbean island.

The case of Puerto Ricans is different. The Caribbean island of Puerto Rico became part of the United States in 1898. Puerto Ricans are U.S. citizens by birth and are free to live anywhere in the United States and its territories. More than one-third of Puerto Ricans live in the mainland United States. They account for

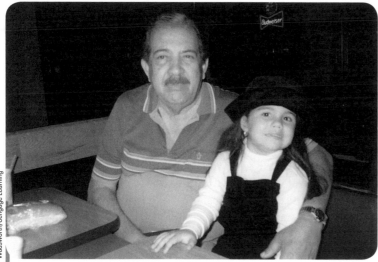

Puerto Ricans are American citizens with Hispano-Caribbean roots.

9 percent of the total Latino population of this country (U. S. Census Bureau, 2010).

The third fastest-growing Latino group consists of those coming from the Caribbean and Central and South American countries, and this group makes up about 20 percent of the total Hispanic population in the United States. Approximately 300,000 from the Dominican Republic are estimated to have settled in New York City alone. Many Hispanics are still struggling for success. For many, language presents a major challenge: less than 30 percent are fluent in English. Of the estimated 30 million, 70 percent live in just four states: California, Florida, New York, and Texas. Separation from their families is also a hardship for many living in the United States. Unfamiliarity with the education and health-care systems also poses serious challenges, making it very difficult to access services. For families of young children, finding out about the available educational and family services is one the most difficult challenges to overcome.

Latino populations are projected to continue to rise in numbers as a result of the second generation. The second generation predominantly consists of young people—two thirds of whom are under the age of 18—who already are or will be citizens of the United States and products of its schools (Suro & Passel, 2003). Their potential contributions to U.S. society make support to the Latino community a national priority.

Native Americans

> *Treat all men alike. Give them all the same law. Give them all an even chance to live and grow.*
>
> Chief Joseph (1840–1904)

Native Americans represent the indigenous inhabitants of the United States. Long before any immigrants came, many Native American nations and tribes already called this territory their homeland. Native Americans are a pluralistic society that should not be viewed as a homogeneous group. The rich history and customs of different nations and tribes are unique and should be studied and presented as individual cultures. Thus, it is difficult to collectively describe the specific family practices, ways, and traditions of Native Americans. Diversity is one of the traits that depicts the Native American people on 314 reservations and trust land areas throughout the country. Yet, we could say that strong family values, respect for their elders, and a high sense of spirituality characterize Native Americans.

The end of the nineteenth century brought about the confinement of Native Americans to designated reservations, many of which were useless patches of wasteland. In addition to having to create a living in these new places, Native Americans were subjected to concerted government efforts to assimilate them into the mainstream culture. These efforts met with great resistance and caused additional clashes between the European Americans and Native Americans. Today, the violent resistance to assimilation has eased somewhat and has been replaced with a cultural revival and an adoption of some political and entrepreneurial models from the mainstream culture.

The 2010 Census showed that Native Americans and Native Alaskans represent less than 1 percent of the population, or 2.4 million people, a rise from 1.4 million in 1990. The increase in the population is partly due to the increased birth rate and more accurate reporting (U.S. Census Bureau, 2010). The four states with the largest Native American populations are Oklahoma, California, Arizona, and New Mexico.

Native Americans have suffered irreparable harm by the government and by the white settlers. The damage that was done to their culture and heritage has caused many problems for the current generations. Having survived centuries of persecution and genocide, the Native Americans are working hard to reclaim their place in U.S. society.

LITERACY CONNECTIONS...

RECOMMENDED BOOKS ABOUT NATIVE AMERICANS

Native American culture abounds in stories and myths focusing on all aspects of life that families pass on to their young from infancy. Here is a selection of books that will familiarize you with some of their rich traditions.

- Goble, P. (2001). *The girl who loved horses.* NY: Atheneum.
- Harjo, J. (2000). *The good luck cat.* NY: Harcourt.
- Smith, C. (2000). *Jingle dancer.* NY: HarperCollins.
- Sockabasin, A. (2005). *Thanks to the animals.* Tilbury Press.
- Van Camp, R. (1997). *A man called Raven.* CA: Children's Book Press.

Middle Eastern Americans

People from the Middle East came to the United States in the late nineteenth century. Christian traders from the Ottoman Empire were probably the first to arrive in the United States in 1875 (Lynch & Hanson, 2008). Other political events led to additional migrations of Iranians, Iraqis, and Afghans. The Iranian revolution in 1978 and the Iran–Iraq war between 1980 and 1988 brought a continuous flow of Iranian immigrants to the United States. During the 1990s and following the Persian Gulf War, many Kuwaiti refugees came to the United States.

To a large extent, the immigrants from the Middle Eastern countries are concentrated in large cities. Those who arrived prior to 1980 are generally educated members of the professional class who possessed a good command of English prior to coming to this country. Those arriving after 1980 seemed to have lower education levels, although most had at least a high school diploma and some knowledge of English (Lynch & Hanson, 2008). Differences exist among the various Middle Eastern groups and, even more so, between the urban and the rural contingents of each group.

Demographically, the Arab American population in the United States increased by nearly 50 percent from the 1990s to 2010, bringing the number to 1.5 million (U.S. Census Bureau, 2010). The three largest Middle Eastern groups represented in the United States are the Lebanese, the Egyptians, and the Syrians. They account for approximately three-fifths of the Middle Eastern U.S. population. Most of them live in large cities, with New York City having the highest number.

Since the tragedy of September 11, Middle Eastern Americans have come under close scrutiny. Before these events, little was known about this ethnic group. Images from the media have focused negative attention on Middle Eastern Americans as a result of the war and security measures. Concerted efforts of educators and responsive individuals are needed to help change these attitudes. In a diverse and democratic society like ours, avoiding any generalizations about an ethnic group is essential. Responding effectively to comments and remarks about Middle Easterners is necessary to prevent prejudice and stereotyping of this group.

Wadsworth/Cengage Learning

Many Middle Eastern families came to our country in the early 1980s as a result of political and religious unrest in their world.

📖 LITERACY CONNECTIONS. . .

RECOMMENDED BOOKS ABOUT MIDDLE EASTERNERS

Stories provide windows into the lives and cultures of people. The titles included in this section address topics ranging from the traditions to the folk tales of people from the Middle East. They provide young children opportunities to discuss, clarify, and learn more about this ethnic group.

- Bunting, E. (2006). *One green apple*. NY: Clarion.
- Ghazi, S. (1996). *Ramadan*. New York: Holiday House.
- Hauff, W., & Shepard, A. (1995). *The enchanted storks: A tale of the Middle East*. Boston: Houghton Mifflin.
- Hickox, R., & Hillenbrand, W. (1999). *The golden sandal: A Middle Eastern Cinderella story*. New York: Holiday House.
- Ichikawa, S. (2006). *My father's shop*. NY: Kane/Miller.
- Kyuchukov, H. (2004). *My name was Hussein*. Honesdale, PA: Boyd Mills Press.
- Matz Sidhom, C., & Farnsworth, B. (2002). *The stars in my Geddoh's sky*. Morton Grove, IL: Albert Whitman & Co.
- Musch, R. (1999). *From far away*. Minneapolis, MN: Sagebrush.
- Nye, N. (1997). *Sitti's secrets*. New York: Aladdin.
- Parry, F. (1995). *The day of Ahmed's secret*. New York: Harper-Trophy.

African Americans

Historically, African Americans were the only group who did not originally come to the United States as immigrants. Removed against their will from their homeland by the unscrupulous human traffickers of colonial times, they were brought to the New World as slaves. This led to the institutionalized inhumane treatment rooted in violence and injustice, which they endured for centuries. In the post–Civil War era, this system was replaced by discrimination and racism sanctioned by legislation.

During the years following the Civil War, racial hatred produced many contradictory social initiatives that altered the fabric of U.S. society for the next hundred years. The founding of the Ku Klux Klan in 1866 signaled the beginning of an era of extreme persecution of African Americans. Additionally, the Black Codes enacted in 1865–1866 to disenfranchise them and the Supreme Court decision *Plessy v. Ferguson* in 1896 that established "the separate but equal" doctrine were all designed to deny African Americans their rightful place in society.

Throughout the twentieth century, racism and discrimination kept African Americans segregated from whites in schools, factories, businesses, housing, public facilities, and services. "Jim Crow" laws, which took the form of literacy tests, "white primaries," poll taxes, and "grandfather" clauses, were all enacted to prevent African Americans from exercising their right to vote. Not being able to exercise this right prevented African Americans from participating in the greatest era of progress in U.S. history. Things did not begin to change until World War II, when the military desegregated and the landmark

According to the Census, African-Americans comprise over 13% of the U.S. population.

case of *Brown v. the Board of Education* in 1954 abolished school segregation (McLemore and Romo, 2005). The late 1950s and 1960s marked the greatest years of social change in recent U.S. history. The civil rights movement became the focus of U.S. society largely as a result of the leadership of African American organizations, such as the National Association for the Advancement of Colored People (NAACP), the Urban League, and the Southern Christian Leadership Conference, as well as individuals, such as Dr. Martin Luther King Jr., Rosa Parks, Thurgood Marshall, and others. The sit-ins, freedom rides, peace demonstrations, and violence associated with African Americans attempting to gain admission to formerly all-white institutions provided the nation with a renewed look at the depth of hatred and racism. Many battles were won during those years, including the Civil Rights Act and Equal Opportunity Act of 1964 and the Voting Rights Act of 1965. The federal government poured much money into social programs intended to assist the poor and the disadvantaged during the 1960s and 1970s. These initiatives and services gave the government the right to interfere in cases of discrimination within the individual states, without which many cases involving African Americans could not be settled.

Data from the 2010 U.S. census (Bureau of Census, 2010) indicate that there are approximately 39.4 million African Americans, representing 12.7 percent of the total population. They are the second largest minority group after the Hispanics. Many are the challenges still faced by African Americans in the twenty-first century. This is partly due to the fact that societal institutions have failed to meet their needs. However, the incredible resiliency, sense of pride, and desire to improve that characterize African Americans will continue to facilitate their progress. Results from the 2008 elections in the United States marked a historical event with the election of an African American, Barack Obama, as president. His election brought about a new dimension in the social and cultural fabric of the nation and set new expectations for the future of racial relationships in a nation defined by diversity.

Pacific Islanders

Pacific Islanders have roots in the islands and archipelagos of the vast Central and South Pacific Ocean also known as Oceania (Novas & Cao, 2004). Many are sovereign nations, and others are affiliated with the United States. Oceania is divided into three major regions: Polynesia, Micronesia, and Melanesia. Polynesia, which includes the Hawaiian Islands, is the largest. Census 2000 was the first census that designated Native Hawaiians and other

Wadsworth/Cengage Learning

LITERACY CONNECTIONS. . .

LEARNING ABOUT AFRICAN AMERICANS

Stories have the power to bring life issues into the world of the child in ways that adults sometimes cannot. The following titles address various cultural aspects about African American traditions and family lifestyles.

- Adoff, A. (2004). *Black is brown is tan.* New York: Harper & Row.
- Anastasia, N. (2001). *I love my hair!* New York: Little Brown.
- Collier, B. (2004). *Uptown.* New York: Henry Holt.
- Dillon, L. (2002). *Rap a tap, tap.* Blue Sky Press.
- Hudson, W. (1993). *Pass it on: African-American poetry for children.* New York: Scholastic.
- Levine, E. (2007). *Henry's freedom box.* NY: Scholastic.
- Manjo, N. (1970). *The drinking gourd.* Englewood Cliffs, NJ: Harper & Row.
- Rappaport, L. (2007). *Martin's big words. The life of Dr. Martin Luther King.* NY: Hyperion.
- Steptoe, J. (2001). *In daddy's arms I am tall: African Americas celebrating fathers.* New York: Lee & Low.
- Woodson, J. (2001). *The other side.* New York: Putnam.

Pacific Islanders (287 islands) as a racial group distinct from Asians (Novas & Cao, 2004). Pacific Islander Americans differ from most immigrants. They did not come to the mainland United States looking for a better life. In their case, the United States came to them through extended borders propelled by the political, economic, and social winds of change.

The two Pacific Islander groups with the highest population in the United States are the Hawaiians and the Samoans. They, like many other colonized people, experienced many changes as a result of Western cultures. Samoa was occupied by the Dutch in 1722 and Christianized by the missionaries by the 1830s. Throughout the twentieth century, the United States, England, and Germany asserted power over this small nation. In 1900, Samoa was partitioned into two parts, one of which, American Samoa, still remains a U.S. territory. The majority of American Samoans came to this country for economic reasons and settled in ethnic enclaves in California. The transfer of this group was also facilitated through the transfer of navy base personnel. Samoans in the United States have been acculturated to a lesser extent than the Hawaiians, whose association with the United States has closer ties.

Hawaiians first came in touch with the Europeans through the explorer Captain James Cook in 1778. Throughout the nineteenth century, visitors from the United States, England, Germany, Spain, Portugal, and other countries influenced massive changes, not only in religious views but also in the political and socioeconomic practices of native Hawaiian people. The Westerners had a devastating effect on the native population, largely attributed to diseases for which the natives had no immunity. Hawaiians are very proactively engaged in preserving their culture, especially in their native islands where they are in the minority.

Before 1950, few Pacific Islanders ventured into the continental United States. Today, however, demographic data indicate that over 58 percent reside in California

LITERACY CONNECTIONS. . .

RECOMMENDED BOOKS ABOUT PACIFIC ISLANDERS

Stories about the people of the Pacific convey these peoples' life experiences and cultures and are part of the rich, diverse mosaic of U.S. society. The following selections are a sample of the many tales, myths, and legends that Pacific Islander families have shared for generations.

- Beamer, N. (2008). *Naupaka*. Kamahoi Press.
- Beamer, N. (2005). *Pua Polu, the pretty blue Hawaiian flower*. Kamahoi Press.
- Nelisi, L. (1992). *Sione's talo*. NY: Scholastic.
- Phillips, L. (2004). *Samoan alphabet*. Bess Press.

and Hawaii (Hobbs & Stoops, 2002). Small percentages are also found in Washington, Utah, Texas, New York, and Florida. The total population of Hawaiians and Pacific Islanders is fewer than a million (U.S. Census Bureau, 2010).

THE UNITED STATES: A KALEIDOSCOPE OF PEOPLE

Today's communities, schools, and workplaces reflect the changing social and cultural landscape of the United States. Everything we know about the demographic patterns indicates that diversity is here to stay. Even though the non-European cultural groups are playing an increasingly more dominant role, the groups of European origin will continue to be an important influence on the development of the country in the twenty-first century. Aside from both being part of the U.S. demography, the groups share another common characteristic: heterogeneity (see Figures 1-5 and 1-6).

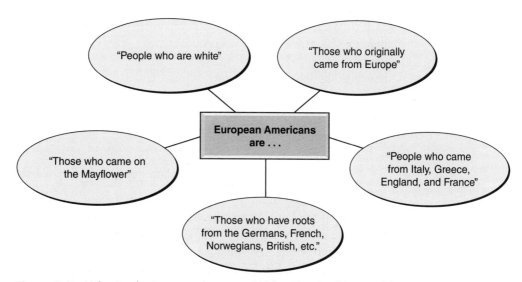

Figure 1-5   Who Are the European Americans? What Else Would You Add?

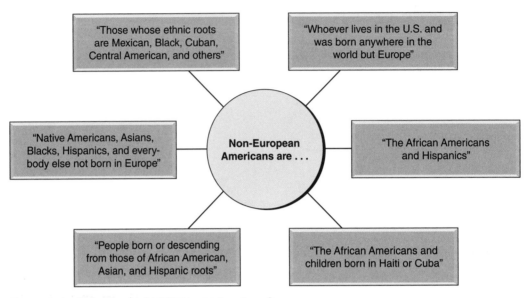

Figure 1-6   Who Are the Non-European Americans?

Terms are useful in identifying a specific quality or shared characteristics. Sometimes, however, a term can oversimplify the meaning or hide its magnitude. Using geographical terminology, like "Hawaiian," in connection with individual non-European American and European American cultural groups does not provide an accurate description of each group.

When a group of early childhood graduate students were informally asked to web their ideas about the terms *non-European Americans* and *European Americans*, their responses showed a wide range of ideas (Robles de Meléndez, 2006). In most cases, some cultural groups, such as the Pacific Islanders and the Middle Easterners, were not included, whereas all failed to identify the European Americans as being a diverse group in itself. What are the implications of these responses? Mainly, there is a need for early childhood educators to build and have accurate knowledge about the various cultural groups if they are to deliver developmentally appropriate programs that are sensitive and responsive to the world of today's children.

CURRENT IMMIGRATION DEBATE

In the last few years, the issue of immigration has advanced to the top of the political agenda in the United States. The lagging economy and high unemployment rate continue to fuel the debate. The issue of illegal immigration in particular is polarizing our society. Some favor amnesty and social programs that will assist those who are law abiding and employed to achieve legal status, while others believe in more extreme measures and tougher laws. According to the Pew Hispanic Center, the economic factors and legal measures have resulted in a 50 percent decrease (300,000) of illegal immigrants crossing the border into the United States from five years ago (Bennett, 2010). In spite of such improvements, currently there are no permanent solutions to the illegal immigrant problem. It is likely that the topic will remain at the forefront of public discussion for a long time to come.

IMMIGRATION

Immigrants entering illegally present a political and economic problem for the United States. The issue will become even more significant if the jobless rate remains high. We are entering a new era of possible conflict over a principle on which our country was founded. Driven mostly by the impact of the economic situation, the Statue of Liberty's motto "Give me you tired, your poor, your huddled masses yearning to be free" is acquiring a different meaning.

Reflect on the statements and share your thoughts and experiences. Consider the impact of this reality on young children and their families.

CALL FOR ACTION

Today, addressing cultural diversity remains a challenge for the United States that civic and professional organizations, such as the National Association for the Education of Young Children (NAEYC), Association for Supervision and Curriculum Development (ASCD), Southern Early Childhood Association (SECA), and National Council for the Social Studies (NCSS), work to overcome. There is a pressing need for early childhood educators to be aware of these past and present efforts in order to assist children in acquiring ways to face the challenges of our continuously growing, pluralistic world.

Now more than ever, educators of young children recognize that the new complex diversity mandates programs that positively affect the learning processes and social adjustments of all school children. As an early childhood educator, providing children with developmentally and culturally appropriate practices (DAP) is at the core of your profession (Bredekamp & Copple, 2009). Today, culture and diversity are acknowledged as elements defining program quality in all dimensions of early education. From classroom instruction to interactions with families and communities, sensitivity to and respect for the child and family's culture is intrinsic to professional practice. The NAEYC's Code of Ethical Conduct and Statement of Commitment (2005) further emphasize the responsibilities of early educators working with culturally diverse children and families:

Section II:

Ideals:

I-2.5. To respect the dignity and preferences of each family and to make an effort to learn about its structure, culture, language, customs, and beliefs.

I-2.6. To acknowledge families' childrearing values and their right to make decisions for their children.

Experiences in early childhood settings show that developmental practices are effectively guided when there is an understanding of the child in the "context of family, community, culture, linguistic norms, social group, past experience and current circumstances" (NAEYC, 2009, p. 10). To create responsive environments, early child-hood educators cannot isolate activities from the social and cultural framework of the child. Educational designs that are based on the principles of child development recognize the undeniable influence culture has on the child (Berger, 2005).

With the increasingly changing nature of the country and world, early childhood professionals must be cognizant of the ongoing social and cultural transformations. This constant state of sociocultural flux affects the physical and social environments of all children. More precisely, the increased growth of the non-European American population, as demographers have predicted, is producing and will continue to produce a distinctively different social climate for children living in the twenty-first century United States.

Research has shown that the way a young child learns to view and respond to the social world depends on the cultural values held in the immediate surroundings (Jarvis, 2003; Wright & Edelman, 2004). Culture, thus, plays a crucial role in the development of the child. If the society of the twenty-first century is to be characterized by a higher degree of diversity, this unquestionably describes an environment where children will find a multiplicity of cultural values. As an early childhood educator, you must consider the following questions:

- *Am I preparing children to live in the twenty-first century?*
- *Am I aware that today's preschoolers, kindergartners, and primary grade students will live their adult lives in a new era very different from mine?*
- *What am I doing about it now?*

Issues raised by these questions constitute a call for action for early childhood professionals. We need to prepare to serve children in consonance with reality. This is not only a need but a mandate if we are to teach children in genuinely developmentally appropriate ways. It is no longer acceptable to just display pictures of groups different from the mainstream culture or to assign a week to celebrate multiculturalism, which are practices still found in many classrooms. Nor is it acceptable to decide what students should learn without regard for the new socio-cultural realities.

Education is a process of guiding and preparing a child to succeed in life. Given the social reality of the future, education of the young will have to encompass the skills and knowledge children need to navigate this pluralistic world. This will include learning to live effectively and productively in a society where diversity is a major factor. The success formula for future generations will include a solid foundation in cultural knowledge of many non-European American groups. The social skills and tools to interact effectively with these groups will be an essential part of everyday life and ultimately the key to survival in the twenty-first century.

One out of three children in 2050 in the United States will be a non-European American (Hobbs & Stoops, 2002). The difference between successful and unsuccessful individuals, at that time, may be the ability to interact effectively with people of various cultures. Early childhood professionals must lay the foundation by offering all children appropriate educational programs that will enable them to become successful individuals in this multicultural environment. This is the position that describes the aspiration for early childhood practices aimed at acknowledging, respecting, and incorporating the children's cultures and diverse characteristics into daily experiences in classrooms everywhere.

Leading scholars in the field of multiculturalism describe the goal of education for diversity as a way of keeping and maintaining the spirit and the essence of the American unum (Banks, 2006; National Council for the Social Studies, 1992). This idea of the American *unum*, literally, "where all are one," and where everyone is equally important, is a reminder of the goals and purposes that define our country: the champion of democracy and equality for all individuals. The authors of this book also believe that the achievement and preservation of the idea of *e pluribus unum* begins with the child. Because early childhood educators play such a vital role in the development of children, the future of our society may well rest in their hands.

YOUR STANDARDS PORTFOLIO

Documenting Your Knowledge about Multiculturalism and Diversity

As you embark on the journey of learning about multicultural education, you will have opportunities to learn about new concepts, strategies, and resources. To document your progress, we invite you to create your own portfolio. A portfolio is a way of demonstrating and documenting your knowledge and mastery of key competencies. Sample artifacts are collected over time to show how you meet expectations of teaching and working with young children and their families.

A portfolio can be created around many different elements such as a job, a hobby, volunteer work, and so on. In education, portfolios are created around significant benchmarks, such as professional standards and state guidelines. Throughout this book, you will have opportunities to use the NAEYC standards for professional preparation as the framework to build your portfolio. We have also broadened the scope of your portfolio by correlating the NAEYC standards with the widely used standards developed by the Interstate New Teacher Assessment and Support Consortium (INTASC).

Purpose of a Professional Portfolio

A professional portfolio has many uses. It is a portrait of yourself as a current or aspiring early childhood professional and a record of your accomplishments. A portfolio can be created according to many professional guidelines that are provided by state agencies, school districts, and professional organizations. You can organize this very personal document to present yourself in the most positive light as a professional. Some of the artifacts that may be included in the portfolio are an autobiographical sketch, a résumé, your philosophy of early childhood education, and any special honors and awards, as well as evidence of mastery of professional competencies as defined by your profession. The portfolio is a creative and personal document that has many applications. The portfolio exercise also allows you to learn more about your beliefs, commitments, and skills. Creating a portfolio is an invaluable experience. We invite you to begin the process now.

Using Standards to Organize Your Portfolio

As stated previously, we have chosen for the framework of your portfolio the professional standards outlined by NAEYC (NAEYC, 2011). These guidelines address quality of professional preparation as well as effective delivery of learning experiences for young children. Seven core standards describe the critical expectations and characteristics of professional early childhood educators:

1. *Promoting Child Development and Learning*
2. *Building Family and Community Relations*
3. *Observing, Assessing and Documenting*
4. *Using Developmentally Effective Approaches to Connnect with Children and Families*
5. *Using Content Knowledge to Build Meaningful Curriculum*
6. *Becoming a Professional*
7. *Early Childhood Field Experiences*

The Interstate Teacher Assessment and Support Consortium (InTASC) standards that have been correlated with the NAEYC standards describe generic principles of best teaching practices to meet the needs of all students.

Standard 1: Learner Development

Standard 2: Learning Differences

Standard 3: Learning Environment

Standard 4: Content Knowledge

Standard 5: Application of Content

Standard 6: Assessment

Standard 7: Planning for Instruction

Standard 8: Instructional Strategies

Standard 9: Professional Learning and Ethical Practice

Standard 10: Leadership and Collaboration

Creating Your Portfolio

Activities located at the end of each chapter are intended to connect the content and your experiences to the specific NAEYC and InTASC standards. The activities allow you to demonstrate your knowledge by creating various artifacts for your portfolio. Artifacts can take many forms, such as written reflections, projects, multimedia creations, lesson plans, or tests, just to name a few.

The portfolio has many purposes. It is an excellent tool for keeping track of your professional growth and progress. We have been told on many occasions that the portfolio is extremely useful in job interviews, and many students have also used their portfolios in formal presentations and workshops. We hope that you will create an exemplary record of your work and knowledge and that it will serve you well in the future.

WHAT WE HAVE LEARNED—CHAPTER SUMMARY

In this chapter, you learned about the origins of multiculturalism in our country. The profiles and short histories of major cultural groups were presented along with some key historical events, the current demographics, and future growth patterns. The concept of immigrants and processes of immigration were emphasized in order to make you aware of what many members of our society, including young children, experience. We discussed the meaning of diversity and its importance in education as well as its growing importance in the future of the United States. Being alike and being different do not need to be polarizing positions for anyone, least of all for educators of young children. Emphasizing our commonalities and expanding the understanding of others are keys to a better world that educators of young children hold as a sacred trust.

MAKING CONNECTIONS . . .

1. Discovering the cultural composition of your neighborhood and of the community of your school helps you gain a practical awareness about the people you live with. Begin by making a list of the cultures present in both environments, your neighborhood and your school. Then, take a field trip and list all the things that reflect diversity (signs, buildings, decorations, etc.). What did you find? Highlight those cultures you feel you need to learn more about. Your school or community library is a good place to continue your search.

2. Are you aware of your own culture? To appreciate cultural diversity, you must first know your own. Get a stack of index cards. On one of the index cards, write the name of the cultural group you think you belong to. Next, find out where (geographical area) that cultural group originates and write it on another card. Use the other cards to describe the things you do that underline your being part of that cultural group. Examine your results and see what you discovered about yourself that you were not aware of before.

3. Get together with two or three colleagues and discuss your backgrounds. Identify the historical event that brought the members of your family or you to the United States. Then, create lists of social, economic, and political events that caused their or your immigration. Discuss what may have happened if they or you never left. How have your and their lives changed as a result of coming to the United States? List the positive and negative elements of the experience.

4. Take action in your classroom by examining your present curriculum for diversity. Highlight those activities and concepts that focus on pluralism.

5. This book will take you on a journey where you will find ways to develop an appropriate multicultural environment for young children. Begin

a diary of your experiences. You may want to get a small notebook where you can record your thoughts and experiences. To begin your diary, enter your responses to these questions:

- *What do I want for children as an individual and as a teacher?*
- *How can I support the needs of children with cultural and diverse characteristics?*

6. Write a description of your community in 2050. While writing, think about what the architecture, recreation, schools, churches, and people may be like. What about language technology, transportation, and so on?

RECOMMENDED INTERNET RESOURCES

- Articles from the Center for Immigration Studies providing historical perspectives on immigration
  www.cis.org/topics/history.html

- Links to relevant sub-topics related to historical and current immigration issues, from the Constitutional Rights Foundation
  www.crf-usa.org/immigration/immigration_history.htm

- The U.S. Census, the main source of data and information on a variety of demographic topics
  www.census.gov

- *National Association for the Education of Young Children* is a professional organization providing leadership and advocacy for young children and early childhood education
  http://www.naeyc.org

YOUR STANDARDS PORTFOLIO

naeyc **Standard 1:** Promoting Child Development and Learning

naeyc **Standard 6:** Becoming a Professional

InTASC Standard 1: Learner Development

InTASC Standard 9: Professional Learning and Ethical Practice

One of the critical characteristics of a professional multicultural educator is the ability to reflect on issues that concern young children, their families, and the impact of classroom practices on their lives. Reflection is a way of being introspective and examining your thoughts and opinions at a deeper level. As you reflect, you acquire additional information and in-depth knowledge. Reflection allows you to critically look at your own practices and identify ways to enhance your professional skills as a multicultural

early childhood educator. Here are suggested activities to address standard 6.

a. Begin a journal of reflections and record your thoughts and ideas as you explore the topics in this book that relate to your experiences and work with children and their families. This book's components, such as "In Action," "Around the World," "Focus on Classroom Practices" and "Think and Reflect," will help you reflect on key concepts of diversity.

Record your reflections on the following questions

• *As an early childhood educator, what do I want for young children?*
• *What do I need to know to support the needs of culturally diverse children and their families?*

b. *Within the framework of diversity, reflect on your own experiences and consider how you have approached the needs of children with diverse characteristics.*

You may want to use the form in the Appendix section to collect your responses.

REFERENCES

Axtel, R. E. (1993). *Do's and Taboos Around the World.* NY: Wiley.

Banks, J. (2006). *Cultural diversity and education: Foundations, curriculum, and teaching* (5th ed.). Needham Heights, MA: Allyn & Bacon.

Banks, J., & Banks, C. M. (Eds.). (2009). *Multicultural education: Issues and perspectives* (7nd ed.). Needham Heights, MA: Allyn & Bacon.

Baruth, L., & Manning, M. L. (2008). *Multicultural education of children and adolescents* (5th ed.). Needham Heights, MA: Allyn & Bacon.

Bennett, B. (December 27, 2010). *Immigration Debate Changes.* Sun Sentinel. Fort Lauderdale, FL.

Berger, K. (2005). *The developing person through childhood and adolescence.* New York: Worth.

Bredekamp, S., & Copple, C. (2009). *Developmentally appropriate practice in early childhood programs* (Rev. ed.). Washington, DC: National Association for the Education of Young Children.

Brown McCracken, J. (1993). *Valuing the primary years.* Washington, DC: National Association for the Education of Young Children.

Campbell, D. E. (2009). *Choosing democracy: A practical guide to multicultural education* (4th ed.). Upper Saddle River, NY: Pearson.

Doctorow, E. L. (2007). *Ragtime.* New York: Alfred Knopf. (Original work published in 1975).

Hobbs, F., & Stoops, N. (2002). *Demographic trends in the 20th century.* (Census 2000 Special Report, Series CENSR-4.) Washington, DC: U.S. Government Printing Office.

Jarvis, A. (2003). *Social learning theory.* New York: RoutledgeFalmer.

Kivel, P. (2002). *Uprooting racism* (Rev. ed.). Canada: New Society Publishers.

Lynch, E. W., & Hanson, M. J. (2008). *Developing cross-cultural competence: A guide for working with young children and their families.* Baltimore, MD: Paul Brookes.

Martorella, P. H. (2001). *Social studies for elementary school children.* New York: Prentice Hall.

McLemore, S. & Remo, H. (2005). *Racial and ethical relations in America.* New York: Pearson.

Migration Policy Institute. *Inflow of New Legal Permanent Residents by Country of Birth, Fiscal Year 1999-2009.* Retrieved from: http://www.migrationinformation. org/datahub/countrydata/files/DH_US_InflowLP RsbyCOB.xls

National Association for the Education of Young Children. (2005). *Code of ethical conduct & statement of commitment: A position statement of the National Association for the Education of Young Children.* Washington, DC: Author.

National Association for the Education of Young Children. (2010). *NAEYC Standards for Early Childhood Professional Preparation Programs. Position statement of the National Association for the Education of Young Children.* Washington, DC: Author

National Council for the Social Studies. (1992). Guidelines for multicultural teaching. *Social Education* 56(3), 274–294.

Nieto, S., & Bode, P. (2008). *Affirming diversity: The sociopolitical context of multicultural education.* New York: Longman.

Novas, H., & Cao, L. (2004). *Everything you need to know about Asian-American History.* New York: Plume.

Parillo, V. N. (2007). *Understanding race and ethnic relations* (3rd ed.). Needham Heights, MA: Allyn & Bacon.

Robles de Meléndez, W. (2006). Activities for the graduate course. *Planning the multicultural environment.*

Summer. Fort Lauderdale, FL: Nova Southeastern University.

Rosales, L. (1992). *Listen to the heart: Impressions and memories of a teacher.* Unpublished manuscript.

Say, A. (2008). *Grandfather's journey.* Boston: Houghton Mifflin.

Suro, R., & Passel, J. S. (2003). The rise of the second generation: Changing patterns in Hispanic population growth. Retrieved from http://pewhispanic.org/files/reports/22.pdf.

U.S. Census Bureau. (2010). *Demographic and housing estimates.: 2005-2009.* Retrieved from http://factfinder.census. gov/servlet.

U.S. Census Bureau. (2010). *Selected social characteristics in the United States: 2005–2009.* Retrieved December 22, 2010, from http:// factfinder.census.gov/servlet.

U.S. Census Bureau. (2010). *United States by states-GCT-TI-R. Population estimates.* Retrieved from http:// factfinder.census.gov/servlet.

U.S. Census Bureau (2005-2009). American Survey. Washington, DC: Department of Commerce.

Wright, A., & Edelman, W. A. (2004). *Faces of hope: Children of a changing world.* New York: New World Library.

The Nature of Culture, the Nature of People

Culture is [a] framework that guides and bounds life practices.
—E. Lynch and M. Hanson (2004)

STANDARDS: THE FOLLOWING STANDARDS ARE ADDRESSED IN THIS CHAPTER:

naeyc **Standard 1:** Promoting Child Development and Learning

naeyc **Standard 4:** Using Developmentally Effective Approaches to Connect with Children and Families

naeyc **Standard 7:** Early Childhood Field Experiences

InTASC Standard 2: Learning Differences

InTASC Standard 4: Content Knowledge

CHAPTER OBJECTIVES

Upon reading this chapter and reflecting on its content, you will identify the ways *culture shapes our lives and influences* the lives of young children.

KEY CONCEPTS

- culture
- socialization
- cultural identity
- cultural diversity
- race
- stereotype
- cultural values

TEACHERS SHARE: AN INDECENT PRACTICE

Ms. Allen believed that her child-care center was the best facility for young children. Every effort had been made to follow developmentally appropriate practices. Recently opened in a suburban area, the center was enthusiastically received by the parents in the community. The children seemed very happy. The staff, hand picked by Ms. Allen, was excellent.

One morning, Ms. Allen was surprised to get a call from a very irate Mrs. García, who informed her that she was moving her 4-year-old daughter to another school. Only a week before, Ms. Allen had personally registered the bright-eyed child and had a pleasant conversation with Mrs. Garcia, who then seemed very impressed by the school. Ms. Allen could not understand the reason for the parent's sudden anger or her actions.

After getting off the phone, the very puzzled Ms. Allen asked if anyone in the office was aware of an incident involving the Mrs. Garcia's child. Her secretary informed her that the child's mother called the day before and complained that in her child's classroom they were doing things that were indecent, "especially for a girl." But the secretary had been so busy that she had forgotten to mention the conversation to Ms. Allen. "This can't be true," said Ms. Allen and went to see the teacher to learn more before calling back Mrs. Garcia.

Ms. Morton, the teacher, told Ms. Allen that Mrs. Garcia visited her daughter's classroom the day before and saw the children's bathrooms, which made her "very irate." Ms. Morton tried to explain that the absence of doors was a safety measure. Despite her efforts to elaborate further, Mrs. Garcia took her child and left very annoyed. "I really don't know why," Ms. Morton said. Ms. Allen thought for a moment and said, "I do." She knew that in some cultures modesty and the need for privacy are perceived differently.

CULTURE, THE MAGIC WEB OF LIFE

Have you ever asked yourself why you are the way you are? Why you act the way you act? Why you believe in what you believe? Why you speak the language you speak? Why you eat what you eat? The answer is culture, a critical factor in everything we do, say, believe, and are.

The definition of culture has been a focus of discussions among social scientists, educators, philosophers, and people in general for generations. No one seems to be able to agree on one definition. However, everybody acknowledges that we all have a culture.

Culture is a part of each individual because it is a part of every society (Geertz, 2000). No one can claim to be exempt from having a culture. This is inherent to human nature. Whether aware of it or not, "everybody has a culture" (Nieto & Bode, 2008). Individuals begin to assimilate culture from birth. As early childhood educators, you have probably noticed the different ways your children respond to experiences and interpret reality in the classroom. This may be even more evident at times when your interpretations diverge from the children's. These variations are largely rooted in their individual cultural patterns.

IN ACTION . . .

WHAT IS YOUR IDEA OF CULTURE?

Before reading any further, you should explore your ideas about culture. Take a piece of paper and fold it into three parts. Title each part as follows: *My ideas about culture, Examples of culture in my family,* and *Examples of culture in my community.* Fill in the first column by writing all the ideas that you believe define culture. As you read through this chapter, complete the rest of the columns. We will get back to this activity later.

The Need for Guideposts: What Culture Does for Human Beings

Imagine a world with no rules. Think about how it would be if there were no guidelines for our existence, no principles to tell us what is right or wrong, no frames of reference to give us clues as we confront things never encountered before. Those are some of the problems we would face if there were no culture.

Culture provides a framework for our lives. It guides humans to find meaning in events, interpret the past, and set aspirations. From very early in life, we learn to follow and apply the recognized guidelines of our groups, sometimes without even being consciously aware of them. For a child, cultural guidelines are discovered through daily interactions with others, observing the environment, and modeling behaviors learned from families and adults. Psychologist Jerome Bruner (1996) indicates that when the child enters into a group, the child does so as a participant of a public process where meanings are shared. This participant status entitles the child to learn the ways of the group. Learning makes the child a member of a group. These "ways of the group" are what we call culture. As social human beings, we all belong to a group, and all groups have culture.

We All Have a Culture

Social scientists—sociologists, anthropologists, and psychologists—believe that culture demarcates all manners people use to interact in the context of society. Culture is necessary for humans to survive in a social group. Bruner (1996) affirms that a major point in human evolution was when culture became a factor in defining the identity of a group, thus the individual. This is what makes culture a thing shared by all social groups.

There are many ways to describe and define culture. For Freire (2000), culture encompasses all that is done by people. Hernandez (2001) says that culture refers to "the complex processes of human social interaction and symbolic communication." Arvizu, Snyder, and Espinosa (cited by Hernandez, 2001) describe culture as an instrument

THINK AND REFLECT...

THIS IS MY CULTURE

Our culture defines who we are and how we live. It permeates most aspects of our lives, including those that are easy to observe and those that are not. Culture can be a safe haven or a battlefield; a cherished possession or a burden.

- *What is my perception about my own culture?*
- *What are some of the aspects easily noticed? Which ones are not?*
- *How has my own culture influenced who I am?*

Figure 2-1
Dimensions of Culture

Through culture we . . .
SEE   PERCEIVE   INTERPRET   REPRESENT
SYMBOLIZE   VALUE   ASSIGN MEANING

people use as they struggle to survive in a social group. The definition used throughout this book identifies culture as the ways and manners people use to see, perceive, represent, interpret, and assign value and meaning (see Figure 2-1) to the reality they live or experience (Banks, 2007; Lynch & Hanson, 2004; Nieto & Bode, 2008).

Looking at Life Through Our Cultures

> *Todo es del color del cristal con que se mira. (Everything depends on the color of the glass you look through.)*
> Pedro Calderón de la Barca (1600–1681), *La Vida es Sueño*

Culture is a glass prism through which we look at life. Like a prism, culture has many facets. Early childhood educators need to be cognizant and aware of these various angles that help explain the behavior, reactions, and manners of children in the classroom.

Some of the key aspects of culture that contribute to understanding and responsively planning experiences for young children and their families are the following:

• *Culture defines the accepted behaviors, roles, interpretations, and expectations of a social group.* Every social group has norms and principles that reflect agreed meanings. For example, in Nepalese society, it is accepted "to pop in and stare at the strange [Westerner] at great length, without thinking twice about it" (Murray, 1993).

• *Culture is present in visible, tangible ways.* Culture also exists in abstract ways that are not physically perceived by the eye. For example, we see the sari dress of an Indian woman and a child's toy truck and recognize them for what they are. However, we do not know why the Indian woman is smiling or why the child is hugging the toy. These reactions are rooted in inner feelings that are not readily visible.

• *Culture offers stable patterns to guide human behavior.* Although constant, culture is also dynamic as it constantly responds to the various influences in the surroundings, affecting changes whenever necessary. An example of this is seen in the concept of a child. Today, a child is considered an individual with unique characteristics and rights, whereas in the past, the child was not valued as a person (Roopnarine & Johnson, 2008).

• *Culture is acquired through interactions with the environment.* The major settings where culture is learned are the family and the school. One of the most evident aspects of culture acquisition is how, through interactions with parents and family members, children learn the language of their group. Cultural expectations also help children to build knowledge about their cultures. For example, in many countries in Africa, children as young as age 5 are expected to take care of younger siblings. Culture was also found to be the critical factor influencing attachment and socialization patterns during the early childhood years (Gardiner and Kosmitzki, 2005; Harwood, Miller, & de Lucca, 1997).

- *We begin learning the patterns and shared meanings of the group we belong to at birth.* This knowledge increases and changes as we grow and develop, both individually and as a member of society. Think about how a 5-year-old interprets a birthday party and compare it with the reactions of a 2-year-old. Compare the ideas held about single parents in the 1950s with those of today.

- *Culture influences all and every different aspect of life.* Nothing escapes the power of culture. Notice, for example, how you dress yourself and how you decide what appeals to you as beautiful in contrast to what you label as not beautiful.

- *Cultural differences also exist among people of the same culture.* Within a same group, differing lifestyles and values are not uncommon. Experiences, including personal and historical circumstances, shape people's views. For instance, ideas and practices concerning child rearing held by urban parents probably differ from the views held by parents in rural areas. Even people belonging to a same family may exhibit differences in terms of their behaviors and ideas.

- *Culture gives people identity.* Sharing ideas, values, and practices gives humans a sense of being part of an entity. There are various factors that make people feel they are members of a group. Having a gender, age, religion, and family background are among the basic factors that provide a sense of identity. Additional traits that define someone's unique persona are derived from experiences and interactions with others within and outside one's cultural group.

Cultural Dimensions

> *"There is no one aspect of life that is not touched and altered by culture."*
> E. Hall (1990)

The influence of culture is so powerful that it covers every aspect of behavior. This includes personality, how people dress themselves (including shows of emotions), the way they think, how they move, how problems are solved, how their cities are planned and laid out, how transportation systems function, and how economic and government systems are put together and function.

Culture is exhibited in *visible* ways (that is, with our body movements, our gestures, and the physical distribution of our cities) and *invisible* ways (such as with our thoughts and ways we solve problems). Also visible to the eye are dress codes, eating patterns, and even the games played by children. Other things remain invisible, but are perceived through actions. Examples of the invisible culture may be seen in emotional reactions to events such as happy occasions or death, how to welcome guests into one's home, or how to interpret an event.

IN ACTION . . .

EXPLORING CULTURE

One of the ways to "see" proof that we all have and respond within a cultural framework is to find two persons and ask them what they think is the right way to celebrate a wedding. Write their answers and compare them with your own.

- Were they in agreement with each other?
- Were you in agreement with them? Why?

Whether visible or not, culture provides patterns to interpret life. We use them every day. Like the skin that covers our bodies and gives us our external individual identity, culture is always with us (Lynch & Hanson, 2004). As a classroom educator, you have probably experienced times when you could easily identify the cultural patterns followed by your students; however, other times, you have probably been unable to do so. This occurs because culture presents itself in ways that are either materially or nonmaterially expressed (see Figure 2-2) (Gardiner & Kosmitzki, 2005; Hernandez, 2001).

The presence of culture transcends all that we do. The material and the nonmaterial sides of culture are constantly working together. You and your children display them

Figure 2-2   Cultural Levels in the Community and the Early Childhood Classroom

Material Culture:
What we see, hear, and experience

- Language—accents, intonations
- Dress—colors, garments, materials, dress codes
- Food and eating—items, preparation, eating habits
- Personal decorations—jewelry, body decorations, head coverings
- Utensils and tools—cooking utensils, living utensils
- Artwork—styles, colors, use of materials, folk art
- Music—instruments, practices, sounds
- Construction—buildings, home decorations
- Household utensils

Nonmaterial Culture:
What is invisible to the eye but perceived through interactions

- Ideas
- Values
- Beliefs
- Feelings and emotions

in the classroom through your actions and interactions. Usually, we can easily note differences in others when they are visible or, to a lesser extent, when they are not observable but perceived. Also, we can more easily observe differences in others, although we often fail to detect our own patterns of divergence. This is the result of our own culture being so embedded in us that we forget it exists. It also happens because we consider our ways the most appropriate for responding to the environment. To further understand how culture is seen in our classrooms, consider the findings of a kindergarten teacher who took a cultural inventory of her children. As you read Figure 2-3, Culture in Action, highlight the similarities between her findings and yours. Diller and Moule (2005) warn that in order to provide responsive experiences, it is essential to become aware of the children's behaviors. These provide insights about their experiences that are shaped by their cultures. Teaching that is developmentally appropriate depends on the teacher's ability to respond to the child's individual and cultural realities. Consider,

Figure 2-3 Culture in Action: Ways Young Children Exhibit Their Culture in the Classroom

Verbal Skills
- Language use
  - Linguistic code-switching by English language learners (ELL)
  - Mixing terms from languages other than English
  - Native language dominance
- Oral expressions
  - Linguistic expressions
  - How they address adults
  - Use of questions
- Voice accent and inflection

Emotions
- Expressing fears and feelings
- Expressions of love and friendship
- Reactions to stories
- Reactions to conflict (while at play, in the playground, during classroom activities)

Behaviors
- Culturally based mannerisms
- Gestures
- Body movements
- Independence and collectivistic approaches

Other ways of exhibiting culture
- Ways of dress
- Food preferences
- Comments about family activities (special events and holidays)
- Expressing preferences
- Sharing pictures and objects from homes

AROUND **THE WORLD**

THE MILESTONE OF THE FIRST WORD IN HAITI

For the Pierre family in rural Haiti, the birth of their first child, Jean Louis, now ten months old, had brought great happiness. He was their first baby boy who had come to join his two sisters. Named after his mother's grandfather, little Jean Louis had a big smile and a head covered with dark brown curly hair.

Today was a special day for young Jean Louis. Just a week earlier, his mom, who was busy peeling and sorting pigeon peas, heard him say his very first word. "He spoke! Did you hear that?" said his mom to her cousin who was helping to sort the fresh peas.

Hugging him, she was excited to know that he had said his first word. "Now it's time," she said looking and caressing his curly baby hair locks. "Yes, it's time for your first haircut." Following their custom, a child's hair was first cut only after the first word had been uttered. For Jean Louis, that moment had just been marked.

Sitting in the barber's chair, Jean Louis' mom watched with emotion as her baby boy's hair fell to the floor. "I'll save this one," she said as she picked up the first lock of hair and put it lovingly in her handkerchief.

for instance, the experience of the child-care center director in the opening scenario to this chapter. Without a doubt, the bathroom facility was designed to provide for the safety of the children in the center; however, from the parent's perspective, not having a door to provide for her daughter's privacy violated her cultural principles, both at the overt and covert levels. Gaining awareness about the interplay of various cultural worlds gives the early childhood educator an opportunity to create environments sensitive to children and to their realities.

DISCOVERING THE CULTURES OF CHILDREN

At birth, we begin to acquire the ways of those with which we live and interact. We learn about our culture and the cultures of others as we interact with people. Because every individual's environment has a culture of its own, we come in contact with many different cultural patterns. Perhaps the best place to see these differences is in the classroom. You probably have noticed already that the children you teach have unique ways. This is easier to see in the context of their interactions when they begin to share their thoughts and feelings.

Culture Establishes Patterns of Life

"Who are you?" said the caterpillar . . . Alice replied rather shyly, "I hardly know, sir, just at present—at least I know who I was when I got up this morning, but I think I must have been changed several times since then."
Lewis Carroll (1832–1898), *Alice's Adventures in Wonderland*

FOCUS
ON CLASSROOM PRACTICES

"SEEING" THE CULTURES OF YOUNG CHILDREN

To help you "see" the many cultures that characterize your children, do the following exercise. Select a story to share with the children; for instance, choose any of Verna Aardema's stories, Pat Mora's stories, or any of the Jafta books by Hugh Lewin. If you want, present an issue for children to ponder and react to. Before sharing the story or issue, write down what is, in your opinion, the central message, point, or moral of the story. Then, share the story or the issue and ask the children to offer their interpretations. Here is where the fun part begins. As you listen to their comments, see how many different ideas are given. Compare their answers with your own. You will find that your students, despite their young age, have an exciting variety of views. Charting their comments will give you additional opportunities to learn how their answers reflect their cultures. This beginning experience will make you aware of two important facts: (1) everyone has a culture, and (2) culture influences our views.

You probably would have answered like Alice if you found yourself in her wonderland. When Alice went down the rabbit hole, she left behind the rules and roles that gave meaning to her life, and she entered a world of unfamiliar ways. We have encountered similar experiences. For instance, how many times have you been in a place where you could not understand what others were doing or saying? Only when a familiar action is observed or expression is understood does the situation make sense.

Everything we do responds to patterns learned through and from experiences with families, individuals, and people from our own social group. In social groups, everyone tends to follow a similar frame of reference that gives meaning to life routines and experiences. This pattern gives sense and direction to our actions and behaviors, which is the essential role of culture. A system of rules, culture serves as the framework people from a group use to make decisions, see and interpret reality, and perceive one's role in the family and society.

Experiences reflect how the members of a group use their frames of reference or scripts. These frameworks are made up of the following:

- values
- beliefs
- shared meanings and interpretations
- rules

Explaining when and why the social patterns of a group were established is difficult. The origins are found in events experienced long ago by elders who, in turn, established ways and ascribed their meanings. Recognizing the need to perpetuate one's traditions, each generation has the responsibility of delivering the message from one generation to the next. How we came to learn and follow social patterns is a result of the social environment in which we were born and live.

Culture as a Main Influence in People's Lives

Underlying our behavior is a set of complex ideas that individuals in our particular group use to interpret experiences and generate actions and behaviors (Spradley & McCurdy, 2004). These are rules, values, beliefs, and principles that, when followed, provide coherence and integrity to human existence. The members of the group know each of these structures or schemes. Despite how unusual rules might look to an outsider, for its members, they are logical. In fact, when practiced, they grant a sense of identity to the collective group (Gardiner & Kosmitzki, 2005; Hernandez, 2001). Cultural schemes are used to define the behavior parameters as well as the needs and aspirations of the group. Practices are also based on the particular interpretations that the group has made of life events. For instance, this is what Milo, the character in *The Phantom Tollbooth*, discovers during his encounter with a magical child:

> Milo turned around and found himself staring at two very neatly polished brown shoes, for standing directly in front of him . . . was another boy just about his age, whose feet were easily three feet above the ground . . .
>
> "Well," said the boy, "in my family everyone is born in the air, with his head at exactly the height it's going to be when he's an adult, and then we all grow toward the ground."
>
> . . . [Milo said] "In my family we all start on the ground and grow up, and we never know how far until we actually get there." (Juster, 1961/2000)

"What a silly system," was the child's reaction to what Milo considered a logical growing style, probably the same comment you would have made had you been part of the boy's culture group.

Each child brings their own unique heritage to the classroom. Together they are a sample of the cultural diversity present in communities across the nation.

Trying to understand the rules, beliefs, and values of other cultures while using our own values is not always effective. Each culture needs to be observed and understood from the perspective of its members. More precisely, the ideas of different cultures cannot be fully equated (Spradley & McCurdy, 2004). For example, individuality, prized in U.S. culture, is not equally valued in other cultures. Lynch and Hanson (2004) remark that in traditional Asian cultures, social orientation is focused on the collective "we" rather than on the individual. Awareness of values and visions of others contribute to our appreciation of diversity.

FOCUS

ON CLASSROOM PRACTICES

CELEBRATIONS, ONE OF CULTURE'S UNIVERSAL TRAITS

Many common elements are shared by different cultures. Perhaps one of the most characteristic is the need to celebrate. Celebrations can happen for a variety of reasons. They can also be observed in many ways, all of which are understood and shared by those who belong to the cultural group. In simple terms, celebrations are happenings that people observe because of the significance they have in their lives. Celebrations become holidays when they are observed by an entire religious group or when they hold national relevance. For early childhood teachers who want to discover more about the cultures of their students, learning how and why celebrations occur opens doors to cultural understanding. In the classroom, you may want to explore the celebrations observed by children and their families. Begin by brainstorming with children about what a celebration is. A good storybook to use is *Birthdays Around the World* by Mary Lankford and Karen Dugan (HarperCollins, 2002). Information about the holidays and celebrations families observe can be obtained by sending home a letter with these two questions:

- What are the three most important celebrations or special days for your family?

- What are the holidays your family observes?

Take time to analyze the answers. They will give you not only a glimpse of the students' cultures but also an idea of what families consider important. With the information gathered, engage the class in creating a mural depicting the holidays and special days they celebrate. You may want to involve students in further exploration of the topic. This can even become the target of an interesting thematic unit. To help you build a thematic unit, here are some essential points that will help you focus on the cultural aspects:

What Constitutes Cultural Aspects in Holidays and Celebrations

1. Meanings: Why is it observed?
   a. religious
   b. personal
   c. national or patriotic

2. Ways in which it is observed: How is it observed? What do people do?
   a. When does it take place? (time, season, dates)
   b. What do people do? (external or physical aspects)
      – colors and symbols
      – decorations
      – traditions (such as gift-giving, food, music)

3. People involved: Who participates?
   a. adults; children
   b. all

4. Places, locations: Where do activities take place?
   a. home
   b. community
   c. school

What we do and plan in early childhood classrooms is influenced by our cultural beliefs and values. Lewis (1991) reports how the view of responsibility varies in Japanese schools and how it influences classroom practices in nursery schools. During her study, Lewis observed how 5-year-olds were given responsibilities at an age when, in the U.S. context, the child is still guided by teachers. As their "brother's keepers," Japanese children were granted the authority to control the behavior of their peers and were held accountable for chores and tasks expected to be carried out by the group. Sanctions for activities or routines not followed emerged from the peers and not the teacher, for she was to remain a conflict-free benevolent figure.

Examples abound of differences in the interpretation of reality. Each interpretation reveals what is logical and correct in a particular culture. Knowledge of these interpretations helps the early childhood educator establish positive interactions and avoid misinterpretations. Take, for example, the extended use of baby language commonly employed by Hispanics in their communication with young children. This practice is not encouraged in the culture of the United States because the members of this group believe that adult language should be used from infancy. Another illustration pertains to visiting Native American families for the first time. Guests should ask for a place to sit, rather than assume any place is acceptable (Joe & Malach, 2004). Although special practices might differ from ours, we must always remember that they are part of what gives members of a particular culture a sense of identity.

A Sense of Identity: Being a Part of the Group

In our society, elementary school children learn far more than reading, writing, and arithmetic. Some of the mere aspects of their knowledge are never taught in a systematic way. They are acquired as part of their culture through interaction with teachers and peers.

James Spradley and David
McCurdy (2004)

Have you ever stopped to consider what prompts you to say "I am . . ."? Are you aware of what saying what you are means? Ask a 5-year-old what she is and see how quickly she states her identity. Even if the answer is, "I am a girl," that child is establishing herself as a member of a gender group. This sense of identification reveals an awareness of a group in which the individual participates and discloses another trait of culture: a sense of identity.

Many factors determine one's cultural identity. These factors vary according to one's individual characteristics, experiences, and affiliations. Your identity may be influenced by gender, age, profession, ethnicity, language, and other factors. This leads us to affirm that we all belong to many more groups than we may be aware of. Some of the elements influencing our individual identity may be any of the elements in Figure 2-4 (Banks & Banks, 2006; Gollnick &

Wadsworth/Cengage Learning

Can you describe the cultural schema of these young Eastern European women who arrived in the United States at the turn of the twentieth century?

Figure 2-4 Elements of Cultural Identity

• ethnic or national origin	• geographical region
• family	• language
• religion	• age
• gender	• socioeconomic level
• educational background	• job or occupation

Christianson, 2008). As you read them, consider those that play a leading influence in defining your own identity.

The interplay of a multiplicity of variables—age, family, ethnicity, religion, socio-economic status, gender, religion, educational experiences, individual characteristics, and others—is what makes us who we are. Garza and Lipton (cited by Hernandez, 2001) state that because individuals are defined by more than just one cultural influence, we are all uniquely multicultural.

LITERACY CONNECTIONS...

USING CHILDREN'S LITERATURE TO LEARN ABOUT CULTURES

Learning about cultures is an exciting adventure. Today, you can obtain information about most cultural groups, which makes it easy for early childhood educators to create appropriate classroom environments where children can learn about each other's cultures. Classrooms where the children's cultures are represented also send the message that the various cultures are valued and welcome.

Sharing experiences through books is an excellent way for young children to find out about their own culture while learning to appreciate the cultures of their peers.

The following selection of books is suitable for pre-schoolers (ages 3–4) and kindergartners.

- Adoff, A. (2004). *Black is brown is tan.* New York: HarperTrophy. (interracial)
- Delacre, L. (1992). *Arroz con leche: Popular songs and rhymes from Latin America.* New York: Scholastic. (Latino)
- Fowler, S. (2003). *Circle of thanks.* New York: Scholastic. (Inuit)
- Grimes, N. (2002). *Danitra Brown leaves town.* New York: HarperCollins. (African American)
- Krebs, L., and Cairns, J. (2004). *We all went on a safari: A counting journey through Tanzania.* Cambridge, MA: Barefoot Books. (African)
- Lets, E. (2008). *The butter man.* New York: Charlesbridge. (Moroccan/African)
- Lin, G. (2003). *Dim sum for everyone!* New York: Knopf. (Chinese)
- Pak, S. (2003). *Sumi's first day of school ever.* New York: Viking Books. (Korean)
- Rumford, J. (2008). *Silent music.* New York: Roaring Brook Press. (Middle-East)
- Uegaki, C. (2005). *Suki's kimono.* Toronto, Canada: Kids Can Press. (Japanese)

A MYRIAD OF CULTURAL IDENTITIES: THE ESSENCE OF CULTURAL DIVERSITY

Many factors make us who we are. A cultural identity, as you have seen already, is based on numerous elements, each having varying degrees of influence on a person's individuality. You have also learned that ethnic or cultural descent is not the only element that defines a cultural orientation. People might share some similar traits, like a culture of origin or religion, but they probably have values that diverge to various degrees from those of others. You as an individual represent many ideas and influences, all blended into who *you* are. They are your unique experiences and will not be like those of others. As you constructed your reality, you processed every bit of it according to your own mental schemes. If, as an early child educator, your ideas about education or about parenting differ from those of your colleagues, it is because you are the sum of your particular experiences. This is an example of diversity on a personal level.

Cultural Diversity Factors

The society of the United States is one of the most complex reflections of social and cultural diversity. This comes as a result of the multitude of different nationalities and ideologies representative of the immigrant nature of this nation. Today, the term *cultural diversity* is freely used whenever we talk about the cultural spectrum found in our communities.

Often, the term cultural diversity is narrowly defined. Cultural diversity entails many more factors than the place of origin (where you or your parents were born or came from) or language. In the social context, cultural diversity describes the variety of social factors that, either singly or interactively, exert influence on an individual's behavior. Some of these key social factors are nationality, race, ethnicity, religion, social class, gender, exceptionalities, gender orientation, and age (see Figure 2-5). Knowledge about how diversity factors contribute to shaping the character and ways of an individual helps educators to better understand children's behaviors and learning characteristics (Banks & Banks, 2006; Copple, 2003). In the early childhood classroom, this knowledge provides the foundation for designing a sound developmentally appropriate program. How

Wadsworth/Cengage Learning

Cities and towns throughout the United States reflect the multiplicity of people's ethnic roots.

Figure 2-5   Elements of Diversity

Nationality	Refers to the country where the individual was born or from where his parents came.
Race/ethnicity	Defines the cultural traditions that serve to shape the individual's identity.
Religion	Refers to the religious affiliations and the freedom to exercise any faith as defined in the First Amendment of the Constitution.
Social class	Determined by income, education, occupation, lifestyles, and values typically held by a group.
Gender	Defines the behavior socially accepted and assigned to females and males, including role expectations.
Exceptionality	Defines the child who has any special needs or who is gifted.
Age	Defines the social expectations for behavior established by society for individuals of different age groups. They vary according to the individual's main cultural influence.

Understanding diversity requires an awareness of many different elements. This figure can serve as a barometer for assessing the levels of diversity in your classrooms.

to respond to those variables in the context of your classroom is presented in the third part of this book.

Many scholars believe that concepts about diversity are socially constructed categories (Banks & Banks, 2006). In fact, these concepts are ideas or representations of physical, cultural, or social traits that individuals might possess. For instance, the social class category is very hard to define concretely, because it entails areas that are exclusive to those said to belong to it. Today, many of the attributes used to profile certain social groups are now also found across other social groups (Banks & Banks, 2006). For this reason, we caution educators to carefully use terminology when describing children and families.

IN ACTION . . .

WHAT IS YOUR IDENTITY?

Could you name the things that make you who you are? To find out, you need a pair of scissors, construction paper in eight different colors, and a piece of white paper. Place the white paper on a desk or table and write your name across the top. Using the colored construction papers, assign cultural elements that define cultural identity to each one. Now, reflect carefully on those factors as they pertain to your identity. Establish which one has the most impact in determining who you are. Consider the importance of the rest of the elements. As you decide their levels of impact, cut the papers in triangles proportional to the priorities they represent. Arrange the triangles in a circular form on the white paper. This is a representation of what you believe defines your identity.

• What are the reasons for your choices?

• Do this exercise with other members of your family and discuss the results.

Cultural Diversity Defines the "American Way"

Today, debate still continues on the accuracy of the term *diversity* when describing people and communities in the United States. Some claim that we all are simply Americans. Others say that cultural diversity will endanger the future of the nation. These comments usually reflect the fact that some people are still unclear about the significance of diversity.

Diversity has been the common denominator of the United States since its inception. As you saw in Chapter 1, people from many different countries came to forge the nation we feel so proud of now. Decades ago, when the founders—the poor, the idealists, and the persecuted of the world—came to this part of North America, they faced many physical, personal, and social adjustments. One of their major tasks was to adapt to their new social reality and become Americans. In this effort, newcomers laid aside their own cultures and blended into a common culture and framework. This is known as the process of acculturation. This concept is commonly described using the metaphor of the "melting pot," in which people dissolved their individual cultural identities and adopted the patterns of the mainstream culture.

Today, the concept of the United States as a "melting pot" where everyone becomes a mainstream American has been challenged by the changing nature of society in the twenty-first century. Today, the process of acculturation is seen more as a "salad bowl" rather than a melting pot by those affirming that it is possible to be productive members of American society while maintaining their own individual cultural heritage. To support this position, we find many examples derived from the stories of immigrants

ANOTHER WAY TO DEFINE OUR CULTURAL IDENTITY

Did you know that you are actually a member of many intermingling cultures? According to Vontress (1976), every individual is a member of at least five different cultures. Of these five, one is shared by all human beings; others are particular to the individual.

- *Universal:* All human beings are alike in their needs and rights.
- *Ecological:* The place where humans live on the earth determines the way they will respond and relate to their natural environment.

- *National:* Depending on the country where they were born, individuals will have characteristics that identify them (language, world views, and so on).
- *Regional:* Based on the region where humans live, they will develop area-specific cultures.
- *Racio-ethnic:* All people have distinct racial and ethnic characteristics.

Adapted from Baruth & Manning, 2008.

Wadsworth/Cengage Learning

Even though they share a common Hispanic background, these children are diverse in their own ways. Teachers need to be aware of using only one variable when addressing children's needs.

who have integrated and adopted American lifestyles while upholding their heritage.

Being a teacher in today's classrooms requires an understanding of the magnitude and significance of new social directions that have emerged out of the increasing presence and nature of diversity. More than ever before, professionals must understand the impact of life in a socially and culturally diverse society on early childhood practices. There is an added responsibility to meet the needs and expectations of young learners and their families. Current social realities also place demands on early childhood professionals to become more cognizant about their own cultures as well as the cultures of children they teach. This understanding is instrumental in setting an atmosphere of mutual respect in our classrooms.

The classrooms of the United States are settings where the country's future is being forged. Preparation for the real world in our society now entails giving children the skills needed to interact with others. This has special meaning in an increasingly diverse society. As early childhood professionals strive to create the best environment for children, including and infusing the realities of society will prove to be the key elements. Teaching the whole child must include considerations of the child's cultural background.

THINK AND REFLECT...

CULTURE AND IDENTITY

Culture plays an important part in the development of young children's identities and shapes their views of the world. Various environments also play essential roles in that process.

• How does the social and cultural environment of the community influence the children's concept of "self"?

• What messages are sent in the classroom regarding the differences in gender and exceptionalities? How do they influence children's emerging sense of self and sense of others?

TALKING ABOUT RACE AND ETHNICITY

Probably no two concepts are more misunderstood than race and ethnicity. Both tend to be included in discussions about culture. The important issues are the relevance they have to culture and the meaning of each term.

Ethnic groups share common histories, customs, values, lifestyles, religions, and languages. In the United States, some ethnic groups have preserved their identities, whereas others have been integrated into the mainstream culture or have merged with other racial and ethnic groups. The particular preoccupation with race in the United States makes it even more difficult to define ethnic groups in absolute terms. For example, Asian Americans can have several different religions, be of different races and lifestyles, and hold totally different values.

The same is true of race. **Race** is a term used to describe the physical characteristics of a large group of people with somewhat similar genetic history (Campbell, 2009). The definition of race as defined by genetic characteristics was important in the European-dominated United States from its inception. Today, the definition of race has become more of a sociopolitical category than a biological phenomenon. The danger to our democracy is not ethnic identity or race, but racism, the oppression of a group of people based on the color of their skin (Campbell, 2009). Prevention of racist ideas

 ## AROUND **THE WORLD**

IN GRANDFATHER'S MEMORY

In the Peruvian sierra, for young Elenita's family, it had been a very busy day. A couple of days earlier she had been with her mom to the local store to get all the ingredients to make the special meals to honor their family members who had passed away. As was their custom, every November 2nd, Day of the Dead, they would pause to honor those family members who had died. It was their tradition to remember them by preparing the meals that their loved ones liked. All would be set on a table to honor their memory and remember happier times. Included in the meals would be *bollos*, a type of baby-shaped bread roll. This year it was a time to also honor the memory of Elenita's grandfather.

Since early in the morning Elenita had been watching her mother and older sister blending and tasting the mix for the *bollos*. Her mom had promised her that this year she would make one especially for grandfather Felipe. Carefully molding the dough, her sister invited Elenita to finish the doll-shaped rolls for her grandfather. With excitement the six year-old tried her best. "My doll is the best one," thought the child, looking at the *bollos* going into the oven. She knew that all the *bollos* would be placed on the special table along with other favorite foods of the departed loved ones. Elenita heard her mother say, "Now, let's get everything ready for the table," as she started to gather the pots on the stove full of rice, *aji con pollo*, fresh corn and potatoes.

A smell of bread and spices inundated the humble house. Candles illuminated the dishes and the freshly made *bollos* were set on the special table. Elenita carefully placed Grandfather's *bollo* in the place of honor.

That evening the family and friends remembered their loved ones with prayers and the sharing of stories.

We thank Ms. Vinda Vázquez who shared her memories about this Peruvian tradition.

needs to take place early in life. Early childhood educators have the responsibility to eradicate racism among young children by addressing inappropriate comments and behaviors in the classroom in developmentally appropriate ways that will help clarify and thus erase what may be the emergence of erroneous concepts about others.

What Is Ethnicity?

Central to the idea of culture is the concept of ethnicity. Ethnicity is defined by three factors: nationality, ancestry, and religious affiliation. A member of an ethnic group might share some or all of these characteristics with other group members (Figure 2-6). Ethnic groups are usually described as people with a common cultural tradition and a clear sense of identity. Ethnicity, thus, becomes the set of features that historically has characterized a particular subgroup in the context of a larger dominant culture (McGoldrick, 2003). At the personal level, ethnicity becomes the sense an individual has of commonality with family and others of the same group to which he or she belongs (Feinstein, cited in McGoldrick, 2003). The family plays an instrumental role in a person's acquisition and development of a sense of ethnicity, serving as the initial source and reinforcer of ethnic characterizations. The impact of ethnicity on people is such that it identifies them within the spectrum of a society. Examples of ethnic groups found in U.S. society are the Amish, African Americans, and Jews. These three groups are good examples because they represent some of the differences you may find when defining ethnicity.

THINK AND REFLECT...

AMERICA, THE MELTING POT

At the turn of the century when masses of immigrants poured into this country, America was referred to as a "melting pot," a place where everyone became one. This socialization process was the ultimate goal of the immigrants from Eastern Europe, Russia, and the Asian countries. Even though many of the ethnic groups lived in their own neighborhoods and practiced their cultural rituals, it was expected that the children assimilate into American society by becoming part of the mainstream culture.

Today, the climate is much different. The "melting pot" has given way to a pluralistic society where assimilation is not necessarily viewed as a priority. Many ethnic, cultural, and religious groups preserve their languages and ways and do not want to become part of the mainstream culture. Many immigrants, particularly in metropolitan areas, live in large self-sufficient communities that allow the members to have meaningful and productive lives without depending on the society at large. This has facilitated the retention of the "mother tongue" and resulted in a lack of English language proficiency and the perseverance of other cultural habits, behaviors, and rituals of the mainstream culture. As the minorities continue to grow to the point that they will soon comprise the majority of the country's population, we are faced with many issues. Are we becoming a fractured society? Has the *unum* (oneness) of America all but disappeared? What are the consequences as well as the current and future goals of the new society of the United States of America?

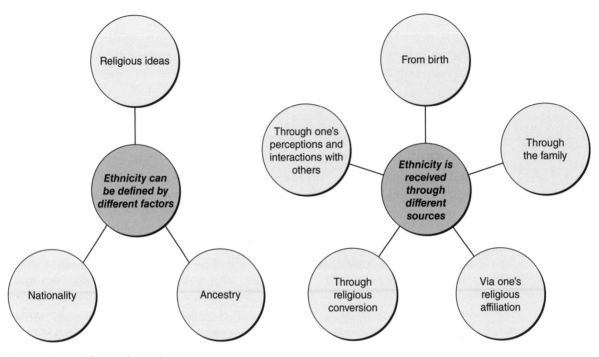

Figure 2-6 What is ethnicity?

Although the Amish have all three basic elements of diversity (religion, ancestry, and nationality) and the African Americans possess two (ancestry and nationality), the Jews, affiliated through their common religious tradition, may only have one. Regardless of what element establishes the character of an ethnic group, we all belong to one.

Baruth and Manning (2008) add another interesting dimension to the concept of ethnicity: the role of self-perception and of outsiders' perceptions about the individual. They assert that ethnicity is a "dynamic and complex concept [that] refers to how members of a group *perceive themselves,* and how, in turn, *they are perceived by others*" (emphasis added).

Subjective perception can lead to very distorted views about individuals and social groups. For example, consider the child who perceives breaking apart a brand-new toy as an exploration, while the parent may interpret the action as misbehavior. Similarly, practicing hand movements with a marker on a living room wall has a different meaning to the child than to an adult. When subjective perception is applied to ethnicity, we find that we do not agree with how others see us. For example, you might see yourself as part of an ethnic group, and yet people might not consider you as part of that group. The same can happen when people see you as part of an ethnicity that you do not perceive yourself as being a part of.

Divergences in ethnic perception commonly occur in connection with non-European American groups. During graduate courses on multiculturalism, we have

Children become aware of their differences and similarities at a very young age.

found repeatedly that non-European American students' ethnic perceptions of themselves differ from those assigned to them by the mainstream society. For example, a student born in Barbados was shocked to find herself defined as "black," when in her country she was not classified that way. She found that her ethnicity was being designated by the color of her skin rather than by her ethnic heritage. Similarly, it was traumatic for light-colored Hispanics to be denied the designation of "white" because of their heritage. One student commented that, for her, it was particularly disappointing to find that her color was primarily used to describe her, whereas her nationality was of secondary importance. One of the authors of this book remembers witnessing how a dark-skinned teacher born in Trinidad was once questioned by her colleagues when she refused to identify herself as an African American. Using solely the element of color, the teacher's colleagues were unable to acknowledge her Caribbean ethnicity. Similar misconceptions are common among Asian Americans, whose ethnicities are usually compounded into one expression, "Oriental," a very misleading term.

Race: A Controversial Concept

Race has been used to establish an unfair separation of human beings in many parts of the world. This practice has also existed in the United States for centuries. The term *race* has been used as a synonym for color, and, whenever color is the sole attribute used to define an individual, it can become a dangerous tool. Banks (2007) warns that nothing has had a more destructive effect on humankind than ideas about races. Montague affirms that it is, in fact, "man's most dangerous myth" (cited in Baruth & Manning, 2008). Recently, the term *people of color* has been coined to depict non-European groups. Some educators disagree with this terminology because of its misleading connotation. We agree that *people of color* emphasizes only one characteristic of a cultural group. We (as well as many others) prefer the more inclusive term *culturally diverse*.

Race is defined as the phenotypical characteristics that designate a group. The term basically refers to the biological features common to a group. Different from ethnicity, race describes characteristics that individuals cannot change. These physical characteristics are transmitted from one generation to another.

IN ACTION . . .

CAN YOU DEFINE YOUR ETHNICITY?

Clarity about your own roots is critical when trying to understand and teach children from various cultures. To establish your ethnic affiliation, ask yourself the following questions:

- How do I define myself?
- How do I know that I belong to a specific group?

- What things do I do that identify me as part of that group?
- How did I receive my ethnic identity?
- How do other people perceive me? Are their perceptions the same as mine?

The concept of race has its origins in anthropology, where it was used to describe the physical characteristics (eyes, skin color, size of head, and so on) of people (Hernandez, 2001). From this anthropological perspective, scientists identified humans according to racial groups. Today, however, even in the scientific sphere, categorizing human beings by such limited attributes is difficult. With the high incidence of

THINK AND REFLECT...

FACTORS INFLUENCING INTENSITY OF ETHNIC FEELINGS

Perhaps you have wondered why all people in a group do not show the same intensity of ethnic traits. According to McGoldrick (2003), this is due to specific factors that are applicable to immigrants all over the world:

- *Reasons for immigration:* What they were seeking when they left their countries.
- *Length of time since immigration and the effects of generational acculturation:* How long it has been since they left and to what extent the families have become part of the mainstream society.
- *Place of residence:* Whether they lived or continue to live in an ethnic neighborhood.
- *Order of migration:* Whether one person migrated alone or with the family.

- *Socioeconomic status:* The socio-economic status of the individual in the home country and upward mobility capability of the individual in the new country.
- *Political and religious ties:* Whether the individual maintains such ties to the ethnic group.
- *Language:* The languages spoken by the individual in the new country: native language versus the language of the new country.
- *Interracial marriages:* Extent of intermarriage with other ethnicities.
- *Personal attitudes:* How the individual feels about his or her ethnic group.

Adapted from: McGoldrick (2003).

interracial marriages, it becomes even more challenging to define the racial make-up of children with diverse backgrounds. Consider the case of a 3-year-old living on the East Coast, whose father is Italian American and whose mother is half Asian and half African American. It would be a hard task to label the child racially. You would need to get a formula to determine the physical racial proportions, which, at the end, would yield no significant information about the child as an individual. Unfortunately, race labels continue to be used even by the United States government. This practice produces inaccurate images of people that ignore the social and cultural heritage of the individual.

There are still many implications to the meaning of race in society. Gollnick and Christianson (2008) point out the following:

- *Race as a concept still carries a strong social meaning in our country as well as in many other societies.* This is despite the extensive movement of people from one geographical region to another and the high incidence of interracial marriages.
- *The concept of race contributes very little to cultural understanding.* Race seldom correlates with cultural groups defined by nationality, language, or religion. The racial identity of people does not necessarily correspond to their nationality.
- *The persistent use of racial, ethnic, and language categories in public and governmental documents provokes more confusion about the U.S. population.* The use of racial and ethnic indicators has proven to be not always effective when trying to assign individuals to a category. An individual could belong to several categories at the same time; therefore, tallying inclusive categories is difficult.

The current racial designations of the major ethnic groups are portrayed in Figure 2-7. They include whites and blacks who declared themselves to be of one race as well as the Hispanic or Latino population. The categories such as Asian, Native Hawaiian, and Pacific Islander also contain other subcategories of other ethnicities. Demographically, the United States is now considered one of the most racially diverse countries in the world. After looking at these numbers, you may want to consider the cultural implications of the United States' racial profile.

Figure 2-7 Racial Profile of the Population of the United States, 2000

White (excluding Hispanics/Latinos)	211,460,626
Hispanics or Latinos	35,305,818
Black or African American	34,758,190
American Indian and Alaska Native	2,475,956
Asian	10,242,998
Native Hawaiian and Pacific Islanders	874,414

Source: U.S. Census Bureau, 2000.

IN ACTION . . .

ALL THE COLORS WE ARE

The story of how we get our different skin colors is told in the book *All the Colors We Are: The Story of How We Get Our Skin Color/Todos los Colores de Nuestra Piel: La Historia de por qué Tenemos Diferentes Colores de Piel,* written by Katie Kissinger (Redleaf Press, 1994). Read the following excerpt and see how she addresses this difficult concept.

The skin color we are born with comes from our parents, ancestors, and where they lived a long time ago. Do you think your ancestors came from a very warm, sunny place or a cooler place with less sunshine? Dark skin, light skin, and skin with freckles are all caused by our ancestors, the sun, and the melanin.

What do you think about her approach? Is it developmentally appropriate?

A New Demographic, Multicultural People

Today, the demographic profile of the United States includes the people classified as "multicultural," a growing group whose existence was officially acknowledged for the first time during Census 2000. Before then, people of mixed-race heritage were defined as the "third culture" (West, 2003). Socially and demographically, the members of the "multicultural" category present another variable in the composition of the ever-increasing pluralistic communities across the nation. Consequently, the presence of multiracial children is already a stable trend in most schools that is projected to grow in the future (National Association of School Psychologists, 2004).

Prejudice and Racism: The Plagues of the Past and the Present

> *Sadly, the world is full of old prejudices.*
> Doris Bergen (2003)

Any discussion about race and ethnicity must acknowledge the presence of prejudice and racism in society. Unfortunately, neither is a stranger to the United States. U.S. history includes numerous instances in which people were victims of unfair treatment because of their differences, and many more will occur unless actions are taken to prevent unfairness.

Prejudice has caused much destruction in the world and is at the root of racism and bigotry. Prejudice is based on holding negative views about others not supported by solid evidence and inspired by fear. The dislikes manifested by those who are prejudiced are based on poor or inadequate knowledge.

Dislikes of others are often demonstrated through deeds, attitudes, and verbal and nonverbal condemnation. Victims of prejudice have been subjected to subtle, covert disparagement, such as a condescending smile or a mocking look, which wounds and often stigmatizes them. Kehoe (cited in Hernandez, 2001), in an analysis of prejudice, found key points that alert educators to its sources. Some of Kehoe's findings are included in the next "Think and Reflect."

Statistics show that hate crimes have increased in the United States during the first decade of the twenty-first century. The crimes range from defimation of Jewish synagogues, attacks to individuals because of their ethnic or sexual orientation, and protests against Muslims, to the subtle patronizing ways in which culturally diverse individuals are often treated. Prejudicial behavior of any kind is damaging and offensive to the victims and to society.

Post–September 11 society has made many more aware of the culturally diverse nature of people. In some cases it has led to prejudice and discrimination against things and individuals unknown to us. The need for more security sometimes results in more racism and greater prejudice against the individuals and groups that are perceived as threatening. Since September 11, incidents against ethnic groups have increased to an alarming level, making the fight against intolerance imperative. Because many adults openly exhibit their feelings and convey their biased views in the presence of children, early educators need to be aware of such information being brought into the classroom. Children may repeat adults' disparaging remarks while they role-play, talk with their peers, or react to stories. Early childhood educators have a responsibility to address such incidents in appropriate and anti-biased ways. This will prevent the formation and reinforcement of prejudiced behaviors.

The Classroom as a Culture of Peace

The best weapon against violence and prejudice is peace (UNESCO, 2000). Peace can be defined as a feeling of harmony and well-being. Tolerance and bias-free attitudes are avenues that lead to peace. A culture of peace begins when adults and children together share and participate in activities as equals. Peace is also found in places where violence is openly rejected and where people are free to express their views and exchange ideas.

Learning tolerance occurs through the interactions with individuals we encounter at home, in school, and in the community. These settings are major places where bias-free behaviors can be learned. For young children, the classroom can become the most powerful bias-free place where they can acquire knowledge about socially acceptable tolerant behavior. Routine activities and interactions characterized by equal treatment for all and by rejection of unfairness promote a culture of respect that leads to peace. Taking time to clarify derogatory and prejudicial comments made by children is a critical step in eradicating prejudice. Because teachers exert an influential role in the behaviors and attitudes of young children, responding and intervening appropriately in prejudice-inspired incidents is essential. As a teacher with this goal, you can do the following:

- Be sure that comments made in the classroom regarding actions of people from diverse backgrounds do not convey criticism.
- Be aware of many different messages your own body language communicates to young children. Remember, they can read you!

- Remember to respond to children's actions clearly and within the context of their actions, and make sure that children understand your responses.
- Acknowledge children's bias-free and tolerant behaviors in real context and through vicarious experiences, such as reading of multicultural books and shared children's stories.

LITERACY CONNECTIONS...

SUGGESTED REFERENCES FOR BUILDING A CULTURE OF PEACE AND TOLERANCE

You may want to review some of the following titles that provide ideas and strategies for supporting tolerance and peace in early childhood classrooms.

- Arnow, J. (1995). *Teaching peace: How to raise children to live in harmony: Without fear, without prejudice, without violence.* New York: Perigee Books.
- Bullard, S. (2003). *Starting small: Teaching tolerance in pre-school and primary grades.* Atlanta, GA: Southern Poverty Law Center.
- Derman-Sparks, L., & the A.B.C. Task Force. (1989). *The anti-bias curriculum: Tools for empowering children.* Washington, DC: National Association for the Education of Young Children.
- Lalli, J. (1996). *Make someone smile: And 40 more ways to be a peaceful person.* Minneapolis, MN: Free Spirit.
- Parr, T. (2009). *The peace book.* New York: Little Brown Books for Young Readers.*
- Radunsky, V. (2003). *What does peace feel like?* New York: Atheneum.*

*Children's books recommended for ages 3–6.

THINK AND REFLECT...

FACTS ABOUT PREJUDICE

- Individual differences in temperament cannot be attributed to race.
- Prejudice and stereotypes are learned, not innate. They are learned in the family and in school without conscious intent.
- Generally, individuals do not realize how prejudiced they are.
- Those prejudiced against one ethnic group are likely to be prejudiced against others.
- Individuals who are not directly competing with minority group members tend to be less prejudiced toward them.
- As a group's character becomes more distinctive, a consensus develops regarding stereotypes associated with that group.
- Stereotypes resist change. However, social and economic conditions, especially of the kind that modify relations among groups, can alter stereotypes.
- Prejudice is a predictor of discriminatory behavior.
- There is considerable agreement within a society about specific stereotypes assigned to particular groups.

Source: Kehoe, cited in Hernandez, 2001.

As multiculturalists and early educators, the need to prepare children to successfully live in and embrace a culture of peace is a priority. The hope and seed for peace and successful life in a diverse society is found in every classroom.

Stereotypes

One of the most damaging ways prejudice is expressed is in the form of stereotypes. A stereotype is an oversimplified, generalized image describing all individuals in a group as having the same characteristics in appearance, behaviors, and beliefs. Although there may be a germ of truth in a stereotype, the image usually represents "a gross distortion, or an exaggeration of the truth, and has offensive, dehumanizing implications" (Council on Interracial Books for Children, in Saracho & Spodek, 1989). The effects of being stereotyped are damaging to the individual and to those who witness it. As found by Kehoe (cited in Hernandez, 2001), stereotypes are learned usually in the context of the family and, unfortunately, in schools. Actions to prevent and stop stereotyping are the responsibility of all educators, particularly during the early years because of the inherent vulnerability of young learners. Developing an antibias curriculum, like the one developed by the staff at Pacific Oaks College in California, is a good way to start (Derman-Sparks, 1989). Familiarizing young children with action-oriented multicultural activities that promote understanding and tolerance is not only recommended but essential.

Racism is a crime many often reject but refuse to stop. It continues to be a "prevailing social practice" (Derman-Sparks, 1989). Hernandez (2001) states that racism is found in those individuals exhibiting behaviors and actions that reflect (a) the conviction that physical, psychological, and intellectual characteristics are inherited and distributed differently among humans and (b) the belief of being racially superior to other racial groups. Throughout history, many individuals and groups have been victimized as a result of these tenets.

As we strive to offer children an education that will empower them to become successful members of society, early childhood educators must realize that the key to *unum* is in their hands. Prejudice and racism must be eradicated for the United States to remain a strong leader in the twenty-first century. Old ideas about superiority of some racial and ethnic groups must be abandoned. As an early childhood educator, remember that change begins with the child. The battles to eliminate prejudice and racism are to be won in your classrooms.

Overcoming Unfairness and Discrimination: Legislative Landmarks

There are many laws and landmark legislations that have been passed to protect the rights of all members of U.S. society. Early childhood educators need to become cognizant of many legislative mandates and laws that directly influence young children in their classrooms. Many state and federal statutes exist that not only protect young children's rights to equal educational experiences but also address the diversity of needs and characteristics of young children.

The passage of the 1960s Civil Rights Act created fertile ground for recognizing the rights of every citizen regardless of his or her characteristics and conditions. Furthermore, the Act acknowledged and reaffirmed the individual rights of culturally diverse people and gave way to additional efforts that directly impacted early childhood education.

The passing of the historic law PL 94-142 of 1975 established the rights of individuals with disabilities to receive educational services according to their needs. This transcendental legislation impacted the social framework of the nation and began to erase the inequitable treatment of children and adults with disabilities. The rights of individuals with disabilities were expanded further by the enactment of PL 101-476 in 1990, the Individuals with Disabilities Education Act (IDEA), and later on by the amendments passed in 1997 that defined early childhood intervention.

LITERACY CONNECTIONS...

USING LITERATURE TO ADDRESS PREJUDICED COMMENTS IN THE CLASSROOM

It is not surprising to hear children make comments and statements reflective of prejudiced or stereotypical views. Most of the time, they repeat what they have heard adults say, unaware of the meaning of the words. Other times, they are repeating what they have heard in the media or on the streets. Rather than ignoring these incidents, responding to their comments and clarifying the meanings is the best way to avoid repetition. Upon hearing an inappropriate comment, use your own words to let the child know that the comment is not appropriate and that you intend to discuss the statement with the child. ("Those are words that hurt and that we don't use.") Be sure to take time to (1) clarify the comment or incident and (2) explain on the child's level why it is inappropriate. These are important steps in building understanding and in avoiding having such behaviors become a part of the child's response repertoire. For example, ask the following:

- Why did you say this?
- Where did you hear such words?
- What made you say that?

- What do you think it means?
- How would you feel if someone were to call you such a name?

Another way for clarifying prejudiced comments in the classroom is to use stories addressing racial and ethnic content. For preschoolers, stories with fantasy characters, like the animals in *What if the Zebras Lost Their Stripes?* are age-appropriate ways to engage them in a lively discussion about words and attitudes that hurt. You may want to try some of the suggested titles included in this section:

- Andreae, G. (2002). *Giraffes can't dance.* UK: Orchard Books.
- Derolf, S. (1997). *The crayon box that talked.* New York: Random House.
- Polacco, P. (2001). *Mr. Lincoln's way.* New York: Philomel Books.
- Reitano, J. (1998). *What if the zebras lost their stripes?* Mahwah, NJ: Paulist Press.

Wadsworth/Cengage Learning

All children should be appreciated for who they are.

Equity in Educational Services for All Children

Unequal programs and services available to the young have presented enduring challenges for multicultural educators. The No Child Left Behind (NCLB) Act, passed in 2002, addressed these critical issues (U.S. Department of Education, 2004). Although the mandate placed emphasis on individual and school accountability, it also brought to the forefront the recognition of the rights of all children to quality educational services. NCLB also addresses the disparities and fair services, a major issue in multicultural education. It reinforces the rights of all children, especially those in poor communities, to receive educational experiences from well-trained teachers. No Child Left Behind establishes high expectations for all, regardless of their ethnic or linguistic backgrounds. Equal treatment is based on the premise that all children have potential beyond racial background or language capability and deserve quality services.

As we move forward in the twenty-first century, we recognize that although much has been gained, much still remains to be changed for the young children and families of the increasingly culturally and linguistically diverse society of the United States.

NCLB focused national attention on much needed reforms for the good of all, but it also raised many concerns with regard to its emphasis on testing and various biases inherent in the process. Today, arguments still abound about the impact and efficacy of NCLB in relationship to developmentally appropriate practices and culturally appropriate approaches.

Stability and Change: The Rhythm of Culture

According to Bowman (cited in Bredekamp and Rosegrant, 2001), all cultures have shared meanings that give direction to the group. Your classroom is the place where children come to explore and discover how to live in their social environment. The playground is another place where children express the views of the world that they have acquired so far. We say "so far" because these views are not static. Being a dynamic process, culture evolves and changes with time. This process affects our personal perceptions and beliefs about people and environments.

IN ACTION . . .

THAT WAS ME . . . BEFORE!

We all have changed some of our ideas, sometimes without being aware of it. To find some of the ways in which you have been a part of this process, visit your closet! Yes, that's right. If anything represents the trends of our society, it's fashion. Search through your clothes and find any outfit you stopped wearing some time ago; in fact, the older the outfit, the better. Now ask yourself why you stopped wearing it and if you think you will wear it again.

- Give yourself two reasons you "forgot" that outfit.
- Examine your own answers and discuss them with a friend.

Your classroom reflects cultural changes in many ways. For example, educational theories of early childhood practices evolved from being teacher-centered to being child-centered. If you had been teaching in the 1950s or 1960s, your classroom would have included more academic materials and activities. A higher number of large group experiences would have dominated your teaching. Children would have probably been found doing many "pencil and paper" exercises while you would have been delivering more information for them "to learn." You also would have looked different. Most likely, your school dress code would not have included sneakers and today's informal, casual clothing. Because our cultural values have experienced modifications, we now have a very different picture of how the early childhood classroom should look.

Change is a characteristic of life and of all cultures. Through change, a group keeps itself alive. Comparing culture to the human organism, we find that in the same manner that the body affects modifications when faced with new circumstances, culture similarly adapts itself to new circumstances. This capacity to adapt itself grants culture the capability to respond to reality. You must remain abreast of current social transformations that take place in society, which will allow you to respond and provide for the relevant needs of children.

Supporting Cultures in Our Classroom: Taking Action

Your classroom is a reflection of our social mosaic. The children you teach bring to the classroom the ideas and experiences that characterize the United States in the twenty-first century. One of the things the children reflect is the diversity of visions found in our communities. As they interact in their social environments—the family, the classroom, the neighborhood, and the community—they learn that not all individuals are alike. For example, they will discover that what makes some people happy might be different from their own ideas of happiness. They will notice that not all people like to wear the same kind of clothes as they do or that other people have a hair texture smoother or curlier than theirs. They will learn that they have ideas of their own and that others see the world differently. While holding their own views, children—and you as a teacher— come to discover that there are other ways to see and interpret reality. Sometimes we will agree with others' interpretations, and other times we will disagree. Not everyone looks at life through the same glasses!

Preparing to serve children who live in a diverse country requires much initiative and imagination. Becoming effective teachers of young children in a multicultural world begins with the following steps:

- *Discover and clarify your own cultural viewpoints.* Begin by ascertaining your own beliefs, values, and practices. To appreciate other cultures, you must be clear about your own. The search for your roots can begin by talking to your relatives and family. Examine official records that document your and your family members' birthplaces, marriages, travels, and other significant events. Analyze your responses to the activities presented in the "In Action" sections throughout this chapter. They are intended to help you clarify ideas about your own cultural identity.

- *Learn to be more culturally competent.* Examine the cultures represented in the community where you live and those in your school. See what cultural groups are familiar to you and which ones you would like to learn more about. One way to choose is to think about those cultures commonly found in your classroom. Remember, we are all learning more about the cultures in this country. Do not feel bad if you lack knowledge about some of them!

- *Honestly examine the stereotypes about other groups that you have in the classroom or that you have encountered.* Do a self-inventory to find out what you know about any stereotypes associated with those groups. You may be surprised to find that they are probably based on very inconsequential and unfair facts.

- *Read about people from other cultures.* The resources in this book are a starting point. Check your local library, where you may also find a variety of publications about different cultural and ethnic groups.

- *Consider the importance that principles of development have on planning and designing classroom experiences.* Along with that, learn to recognize and appreciate the influence of the family in the child's overall development. These two points will be examined in Chapters 3 and 4.

WHAT WE HAVE LEARNED—CHAPTER SUMMARY

The main topic of this chapter is culture. We defined what culture is and discussed many ways in which it shapes our behavior and our lives. Culture is the most potent single influence that defines our identity. There are many aspects of culture. Some of the elements of culture are very visible (material) while others are very covert and deal with the emotional and thinking patterns (nonmaterial) of individuals and groups. Because one's sense of identity is very closely related to one's culture, it is important for all of us as individuals to know as much about each other's cultures as possible and to understand their influences on ourselves and on the world around us. Educators of young children are expected to learn about various cultures and their rituals in order to teach and nurture young children. Through education comes understanding and tolerance that allow us to create classrooms of peace. We are all responsible for overcoming unfairness and discrimination as well as ensuring the equity of educational services provided to all children regardless of their culture, religion, or the color of their skin.

MAKING CONNECTIONS . . .

1. Based on the **discussion** about culture presented in this chapter, create your own definition of *culture*.

2. Visit your community or neighborhood and make a list of its cultural elements. How many of these are visible to the eye? How many are not visible?

3. Observe two young children (ages 2–5). Identify how they exhibit their cultural heritage.

4. List the ways you share your own culture with others. Include both material and nonmaterial items.

5. Find an early childhood textbook and review two or three chapters for stereotype language and concepts.

6. Engage a group of friends or family members in a conversation about stereotypes. Make a list of the terminology that was used. What did you learn about their level of acceptance of others?

RECOMMENDED INTERNET RESOURCES

- "Building the legacy of IDEA 2004," U.S. Department of Education, which provides details about the legislation and services for children and people with disabilities

    Retrieved from http://idea.ed.gov/explore/home

- *Colorín Colorado*, a website that provides a variety of resources to support the needs of young English language learners

    www.colorincolorado.org

- Culture and Ethnic Groups, a portal that provides resources and information from the government about the different cultural and ethnic groups in the United States

    www.usa.gov/Citizen/Topics/History_Culture.shtml

- *Race, the Power of an Illusion*, a PBS series that examines issues related to race and their implications for society

    www.pbs.org/race/000_General/000_00-Home.htm

YOUR STANDARDS PORTFOLIO

naeyc **Standard 1:** Promoting Child Development and Learning

naeyc **Standard 4:** Using Developmentally Effective Approaches to Connect with Children and Families

naeyc **Standard 7:** Early Childhood Field Experiences

InTASC Standard 2: Learning Differences

InTASC Standard 4: Content Knowledge

Culture is one of the factors that influence the child's development and learning processes. Teaching and responding to the child's unique needs requires a clear understanding of the experiences, cultural and linguistic contexts in which children grow and develop. To demonstrate how you build effective and responsive relationships, select and complete one of the following activities which serve to evidence how you meet NAEYC's Standard 4a.

- Create a pictorial cultural profile of the community where you live or teach. Include aspects such as cultural groups, religious groups, languages used, businesses, places of interest, community celebrations, and any other details. Reflect on how these elements influence and play a role in the children's development.
- Prepare a chart about the linguistic environment in your community. Identify languages used by people and in signage in streets; names of businesses; newspapers; media, including radio and television programs; materials at the library; and any other places. Comment on your findings and reflect on how the nature of the linguistic environment may influence children.
- Stereotypes often can be found in the visuals, children's books, and materials used in the classroom environment. Conduct observations in at least three classrooms of different age groups and look for any stereotypical content in pictures, posters, children's literature, and manipulatives. Pay attention to the children's reactions to the materials. Comment on your findings and reflect on how they may influence development. Suggest alternative materials to prevent stereotypes in the classroom.

REFERENCES

Banks, J. (2007). *Multicultural education* (4th ed.). Needham Heights, MA: Allyn & Bacon.

Banks, J., & Banks, C. M. (2006). *Multicultural education: Issues and perspectives* (6th ed.). Needham Heights, MA: Allyn & Bacon.

Baruth, L. G., & Manning, M. L. (2008). *Multicultural education of children and adolescents* (5th ed.). Needham Heights, MA: Allyn & Bacon.

Bergen, D. (2003). *War and genocide: A concise history of the Holocaust.* Lanham, MD: Rowman and Littlefield.

Bowman, B. (2001). Reaching potentials of minority children through developmentally and culturally appropriate programs. In S. Bredekamp & T. Rosegrant (Eds.), *Reaching potentials: Appropriate curriculum and assessment for young children* (pp. 129–135). Washington, DC: National Association for the Education of Young Children.

Bruner, J. (1996). *Acts of meaning.* Cambridge, MA: Harvard University Press.

Campbell, D. E. (2009). *Choosing democracy: A practical guide to multicultural education* (4th ed.). Upper Saddle River, NY: Pearson.

Carroll, L. (1987). *Alice's adventures in wonderland.* New York: Philomel Books. (Original work published in 1865.)

Copple, C. (Ed.). (2003). *A world of difference: Readings on teaching young children in a diverse society.* Washington, DC: National Association for the Education of Young Children.

Diller, J., & Moule, J. (2005). *Cultural competence: A primer for educators.* Burbank, CA: Thomson Learning.

Freire, P. (2000). *Pedagogy of the oppressed.* New York: Continuum International.

Gardiner, H., & Kosmitzki, C. (2005). *Lives across cultures: Cross-cultural human development.* Boston: Allyn & Bacon.

Geertz, C. (2000). *The interpretation of cultures.* New York: Basic Books.

Golnick, D. M., & Christianson, R. C. (2008). *Multicultural education in a pluralistic society and exploring diversity package.* (8th ed.) New York: Prentice Hall.

Hall, E. T. (1990). *The silent language.* New York: Fawcett.

Harwood, R., Miller, J., & de Lucca, N. (1997). *Culture and attachment: Perceptions of the child in context.* New York: Guilford Press.

Hernandez, H. (2001). *Multicultural education: A teacher's guide to content and process.* New York: Merrill.

Joe, J., & Malach, F. (2004). Families with Native American roots. In E. Lynch & M. J. Hanson (Eds.), *Developing cross-cultural competence: A guide for working with young children and their families* (pp. 89–120). Baltimore, MD: Paul Brookes.

Juster, N. (2000). *The phantom tollbooth.* New York: Random House for Young Children. (Original work published in 1961).

Lewis, C. (1991). Nursery schools: The transition from home to school. In B. Finkelstein, A. Imamura, & J. Tobin (Eds.), *Transcending stereotypes: Discovering Japanese culture and education* (pp. 109–118). Yarmouth, ME: Intercultural Press.

Lynch, E. W., & Hanson, M. J. (2004). *Developing cross-cultural competence: A guide for working with young children and their families* (3rd ed.). Baltimore, MD: Paul Brookes.

McGoldrick, M. (2003). Ethnicity, cultural diversity, and normality. In F. Walsh (Ed.), *Normal family processes* (p. 341). New York: Guilford Press.

Murray, G. (1993). The inner side of experiential learning. In T. Gochenour (Ed.), *Beyond experience: The experiential approach to cross-cultural education* (Rev. ed., pp. 159–174). Yarmouth, ME: Intercultural Press.

National Association of School Psychologists. (2004). Multiracial children: Practical suggestions for parents and teachers. *NASP Communiqué* 32(7), 174.

Nieto, S. & Bode, P. (2008). *Affirming diversity: The sociopolitical context of multicultural education.* New York: Longman.

Roopnarine, J. L., & Johnson, J. E. (2008). *Approaches to early childhood education* (3rd ed.). New York: Prentice Hall.

Saracho, O., & Spodek, B. (Eds.). (1989). *Understanding the multicultural experience in early childhood education.* Washington, DC: National Association for the Education of Young Children.

Spradley, J., & McCurdy, D. (2004). *The cultural experience: Ethnography in complex society.* Chicago: Waveland Press.

UNESCO. (2000). Education for a culture of peace. Retrieved from http://www.unesco.org/education/ecp/index.htm.

U.S. Department of Education. (2004). *No child left behind: A toolkit for teachers.* Retrieved from http://www.ed.gov/teachers/nclbguide/nclb-teachers-toolkit.pdf.

Vontress, C. (1976). Counseling the racial minorities. In G. Belkin (Ed.), *Counseling: Direction in theory and practice* (pp. 277–290). Belmont, CA: Wadsworth.

West, M. (2003). Teaching the third culture child. In C. Copple (Ed.), *A world of difference: Readings on teaching young children in a diverse society.* Washington, DC: National Association for the Education of Young Children.

Families in Our Classrooms: Many Ways, Many Voices

No matter the size,
No matter the name.
One thing in families
Is always the same . . .
LOVE, LOVE, LOVE!

—The Kindergarten Children of Westfield School, Sacramento,
California (1995)

Wadsworth/Cengage Learning

CHAPTER OBJECTIVES

Upon reading this chapter and reflecting on its content, you will understand the characteristics of family structures and their role in the transmission of culture to the young child.

KEY CONCEPTS

- family
- family configurations
- traditional family
- kinship care

STANDARDS: THE FOLLOWING STANDARDS ARE ADDRESSED IN THIS CHAPTER:

naeyc Standard 2: Building Family and Community Relations
naeyc Standard 7: Early Childhood Field Experiences
InTASC Standard 9: Professional Learning and Ethical Practice
InTASC Standard 10: Leadership and Collaboration

TEACHERS SHARE: MEET MILAGRITOS

Teachers were getting ready to begin their round of home visits, as was the practice at the local early childhood center. The visits always provided great opportunities not only to meet the families of the children they were teaching but also to learn more about them.

For Ms. Harold, her first visit was to the home of Milagritos, a bright-eyed four year-old Filipino girl, who lived not too far from the child development center. She had looked forward to visiting her, especially since she had not yet met Milagritos' parents. It was early in the afternoon when she rang the bell. While she waited, she noticed the religious portrait on the door and heard music, which went silent as the door opened.

A pretty teenage girl smiled at her while an older lady came to greet Ms. Harold. Introducing herself, Ms. Harold soon discovered that she was in the company of Milagritos' grandmother and older sister. Timidly, Milagritos, who was also present, smiled at her teacher as she peeked bashfully from behind her grandmother. "She's the baby," said the grandmother referring to Milagritos, as the teenager translated. Sitting between her sister and the grandmother, Milagritos quietly listened while her sister translated how proud "Mami" was of her young grandchild. In the small and humble but neatly kept house Ms. Harold noticed many family photos on the living room wall. "This is my daughter, Milagritos' mother," said the grandmother, pointing to one of the photos on the wall. "Is she here? I'd love to meet her," said Ms. Harold. "Oh, no," said Milagritos' teenage sister. She then explained, "Mama works in another state and grandma and I take care of everything here." As the teenage clutched her grandmother's hand, Ms. Harold could read in her eyes how proud and certain she was that all was fine.

FAMILIES—A CONSTANT IN OUR CHANGING SOCIETY

Call it a clan, call it a network, call it a tribe, call it a family. Whatever you call it, whoever you are, you need one.

Jane Howard (1978)

Constant change remains the force that continues to mold life patterns in society. Fortunately, one of the few constants in life is the family, an essential social unit of varied configurations that enfolds each and every one of us. In spite of the many changes the family has experienced, it continues to be a fundamental force in creating and perpetuating humankind. The family is still the basic channel for learning because of its essential role in transmitting culture. This is particularly important in multicultural early childhood education, where learning about the families of young children is the best way to discover the diversity of our students.

Most of us have encountered a kaleidoscope of family configurations in the neighborhoods and in the communities where we live. Through this chapter, we will tour the world of the family with special emphasis on those characteristics that make families alike and yet so different. As we examine the nature, the composition, and the role of families in culture, you will learn about the role of family in the lives of young children.

WHAT IS A FAMILY?

Families comprise persons who have a shared history and a shared future.
Monica McGoldrick and Betty Carter (2003)

Defining family is not an easy task, particularly in today's society. You probably have read and heard people say that families are no longer what they used to be, that today's families are too different and complex, and even that the family no longer exists. The reality is that the family as a social unit is very evident, but it has evolved along with our society. The traditional family unit, consisting of mother, father, and children, has changed so much and assumed so many different formulas that even the United Nations prefers using the plural term *families* to more accurately describe the current nature of this social unit (United Nations, 1994). In working with children, we come to understand that "our image of what a family is and what it should be is a powerful combination of personal experience, family forms we encounter or observe, and attitudes we hold" (Gilbert, 2007).

Diversity—The Ever-Present Characteristic of Families

Because of today's social changes and diverse perceptions regarding the family as a unit, trying to find just one model is impossible. In discussing the family, Walsh (2003) reminds us of the ever-existing diversity of the family and how today's families reflects the changing and complex nature of contemporary society. We need not travel far to state with certainty that the diversity of family configurations is one of society's essential characteristics. Our classrooms present the most vivid examples of this. While it is generally acknowledged that the model of the traditional family has changed, it is also encouraging to know that the family as an institution continues to exist. In fact, the family is still the most basic social unit (United Nations, 1994) that is important for individual and social survival.

Defining the Family: What the Literature Says

Today, families are of such interest that they have become the focus of study across many other disciplines. Numerous ideas defining the family have been proposed over time, as researchers attempted to answer the question: "What is a family?" One idea on which they all agree is that establishing only one definition is difficult. By examining what several social scientists have observed, you will get a better idea of what a family is.

According to Garbarino and Abramovitz (1992), families, "the headquarters for human development are the most basic and enduring of social institutions." The authors also offer the dual perspective on the family "as a small group of people sharing love, intimacy, and responsibility for children; and, as a social institution that serves and reflects the American macrosystem."

Bronfenbrenner's (2004) theory places family at the core of influences for individuals. Based on Bronfenbrenner's ecological theory, the family is the main source of influence within the microsystem that describes the network of firsthand

Culture

Values
Ideas
Beliefs
Traditions
Acceptable behaviors

Culture is influenced by the
environment, language,
and historical events

Family members
interpret and pass on
culture to children

Figure 3-1   Like a Filter, the Family Serves
As a Mediator of Culture

social experiences individuals confront across cultures. According to this theory, families are the heart of the process in which each person becomes who he or she is. Serving as interpreters and mediators between the individual and the society, families teach individuals how to be family members and how to become members of the immediate socio-cultural environs (see Figure 3-1). When we are cognizant of the powerful influence families have on children, we recognize the need to work in close collaborations with families.

Children Define the Family

In our search to gain better understanding of young children's perceptions of families, we asked some of our graduate students to ask their children to define *family*. To elicit more information, the teachers asked the children to draw their families prior to being asked the following questions: "Is this your family?" "Who is in your family?" "Can you tell me what you like best about your family?" The array of answers was fascinating, mainly because they highlighted what children perceive as meaningful about their families. They also shed light on the differences found across cultures. Their answers revealed views about family membership that included grandparents, other relatives and significant adults, and even pets.

One of the best ways to define the family is expressed by Gina and Mercer Mayer (1999) in their story *This Is My Family*:

> This is my family. Each of us
> is different, but we love each
> other a lot. I think that's what a
> family is all about.

Beyond diversity, families are alike in the roles, tasks, and functions they perform. Let us explore what makes our families similar.

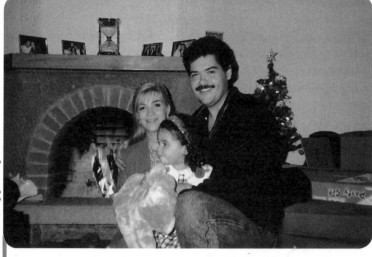

Families come in all shapes and sizes, but they all have the same roles and functions. What are the family configurations most common in your community?

FAMILY MODELS

Today's families come in many different configurations. The concept of a traditional family model is based on our personal experiences, our culture, and the environment in which we live. Ask yourself the following:

What is my idea of a family? What do I consider to be a family?

How does my idea of family compare to the actual families in my community?

What Are the Functions and Roles of the Family?

Society needs families to prepare the young to become constructive members of society. This is accomplished through the transference of expectations, social responsibilities, and behaviors to the future generations of adults. All families share these basic social responsibilities even though cultures define the ways those functions are performed. Social researchers have defined these functions as being both basic and complex tasks. There are divergent opinions regarding the ways these specific responsibilities are carried out by families. As we describe each of them, remember that they are activities expected of *all* families, but that the way they are performed may differ as a result of each family's culture.

According to educators and sociologists, families perform several key tasks, or functions. These functions are essential to meeting and supporting the needs of family members and to the family's success as a group. Some of the key functions of the family include the following (Epstein, Bishop, Ryan, Miller, & Gabor, 2002; Hildebrand, Phenice, Gray, & Hines, 2008):

- *Basic needs:* All families need to have their basic needs met. These include food, shelter, and financial stability.
- *Socialization tasks:* One of the key functions of the family is to socialize children by teaching them the accepted behaviors of society. This is a process that encompasses all the activities and rituals that pass on the social behaviors and ways deemed appropriate according to the family's culture and heritage. Parenting and caregiving responsibilities are central to the successful socialization of the child and family as a group. Through interactions with family members, peers, and adults, children learn the values and beliefs of their culture. Affection, sense of respect, morality, and ways to respond to others are among the behaviors learned during the early years.

Through time, families have played a leading role in passing on traditions to the young.

The family is the major facilitator of cultural ways and traditions.

- *Emotional support and spirituality:* The family is also the source of emotional support for individuals. For the developing child, this critical support provides a sense of love, trust, respect, and connectedness to the family. Emotional support is also essential to building a sense of security and safety. Families also instill in their members a sense of spirituality, ideals, and beliefs, which contribute to feelings of emotional stability. Researchers have identified spirituality as an integral element that is instrumental in keeping the family together and which contributes to overcoming adversity (Walsh & Pryce, 2003).

- *Economic tasks:* All families need a stable environment where necessary resources are available. Stable jobs and income allow families to be self-sufficient and to satisfy the financial needs and responsibilities.

- *Educational tasks:* The family is also responsible for providing the young with appropriate learning and schooling experiences. At home, families fulfill the task of helping children to learn important skills and responsibilities as a member of the family and of the community. Families also teach their young about cultural knowledge, including traditions, values, and beliefs. Promoting education and supporting educational goals is also a key function of the family. Views regarding education are culturally defined.

- *Crisis management tasks:* Sharing ideas about how to face challenges is an integral task of families. This includes all the skills and responses families use during emergencies and difficult situations that may arise (such as family illnesses, accidents, moving, loss of income, and death). How families respond to crises and how they engage in coping is culturally influenced.

- *Shared family functions (See Figure 3-2):* These are common to all families across cultures. However, how these are carried out and by whom varies with culture.

Figure 3-2   Shared Functions of Families

To understand the meaning of *family*, we asked a group of early childhood educators representing several ethnic groups (European American, African American, Afro-Caribbean, and Hispanic) to define the basic tasks and responsibilities of the family. As you read their answers, think about other descriptors or details that you may want to add to this list.

Families are a group of people who . . .
- Provide love and nurturance to their members
- Keep people together
- Meet the basic needs of their members
- Provide role models for their younger members
- Support each other in *all* circumstances
- Transmit values and beliefs to their members
- Teach their members to respect others
- Model problem-solving skills to their members
- Model how to live in a social group
- Transmit a sense of pride about their own cultural heritage to their members
- Establish a sense of cultural identity
- Create an invisible but strong bond among their members

IN ACTION . . .

WHAT IS A FAMILY?

To find out what children think about the concept of family, select several children, preschoolers through primary-age, and have them draw their families. Afterwards, talk with each child and let him or her describe the drawing. You may want to ask questions such as these:

- *Tell me, what is a family?*
- *Is this your family? Who is in your family?*
- *What is your family like?*
- *What do you like about your family?*

Note the similarities and differences in their responses. See whether differences are based on the children's cultural backgrounds. Look for family elements such as memberships in clubs or social groups and participation in sports or other activities. Considering all their responses and illustrations will shed some light on children's perceptions of family. Think about what makes them alike and what makes them unique.

- How can you as an early childhood educator support the families of your students?
- What are the ethical responsibilities early childhood educators have toward the students' families?

CULTURE AND THE FAMILY

Culture establishes meanings shared and understood by those who belong to it (Spradley & McCurdy, 2004). Because we all live in and respond to the patterns of our cultures, interpretations of how to perform a specific function vary. Living in a multicultural environment like the United States means that we need to realize that

IN ACTION . . .

CHILDREN'S VIEWS OF THE FAMILY

A group of early childhood teachers in Florida and Las Vegas asked their students to tell them about their families. Their findings proved very interesting. Through their responses, children ages 4–6 described the family in terms of the functions and roles they perceived. Essentially, two main roles were elicited from their responses:

1. Nurturance and a sense of a warm environment ("My family loves me." "My mommy is always with me." "Nana reads me stories.")

2. Provision of basic needs ("Daddy buys me ice cream." "We play together." "Mi familia cocina [My family cooks]." "Grandpa bought me these sneakers." "Mom makes me cookies.")

Although their responses are characteristic of the still-egocentric child, they reflect an early perception of what being a part of a family means.

what one person holds as an expectation might diverge from that of another. This is the paradigm and challenge of life in a multicultural society. Working with families of different cultural backgrounds affords teachers an opportunity to experience the variety of views and interpretations of social roles and functions. Even the simplest task is viewed differently when examined cross-culturally, which punctuates that what is valued as necessary for social survival in a group becomes a task expected for families to perform. Take, for instance, the function of education, which teachers expect families to support. Although it is true that valuing education represents a shared view among all cultures, not all cultures will expect children to acquire the same kind of knowledge. Because the concept of what is to be learned differs from culture to culture, what a young child learns by the time he or she reaches school age differs among groups. For example, children in the United States are expected to master the "Three Rs," whereas families from New Guinea believe that learning their tribal history and mastering hunting and fishing are important because these skills are related to survival (Konner, 1992). This remote example illustrates that each cultural group assigns expectations that respond to its own needs and circumstances.

A Child Is Born

Consider these comments made by future parents we interviewed: "She'll be an important person, maybe even a president!" "We want her to be a good wife and mother." "My baby will be proud of his color." "Whether it's a boy or a girl, I want our baby to be a good person." "He'll be a minister like his father." "We want our child to live in a country where there is freedom."

AROUND **THE WORLD**

INDIAN NAMKARAN CEREMONY

Busy preparations had kept the Rivani family working for several days. Many family members had come from far away to attend the Namkaran, or naming ceremony, of the Ravani's newborn son, As part of the Hindu tradition, a priest was called to consult the newborn's horoscope, which he used to determine the most auspicious name for the child. Following the custom, the priest advised the Ravanis that if the name he selected was not to their liking, they could substitute it for another, as long as it started with the same letter. By coincidence, Jai, the name chosen by the priest, was also the Ravani's favorite. That afternoon, the parents and the grandparents took part in the ceremony with the priest. At the end, Jai's father whispered his little son's new name in the right ear three times, according to custom. An elaborate feast followed that marked the beginning of little Jai's welcome into society.

What we read in these parents' comments are not only their desires for a bright future for their children but also the unique ideals and expectations for the new members of their culture. The thoughts parents have about their children provide glimpses of their values and ideals, knitted by the cultures to which they belong. For some, the arrival of a new child brings new hope for the survival of the group; for others, it is a way to continue the family tradition; for others still, it means a new opportunity to accomplish some unrealized dreams. Regardless of what expectations families have for their children, they represent the interplay of the cultural and personal characteristics of the group's members. Culture begins its profound influence on individuals through their families from the moment of conception. Family rituals, child-rearing practices, and the structure of the family into which children are born are factors that contribute to socialization and passing on of cultural knowledge.

Family Rituals

For those who have younger siblings or children of their own, they know that the arrival of a new child entails a number of family activities. Among those activities, many represent traditional rituals that people have carried out for centuries. They are important because they keep alive the essence of cultures. Some of these rituals are observed before the child is born, whereas others happen after the birth.

Many family rituals begin before birth. Selecting colors and clothes for the new baby are among the many rituals that are performed across cultures. For instance, preparing a *canastillo*, a basket with all the items the new baby will need, is a traditional activity among Hispanic families. A similar practice commonly found in the United

IN ACTION . . .

OUR NAMES

Names are a very important element of our identities. Many of us have names that were inherited from family members, names that denote historical persons, or names that are rooted in the culture to which we belong.

• Do you know why you were given your name?

• Find out and see if it corresponds to any of the reasons listed in this chapter.

• What other reasons and motivations do you feel people have for naming a child?

• In what ways do names reflect family and cultural values?

Across cultures, love and caring are essential to appropriate development. Daily routines such as feeding are special times for parents and other adults to nurture their relationships with the child.

Wadsworth/Cengage Learning

States is a baby shower, a gathering where everyone pitches in with needed items to help the family prepare to welcome the newborn. Other rituals include preserving personal items across generations. Some families keep and pass on baby clothes worn by their elders; others use the same crib their grandparents used.

Author Margy Burns Knight has collected stories of child-welcoming practices from around the world. In *Welcoming Babies*, Knight (1998) describes a series of informal and formal practices, all depicting the ways in which each society marks the arrival of its new members. Some practices involve everyone in the community, whereas others are performed by the parents and close relatives. For example, in Nigeria, some women sing after learning that the child is born, whereas in Afghanistan, a newborn's father whispers prayers into each of the baby's ears (Knight, 1998).

More than Just a Name

Perhaps one of the most interesting rituals families perform concerns choosing the name for the new baby. Selecting a name for a child not only provides identity but may also reflect cultural heritage and define the individual's roots. For example, in some Asian cultures, names are a way of honoring ancestors. Names are also a good way to note the influence of the times. During many years that we have taught and worked in children's classrooms, we have enjoyed learning from parents the reasons behind the choices of names for their offspring. Although there are always tendencies to choose fashionable names, there are several other motivations for selecting names, which are sometimes shared across cultural groups. Some of the main reasons include the following:

1. *To honor someone:*
   - An ancestor—usually grandparents' names are given to a first child, especially if the child is a boy.
   - A close relative, family member, or friend—names of uncles and aunts or the most recently deceased relatives. Honoring a special friend by naming a child after him or her is another common practice.

2. *To follow a tradition:*
   - Naming children according to their parents' names, that is, a boy with the father's name and a girl with the mother's name.
   - Having a religious authority select the most auspicious name for the child and holding a naming ceremony.
   - Choosing names that are considered acceptable to the parents' religion, such as biblical names or names that honor a religious figure or symbol.

3. *To highlight ethnic identity:*
   - Selecting names that depict ethnic origin or affiliation. Names of specific ethnic groups are sometimes used to name children (for example, *Taina* or *Ashanti*).
   - Selecting names of local and national ethnic heroes or events of special national significance (such as *Bolivar* or *Washington*).

4. *To remember feelings or emotions:*
   - Names that depict a feeling or emotion based on the significance of the child's birth (such as *Milagros* [miracle]).
   - Name of a wonderful feeling (Joy or Aimée [the loved one]).

   It is important to respect and accept a child's name, regardless of how hard it might be to write or pronounce. One of the best ways to demonstrate our respect toward a family's culture is by respecting their names and avoiding the tendency to "Americanize" them.

Wadsworth/Cengage Learning

Cultural heritage influences the names we are given.

Following are some suggestions for dealing with names:

1. Always ask the family what name they prefer their child to use. Respect their choice.

2. Ask parents why they named their child that way. This will help you not only to value the child's name but also to find ways to enhance the child's self-concept.

3. If the name is difficult to pronounce, ask the parents to help with correct pronunciation. Try writing it phonetically, or you may even make an audio recording of the parent pronouncing the name.

4. If a child's name has an English translation, share it with the class. This can also become an opportunity to introduce children to a thematic unit in which they can investigate origins, meanings, and other aspects of names.

5. Some children might want to adopt a nickname. Share this with parents so that they know it is the child's desire to do so.

6. Always emphasize respect toward names. Intervene whenever a child is the target of name-calling or ridicule because of his or her name. This is both damaging and humiliating for the child.

FOCUS
ON CLASSROOM PRACTICES

WHAT'S IN A NAME?

A name is one of the best ways to show pride in our own culture and family. It is also a way to showcase who we are. For young children, names represent and exhibit their emerging sense of self-identity. Helping children to be proud of themselves is a critical developmental task. At times, children with names in their native languages can face challenges as they try to become part of the group. This is the case of the little girl in the story *My Name Is Yoon* by Helen Recorvits (Farrar, Strauss and Giroux, 2003). After sharing the story with children, teachers can use the activities shown here to help children ages 3–6 appreciate and become proud of their names.

My Name is Yoon.

Before Reading:

Purpose of Activity:

> To have each child feel important.

> To increase knowledge of the alphabet.

> To increase knowledge in phonics.

Each child writes his/her name on squares of paper (one letter per square). The consonants will be one color and the vowels another. See "KAREN" below.

1. Have children make their names with the letters. Each child scrambles the letters and rebuilds his or her name. Students may look at sample word cards of their names, but the goal is to build them from memory.

2. As children are sitting in small groups looking at the names in front of them, ask questions such as "Who has a name that begins like yours?" and "Whose name ends like yours?" The students can make comparisons between their names and others.

3. (Small group activity) Have children put the first letter of their name upside down in a pile in the center of the table. Each child takes a turn drawing a letter, saying the sound, and telling whose name begins with the sound of that letter.

4. Put all the letters upside down in the center of the table. Have children take turns selecting one letter at a time. If the letter belongs in their name, they keep the letter; if not, they return it to the pile. (This reinforces letter recognition and sequencing of letters for words.)

5. (For children in grades 1 and 2) Have students work in pairs (as more letters than just one student's are needed) to make two-letter words, three-letter words, four-letter words, and the longest word they can. Have them record their words on the sheet attached.

Read the Story
When you look at the cover, what do you wonder? What makes you wonder that; what evidence do you see that helps you to wonder that?

1. Everyone's name is special. What do you think of when you say your name? Draw things that will tell people about you.

2. Paste the letters of your name at the top of a large piece of paper. Find pictures or words that start the same way as your name.

My name is _____. My name is special. When I say my name, it makes me think of _____
_____.

My Name is Yoon
My name is _____.
My friend's name is _____.
These are the words we can make from our names:
_____
_____.

We thank Karen Burke EdD, reading specialist, who contributed this activity.

DIVERSITY IN CHILD-REARING PRACTICES

Child rearing is an essential function of families. The child-rearing customs and practices do not have shared meaning across cultural groups. Even across people of the same cultural group, it is not uncommon to find different views regarding how to raise a child. Although families in U.S. mainstream culture perceive children as young individuals whose development of independence is strongly supported and valued, it is not so among other cultural groups. For example, in families with Latino roots, young children are believed to be totally dependent on the adults, a fact that explains the pampering and long nurturance parents provide throughout

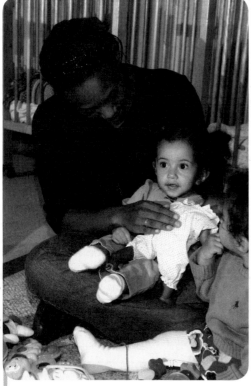

Wadsworth/Cengage Learning

Cultural traits are learned from infancy.

the entire early childhood period. Contrary to families in U.S. culture, Hispanic parents tend to be very nurturing, permissive, and indulgent with their children (Zuñiga, 2004). Families encourage dependency, which gives all the family members an opportunity to create stronger bonds with the child and vice versa. Zuñiga (2004) points out that rather than pushing the child to develop early skills and independence, Hispanics "placate" their children. Independence, a highly valued behavior in U.S. mainstream culture, is not as relevant for Hispanic families. A Hispanic child is often encouraged to keep a "babyish" behavior well beyond infancy and sometimes even until school age. In Hispanic culture, the need for a child to attain independence is not as desirable because, traditionally, children are brought up in a network of caring relationships defined by parents, siblings, and other family members. The family places more importance on strengthening and reassuring the child's emotional ties with the family, which extends beyond the immediate family members. This, in turn, also affords the opportunity for the child to develop a collective orientation rather than an individualistic one. This collective orientation is also found in traditional Native American and Middle Eastern families.

Similar practices are found among Asian American families. Chan (2004) reports that Asian parents consider their children until age 3 as "being relatively helpless," which explains the tolerant and permissive attitudes they exhibit. Emphasis on creating an emotionally supportive family environment causes attention to supersede development of independence in the first 3 years of life. As Asian children reach the preschool stage, Asian families prepare their children to assume responsibilities. The preschool years become a transitional stage in which children are led to achieve self-discipline (Chan, 2004). Life formalities are then emphasized and learned through the direct participation of children in adult activities.

Families are also expected to teach their younger members rules of social interaction. For example, children must learn the rules for interactions with adults and elders. The manner in which a child speaks and responds to adults will be different based on the family's culture. For example, U.S. parents tend to exhibit a more permissive attitude when children interrupt adults' conversation. However, this is not acceptable in many other cultures. Generally, families with Middle Eastern, Hispanic, Native American, Asian, and European roots expect their children to refrain from interrupting when adults are talking. They also demand from their children acceptance of adults' decisions, for parents strongly believe that authority is not to be questioned by the young.

Although in a mainstream U.S. family a child tends to talk back to adults, this is considered unacceptable in the context of Middle Eastern, Hispanic, Asian, European, and Native American families (Joe & Malach, 2004; Sharifzadeh, 2004; Zuñiga, 2004).

Respect toward elders is another concept learned through the family. Traditionally for many cultures, the elders, whether they are relatives or not, represent a source of authority and wisdom, which, in turn, is acknowledged by exhibiting respect and honoring them (Chan, 2004; Joe & Malach, 2004). In Asian, Hispanic, and Caribbean cultures, the extended family, usually grandparents and elder family friends, commonly take direct part in child rearing. This is also a practice observed in many immigrant families, in which it is not uncommon to find grandparents assuming child-care responsibilities.

CHANGES IN THE FAMILY STRUCTURE

One of the most evident societal transformations is the emergence of a variety of family configurations. As a result of societal changes, in addition to the traditional family model headed by mother and father, several other family structures have emerged.

FOCUS
ON CLASSROOM PRACTICES

A CLASSROOM HOLIDAY TIME LINE

Holidays or special celebrations are a part of every cultural group. They also demonstrate the diversity of children's and families' cultures. Because holidays symbolize many of the values and beliefs of a group, they need to be acknowledged in the classroom. Recognition of the holidays other people celebrate is another way for children to become aware of diversity. Unfortunately, because many holidays have religious origins, they are usually omitted in schools. However, there is nothing wrong with becoming aware of the names and times when other groups observe holidays.

One of the ways to acknowledge the different holidays is to create a time line that is developed throughout the school year. Unlike a calendar, where holidays are lost among other events, a time line can provide a linear and clear perspective of all the celebrations observed by the children's families. Displayed conspicuously, children and families can become familiar with celebrations year-round.

This activity also helps children learn about the concepts of time and space.

To create your time line, you need to find out from families the holidays they observe. Gather your data and organize the holidays chronologically. If you are not familiar with some of those listed, remember to ask families about them, including the time of year they are celebrated. For the time line, you can either use a roll of manila paper (size 8 in. by 11 in.) or plain wallpaper (the size for borders is very handy). On the time line, enter the name of the holiday and, if possible, use any of its symbols or colors. Write the names of the families that observe each holiday. As holidays approach, share them with the class. Because you are acknowledging their existence and creating awareness of the holidays, simply mention the name of the holiday and any of the traditions attached to them. In this way, children will know that the family of a classmate is observing a special occasion.

Who Are the Members of a Family?

The best way to determine the family configuration is by finding out who its members are and what roles they have within the family. Membership implies being an active participant of the family unit with relationships to the other group members. Today, social and family researchers agree that family membership is characterized by a wide spectrum of possibilities. No longer is family membership defined by blood or legal status (Lynch & Hanson, 2004). Membership in a contemporary family is often defined by the particular circumstances and even crises that the family has experienced. Early childhood practitioners need to be aware of these circumstances, which may help to explain the unique family structures of their students.

Although most agree that a family is comprised of adults and, in most cases, children, we cannot so easily agree on the membership of others in a family. While the original concepts of family membership are lost in time, each of us has inherited ideas about family membership from our own experiences as family members.

The fact that our society is a mosaic of family configurations was shown in the 2010 U.S. Census (U.S. Bureau of Census, 2010). The data in Figure 3-3 present interesting facts about the diversity of family structures.

Although these findings cannot be used to make any generalizations, they do help show that families are characterized by a diversity of configurations. Identification of the members of a family varies greatly in our society across cultures and even among our own relatives. What really matters is that, regardless of perceived family membership, a group of people can function as a unit and fulfill the roles of a family. The strong sense of "being a family" proves their validity as a social unit.

To fully understand the spectrum of dimensions of the present family, we need to examine the factors that have caused it to transform into its present state.

Figure 3-3
Households by Type

HOUSEHOLDS BY TYPE
- Total number of households is 112,611,029.
- Married-couple families make up 49.7 percent.
- Female householder, no husband present, make up 12.5 percent.
- Male householder, no woman present, make up 4.5 percent.
- Grandparent households, responsible for grandchildren for 5 years or more, make up 9.8 percent.

Source: U.S. Bureau of Census (2010). Selected Social Characteristics of the United States 2005–2009.

IN ACTION . . .

HAS YOUR FAMILY ALSO CHANGED?

Early educators need to be aware of their own family characteristics. Before we continue exploring the concept of the family, you should consider how and whether your family has changed. To do so, complete the following questions. They are adapted from the characteristics that traditionally depict a family (Curran, 1983).

1. Who are the members that constitute your family?
2. Are they all related by blood or marriage?
3. Does your family provide for your economic survival?
4. Is your family your source of protection?
5. Has your family been the main source of social and cultural learning?

6. Is there a sense of mutual and shared responsibility among all your family members?
   - What did you find out?
   - What are the changes, if any, that surprised you the most?
   - What implications can you derive from your findings?

You can determine the level of privacy of your answers and if you are comfortable sharing them with others. What is important is that you find out how change may be present in your own family.

When Did the Family Begin to Change?

The U.S. family began its most dramatic transformation in the second half of the twentieth century as a result of political events and economic trends. Job security became a thing of the past as early as the 1930s with the unstable economy of the Depression years. The need for higher income forced both marriage partners to seek work outside the home (Couchenour & Chrisman, 2004). The participation of women in the workforce became widespread during World War II and started a long trend of U.S. women as active wage earners. This pattern also established the role of working mothers, which, in turn, drastically altered the roles and patterns of the traditional U.S. family. Today, this practice is reflected in statistics that show that 60 percent of women with children under five years old are a part of the workforce (United States Bureau of the Census Research, 2010). The implications for early education are obvious.

As stated earlier, the changes being experienced by U.S. families were caused by the major changes in the society and in the world (see Figure 3-4). Some of the societal changes that began during the 1960s contributed to the transformation of the family. New lifestyles and a broader acceptance of family memberships and responsibilities led to different views of the family. These social factors directly and indirectly produced new and unique family configurations. With newly developed lifestyles, the family as a social organism was forced to adapt itself (Walsh, 2003).

A new wave of immigrants to the United States, particularly since the 1960s, added another element that further diversified the traditional family. The variety of family patterns, as well as customs and traditions brought by different ethnic groups, further altered the old concept of family.

Figure 3-4 Factors Contributing to the Transformation of the Family: How Many Are Evident in Your Community?

1. *Economic situation:* The unstable economic situation has changed the financial stability of families. Responsibility for supporting and contributing to the family's economic resources may include any wage-aged member.

2. *New lifestyles:* Traditional values and ideas about personal relationships are continuously changing. Emphasis on individuality and liberal views about family, sex, and interpersonal relationships has contributed to the change in family lifestyles.

3. *Wave of immigration:* New waves of immigrants continue to add diverse elements to the fabric of the U.S. society. With this comes new family configurations based on the members' cultures.

Culture Influences Family Membership

Exploring who is considered "part of the family" is an interesting way to observe the differences among cultures. For example, some people in the U.S. define their family as consisting of the mother, father, and children. In our mainstream culture, extended family members, although valued as important members, are not referred to as "family" but as "relatives" (Hanson, 2004). This view of the family, which focuses on the immediate family members or the nuclear unit, is different from what other cultural groups acknowledge and call "my family."

According to Willis (2004), African Americans commonly describe their families as including more than just simply parents and children. With terms such as "'my family,' 'my folks,' 'my kin,' 'my people' to identify blood relatives and to denote relationships with special friends or 'cared for' individuals who are not related,'" they describe a wider concept of the family. Families with Native American roots also view the family as consisting of more than just the immediate members. Families in both these cultures are defined as including the nuclear and the extended family members (Joe & Malach, 2004). Similar views are also found among Hispanics (Zuñiga, 2004) and Italian Americans (McGoldrick, 2003), who value and regard as family the extended members as well as those with whom there might not exist a legal relationship. For example, in both groups, godparents, the Italian *comparaggio* and the Spanish *compadrazgo*, describe a way through which outside members, usually neighbors or close friends, become part of the family. Considered an honor, the *compadres* (godparents) assume an active role, much like that of parents, and are expected to watch over the lives of their godchildren or *ahijados*. It is not unusual to find children in the care of a godparent (*madrina* or *padrino*), especially in moments of crises.

Wadsworth/Cengage Learning

Families headed by grandparents are becoming more common in present-day society.

A DIVERSITY OF FAMILY CONFIGURATIONS

The various family configurations of the children in most early childhood classrooms include single-parent families, blended families, extended families, foster families, and two-parent families (see Figure 3-5). No longer is there a single model of the family. The most basic social unit has been changed, much like the other spheres of society, and today's families are structured in both traditional and nontraditional forms. In fact, nontraditional families already outnumber traditional families as the result of the high divorce rate in the United States, the pregnancy rate among teenage girls, and sexual orientation patterns.

AROUND **THE WORLD**

WAITING FOR BABY IN SWEDEN

Erik and Agda are a young Swedish couple who met at a bistro and fell in love three happy years ago. Motherhood is something Agda has been looking forward to ever since she and Erik started living together. It finally happened, and the baby is on its way. Agda's and Erik's parents were ecstatic at the prospect of being grandparents, even though Agda and Erik were not married. Now, it's Agda's last month of pregnancy and she is home from work on paid maternity leave planning the future for her new baby boy. Erik and she have been going to free childbirth education classes at the local public nursery and Agda feels they are well prepared to welcome their new son. With Erik at her side during the birth and paid paternal home leave, Agda is sure that they will master all the tasks required of good parents. They plan to have the baby sleep with them for the first few months, the way she and Erik slept with their parents when they were babies. Thinking about it makes Agda feel warm all over. Of course, she will breast-feed their son. Agda looks forward to joining the other mothers who breast feed their babies in the sunny neighborhood park. Last night, she and Erik were getting ahead of themselves as they mused about whether to let the baby go to the government public nursery or to hire a "child minder" to be in their home when she and Erik go back to work. Either way, the services are publicly funded and will not cost them anything. She also thinks that they should continue with more parenting classes at the nursery center. There is so much to learn and the instructional staff is excellent. Free classes include child development, nutrition, hygiene, creativity, and many more. Agda thinks to herself, "It takes a lot to get ready for baby but now I feel it's worth it."

Figure 3-5
Family Models

Traditional model

Intact family
(*Two-parent heterosexual couple*)

Blended family
(*Stepfamily or multiple-marriage heterosexual couple*)

Nontraditional model

Single-parent family

Grandparent family

Foster family

Sibling-headed family

Gay or lesbian family

Traditional Family

The traditional family consists of a heterosexual couple and the biological or adopted children. This is also known as an *intact family* (Olsen & Fuller, 2003). In recent decades, the high divorce rate has produced the *blended family* model, where the children from previous marriages are assimilated into a newly formed family unit. Present statistics indicate that married-couple families represent about one-third of all families in the United States. What makes the intact and blended family models traditional is the fact that a heterosexual couple performs the traditional roles of a mother and a father.

Single-Parent Families

Single-parent families have become the most common type of nontraditional family structure due to the steadily increasing divorce rate and the high incidence of teenage pregnancy. An estimated 40 percent of all children are born into single-parent families (National Vital Statistics Report, 2009). Most of these families are headed by mothers; however, single-parent families headed by fathers are gradually increasing across the country. Single-parent families face the additional challenge of having one parent carry out all the family responsibilities. In spite of that, such families can successfully meet the needs of the child and provide a healthy family environment.

Grandparenting—A Trend in Today's Family Configurations

Today, many children live with and are in the care of grandparents. Grandparent families are growing in numbers as a consequence of various social problems in our society. An estimated 2.5 million or 41 percent of all grandparents are parenting nearly six million children (United States Bureau of the Census, 2005–2009). Families headed by grandparents have been a practice among some Native American groups and Latinos, but they have not been common in mainstream society (Olsen & Fuller, 2003). Immigration, teenage mothers, loss of a parent, and economic pressures are among the factors leading to an increase in grandparents raising their young grandchildren. The number of grandparent families is growing to the point that support groups are forming across the country and social reforms are taking place to assist grandparents with the upbringing of grandchildren.

LITERACY CONNECTIONS . . .

RECOMMENDED READINGS ABOUT GRANDPARENT FAMILIES

- De Toledo, S., & Brown, D. (1995). *Grandparents as parents: A survival guide for raising a second family*. New York: Guilford Press.
- Kornhaber, A. (1995). *Contemporary grandparenting*. Thousand Oaks, CA: Sage Press.
- Kornhaber, A. (2002). *The grandparent guide*. New York: McGraw-Hill.
- Osborne, T. (2003). *Ticklebelly Hill: Grandparents raising grandchildren*. Bloomington, IN: Authorhouse.

Gay and Lesbian Families

One of the alternative family configurations is the gay or lesbian family. Families headed by gay men or lesbian women span the socioeconomic spectrum of society, much like heterosexual couples. It is estimated that same-sex households in the United States are increasing. Estimates suggest that gay and lesbian parents are raising 4 percent (approximately 65,000) of all adopted children (Gates, Badgett, Macomber and Chambers, 2008). These demographers indicate that gay and lesbian parents raising adopted children are older, more educated, and have more economic resources than other adopted parents. Same sex parents tend to adopt younger children, many of who are foreign born. Gay and lesbian parents have additional child-rearing tasks as they prepare their children for controversy and possible negative experiences associated with social pressures (Clay, 2003). However, research has shown that parenting experiences for adoptive children of gay and lesbian families are comparable to those of peers growing up in heterosexual families (USA Today, 2009).

LITERACY CONNECTIONS . . .

BOOKS ABOUT NONTRADITIONAL FAMILIES

Gay and lesbian families

- Hann, L., & Nijland, S. (2003). *King & King*. New York: Tricycle.
- Valentine, J. (2004). *One dad, two dads, brown dad, blue dads*. New York: Alyson Wonderland.
- Vigna, J. (1995). *My two uncles*. New York: Albert Whitman.

Foster families

- Blomquist, G., & Blomquist, J. (1991). *Zachary's new home*. Washington, DC: Magination Press.
- Wilgocki, J., & Wright, M. (2002). *Maybe days*. Washington, DC: Magination Press.

Adopted families

- Bunting. E. (2000). *Train to Somewhere*. New York: Sandpiper.

- Girard, L. (1991). *Adoption is for always*. New York: Albert Whitman Publishers.
- Kirk, D. (1999). *Little Miss Spider*. New York: Scholastic.
- McCutcheon, J. (2008). *Happy adoption day*. New York: Little, Brown.
- Zisk, M. (2001). *The best single mom in the world*. New York: Albert Whitman.

Homeless Families

- Bunting. E. (1993). *Fly Away Home*. New York: Sandpiper.
- DiSalvo, D. (1997). *Uncle Willy and the soup kitchen*. NY: Mulberry Books.
- Martin, C. (1996). Rosie: *The shopping cart lady*. NY: Hohm.
- Gunning, A. (2004). *A shelter in our car*. CA: Children's Book Press.

Families Facing Challenges

Life situations vary and may lead some families to experience extreme stress while dealing with challenges. While well-functioning families support and nurture their children to happy and productive independence, families experiencing difficult times may not. Families of all configurations and cultures face challenges ranging from economic to social. Some families may be able to provide for the basic needs of their children while being unsuccessful in providing the emotional security necessary for healthy development. A family facing challenges is usually plagued by distrust, anxiety, and unpredictability. Adults and other family members may also exhibit low self-esteem, distrust, inability to have fun, and sometimes a sense of shame. Children of challenged families often exhibit behaviors such as anger and sadness; many are unable to experience intimacy with peers or with other adults. Unless they receive support and positive intervention that allows healthy emotional and physical development to take place, children of challenged families may face difficulties that last throughout their lifetimes (Olsen & Fuller, 2003).

Homeless Families

Life circumstances and social and economic conditions have led many individuals and their families to lose their homes. Homeless individuals are defined as those who do not have a permanent home. It is estimated that about 1 percent of the U.S. population may experience "a spell of homelessness at least once during a year" (Urban Institute, 2000). It is not simple to establish an ethnic profile of the homeless, for homelessness affects people across cultural, economic, and racial lines.

In recent years, communities across the country have seen an increase in the number of families with children who are homeless. It is estimated that there are 65,000 homeless children enrolled in schools (National Coalition for the Homeless, 2009). There are many causes for homelessness, and among the leading reasons are poverty and the lack of affordable homes (National Coalition for the Homeless, 2010). Other reasons include domestic abuse. Frequently, the mother is the victim, forcing her to end a relationship with a spouse or other family member. Unfortunately, the homeless are often victims of discrimination and violence. Many national and local agencies advocate and provide services, including shelter, for homeless individuals and families. Federal legislation establishes the rights and provides funding for educational services to children who are homeless. Programs like Head Start provide direct services to homeless children and their families. More support and understanding is required to address the multiple issues faced by children and families who are homeless.

Immigrant Families

Immigrant families have always been a part of U.S. society. Today, with the continuous increase in immigration, the number of families of immigrants living in communities everywhere in the country has risen. Demographical statistics show that in 2005, close to 21 percent of children under age 6 living in the United States were from immigrant families (Matthews & Ewen, 2006; Matthews & Jang, 2007). The majority of these children are U.S. born with at least one parent born outside the United States. Census data show that more than half of foreign-born parents are Hispanics followed by Asians (United States Bureau of the Census, 2010).

Immigrant families in the United States share many characteristics. Among these are the desire to build a better future for their children, a high sense of commitment to their new life, and a good work ethic. Unfortunately, the immigrant families' adjustments to the new life in the United States is often accompanied by exploitation, poverty, and language isolation (Hernandez, Denton, & Macartney, 2007). Lack of mastery of English language on the part of the parents often hinders access to employment opportunities and social services. Because of this, children from immigrant families are less likely to benefit from good education and appropriate social services. Some families also face difficulties due to their immigration status. In the context of immigration law and policies, many families are faced with uncertainty about their future. This causes additional burdens for children. With immigration projected to continue, policy and legislation to support the needs of immigrant families and their children is a priority.

Extended and Kinship Families

The term *kinship care* describes a family situation in which a grandparent or other extended family member is raising a child whose parents cannot (Children's Defense Fund, n.d.). Among kinship care families, recent trends show that a large number of children live with and are cared for not just by grandparents, but by relatives and friends. Awareness of the broader concept of family membership is important for the early childhood practitioner. Knowing that a relative, whether an uncle, a cousin, or even a close family friend, shares and cares for the child as the parents do helps intervention and development of appropriate services. This sense of kinship that bonds many different family members, as well as close individuals, becomes a significant social asset for the family and for the child. This collective spiritual, emotional, and physical frame of reference becomes a resource that the child can draw upon to successfully solve problems and overcome challenges of the present and the future. From the perspective of the child, it widens the circle of people who care and participate in his or her upbringing.

Families of Children with Special Needs

A family of a child with special needs is not officially classified as a demographic unit. We chose to discuss it as a model because so many early childhood practitioners encounter children with special needs in their work settings. The latest census indicates that 19 percent of the U.S. population has disabilities (U.S. Bureau of the Census, 2010). Of these, five percent are children ages 5-17. The laws that protect children and adults with disabilities and guarantee them equal treatment under the law were enacted with the passing of the Individuals with Disabilities Education Act (IDEA) in 1990 and the IDEA 2004 amendment. The laws specify and define the rights, services, and accommodations for people with special needs. Services for children and their families are also regulated through and embedded in this legislation.

Accepting a child's disability is a difficult emotional and intellectual process for the family. Many have equated it to a loss of a loved one (Turnbull et. al, 2011). Finding the necessary support and understanding from family members, friends, and professionals becomes critical. As with other aspects of life, cultural beliefs and ideas play a leading role in how a family may view a child's disability. Culture, personal experiences, and circumstances influence how families respond to the news about having a child with special needs (Harry, 2002). The type of condition as well as the age of the child may also impact their reaction.

Disabilities in children are viewed differently through the prism of culture. Perspectives aside, families of children with special needs require sensitive, responsive, and caring professionals with whom they can build a sense of trust. With the practitioner's support the family will be able to learn about the rights, the array of services, and programs available for their child.

THINK AND REFLECT...

MY BABY, MY PRECIOUS BABY!

When they saw their baby boy for the first time, Tina and Tyrone said to themselves with great relief, "He's healthy and beautiful! Lots of hair, ten fingers, ten toes, what more is there?" The months ahead were full of happiness. But at four months, Ben was not responding in the ways that Tina had read about in her child rearing books and magazines and she became concerned. He was not smiling, or following any movements, or making noises. She and Tyrone decided to consult Ben's pediatrician. After the doctor examined Ben, the young parents learned that their baby had a disability. Their first reaction was disbelief, "He's my baby, my precious baby!" cried Tina. "He's too young to have a disability of any kind! It's my fault. I should have stayed home and not worked! I should have rested more and not exerted myself going on vacation to hike and swim so much while I was pregnant."

- What do you think about Tina's reaction?
- What would you say to the parents of this child?
- What types of support are available in your community for parents like Tina and George?

SUCCESSFUL FAMILIES

Do you ever consider what makes a family successful? Is there such a thing as a successful family? No matter what the configuration of the family, there are common characteristics that make a family "successful" (see Figure 3-6). When adopted by its members, these traits, found to be common in families across cultures, make the family function harmoniously, positively, and effectively.

Successful families have a set of identifiable values. These values are the principles that guide the decisions and the behaviors of the family members. Primary caretakers—whether grandparents, siblings, mothers, or fathers—try to model behaviors consistent with the values held by the family.

Spirituality has been identified as a key value that holds the family together, particularly during trying times; it is the "glue" that binds the family and a source of shared ideas. Spirituality stems from a family's religious affiliation or spiritual inclination. A family's spiritual sense provides guidelines that may define family lifestyles. It also serves as the source for value-based behaviors such as morality, sense of respect, and responsibility toward elders and family members. African American families have been characterized by their strong spiritual bonds, as have Latino and Jewish families, whose religious ideas form the core of many of their traditions and family roles. How strongly the religious codes will be followed is decided by each family. External elements, such as dress codes, food preparation, and food selection, can be tied to a family's religious beliefs and values. This link can be observed among many ethnic and cultural groups, such as Hindu, Middle Eastern, and Christian families.

Beyond the external aspects, family values, sense of respect, and morality may also influence factors such as the role relationships among family members, child-rearing

Figure 3-6
Characteristics of
Functional Families

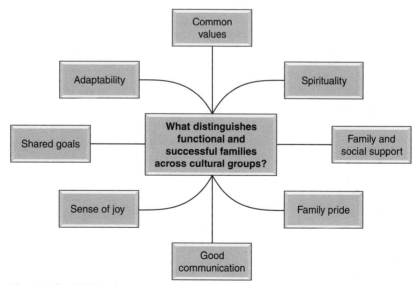

Source: Olsen & Fuller, 2003.

patterns, and developmental expectations (Lynch & Hanson, 2004). Awareness of different religions and spiritual values is essential for early educators to know how to be responsive and respectful to the families of young children they serve.

Healthy families practice and believe in *family support*, which fosters growth and understanding of each other. An important part of family support is the commitment to spend time together and stay together, even during difficult times. In addition to family support, functional families demonstrate social support for others in their communities, schools, and neighborhoods. They take social responsibility for the world they live in and contribute in positive ways. Consider, for instance, the support families display toward each other during natural disasters and other emergency situations.

They also set *shared goals*. All members see themselves as key participants in achieving their aspirations. In their own ways, the members of each family collaborate to see their dreams become a reality. Good *communication skills* are essential for a well-functioning family. Members need time to learn how to express themselves as well as how to listen to others. Family members that communicate well appear to have fewer problems and experience more harmony together and individually.

Adaptability and the willingness to make changes are very important in today's society. Families must be able to adapt to social, economic, and emotional pressures brought on by internal and external forces. Change in traditional roles is a good example of family adaptation. For example, taking care of the baby is no longer the exclusive job of the mother. Cooking is a shared responsibility, as is earning an income for the family.

Healthy traditional and nontraditional families show *pride* and demonstrate *loyalty*. They demonstrate their sense of pride in their success stories and in their behaviors. Family members help each other and solve problems together. They cooperate and work together as a unit when faced with adversity.

In every healthy and successful family, there must be time for *joy* and laughter. Celebrating together is one of the oldest human rituals. Successful families exhibit joyfulness, spontaneity, and enjoyment of life. Celebrations become opportunities to share a sense of happiness through interactions and the ways family members respond to the needs of other members. Formal celebrations, such as birthdays, weddings, anniversaries, and cultural holidays, are times to express joy while reaffirming culture. Informal celebrations take place anytime: during mealtimes, on family outings, while playing together, and even while doing family chores. They are times when family members express their togetherness and support to each other.

IN ACTION . . .

EXTENDED FAMILY

A well-known African saying states:

It takes a whole village to raise a child.

In the context of the extended family, what is the meaning of this phrase? How does it reflect the reality of today's U.S. families?

THINK
AND
REFLECT...

REMEMBERING SPECIAL FAMILY TIMES

Day to day experiences with family members leave indelible marks in our memory. Take time to remember any of the special times spent with your family. What stories can you share about either a happy or sad time experienced with your parents, other family members, or relatives? Think about the feelings that you experienced. How did the experience contribute to your concept of family?

Although healthy families are not guaranteed to produce well-adjusted, productive, happy children every time, it is reasonable to assume that the children from well-functioning families will do better than the children raised in families that have difficulty adjusting to challenges. The hope is that children raised in the context of a supportive family environment will go on to replicate their experiences later on in life when they form their own families.

THE FAMILY—THE MOST IMPORTANT PART OF OUR LIVES

We are all part of a family. We are largely who we are because of what we received and learned from our families. The family is a basic social and cultural institution and a common element of cultures. This sociocultural unit imparts traditions and teaches shared meanings and behaviors to the individual. We only need to look at ourselves to recognize the power embedded in a family. In general, our tastes and dislikes, our beliefs, food preferences, and even some of the phrases we use are grounded in what we learned from our families.

LITERACY CONNECTIONS . . .

LEARNING ABOUT FAMILY DIVERSITY THROUGH CHILDREN'S LITERATURE

Many stories can help children learn and discover more about their own families. Following are a few of the many that you may want to share with children:

For younger children (ages 3–5)

- Barnwell, Y. (2005). *No mirrors in my Nana's house*. San Diego, CA: Harcourt Brace.
- Crews, D. (1998). *Bigmama's*. New York: Mulberry Books.
- Gunning, M. (2004). *A shelter in our car*. San Francisco: Children's Book Press.
- Kerley, B. (2010). *You and me together: Moms, dads, and kids around the world*. Washington, DC: National Geographic.
- Lee, J. (2002). *Bitter dumplings*. New York: Farrar, Straus & Giroux.
- Mora, P. (1997). *A birthday basket for Tia*. New York: Aladdin.
- Morris, A. (2000). *Families*. New York: Scholastic.

For primary-age children (ages 6–8)

- Galindo, M. (2008). *Icy watermelon*. Houston: Arte Publico.
- Ryland, C. (2004). *The relatives came*. New York: Live Oak Media.
- Woodruff, E. (1999). *The memory coat*. New York: Scholastic.

THE CLASSROOM, THE MIRROR OF THE CHILDREN'S FAMILIES

Your classroom is perhaps the best place to observe how relevant and powerful families are. During the early years, families play the principal role in the lives of children. When we know the members of a child's family, even the nuances and gestures exhibited by them are understood as being characteristic of certain family members. Because families perform the role of culture interpreters for the younger generations, the ways children behave also reflect the cultures they belong to.

One of the more common ways to "see" the influence of the family is in the words and phrases children use. What the family members do, say, and wear is always noticed and modeled by children. Observing children during pretend play gives teachers excellent windows into their lives and lets them know what impacts the children the most. During one of our courses, a graduate student shared the following incident she observed involving one of her prekindergartners:

> I was fascinated by what Teresita, a 4-year-old whose parents came from the Dominican Republic, did. She was playing in the housekeeping area when I started this observation. Two other girls were with her and they were all getting dressed. She opened the handbag she was playing with and went to the mirror where she started to put on some eye make-up. As I came closer, I saw her using a black marker to draw a line around her eyes. Of course, she looked as if she had been hit by someone! When I asked her what she was doing, she remarked: *"Me estoy poniendo la raya para pasear* [I am putting on the eye-liner to go out]"; I knew instantly that the idea came from her mother, a young woman who always wears noticeable eye makeup. For Teresita, getting ready to go out implied using makeup. More importantly, this example demonstrates that even at her young age, Teresita was already modeling the ways of her family.

IN ACTION . . .

AM I LIKE MY FAMILY?

We learn so many things from our families that it is sometimes hard to realize the true realm of their influence. To find out how your family has influenced you, begin by finding the material things that reflect its influence. Looking around your own house, identify those things that directly or indirectly reflect the objects, items, and patterns that were found in your family's home. Consider, for instance, the colors, the kind of objects and the ways they are displayed, the way your rooms are arranged, the "messes" in your kitchen, and, of course, the food you cook. How many similarities with your family did you find? If you did not find a lot of resemblances, ask yourself why you are different from your family. You will probably discover that in the similarities, as well as in the differences, the influence of your family is a common denominator.

FOCUS
ON CLASSROOM PRACTICES

A CLASSROOM FAMILY COOKBOOK

One of the exciting things about cultural diversity is learning about ethnic eating habits and food patterns. Discovering what the families represented in your classroom eat is not only a source for cultural awareness but also another way to emphasize likenesses and differences among families. Because all families have a favorite dish (probably several favorite dishes), a good way for children and for teachers to learn about themselves is by creating a cookbook. The classroom cookbook is basically a collection of recipes of simple favorite dishes enjoyed by families. This project provides opportunities to integrate literacy, math, and science. Using a big book format, families would be assigned a page each (or two depending on the enrollment). A picture or a drawing made by the child or any family member would illustrate the pages. To collect the recipes, teachers need to send a letter to the families explaining the purpose of the activity. Ask families for very simple recipes or those that can be made in the classroom. Possible dishes include salads, beverages, desserts, or bread-based recipes.

As recipes are collected and added to the cookbook, test them in the classroom. Give credit to the child's family whenever a recipe is prepared. On the bulletin board, announce the dish with a sign reading: "Today's special dish is ____ contributed by the ____ family." If possible, display the recipe's ingredients early so that children can examine them. Plan to take pictures or videotape children while recipes are tested. These can be used for later discussions and to review specific aspects. Discuss the food value of the recipe and help children look for similarities and differences among the various dishes.

This is a project that could increase participation of families in the classroom. It also gives teachers another opportunity to learn about the specific families' cultures. For the children, learning what their classmates eat and the ingredients used will provide another window into how alike and different they are.

FAMILIES—THE ESSENCE OF SOCIAL AND CULTURAL LIFE

The family serves as one of society's prime agents for cultural learning. Through day-to-day activities and interactions, families pass on to the younger generations the ideas and accepted behaviors of their cultural group. The power the family exerts covers every aspect of life. The younger the individual, the more definitive and influential the power of the family becomes. Even before birth, we begin experiencing the influence of families, and, through them, we experience the culture to which they belong. Through our families, we acquire the meanings and views that make us a part of our social group.

Teaching young children presents a unique opportunity to discover their families. In every classroom in this country, we can begin not only to learn about families, but also to appreciate and value them. This is a unique opportunity to begin to understand what it means to live in and be a part of this diverse U.S. society. Because early childhood practitioners are constantly trying to find novel ways to help children, no better source and channel is found than the children's families. As we search for new ideas to reform our teaching in a responsive manner, the families in our classroom will be our first resource. In the next chapter, you will explore the needs of the child and see more evidence of how relevant the family is to knowing the children you teach.

THINK
AND
REFLECT...

IN SEARCH OF A DREAM

When Aida Ramos made the decision to leave her native Puerto Rico, she had only one thought: to build a better future for her and her 1-year-old child. A single parent, she came to New York almost 40 years ago with only a little knowledge of English and a firm desire to succeed. For a woman from a Spanish-speaking island, life in the United States in the 1950s and 1960s was not always easy. With limited knowledge of English, Aida never gave up, despite the many hardships she faced. Later on, after remarrying, Aida and her husband Angel struggled to give their five children a better life in Chicago where they settled. They succeeded in keeping their cultural traditions and proudly passed them on to their children and today to their grandchildren.

Today, Aida looks back not with nostalgia but with a well-earned sense of pride. Times were difficult, but Aida agrees that there was always the knowledge that, with their desire to succeed, they would make it. And they did.

Wadsworth/Cengage Learning

WHAT WE HAVE LEARNED—CHAPTER SUMMARY

Family is the social unit most responsible for creating the child as a social, emotional, cultural, and psychological being. The learning that takes place during the formative years is most influenced by the immediate and extended family as well as by the environment. Culture and child-rearing practices, as they are transmitted through family members and encountered in the immediate environment, play major roles in the development and socialization of the child. The value system of the child is greatly affected by cultural predispositions instilled at an early age. The changes in our society have also influenced changes in the traditional family model consisting of a mother, a father, and children. Now, it is more common to encounter a variety of nontraditional configurations, such as grandparent families, gay or lesbian families, single-parent families, and foster families. Regardless of its makeup, every family needs to be the conduit of effective and positive development for each child. Given today's socioeconomic, racial, and religious pressures, this is not an easy task. In order to effectively assist in the positive development of their students, early childhood educators must have a firm grasp of the influence the family structure and culture play in the development of each child.

MAKING CONNECTIONS . . .

1. An excellent way to learn about families in a multicultural context is to find out how they see themselves. Begin by asking a sample of your own colleagues or classmates about their ideas regarding families. You may want to ask the following questions:
   - *How do you define family?*
   - *What makes your family a family?*
   - *What would you say makes your family special or different from others?*

   After you have collected their answers, find the things in common and the things that differ. Summarize your findings and share them with your colleagues.

2. A good way to continue learning about families is to learn about their daily routines. Routines help us to "see" the culture of the family. Begin a collection of family routines. Ask your friends, colleagues, and some of the parents of the children in your class to share some of the routines they observe during breakfast, dinner, on Saturday and Sunday, and when having visitors at their house. After collecting your data, analyze them to find trends in common, unusual patterns, and other peculiarities that characterize the families surveyed.

3. Because we all have an interest in learning more about different cultures, select one culture and do some library research about some of its family customs. Possible aspects to research are birth practices, child-rearing ideas, family tasks, funeral practices, and others. Write a paper about your findings and share it with your colleagues.

4. Using the findings from the activity in which you surveyed the family configurations in your classroom, select a minimum of five children's books reflective of those configurations. Design a classroom activity to share the books with your students.

RECOMMENDED INTERNET RESOURCES

- The Annie E. Casey Foundation (serving children and families), the foundation raises awareness about disadvantaged children and their families and sponsors actions and reforms for their betterment
  www.aecf.org/

- Center for Law and Social Policy (CLASP), the organization promotes legislation that benefits the disadvantaged, including children
  http://www.clasp.org/

- The Children's Defense, Fund, the site is an independent voice for all children in America
  www.childrensdefense.org

- The National Coalition for the Homeless, the Coalition provides latest data and information about the homeless in the United States that includes homeless children
  www.nationalhomeless.org/index.html

- "Resources for Child Care Providers" from the Child Care Bureau
  www.acf.hhs.gov/programs/ccb/providers/index.htm

- American Academy for Child and Adolescent Psychiatry, a series of articles includes important topics about young children and families
  http://www.aacap.org/cs/root/facts_for families/facts_for_families_numerical_list

- Family in America, site includes many topics about the family including composition of the U.S. Household that provides information about young children
  http://www.family in America.org

YOUR STANDARDS PORTFOLIO

naeyc **Standard 2:** Building Family and Community Relations

naeyc **Standard 7:** Early Childhood Field Experiences

InTASC Standard 9: Professional Learning and Ethical Practice

InTASC Standard 10: Leadership and Collaboration

Knowledge about diverse families is central to successful collaboration between parents (or families) and schools. Early childhood practitioners must be aware of the role that the family plays in the life of a young child. Getting to know more about the make up and the characteristics of families will assist in providing appropriate experiences and building successful relationships that will benefit the child. To evidence how you meet this standard, complete the following activities:

- Find out about the cultural make up of families in your community and create a concept web to graphically represent your findings.

- Interview a family with cultural diverse backgrounds and find out about their family customs and family composition. Reflect on your findings and highlight commonalities and distinct elements related to the family's culture.

- Identify resources in your community and on the Internet that may assist families with cultural and linguistic differences.

REFERENCES

Bronfenbrenner, U. L. (2004). *Making human beings human: Bioecological perspectives on human development.* San Francisco: Sage.

Chan, S. (2004). Families with Asian roots. In E. Lynch & M. Hanson (Eds.), *Developing cross-cultural competence: A guide for working with young children and their families* (3rd ed., pp. 251–354). Baltimore, MD: Paul Brookes.

Children's Defense Fund. (n.d.). *Kinship care resource kit for community and faith-based organizations: Helping grandparents and other relatives raising children.* Washington, DC: Author.

Clay, J. (2003). Working with lesbian and gay parents and their children. In C. Copple (Ed.), *A world of difference: Readings on teaching young children in a diverse society* (pp. 64–67). Washington, DC: National Association for the Education of Young Children.

Couchenour, D., & Chrisman, K. (2010). *Families, schools, and communities: Together for young children* (4th ed.). New York: Delmar.

Curran, D. (1990). *Traits of a healthy family.* New York: Doubleday.

Epstein, N., Bishop, D., Ryan, C., Miller, I., & Gabor, K. (2003). The McMaster model: View of healthy family functioning. In F. Walsh (Ed.), *Normal family processes* (3rd ed., pp. 581–607). New York: Guilford Press.

Garbarino, J., & Abramovitz, R. (1992). The family as a social system. In J. Garbarino, *Children and families in the social environment* (2nd ed., pp. 72–98). New York: Aldine de Gruyter.

Gates, G.J., Badgett, M.V., Macomber, J.E., & Chamber, K. (2008). *Adoption and foster care by gay and lesbian parents in the United States.* Retrieved from http://www.law.ucla.edu/williamsinstitute/publications/FinalAdoptionReport.pdf

Gilbert, K. (2007). Varied perspectives on the family. In *Annual Editions: The family* (p. 1). Dubuque, IA: McGraw-Hill.

Hanson, M. (2004). Families with Anglo-European Roots. In E. Lynch & M. Hanson (Eds.), *Developing cross-cultural competence: A guide for working with young children and their families* (3rd ed.). Baltimore, MD: Paul Brooke.

Harry, B. (2002). Trends and issues in serving culturally diverse families of children with disabilities. *Journal of Special Education, 36*(3), 131–138.

Hernandez, D., Denton, N., & Macartney, S. (2007). Children in immigrant families—the U.S. and 50 states: National origins, language, and early education. *Child Trends* Pub. 2007–11. Retrieved from http://www.childtrends.org/Files/Child_Trends-2007_04_01_RB_ChildrenImmigrant.pdf.

Hildebrand, V., Phenice, L., Gray, M., & Hines, R. (2008). *Knowing and serving diverse families* (3rd ed.). Upper Saddle River, NJ: Merrill.

Howard, J. (1978). *Families.* New York: Simon and Shuster.

Joe, J., & Malach, R. (2004). Families with Native American roots. In E. Lynch & M. Hanson (Eds.), *Developing cross-cultural competence: A guide for working with young children and their families* (3rd ed., pp. 127–164). Baltimore, MD: Paul Brookes.

Kindergarten Children of Westfield School. (1995). *My family, your family.* Morristown, NJ: Modern Curriculum Press.

Knight, M. (1998). *Welcoming babies.* Gardiner, ME: Tilbury House.

Konner, M. (1993). *Childhood: A multicultural view.* New York: Little, Brown.

Lynch, E., & Hanson, M. (2004). (Eds.). *Developing cross-cultural competence: A guide for working with young children and their families* (3rd ed.). Baltimore, MD: Paul Brookes.

Matthews, H., & Ewen, D. (2006). *Reaching all children? Understanding early care and education among immigrant families.* Washington, DC: Center for Law and Social Policy.

Matthews, H., & Jang, D. (2007). *The challenges of change: Learning from the child care experiences and education of immigrant families.* Washington, DC: Center for Law and Social Policy.

Mayer, G., & Mayer, M. (1999). *This is my family.* New York: Golden Books.

McGoldrick, M. (2003). Ethnicity, cultural diversity, and normality. In F. Walsh (Ed.), *Normal family processes* (3rd ed., pp. 235–259). New York: Guilford Press.

McGoldrick, M., & Carter, B. (2003). The family life cycle. In F. Walsh, (Ed.), *Normal family processes* (3rd ed., pp. 375–298). New York: Guildford Press.

National Coalition for the Homeless. (2009). *Who is homeless? Fact sheet.* Retrieved from http://www.national-homeless.org/factsheets/who.html

National Vital Statistics Report. (March 18, 2009). Vol. 57. No. 12.

Olsen, G., & Fuller, M. L. (2007). *Home–school relations: Working successfully with parents and families* (3rd ed.). Boston: Pearson Education.

Robles de Meléndez, W. (2006). *Family and school collaboration* (study guide). Fort Lauderdale, FL: Nova Southeastern University.

Sharifzadeh, V. (2004). Families with Middle Eastern roots. In E. Lynch & M. Hanson (Eds.), *Developing cross-cultural competence: A guide for working with young children and their families* (pp. 441–482). Baltimore, MD: Paul Brookes.

Sloan Work and Family Research Network. (2009). Boston: Boston College. Retrieved from http://wfnetwork.bc.edu/pdfs/womenwork.pdf

Spradley, J., & McCurdy, D. (2004). *The cultural experience: Ethnography in complex society.* Chicago: Waveland Press.

Turnbull, A., Turnbull, R. Erwin, E., Soodak, L., & Shogren, K. (2011). *Families, professionals and exceptionality: Positive outcomes through partnerships.* MA: Prentice Hall.

United Nations. (1994). *International year of the family.* New York: Department of Public Information.

United States Bureau of the Census. (2010). *Selected social characteristics in the United States 2005–2009.* Retrieved from http://factfinder.census.gov/ADPTable?_bm=y/7geo_id=01000US&-ds_name=A.

United States Census Bureau Research. (2010). *Women leaving and re-entering the workforce.* Retrieved from http://www.catalyst.org/publication/249/women-leaving-re-entering-the–work-force

United States Bureau of the Census. (2010). *Newsroom: Facts for features. 20th Anniversary of Americans with Disabilities Act.* Retrieved from http://www.census.gov/newsroom/releases/archives/facts_for_features_special_editions/cb10-ff13.html

USA Today. (November 5, 2009). *Gay couples a close look at this modern family, parenting* by Sharon Jason. Retrieved from http://www.usatoday.com/nes/health/2009-11-5-gayparents05_ST_N.htm

Urban Institute. (2000). *A new look at homelessness in America.* Washington, DC: Author. Retrieved from http://www.urban.org/url.cfm?ID=900302.

Walsh, F. (2003). (Ed.). *Normal family processes* (3rd ed.). New York: Guilford Press.

Walsh, F., & Pryce, J. (2003). The spiritual dimension of family life. In F. Walsh (Ed.), *Normal family processes* (3rd ed., pp. 337–372). New York: Guilford Press.

Willis, W. (2004). Families with African American roots. In E. Lynch & M. Hanson (Eds.), *Developing cross-cultural competence: A guide for working with young children and their families* (3rd ed., pp. 165–209). Baltimore, MD: Paul Brookes.

Zuñiga, M. (2004). Families with Latino roots. In E. Lynch & M. Hanson (Eds.), *Developing cross-cultural competence: A guide for working with young children and their families* (3rd ed., pp. 209–250). Baltimore, MD: Paul Brookes.

Who Is the Child? Developmental Characteristics of Young Children in a Diverse Society

Wadsworth/Cengage Learning

All *children are born capable of learning.*
—Jean-Jacques Rousseau (1712–1778)

CHAPTER OBJECTIVES

Upon reading this chapter and reflecting on its content, you will understand key aspects of child development as well as the distinctive traits that give every child a unique identity.

KEY CONCEPTS

- child development
- developmentally appropriate practices (DAP)
- socialization
- racial awareness
- prejudice

STANDARDS: THE FOLLOWING STANDARDS ARE ADDRESSED IN THIS CHAPTER:

naeyc Standard 1: Promoting Child Development and Learning

naeyc Standard 4: Using Developmentally Effective Approaches to Connect with Children and Families

naeyc Standard 7: Early Childhood Field Experiences

InTASC Standard 2: Learning Differences

InTASC Standard 8: Instructional Strategies

TEACHERS SHARE

Miss Tyler had been teaching 3- and 4- year-olds for several years in a multiethnic metropolitan community. One of the things she particularly enjoyed about her job was interacting with children of so many diverse cultures. . . . Today during center time, she witnessed an incident that baffled her especially because of the young age of her students. Lilly, a lively 4- year-old girl, was playing in the block area along with several boys. They were building what seemed like a road and "driving" the trucks on it. All of a sudden, Lilly's friend Jena ran over and pulled her out of the center shouting to Lilly that she was a girl and she was not supposed to play with boys, much less with trucks. Lilly protested and soon the argument attracted other children, who began taking sides. Lilly kept saying that she was having fun, while Jena commanded her to stop. "That's not for girls," Jena said leaving angrily. In the end, Miss Tyler got everyone settled down, but it was clear that many of the children did not understand what the argument was about. Only one other girl took Jena's side and commented "Girls don't play with boys". . .

That evening reflecting on the incident, Ms. Tyler realized that gender roles and expectations are learned through the family. Smiling, she also remembered what she had been taught herself when she was growing up. Gender roles would be something she would have to address with her group.

LOOKING AT CHILDREN: SO ALIKE AND YET SO DIFFERENT

In all children, you will find the one.
Carmen Martínez, school teacher (1972)

DEVELOPMENT: THE PROCESS OF BECOMING

Every time a child is born it brings with it the hope that God is not yet disappointed with man [humankind].

Rabindranath Tagore (1861–1941)

Each child is different and yet the same. Although these two children are siblings, beyond gender differences, they are distinct in their own ways. In the classroom, children may share the same chronological characteristics and even cultural backgrounds. But each one will still have very clear characteristics defining him or her as an individual.

Whenever you enter a classroom of young children, you are faced with the wonder of life in its most vibrant form. Smiling faces, curious looks, and lively sounds all epitomize the energy of new life that children personify. Each child is a separate and distinct person as well as a member of the collective of children. Preparing to offer the children the best learning environment requires a careful analysis of the characteristics that make them similar and yet individual. Of particular importance to early childhood practitioners is how children develop the beliefs, attitudes, behaviors, and ideas about others that they exhibit in the classroom. They are also what help us understand the role of culture and how it influences children's responses like those in the opening scenario. This knowledge will both promote better understanding between the practitioner and the child

Many elements in the environment contribute to the positive development of the child. What elements are depicted here?

and provide valuable information to guide the instructional practices that foster multiculturalism. The first step to this knowledge is to explore what makes people alike: the process of development.

What Is Development?

At the moment of conception, all humans enter a continuous dance of change and development, which is completed at the end of our existence. The constancy of change that characterizes development is also what defines it. Development is an integrated and systematic process experienced by all individuals.

Because development is common to all people, children everywhere in the world grow in developmentally similar ways. Development is a process of dual character; one of its functions is to continue the process of establishing basic and similar milestones, while the other is to facilitate the development of individuals' unique personalities.

According to Brazelton and Greenspan (2000), all children must have several specific needs met if they are to grow and thrive successfully:

- Ongoing positive and nurturing relationships
- Physical protection, safe environments, and regulation
- Developmentally based experiences that consider their particular needs
- Reasonable expectations and predictable structure and routines
- A stable and supportive community
- Cultural continuity across home, school, and community

Universal Characteristics of Development

Children of the same age share similar physical, socio-emotional, and cognitive developmental milestones whether they live in Oceania, Africa, or in the United States. Reaffirming the universal character of development, Konner (1991) explains, ". . . infants in all cultures start out with the same biological

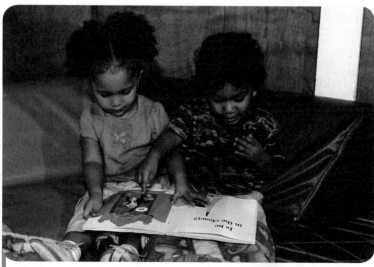

Development consists of similar and diverse milestones. Awareness of developmental commonalities and differences provides guidelines for classroom teachers.

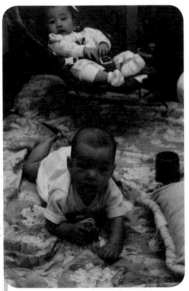

The concept of developmentally and culturally appropriate practice (DCAP) is based on the belief that all children experience common growth and development milestones while recognizing the role of culture as a factor that influences and shapes development.

equipment." This universality establishes the common developmental characteristics of children and of people in general. Cross-cultural research has shown that the stages of physical growth do not vary, although the tempo may vary by race, genetic inheritance, or the physical circumstances in which a child is raised. For example, all children experience shared developmental events such as growth of baby teeth, greater control of arms than legs, replacement of fetal cartilage with bone, and the need to belong to a peer group (Berk, 2006; Konner, 1991; McDevitt & Ormond, 2002; Paludi, 2002).

Language development is another example of developmental characteristics shared by all children. From the time the linguist Noam Chomsky first defined sets of language structures common to all languages, linguists, psycholinguists, and developmental psychologists have studied how children learn these structures (Berk, 2002). They have found that language structures emerge following the same developmental progression regardless of the child's native language. For instance, babies go through stages of random vocalizations that are slowly modified as infants emulate the sounds used by parents and other caregivers. Also, children go through a stage of over-generalizing the rules of grammar in their native language, whether, for example, in English or Russian. An example of this phenomenon is the child's use of "foots" instead of "feet" as the plural of "foot."

The common developmental patterns serve as guidelines to organize teaching and learning experiences responsive to children's developmental milestones. For example, because of the common developmental characteristics of all 4-year-olds, teachers are able to design learning experiences based on the general requirements of all children of that age. Developing activities that respond to the common characteristics of all children is also a basic principle of multicultural education.

Individuality: How We Become Who We Are

Each child is a unique individual. Even children from the same family have very distinct and particular traits that give them an individual character. Many factors contribute to the uniqueness of every child. Four of those are: genetic traits, prenatal environment, home environment, and culture (see Figure 4-1). The first one concerns the biological nature of each child as it relates to the genetic traits of the parents. Stamped at the moment of conception, each child comes into this world equipped with a personalized inherited genetic code. This code determines whether the child has light or dark skin, curly or straight hair, is tall or short, and so on. Many developmental psychologists tell us that genetic traits determine much more than the physical make up of each individual. Whatever your belief, genetics play a very important role in each child's identity.

Figure 4-1 Universal Factors That Influence Development

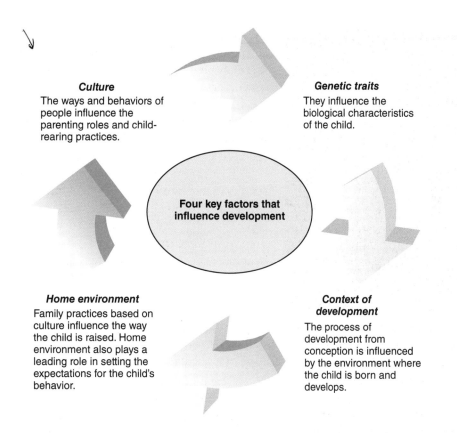

Culture
The ways and behaviors of people influence the parenting roles and child-rearing practices.

Genetic traits
They influence the biological characteristics of the child.

Four key factors that influence development

Home environment
Family practices based on culture influence the way the child is raised. Home environment also plays a leading role in setting the expectations for the child's behavior.

Context of development
The process of development from conception is influenced by the environment where the child is born and develops.

The second factor concerns the prenatal environment. Research confirms that the prenatal development of the child is influenced by the circumstances, culture, lifestyle, and habits of parents during the nine months before birth. Such things as the mother's emotional readiness to accept parenthood, nutritional practices (including the presence of drug use), access to and availability of medical care, and health conditions affect the development of the unborn child. Recent evidence also demonstrates that high emotional stress levels in the mother are a risk to the child.

A third factor is the home environment into which each child is born. For example, a 5-year-old boy born in a Masai village may be given the responsibility of shepherding grazing animals. Compare this responsibility with what is expected of children of the same age in the United States. You can easily see how the environment sets different behavior patterns and expectations for a child. The physical environment plays a very important role in a child's life because it provides the comfort and security that allows the child to develop. Studies have shown that an unfriendly and insecure environment has a negative impact on the social and emotional development of the child. This is something that early childhood professionals need to consider when creating learning environments that meet the needs of young children.

AROUND **THE WORLD**

A BIRTHDAY LUAU

For Jordan's parents, his first birthday was a very special day. "The first year of life is a special milestone," thought his mom, Jolette, a young Hawaiian, knowing that it was an opportunity to be grateful for the healthy child and the promise of a successful future. "It will be the best *luau* our family has ever had," she said to her husband as they started planning. Following Hawaiian tradition, reaching the first birthday was a special time to celebrate life with a *luau*. For Hawaiians, luaus are a traditional way to commemorate a special occasion, particularly first birthdays, high school graduations, and weddings.

Jolette remembered what her parents told her about the significance of the luau. It used to be a special feast of the Polynesians meant to please the gods. *Luau* is actually the name of a traditional dish made of chicken, coconut milk, and taro, a staple of the Hawaiian and other Polynesian people. In ancient times, the luau feast, full of symbolism and religious meaning, was only for royalty. Over time, the tradition changed and the feast came to signify a celebration of important events for all Hawaiian people.

Finally, the long-awaited day arrived. Little Jordan was radiant, as if he sensed that it was indeed his very special day. Family members and relatives had traveled from everywhere to participate in his birthday luau. Everyone was sharing memories and happily waiting to see the birthday boy, who arrived with his parents in the arms of his father. Everyone applauded. Jolette had carefully picked matching flowery shirts for Jordan and her husband and a traditional Hawaiian dress of the same fabric for herself, all signifying their unity as a family and their commitment to their little boy. Soon, all went quiet. It was then that Jolette's great uncle came forward and, looking at Jordan, gave the traditional blessing in the ancient Hawaiian language. After the great uncle finished, all joined in wishing little Jordan a good and long life. Then it was time for the luau and the birthday celebration.

Wadsworth/Cengage Learning

Note: We thank Dr. Jolette Apela, who shared her experiences about her first son's birthday luau.

Wadsworth/Cengage Learning

Uniqueness is the most common characteristic of all children. What similarities do you observe in these four children? What individual traits are also observable among them?

A fourth factor that affects child development is culture. We have already indicated in the previous chapters that culture plays a leading role in the way the child learns to view the world. Developmental psychologists recognize that culture greatly impacts the developmental milestones of children (Berk, 2006; Charlesworth, 2010). For instance, for most people in the United States, "sleeping through the night" is considered an expectation for infants by the time they are four to five months old. This is not so in cultures where infants sleep with their mothers and nurse themselves without hardly interrupting the adults. Infant sleeping arrangements are also influenced by culture. While it is common in the United States to find infants sleeping in a crib and often in a separate room, co-sleeping is practiced by people from countries around the world. For example, in Cambodia and among Central American Guatemalan Mayans, co-sleeping is a common practice believed to help in building a strong parent–child bond (Berk, 2006; Paludi, 2002). Teachers of young children are discovering daily that culture is a major contributor to the identity and individuality of each child in the classroom. As we get to know more about the children's cultures, we get to learn more about how to better address and respond to their individual needs.

THINK AND REFLECT...

THE ENVIRONMENT AS A SOURCE OF INTERACTIONS

One of the important characteristics of environments is that they provide opportunities for people to interact with one another. Direct and indirect interactions are effective catalysts for young children to learn the social and cultural codes of their group. For most of us, those we admire or feel emotionally attached to serve as models and learning sources. Take time to think about the person or persons who exerted a significant influence on your life and from whom you learned the social rules of your community.

- How did they influence you?
- Who were they?
- Were they from your family?
- Were they from your community?
- Why do you think they played such an influential role in your socialization?

VIEWS ABOUT DEVELOPMENT

There are many giants in the field of developmental psychology who have laid the groundwork for understanding how we develop, learn, and experience life. Among them are Freud, Erikson, Piaget, Vygotsky, Bronfenbrenner, and many others. Their observations and ideas are captured in the different theories they proposed—psychoanalytic, cognitive, behavioral and social cognitive, ethnological, and ecological—to help explain development. While no single theory exists to explain the developmental process, becoming familiar with the major theories provides the framework to understand children (Santrock, 2009). We are particularly supportive of the cognitive, sociocultural, and ecological theories, which provide perspectives especially relevant to working with diversity.

Jean Piaget was a Swiss developmental psychologist who concluded that children actively construct knowledge. In his theory of cognitive development, he stated that, universally, individuals go through four stages of cognitive development: sensory motor, pre-operational, concrete operations, and formal operational. These stages follow one another and describe what children are able to do at different points during life. All the stages are made operational with levels of adaptation to the environment and increasingly complex organization of knowledge, allowing children to interpret the world around them and build ideas (Santrock, 2009). Piaget's theory helps us understand why children do the things they do at a certain time of life and why they may not be capable of performing other tasks until they are physically and cognitively ready. Much of Piaget's research forms the foundation of early childhood education practices.

Lev Vygotsky, a Russian developmental psychologist, also researched cognitive development but from another perspective. His findings examine the impact of the environment and culture in the development process. Vygotsky's theory of sociocultural cognitive development is particularly relevant for educators working with children of diverse backgrounds. According to Vygotsky, nurturing interactions provided by parents, family members, and adults help children to build ideas about the reality in which they live (cited in Berk, 2006). Home, parents, and the environment in which the child grows and develops all provide the knowledge and skills vital to successfully meet the challenges of daily life. Vygotsky also recognized the role of language as a tool that facilitates how the child makes sense of the social conventions and concepts meaningful to the family and their culture. Talking about experiences with family members and peers and listening to conversations provides the child with a valuable avenue for learning about the things important in the culture.

The role of the environment was further emphasized by developmental scientist Urie Bronfenbrenner. His views are of particular relevance to multicultural education. In his studies, Bronfenbrenner showed that children in our classrooms reflect the many influences present in their environments (cited in Berk, 2006). The environment includes the family, relatives, school, and peers as well as the physical attributes of the home, community, and neighborhood, all of which impact the child's interpretation

NONVERBAL COMMUNICATION

One form of evidence of children's similarities across cultures comes from the work of the German ethnologist Irenaeus Eibl-Eibesfeldt. For more than two decades, Eibl-Eibesfeldt filmed candid instances of nonverbal communication in cultures throughout the world. He captured the behaviors of people in primitive cultures, such as the Yanomano of Brazil, the Kung of Botswana, and the Tasaday of the Philippine jungles, as well as different European groups. Through his research, he was able to document similar nonverbal responses to environmental stimuli. For example, he documented similar nonverbal responses in expressing disgust at a foul odor, in hitting combined with an angry expression, and in toddlers playing with one of their mother's nipples while breastfeeding. Eibl-Eibesfeldt's evidence includes observations of similar cross-cultural reactions in adults. He further documented parents showing the same facial expressions when they interacted with an infant: broad smiles, wide-open eyes, raised eyebrows, and a bobbing up and down of the head accompanied by a high-pitched, somewhat musical vocalization.

Source: Adapted from Konner, 1991.

and views of life. Even within the same family, each child is impacted differently by the environment. To effectively provide appropriate and meaningful learning experiences, early childhood practitioners must learn about the environments and how they affect the lives of young children.

In more recent research, Gonzalez, Moll, and Amanti (2005) tell us that ideas and concepts learned from home and family interactions become an individual's body of ideas about the behaviors and ways of the group. These "funds of knowledge" are "the historically accumulated and culturally developed bodies of knowledge and skills essential for household or individual functioning and well-being" (Gonzalez, Moll, & Amanti, 2005; Moll, Amanti, Neff, & Gonzalez, 1992). The concept of the "funds of knowledge" possessed by each child helps explain the influence of the environment and culture on the process of development. It also highlights the importance that culture has in shaping individual ways and behaviors.

Wadsworth/Cengage Learning

Adults play a leading role in the socialization of children.

SOCIALIZATION: LEARNING TO BE WITH OTHERS, LEARNING TO BE OURSELVES

Typically, young children in every culture exhibit the ability to establish social relationships. When children come to school, they bring an array of strategies to help them cope and get along with others. Think about the smiles on their faces, the compliments they make about your clothing, or the way they get closer to you to catch your attention. All these actions show that children know ways to gain social acceptance by others. These and other behaviors are acquired through the process of socialization.

Because we live in social groups, each culture has developed patterns and customs for regulating relationships among its members. This is known as socialization. Socialization is an ongoing process that assists individuals in learning to function effectively in a society. From birth, children are introduced to the cultural formulas of their group. Interactions with family members, caregivers, and adults provide examples and guide children in acquiring the responses and ways acceptable in their culture. You can imagine the extent of learning that must take place when preparing a child for an entire lifetime. From the simplest manners to attitudes about others, all is derived through the socialization process that lasts as long as we are in this world. Environments provide settings for this lifelong process experienced by all of us. In the early years, the various environments the children are exposed to help them learn how to do the following:

- Interact with adults and peers
- Distinguish what is good or acceptable from what is not
- Behave in daily life situations
- Express feelings, such as happiness and sadness
- Perform basic activities, such as eating
- Respond when faced with the unknown
- Demonstrate affection, including knowing to whom to show affection
- Show interest in something
- Differentiate between likes and dislikes
- Think about and regard others

Socialization Happens All Around Us

Developmental psychologists Super and Harkness (1995) proposed the idea of a developmental niche, or milieu, where children are socialized into the cultural ways of their society. Socializing forces in this setting come from adults, peers, and the environment itself. Through interactions with family members, caregivers, and the environment, cultural ideas and meanings are conveyed to the young. Each is a source of learning about the beliefs, ideas, and practices acceptable to the social and cultural setting where children grow up (Figure 4-2). The people whom the child spends time with, such as

Figure 4-2
Socialization Factors

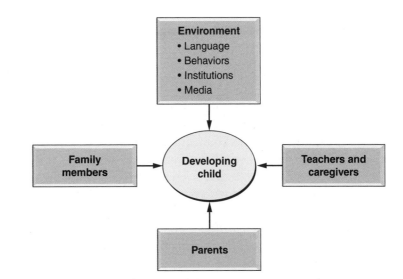

parents, relatives, and teachers, together constitute the most influential groups in shaping behaviors and learning about the specific culture.

What are some settings where learning takes place? If your response is "everywhere," you are correct. Contexts for learning occur as the child comes in contact with the family, the neighborhood, the school, the peers, and with all those in the environment. But, which contacts are more important than others? As you probably know, the family plays the leading role in transmitting to the child the accepted ways of their culture. With the rise in the number of working parents, however, child-care programs have become an influential socialization force as well. Many children are now being exposed to the ideas and views of other adults and their peers earlier in life (see Figure 4-3).

Figure 4-3 Elements That Influence the Process of Cultural Socialization

THINK AND REFLECT...

THE ENVIRONMENT IN ACTION: CULTURE INFLUENCES CHILDREN'S ACTIVITY LEVELS

The child's sociocultural environment plays an important role in forming behavior. Findings from child development research reveal that the cultural environment influences the way a person talks, smiles, and interacts with others. Being aware of the role culture plays in determining how we interact with others can help teachers understand that behaviors considered normal in some cultures would not be considered normal in their own. For instance, for Hispanics, as well as for some groups with roots in the Middle East, the use of hand gestures to emphasize what is being said is considered normal. Persons from these groups tend to be very animated when talking together. In the eyes of persons with Northern European roots, a normal conversation among Hispanics can seem emotional and agitated, much like an argument.

Several studies have found that teachers tend to view behavior that may be culturally normal for Hispanics as disruptive or as indicators of problems. Zigler and Finn Stevenson (1993) cited one study done with Puerto Rican students. In this case, mainstream culture teachers often misinterpreted the social and emotional response styles of children of Puerto Rican origin and considered them disruptive. They also interpreted culturally acceptable interactions, such as three children talking at the same time, as signs of inattentiveness and overactivity (Bauermeister, Berrios, Acevedo, & Gordon, 1990). Using a sample of teachers, some with Puerto Rican roots and some with European American roots, the study showed differences between the ways in which Puerto Rican and European American teachers rated specific behaviors. Many behaviors of Puerto Rican children accepted by Puerto Rican teachers were considered distressing or in need of intervention by non-Hispanic teachers (Achenbach et al., cited by Zigler & Finn Stevenson, 1993). The different perceptions were probably due to the fact that the Puerto Rican teachers were aware of the normal behavioral responses in their culture. Although more research is needed in this area, teachers must be more aware of how children's cultural experiences shape their behavior. Perhaps a rule of thumb is to avoid making hasty judgments when children have a different social and cultural background from our own.

Source: Adapted from Zigler & Finn Stevenson, 1993.

Along with the more traditional human socialization sources, contemporary social scientists have found that mass media has become a significant factor. Today, the media has provided a more accurate portrayal of the racial and ethnic demographics of U.S. society. Some decades ago, for example, we would never have found so many news reporters, show hosts, and artists of ethnicities other than European American. This diversity is also reflected among the individuals who are members of that industry. For today's young child, who typically spends a significant amount of time in front of the television and who is socialized by it, finding out that people of all ethnic

Caring and secure relationships with adults contributes to building a positive sense about one self.

and racial backgrounds can succeed sends a strong positive message about diversity. But the influence of mass media is not limited to the child. Families and parents are also influenced by ideas and behaviors broadcasted over television, the Internet, and other types of electronic communication. Many traditional culturally based child-care expectations, nutritional practices, and even parent–child interactions are being transformed by what is seen and heard through the media. The influence of the media is so powerful in today's society that it affects ways families practice child rearing. Consider the way infants are dressed, the toys they play with, and even the type of food they eat. In all of these areas, you will find that many practices and behaviors are influenced by what both the child and parents watch and hear from the media.

Learning to See the Individual in Ourselves

"I am what I am," goes a line of a song in the movie *Popeye*, reflecting the self-confidence of the main character. For children to reach that same point, at which they can proudly affirm who they are, takes time and effort. One of the principal goals of education for diversity is to implement practices in the classroom that contribute to the students' realization of their identities. Social identity also occurs through the experience of socialization. Erik Erikson postulated that the optimal outcome of development is the achievement of identity. Miller (2009) notes that "for Erikson, the essence of development is the formation of identity that gives coherence to one's personality." How does this happen? How does the child come to see himself or herself? According to social development theory, the perception of one's identity emerges as the individual begins to perceive oneself as a separate person. It is also gradually developed as the child constructs a sense of his or her characteristics, roles, and attributes. Recognizing one's name and responding to comments made by others are experiences that contribute to the formation of identity. Additionally, home and schooling experiences play a significant role in establishing a sense of belonging to a group.

Forming Ideas about the Self

Social development is one of the most important developmental tasks of early childhood. During the first three years of life, awareness about the self, as an individual distinct from others, emerges and grows. Comments like "I can jump high," "I am Carmen," or "I have new shoes" testify to the child's emerging concept of self. These initial descriptions focusing on specific elements of "who I am" and "what I can do" are the building blocks of the child's identity (Berk, 2006). Along with the emergence of a self-concept, self-appraisals begin to take shape. Judgments about one's worth or self-esteem are central to the positive development of self.

Early Years as the Roots of Identity

Psychologist Erik Erikson (1994) defined identity as "a sense of psychosocial well-being . . . a feeling of being at home in one's body, a sense of 'knowing where one is going,' and an inner assuredness of anticipated recognition from those who count." Although identity development is seen mainly as the task of adolescence, its beginnings are undeniably found in the early childhood years (Noguera, 2003). Experiences and interactions with adults during the early years play a leading role in the formation of who we are. How others—parents, caregivers, teachers, and peers—see us influences the evolving concept of self and, thus, contributes to the construction of our individual identity.

Early Childhood: The Beginnings of Cultural and Ethnic Identity

As discussed previously, culture is a main element in the formation of identity. Although ethnic identity evolves throughout one's existence, children gain awareness of their connections to a culture and to an ethnic group early on in life. Studies show that during the preschool years, children are able to identify themselves as members of an ethnic group. What, then, seems to trigger this early sense of cultural identity? First and foremost are home experiences and interactions with the family. They are, in fact, the most significant forces contributing to a person's self-identification as part of a cultural group. Language is one of the most essential traits of a culture and is learned early in life. Being able to communicate opens doors to acquiring key knowledge about one's culture that will progressively grow throughout the preschool and primary years. As young as 4, children are able to describe themselves as members of an ethnic group, and by age 8, they are able to notice the traits of other cultural groups (Cristol and Gimbert, 2008; Phinney & Rotheram, 1987).

LITERACY CONNECTIONS...

USING CHILDREN'S BOOKS TO BUILD POSITIVE SELF-CONCEPT

During the preschool years, children begin to acquire a self-concept. Validation of one's heritage contributes to the development of a positive self-concept. Selecting and sharing age-appropriate stories about different cultural groups is an effective strategy to enhance children's sense of self and instill pride in their heritage. Stories also help young children clarify ideas and views about the behaviors of others. The following titles are suitable for helping preschoolers and kindergartners learn about childhood experiences that represent a variety of ethnic and cultural groups.

- Ada, A. F. (2010). *Let me help! Quiero ayudar!* San Francisco, CA: Children's Book Press. (Hispanics)
- Augur, D. (2008). *Mwakwa talks to the loon: A Cree story for children.* New York: Heritage House. (Native Americans)
- Barnwell, Y. (2005). *No mirrors in my Nana's house.* San Diego, CA: Harcourt Brace. (African Americans)
- Best, C. (2003). *Three cheers for Catherine the Great!* London: DK Publishing. (European Americans)
- Davol, M. (1993). *Black and white, just right.* New York: Whitman and Co. (African Americans)
- Dorros, A. (1997). *Abuela.* New York: Puffin Books. (Hispanics)
- Henderson, A. T. (2002). *Call me black, call me beautiful.* New York: Royal Regal Books. (African Americans)
- Pak, S. (2001). *Dear Juno.* New York: Viking Books. (Koreans)
- Parry, F. (1997). *The day of Ahmed's secret.* New York: HarperTrophy. (Middle-Easterners)
- Shange, N. (2004). *Ellington was not a street.* New York: Simon and Schuster. (African Americans)
- Stock, C. (1995). *Where are you going, Manyoni?* New York: HarperCollins. (Africans)
- Wing, N. (1996). *Jalapeño bagels.* New York: Atheneum. (Multiracial)

Storytelling is a common element of all cultures and another way that young children learn about their heritage. Through the sharing of traditional stories, family anecdotes, and individual accounts of life events, cultural values are passed on, helping to build a sense of connection to one's cultural group. Stories shared by parents and families with moral messages not only contribute to the social development of the child but also convey the cultural values of the ethnic group.

Day-to-day conversations with families are another powerful avenue that influences early formation of a sense of membership in a cultural group. Proverbs and sayings, such as the *refranes* or *dichos* (sayings) in Latino culture, become cultural vehicles that introduce children to the values and beliefs of their culture.

Children's folk music is another example of early cultural induction that influences the formation of identity. Over time, these cultural elements become part of the core of values and beliefs of the child's emerging identity.

ABOUT STORYTELLING

Families have long used storytelling as a tool for teaching children about the experiences and struggles of their cultures. Think about the stories shared by family members you remember that communicated cultural messages. What values did they communicate? What did you learn from them?

Additional Factors That Influence Identity Formation

Additional factors that influence the formation of identity are: context, acculturation, social class, and historical time.

- *Context* is defined as an assortment of external factors and processes that combine to form a setting that makes someone feel "at home." Some of the external elements include objects, colors, flavors, dress codes, language, music, voice, and accents found in the child's cultural environment. Cultural context also consists of processes, such as acculturation; social descriptors, such as family social class and economic status; and chronological elements, such as the historical setting where a person grows up. All of them combined are a strong influence on the child's emerging sense of self. Some of the leading experiences and processes that influence the formation of an identity are the following:

- *Acculturation:* A process occurs where a mainstream (majority) culture and subordinate (minority) cultures coexist in society. The process of acculturation occurs over time when the members of the minority culture adopt some of the ways of the mainstream culture. The result is a blurring of cultural lines. For example, children of Chinese origin may adopt Western eating habits. Or, Indian girls may abandon the sari and wear jeans instead. Acculturation happens more quickly among the members of the second generations and in cross-cultural marriages.

- *Social class:* All individuals belong to a social class or group. Social class is another dimension of a person's identity. The rules and norms of a social class often define the behaviors and expectations for the individual. Membership in a social class is defined by the family's economic status, occupation, where the family lives, and participation in hobbies and organizations.

- *Historical time:* Chronologically, birth ascribes characteristics and predisposes the individual to certain experiences. Current cultural trends and

VIDEO CASE 4.1 ▶❙❙

Watch the video *Developmental disabilities* and answer the following questions:

- In what way do the classroom activities promote a positive perception about individual differences?

- What evidence of acceptance and empathy do you notice toward children with diverse characteristics?

mores define expectations, behaviors, and beliefs that contribute to who a person is. Because each generation has its own frame of reference, children are influenced by the ideas of their time. For example, the notion of a family in the twenty-first century is vastly different from the family model of the mid-twentieth century.

DISCOVERING THAT YOU ARE NOT LIKE ME

As children acquire the rules of the social game, they learn to distinguish people by their attributes. However, not all that young children learn equips them with social tools that are valid and acceptable in a society as diverse as ours. Sometimes they acquire negative and erroneous views of those whose physical characteristics and convictions are different from their own.

Although many still maintain that children are oblivious to racial differences, research shows that even very young children can notice differences and decode the differences in their social contexts. Children begin to discriminate the existence of differences in objects and in people as early as infancy. For instance, infants are capable of distinguishing and reacting to different facial expressions and the sound of the voice. Perception of other differences, such as race, gender, social class, exceptionalities, and physical challenges, also occurs early in life.

Developmental theory provides the best basis for arguing that early intervention is needed if children are to accept persons different from themselves. According to the theory of differentiation postulated by Eleanor Gibson (cited in Berger, 2005), the process of discriminating the details that establish the differences in objects and in people begins in infancy. Gibson saw the infant as an active explorer engaged in discerning the attributes of the things encountered. She also pointed out that with experience, the child increases the ability to notice details (Miller, 2009). Researchers have found evidence that young children perceive details such as gender, age, and color (Brown and Bigler, 2005).

Wadsworth/Cengage Learning

The classroom plays an influential role in helping children discover diversity and see it as part of daily reality.

FOCUS
ON CLASSROOM PRACTICES

A CLASSROOM QUILT

Quilts are symbols of American tradition. Because a quilt is essentially a harmonious combination of different pieces otherwise not related, it can effectively represent the diversity found in a classroom. Creating a human quilt using your young students can help them become aware of themselves. With children as the theme and the main artists, a class quilt can be developed early in the year. This project can be used as a culminating activity for a unit on learning about themselves.

Besides helping children discover who they are, this project will allow children to experience working cooperatively, a valuable and needed skill for social survival.

1. Introduce the children to the tradition and meaning of quilts. Bring in a quilt for children to see and manipulate. If you do not own a quilt, parents or a colleague may be able to lend you one. Share any of the stories about quilts, such as *The Patchwork Quilt* by Valerie Flournoy (Dial, 1985), *Luka's Quilt* by George Guback (Greenwillow, 1994), or *The Keeping Quilt* by Patricia Polacco (Aladdin, 2001). Discuss what a quilt is and the purposes of making and having one.

2. Depending on the age and level of the children, you may want to vary the materials used. However, using the simplest materials works best. (Later on, if the interest is still there, you may move on to more elaborate constructions.) Use paper plates of different sizes and colors, which children can easily tie together with pieces of yarn.

3. Because this quilt is about the children in your classroom, each child should be represented. Give three plates to each child. On one plate, have them draw a picture of themselves, and on the other two plates, have them describe their favorite activity and their preferred story or story character.

4. After the children have completed their plates, they can begin "quilting" the pieces using yarn. Have children make a hole on each side of the plates. Holes can be made by punching a pencil through the plate or by using a paper hole punch. Working in small groups, children can "quilt" the pieces by threading yarn through the holes and tying them together. As each group finishes their piece of the quilt, discuss what it shows about the children represented. Begin by emphasizing the likenesses, and continue by noting the things that make each child unique.

5. The completed quilt can be displayed in the classroom, where it will certainly generate many interesting discussions.

Perceptions of Gender Differences

Scientists say that gender awareness occurs early and is shown through the verbal labels children use. Beginning at age 2, children show knowledge of their own sex. Using external indicators such as dress, activities, and toy preference, children can identify the gender of themselves and others. Assignment of gender roles is a function of culture; therefore, children learn to differentiate gender roles through the process of socialization. Each culture determines the tasks and the behavioral expectations for males and females. For instance, you may have observed that male Eastern Europeans often greet each other with a double kiss or walk arm in arm with male friends. These practices are

LITERACY CONNECTIONS...

BOOKS TO FOSTER POSITIVE VIEWS ABOUT DIVERSITY

Sharing stories is an effective strategy for building diversity concepts. The following books for preschoolers and kindergartners address cultural diversity and individual differences. You may want to continue adding other titles to this list.

- Fox, M. (2006). *Whoever you are.* New York: Voyager Books.
- Hallinan, P. (2006). *A rainbow of friends.* New York: Ideals Publications.
- Hamanaka, S. (1999). *All the colors of the Earth.* New York: HarperTrophy.
- Kates, H. (1992). *We're different, we're the same.* New York: Random House.

- Katz, K. (2002). *The colors of us.* New York: Owlet Paperbacks.
- Lyengar, M. (2009). *Tan to tamarind.* San Francisco, CA: Children's Book Press.
- Miller, J. (2005). *We all sing with the same voice.* New York: HarperTrophy.
- Schette, S. L. (2006). *I have self-respect.* New York: Capstone Press.
- Zobel Nolan, A. (2009). *What I like about me!* New York: Readers Digest.

typically not acceptable for males in other groups, such as U.S., Muslim, or Hispanic cultures. Like many other behaviors, what is socially established by gender is learned by participation in the culture. It follows, then, that young children become cognizant of gender role behaviors early in life.

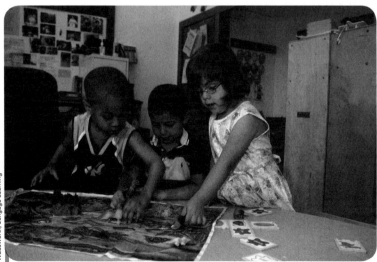

Wadsworth/Cengage Learning

During childhood, classroom interactions contribute to helping children develop a concept of gender-based behaviors.

Working with young children gives you a good opportunity to "see" how they are progressing in their development of gender roles. You have probably observed that although 3-year-old children use terms that describe gender awareness, in reality they do not yet fully understand what "boy" or "girl" really means. Still depending on external clues (physical and societal), they have not yet developed gender consistency: the concept that their gender will remain the same. Perhaps you have also noticed that between ages 4 and 5, children are more likely to express and use gender

FOCUS
ON CLASSROOM PRACTICES

USING PROP BOXES TO PROMOTE AWARENESS ABOUT DIVERSITY

Helping children to become aware of diversity is one of the major goals of early childhood education. Although many planned activities promote awareness, practitioners should also take advantage of the indirect or unplanned activities happening in the classroom. Particularly relevant are the experiences that occur during free play at the learning centers. Use of prop boxes (which can be located in the dramatic center) is a good way to promote awareness of diversity. Essentially, a prop box is a thematic collection of items suitable to foster dramatic play, role-playing activities, and open exploration. To create your prop box, you need a sturdy box with a lid. The box should be easy to handle by children and of a suitable size to facilitate storage. Next, identify themes for your prop boxes that are influenced by things you have observed while talking or discussing with children and questions they have posed about any aspects of diversity.

Here are some suggested themes for prop boxes and some sample props you may want to include:

1. Cooking and eating ethnic foods

   • Typical ethnic utensils, such as a wok, a *caldero* or pot, chopsticks, a cloth coffee colander or *colador*, a small barbecue grill, Indian metal serving trays, Asian and European teapots and cups, typical Amerindian serving dishes (made from clay or gourds), place mats, and so on
   • Empty boxes and cans of ethnic food; empty containers of seasonings; plastic or laminated pictures of typical ethnic vegetables and fruits

2. Hair styling and makeup place

   • Empty bottles of hair products; typical ethnic hair pins and barrettes; ribbons, veils, scarves, and other ethnic hair ornaments; combs, brushes, hair rollers, a hairdryer, and a curling iron (without the electric cords); ethnic dolls with different hair textures or wigs and a wig stand; pictures of different ethnic hairstyles
   • Eyeliners, kohl pencils, blush, and any other ethnic makeup items
   • Earrings, necklaces, bracelets, and others

3. Holiday decoration place

   A series of boxes for the holidays typically observed by children as well as other ethnic celebrations. Items to include are the following:

   • Typical holiday home decorations
   • Songs and music
   • Typical symbols
   • Holiday greeting cards
   • Empty boxes of typical foods
   • Stories

   Sample themes for holiday boxes are the following:

   • Birthdays
   • Wedding celebrations in different cultures
   • December celebrations: Kwanzaa, Christmas, Hanukkah
   • January gift-giving traditions such as the Three Kings (Spain and Latin America) and Befana (Italy)
   • Children's Day in Korea and Japan

4. Clothes for special occasions; the sewing and dressing place

   • Fabric scraps (of different textures, colors, and prints)
   • Pictures of clothing typically worn by people of different ethnicities in the community and in other American communities
   • Pictures of clothing worn during special occasions
   • Fabric glue (to be used instead of needles)
   • A variety of sewing notions to include ribbons, yarn of different colors, buttons, sequins, and so on
   • Accessories such as veils, scarves, gloves, shawls, and hats

5. Ethnic music and dancing

   • Typical musical instruments
   • Pictures of musical instruments
   • Recordings of different vocal and instrumental ethnic music
   • Pictures and videos of folkloric dance

Note: Always be mindful of children's allergies and remember to follow local policies about activities involving cooking and food.

126

VIDEO CASE 4.2 ▶❚❚

View the video *Gender in early childhood* and answer the following questions:

• What are some of the gender stereotypes that these children expressed in their conversation?

• What may be some of the sources of those stereotypes?

VIDEO CASE 4.3 ▶❚❚

Go to the early childhood education video website, watch the video *Gender in infants and toddlers*, and answer the following question:

• Based on the video, how are the mothers conditioned to the gender of their infants?

• How is the environment influencing the infant's gender view?

stereotypes as they play (Shapiro, 1994). What this reveals is that preschool children are in the process of establishing their concept of gender roles. This knowledge becomes more precise over time through increased informal social experiences. In fact, some developmental psychologists believe that clarity about one's own gender does not appear until age 7 or 8.

The early childhood years are an important phase for creating awareness of gender equality. Laura Shapiro (1994) maintains that once children have achieved a sense of their own gender, "the powerful stereotypes that guided them don't just disappear . . . images of the aggressive male and the nurturing female are with us for the rest of our lives." This statement suggests that waiting until children are more mature to address gender equality may not be as effective as dealing with it at the developmentally appropriate time.

Classroom experiences play a leading role in helping children form their concepts of gender roles. A classroom climate characterized by equal relations and opportunities for boys and girls contributes to a sense of equality. When teachers organize their classrooms to provide experiences that invite social interactions among both boys and girls, boundaries created by gender are lessened (Thorne, 1993). More attention is required to what the classroom offers and "says" to the child. Equally important are the behaviors of professionals that children use as models. Specific attention should be given to the kinds of play occurring in the classroom. Teachers must take time to observe the gender role behaviors, labels, and activities children exhibit as they play. Derman-Sparks (1989) recommends that after an analysis of our observations, we should reorganize the classroom learning areas to reflect a more balanced view of gender roles and to encourage "more cross-gender play choices." Changes should affect the entire curriculum. Literature about gender equity should be incorporated regularly into the curriculum.

THINK AND REFLECT...

ABOUT GENDER ROLES

Gender roles are socially and culturally bound. Young children learn to distinguish gender tasks based on the behavior of significant adults. They also acquire gender frames of reference through messages in the media and in the environment. Images in the world at large as well as comments from individuals communicate gender stereotypes on a regular basis.

• Take time to preview television programs. What gender messages do they send? Are there any stereotypes? What would you propose as ways of eliminating gender stereotypes?

• Visit an early childhood classroom and note the messages about gender roles that are displayed in the materials, pictures, and posters. What do they communicate to children regarding their gender?

• Preview videos and software for classroom use such as those used in literacy programs and identify any stereotypes or biases. Are they free of stereotypes?

THINK
AND
REFLECT...

COUNTERACTING GENDER STEREOTYPES IN THE CLASSROOM

Here are some practices early childhood practitioners can implement to counteract stereotypes:

1. Begin by examining your own gender stereotypes and be determined to avoid them. Remember that, second to parents and family, teachers are the children's most influential models.

2. Provide opportunities for appropriate development of gender identity. Include materials that will help children form correct ideas about their anatomy and that will help them understand sex differences. Inform parents of the reasons for using materials (such as dolls, books, and puzzles) and vocabulary that are anatomically correct. Extend it to the home by providing parents with suggestions about what terms to avoid because of the confusion they create in the child.

3. Learn about the gender roles that are assigned in the children's cultures. Be responsive to them by including opportunities for children to see that some people may hold different views.

4. Encourage participation across genders in activities traditionally assigned to either gender. For example, encourage boys to play in the housekeeping area and girls to play in the block area.

5. Select more children's stories about roles across gender lines and include biographies of people whose accomplishments were not restricted by gender biases.

6. Take a proactive stance and intervene whenever children express stereotypical labels.

Source: American Association of University Women, 2008; Derman-Sparks, 1989; Streitmatter, 1994.

IN ACTION . . .

"GIRLS' WORK"

The following is a conversation between two 5-year-old preschoolers that took place in the classroom housekeeping area:

"Guess what? The baby is dirty," Yani said, pinching his nose to indicate that the doll smelled bad. "Yani, you better change his diaper. You are the daddy and my daddy does that at home," Yani's playmate Sarah explained. Upset, Yani moved away from the doll. "I'm not doing that. That's girl's work and I'm a boy. I don't want to play anymore," he added, leaving the play area abruptly.

- Do you think an intervention is needed? Why or why not?
- What stereotypes are depicted here?
- What actions would you take to clarify gender stereotypes?

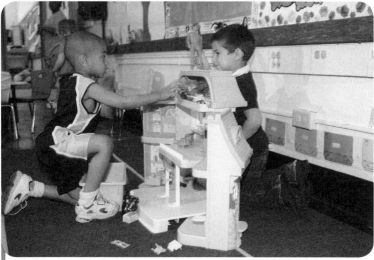

Dramatic play provides children opportunities to learn about gender roles. Think about how allowing these boys to play in this area contributes to counteracting gender stereotypes.

Awareness of Physical Differences

One of the common areas addressed in the early childhood curriculum includes the ability to recognize and discriminate details (such as color, form, and shape). Because we live in a world of forms and colors, learning to notice these characteristics is an important way of discovering what surrounds us. This same ability enables the child to see that not all people share the same physical characteristics. Preschool children are able to discern differences such as color of skin, color of eyes and hair, texture of hair, shape of the lips and nose, and other physical differences, including disabilities. Three-year-olds often reveal their awareness of these traits through their questions and comments (Katz & Kofkin, 1997; Miller, 2007). Although the timing of young children's development of awareness of specific racial and ethnic characteristics during the first three years of life is not yet clearly established, it can be argued that it derives as part of the intensive process of cognitive construction that takes place during the first 36 months of their social life. However, research does indicate that awareness of differences as representative of race or ethnicity is developed through the influence of the family and the social environment (Banks, 1992; Bigler & Averhart, 2003; Katz & Kofkin, 1997; Robles de Meléndez, 2000). The ideas and attitudes of the child's culture shape the notions that the child will express.

Racial Awareness

The problem of the twentieth century is the problem of the color-line.
W. E. B. Du Bois (1868–1963)

Race is a very misleading concept. So is color when we use it to try to characterize human beings. However, because society still uses race to describe people, children learn this concept through the process of socialization. Most of what the literature says about racial preferences in children comes from studies done primarily with African American children (Derman-Sparks, 1989; Kendall, 1999). However limited, their findings are relevant for the early childhood educator.

INFLUENCE OF PARENTS IN THE PERCEPTION OF GENDER ROLES

Research about gender awareness and roles in children has shown that parents are a leading influence. Summarizing research findings, Anselmo and Franz (1995) found that there are at least three major ways in which parents influence children's perception of gender roles:

- Interaction with girls is characterized by being more proactive than with boys. Research shows that mothers show a significantly higher level of protection toward girls than toward boys. Mothers tend to stay closer to girls than to boys. For example, when children fall, girls are comforted while boys are guided "to dust themselves off and get back into action."

- Parents reward boys and girls differently. There is a difference in the kind of behavior that gets rewarded by parents. For instance, boys are encouraged and rewarded when they exhibit more active exploratory behaviors. Girls are rewarded for their social responsiveness.

- Parents tend to choose gender-related toys. Girls are encouraged to play with dolls and replicas of housekeeping items, whereas boys are guided toward traditional male toys such as cars and trucks.

Source: Adapted from Anselmo & Franz, 1995.

LITERACY CONNECTIONS...

RECOMMENDED BOOKS ABOUT GENDER EQUITY

Following are some selected titles addressing multiculturalism and gender topics suitable for young children ages 4–6:

- Hazen, B. (1992). *Mommy's office*. New York: Atheneum.
- Hoffman, G. (1991). *Amazing Grace*. New York: Dial Books.
- Howe, J. (1996). *Pinky and Rex and the bully*. New York: Atheneum.
- Klein, N. (1973). *Girls can be anything*. New York: Dutton.
- Low, A. (2002). *Mommy's briefcase*. New York: Scholastic.
- Luen, N. (1999). *Nessa's fish*. New York: Econo-Clad Books.
- Martin, B., & Sampson, M. (2001). *Little granny quarterback*. Honesdale, PA: Boyds Mills.
- Quinlan, P. (1987). *My daddy takes care of me*. New York: Annick Press.
- Zolotow, C. (1985). *William's doll*. New York: HarperTrophy.

Many believe that race is a concept incomprehensible to children. Interactions and observations of young children, however, reveal that they do perceive racial differences from very early in life. As early as infancy, children perceive multisensorial racial signals such as accent, physical characteristics, and hair texture. By the time they enter preschool at age 3 or 4, children already have a sense of racial attributes (Cristo and Gimbert, 2008; Katz, 2003; Sheets & Hollins, 1999). This knowledge is confirmed through their comments when retelling stories and describing story characters, people, or images in books and the media.

Studies have revealed the existence of an early awareness of one's own color. In studies by Spencer and Cross (cited in Banks, 1992), African American children showed a preference for materials (such as dolls and pictures) and people with European features. One of the interesting points regarding children's awareness of color stems from the research done by Spencer, which confirmed that children were not only aware of their own race but also could "read" how others perceived African Americans as well as whites. Discussing Spencer's findings, Banks (1992) points out that the following was established:

> Young African American children are able to distinguish their personal identity from their group, can have a high self-esteem and yet express a white bias, and that the expression of white bias results from a cognitive process that enables young children *to accurately perceive the norms and attitudes toward whites and blacks in American society* [emphasis added].

Racial awareness has also been linked to the color preferences exhibited by children. Observations of young children across social and cultural groups reveal a color bias when it comes to choosing between white and black. This bias is more of a symbolic nature, which highlights the influence of social experiences in ascribing meaning to the colors white and black. Interestingly, this behavior has been found to be common among children not only in the United States but also in other countries. The existence of a color bias, found among children as young as age 3 (Duckitt, Wall, & Pokroy, 1999; May & May, 1981), refutes the idea that children are "color-blind."

Studies on the perception of color describe the role and significance of social experiences in children's racial preferences. Using messages from their environment—family, classroom, community, and media—children will exhibit color preferences that, in turn, define their inclination toward racial groups. Without interventions, color bias may be a factor in the formation of racial prejudice. Research on color bias also proves that when children are exposed to a bias-free environment, color bias can be effectively reduced (Duckitt, Wall, & Pokroy, 1999). This finding has clear implications for early childhood educators, pointing to the need for including classroom strategies that address color preferences. An example of a developmentally appropriate strategy is the antibias approach (Derman-Sparks, 1989), which is centered on creating experiences and an environment that convey a sense of equity and respect for diversity. Suggestions about classroom activities that foster positive views about racial differences are described in the next Focus on Classroom Practices section.

Louise Derman-Sparks (1989), in an examination of research about biases and prejudice, found that the formation of racist views "damages White children intellectually and psychologically." The implications are clear: all young children are affected. Individual research of the effects of racism conducted by Bernard Kutner, Kenneth Clark,

The classroom is another place where children become aware of racial similarities and differences.

and Alice Miel (cited in Derman-Sparks, 1989) demonstrated the following two main negative consequences for European American children:

1. It affected the reasoning ability of children and misled their perception of reality and thus of judgment (Kutner).

2. Children were taught to hide their own feelings toward people of other races, which encouraged the moral hypocrisy of maintaining prejudices while giving lip service to the concept of equality (Clark, Miel).

Evidence from research and from daily life strongly confirms that contrary to what some adults still want to believe, children do see color and racial differences (Kendall, 1999). Copying the behavior of those they consider their models, whether parents, relatives, or neighbors, children learn to negatively discriminate against others who are not like them. By the time they enter middle childhood, most children hold racial perceptions as truths.

AROUND **THE WORLD**

THE WHITE GIRL IN THE CLASSROOM

Miss Strand came to St. Thomas, U.S. Virgin Islands, from Chicago to teach kindergarten. Although she was from a very multicultural city, she never had an entire class of Afro-Caribbean children. The morning she arrived at her new kindergarten classroom, all eyes were on her; she was the only white teacher in the school. All the children wore uniforms and were "so neatly dressed," she thought. The little girls had colorful hair ribbons and beads in their hair and the boys had a variety of different haircuts that made them stand out. Miss Strand also noticed that the children's skin color varied from dark ebony to an almost "olive" color, as it had been called in Chicago. The children were happy, boisterous, and full of energy, and Miss Strand loved being their teacher.

The second week of class Antoinette arrived. She had been born in a nearby Caribbean island, but had very light skin and naturally blond curly hair. As she came through the door, other little girls shouted, "The white girl is here!" Some even came to tell her, "I want to be your friend!" Even one of the boys said bashfully, "She is pretty." It was clear to Miss Strand that these beautiful children valued the light-colored skin of their classmate more than their own. She thought that this appreciation of lighter color skin was an attitude that survived the colonial days of the Virgin Islands, but it was difficult to understand its existence in the twenty-first century, on a Caribbean island.

Timely action from early childhood teachers becomes the best antidote against perpetuation of misleading interpretations and concepts.

Developing a Concept of Ourselves as Part of an Ethnic Group

Self-perception of one's own race develops with the onset of the awareness of other racial groups. For children with non-European American backgrounds, their perceptions of being different from others form early. The sources of their perceptions are many. Let's consider three of them: parents and family, peers and other adults, and the environment.

The first one to examine is the influence of the child's parents and family. Family members who are proud of their racial or ethnic identity will create similar perceptions in the child. The family will also provide a model for dealing with negative comments about the child's race or ethnic group. A positive and solid self-concept is likely to be

FOCUS
ON CLASSROOM PRACTICES

FOSTERING POSITIVE IDEAS ABOUT RACIAL DIFFERENCES

- At all times, provide equal opportunities to all children to work and participate in activities. As a practice, include children from diverse backgrounds in all activities (for example, classroom helpers, leaders during play, and cooperative activities). Your behavior will communicate to children that each one is a valuable member of the group.

- Use an inclusive approach to experiences. Encourage children to work with peers with different racial characteristics. Plan cooperative learning experiences where children can work and interact together.

- Create a visual environment that exhibits diversity and equality. Display positive images of different racial groups. Provide pictures, posters, and media images that include a variety of racial groups.

- Facilitate play with materials representing diversity. Play, a learning tool for children, provides opportunities to reenact situations and pretend with materials that characterize different racial groups. Include a variety of dolls representative of racial groups in the play areas. Clothing and other articles associated

with different ethnic groups should be also included in the pretend play area.

- Select and share stories with characters of different racial groups. Story characters can provide powerful sources about individuals with different ethnic and racial characteristics.

- Present images and stories that portray the good deeds of people from diverse ethnic and racial groups. Display posters with images representing individuals with diverse ethnic characteristics engaged in a variety of activities, including jobs and professions. This will help children see that contributions come from all people.

- When describing people with racial and ethnic characteristics, use accurate terms. If derogatory terms are heard or used by children, take time to clarify why these are not acceptable.

- Talk with children and listen to their comments about racial differences. Always take time to discuss their observations and provide explanations. You are key in dispelling prejudicial ideas.

IN ACTION . . .

ARE CHILDREN AWARE OF COLOR OR RACE?

The following incident happened in a classroom of 4-year-olds. The group was mainly Hispanic. As you read, consider the implications of what the children said.

Adela, a fair-skinned Hispanic girl, was playing in the literacy area when several other girls joined her. One of the girls was Lilly, who had very dark skin.

Adela looked at Lilly and said in a commanding voice, "*Vete!*" (Go away.) Soon, a discussion began between the two children. When the teacher asked Adela why she wanted Lilly to leave, Adela answered: "*No es como nostros.*" (She is not like us.)

- Why did Adela react to Lilly as she did?
- What are some explanations for Lilly's reaction?
- What are the implications of this incident?
- What would you do if you were the teacher?

developed by children who, nurtured by their families, see their racial or ethnic identity as equally valid as any other. When children find their classrooms, in addition to their families, supportive of their racial identities, they will grow confident and able to overcome most challenges.

The second force that shapes how we feel about our racial and ethnic identity is how others see us and what others say about us. Children are most likely to be deeply damaged for life by racial slurs and negative comments made by their peers. Research has indicated that the origins of negative comments are found in the views and ideas of the children's parents and community. Instances where children replicate the words and behaviors of their parents are many. A graduate student who teaches kindergarten told one of the authors of this book of an incident that portrays this. The student, an African American, was teaching in a predominantly white community when one of her 5-year-olds told her that she was nice but that she was "the wrong color." Feeling shocked, she asked the child why he thought she was the wrong color, and the boy answered that his father had told him so. Obviously, there is no such thing as the "right" or "wrong" color.

Figure 4-4
Physical Characteristics Frequently Noticed by Children

Children tend to notice the following:

- Hair texture
- Skin color
- Color and shape of eyes
- Tone of voice
- Physical size (height and weight)
- Impairments (orthopedic, visual, hearing, physical)
- Neurological impairments (particularly when they affect movement)

WORKING TOWARD PREJUDICE REDUCTION

According to Allport (cited in Banks, 1992), prejudice can be reduced when interracial situations are characterized by the following:

- The situations are cooperative rather than competitive.
- During the situation, each individual feels of equal status to others.
- All individuals share similar goals.
- The contact has the approval of parents, teachers, and other authority figures.

There are obvious implications for developmental teaching in Allport's suggestions. These four characteristics indicate ways to plan and organize activities for young children that also respect the developmental principles. Essentially, what Allport recommends is the provision of more cooperative experiences where children will be racially intermixed and will find that participation has the endorsement and support of relevant adult figures. Cooperative activities must also be extended to include experiences with children and adults from diverse cultural groups. Learning to participate and work in a group is a necessary skill children must acquire because it serves as the basis of successful social interaction. When they form groups, practitioners need to include children with different characteristics regarding race, ethnic origin, gender, and other characteristics. However, for these suggestions to be effective, they must become standard practice.

Source: Adapted from Banks, 1992.

Unfortunately, episodes like this one occur in everyday life. The lesson we can learn from this is clear: perception of racial differences is learned early in life. Early childhood practitioners must take every opportunity to counter such harmful perceptions by providing learning experiences and opportunities for children that will help build positive attitudes toward self and others. Although parental influences are very strong, teachers are also instrumental in reducing prejudice by providing opportunities to view and exercise equality in the classroom.

What the environment "says" is the third force that influences how we feel about ourselves. Messages in the environment play a powerful role in building a concept of one's racial characteristics. The media and the environment have often fostered negative views of certain racial groups. Cases abound of African American children asking why they are black or why they cannot have straight hair. On several occasions, one of the authors had 4- and 5-year-olds of Latin descent with Amerindian features question why their eyes were not "claros", clear, like those of the dolls they play with. When asked why they preferred clear eyes, they simply said, "Son más bonitos" (They are prettier). Along the same lines, a 3-year-old African American told his teacher that he wanted to have blond hair like hers instead of his own dark hair. Educators need to be particularly attentive to subtle messages that might convey a negative attitude toward a child's race or ethnic group. Addressing these when they happen contributes to clarifying views and preventing formation of misleading concepts.

THINK AND REFLECT...

MEMORIES STAY WITH US

What our teachers, classmates, and people in the neighborhood told us in our childhood is part of the baggage we carry with us through life. This is what Kathryn Noori (1995) found through the stories written by her college students, all prospective teachers. We chose two of them to share with you. Both stories concern African American students and reveal how the negative and positive attitudes of others can influence our lives.

The first story tells about the influence that teachers can have on the self-esteem of a child:

I was always one of the African American students enrolled in the public school system [in New Mexico]. Not only was I aware of my "blackness," I was also reminded of it every time a fellow classmate or the teacher made a racist comment. I expected it from my classmates, more or less, but from my teacher—never. The remarks were often cruel and intended to make me feel like a second-class citizen (or, so I thought). For example, in first grade, my teacher asked me to sing, "Eenie, meenie, miny, moe, catch a nigger by the toe." When I

wanted to try out for the debate team in fifth grade, my teacher told me that people of color usually do best in athletics.

In contrast, the following story presents the positive influence that teachers may have on a child:

Mrs. Gage, my second-grade teacher, was the person that inspired me to join the teaching profession. Mrs. Gage took a child with low self-esteem and boosted her up to the sky. She was a Caucasian teacher who treated everyone equally. She didn't let your skin color determine her expectations and perceptions of you.

Because of Mrs. Gage's kindness and caring, I have decided to become a teacher, a teacher who will encourage all students regardless of their gender, religion, race, or background to be the very best they can be.

Which of these elements do you consider most influential for children? Why?

Source: Noori, 1995.

Children's Perceptions of Disabilities

Acceptance and integration of people with disabilities was mandated with the approval of Public Law 94-142 in 1975. The Individuals with Disabilities Act of 1990 reaffirmed the rights of the exceptional. As a result, children are more frequently exposed to people with different kinds of disabilities. This has increased the need to help children develop positive attitudes toward people with disabilities, a segment of the population contributing to diversity. As with racial awareness, children begin as early as age 3 to notice the physical disabilities of others. Because children are constant explorers, it is logical to find them asking and wondering about the physical differences they see. These questions provide an opportunity to guide children to accept disabilities as another characteristic some people have. When trying to fight biases concerning disabilities, teachers need to act promptly any time labeling or rejection is observed among children. This early response will stop misinterpretations and behaviors from becoming permanent.

Wadsworth/Cengage Learning

Inclusive environments promote equality and diversity as part of daily life.

By now, it should be no surprise to know that culture influences perceptions of disabilities. For example, disabilities may be seen as a stigma for the family and the child. Some families may blame their child's disability on their own mistakes and feel guilty about it. Others, like some Hispanic and Filipino families, may consider the disability as "God's will." Families with Chinese-American roots may attribute the disability to something supernatural (Lynch and Hanson, 2004). Early childhood practitioners must be cognizant of the fact that views about disabilities are rooted in cultural beliefs and customs of the families with diverse backgrounds and that those views may differ from those of the practitioner.

Opportunities must be provided for children to clarify their perceptions and feelings about children with disabilities. Barry Friedman and Sharon Maneki (1995) developed an experience designed to create awareness about blind people as the disability for their project because Maneki is a non-sighted educator. They selected a group of third graders to whom they taught the Braille alphabet. Maneki not only demonstrated how to write messages in Braille, but she also introduced the children to the special qualities of people with blindness. The experience helped children clarify their ideas and become more tolerant of people who are blind.

Building awareness about people with disabilities can happen by using stories that involve characters with special needs. Stories such as Jane Cowen-Fletcher's *Mama Zooms* (Scholastic, 1993), Patricia McMahon's *Listen for the Bus: David's Story* (Boyds Mills, 1995), Meg Girnis's *1, 2, 3 For You and Me* (Albert Whitman, 2001), and Virginia Fleming's *Be Good to Eddie Lee* (Putnam, 1997) are among those with plots that provide accurate representations of people with special needs. These books are also good avenues for sharing experiences and talking about disabilities, which counteracts prejudice.

WHAT WE HAVE LEARNED—CHAPTER SUMMARY

In this chapter, we explored the influence of culture on the process of child development. Successful multicultural teaching that meets the needs of young children can only happen when the early childhood professional considers the developmental characteristics of young learners. Culturally responsive teaching follows the principles of developmentally appropriate practices (DAP). The process of development is an experience common to all children. While all children follow predictable developmental changes, there are other influences that impact each child. Culture is one of the factors that accounts for the diversity observed in each child. One of the most evident influences of culture is on child-rearing practices, as each group may have different views about the right way to raise a child. Family experiences and the environment are the driving forces from which children learn the acceptable social behaviors of their culture. Ethnic identity develops during the early years and continues to form during the primary years. Family and classroom experiences are central to forming a sense of identity. They are also instrumental in preparing the child to see differences as part of social life.

MAKING CONNECTIONS . . .

1. Knowledge about what makes children uniquely individual is important for an early childhood practitioner. Select three children from diverse families and begin learning about their individual characteristics. Examine their physical traits, their families, and the elements of diversity (religion, ethnicity, language, social class, exceptionality, and gender) that characterize them and create a chart of your findings.

   Child's name: _____ Age: _____

   Physical Characteristics: _____

   Family Diversity Characteristics: _____

2. The media is a powerful instrument for disseminating ideas about people. Observe any program designed for children for an hour during one week and determine what messages are presented about gender, ethnic groups, and the individuals with disabilities. As part of your observation, include the commercials presented. Write a report about your findings. If you feel that changes are needed, propose them and explain your choices.

3. Considering the developmental needs of the children in your class, design two experiences targeting differences that will help children build a positive view of diversity.

RECOMMENDED INTERNET RESOURCES

• Developmental information for parents from PBS
  www.pbs.org/parents/childdevelopment/

• Inclusive communities from PBS
  www.pbs.org/parents/inclusivecommunities/

• Council of Exceptional Children (CEC) is a major advocacy agency for children with exceptionalities
  http://www.cec.sped.org//AM/Template.cfm?Section=Home

YOUR STANDARDS PORTFOLIO

naeyc **Standard 1:** Promoting Child Development and Learning

naeyc **Standard 4:** Using Developmentally Effective Approaches to Connect with Children and Families

naeyc **Standard 7:** Early Childhood Field Experiences

InTASC Standard 2: Learner Differences

InTASC Standard 8: Instructional Strategies

A thorough understanding about the developmental process assist early childhood teachers in planning experiences for young children. Realizing that development occurs on many different levels, that it is influenced by the environments, and is influenced by many individuals and groups helps practitioners in meeting the needs of the children. Complete the following activities that demonstrate your understanding of the standards.

- Interview an early childhood teacher and find out about practices followed to support developmentally and culturally based experiences for children with diverse backgrounds. Review your findings and select those that you would like to implement in your own classroom.

- Interview two families of diverse cultures and compare their ideas about raising a child with yours. What did you learn? What ideas were in common, and which ones were different?

- Observe children in a preschool classroom for at least an hour. Based on your observations and on the children's developmental and diverse characteristics, prepare an inventory of learning materials that contribute to and support positive ethnic identity.

REFERENCES

American Association of University Women. (2008). *Where the girls are. The facts about gender equity in education.* Washington, DC: Author.

Anselmo, S., & Franz, W. (1995). *Early childhood development: Prenatal through age eight* (2nd ed.). Englewood Cliffs, NJ: Merrill.

Banks, J. (1992). Reducing prejudice in children: Guidelines from research. *Social Studies and the Young Learner, 5*(2), 3–5.

Bauermeister, J., Berrios, V., Acevedo, L., & Gordon, M. (1990). Some issues and instruments for the assessment of attention deficit hyperactivity disorder in Puerto Rican children. *Journal of Clinical Psychology, 19,* 9–16.

Berger, K. (2007). *The developing person through childhood and adolescence* (7th ed.). New York: Worth.

Berk, L. (2006). *Infants and children: Prenatal through middle childhood* (6th ed.). Boston: Allyn & Bacon.

Bigler, R., & Averhart, C. (2003). Race and the workforce: Occupational status, aspirations, and stereotyping among African American children. *Developmental Psychology, 39*(3), 572–580.

Bredekamp, S., & Copple, C. (2010). *Developmentally appropriate practice in early childhood programs: Serving children from birth through age 8* (3rd ed.). Washington, DC: National Association for the Education of Young Children.

Brown, C., & Bigler, E. (2005). Children's perception of discrimination: A developmental model. *Child Development, 76*(3), 533–553.

Charlesworth, R. (2010). *Understanding child development* (8th ed.). New York: Delmar.

Cristo, D & Gimbert, B. (2008). Racial perceptions of young children: A review of the literature post 1999. *Early Childhood Education Journal, 36,* 201–207.

Derman-Sparks, L., & the A.B.C. Task Force. (1989). *Antibias curriculum: Tools for empowering young children.* Washington, DC: National Association for the Education of Young Children.

Duckitt, J., Wall, C., & Pokroy, B. (1999). Color bias and racial preference in white South African preschool children. *The Journal of Genetic Psychology, 160*(2), 143–154.

Erikson, E. (1994). *Identity: Youth and crisis.* New York: W. W. Norton & Company.

Friedman, B., & Maneki, S. (1995). Teaching children with sight about Braille. *Childhood Education, 71*(3), 137.

Gonzalez, N., Moll, L., & Amanti, C. (2005). *Funds of knowledge: Theorizing practices in households and classrooms.* Mahwah, NJ: Erlbaum.

Katz, P. A. (2003). Racists or tolerant multiculturalists? How do they begin? *American Psychologist, 58*(11), 897–909.

Katz, P. A., & Kofkin, J. A. (1997). Race, gender, and young children. In S. S. Luthar, J. A. Burack, D. Cicchetti, & J. R. Weisz (Eds.), *Developmental Psychopathology* (pp. 51–74). NY: Cambridge Press.

Kendall, F. (1999). *Diversity in the classroom: A multicultural approach to the education of young children.* New York: Teachers College Press.

Konner, M. (1991). *Childhood: A multicultural view.* Boston: Little, Brown.

May, J., & May, J. G. (1981). Effects of age on color preference for black and white infants and children. *Perceptual and Motor Skills, 52,* 255–261.

McDevitt, T., & Ormond, J. (2009). *Child development and education* (4th ed.). Upper Saddle River, NJ: Merrill/Prentice Hall.

Miller, P. (2009). *Theories of developmental psychology* (5th ed.). New York: Worth.

Miller, S. (2007). 3–4: me and you. *Scholastic Parent and Child, 15*(4), 60.

Moll, L., Amanti, C., Neff, D., & Gonzalez, N. (1992). Funds of knowledge for teaching: Using a qualitative approach to connect homes and classrooms. *Theory Into Practice, 31*(2), 132–141.

Noguera, P. (2003). How racial identity affects school performance. *Harvard Education Letter.* Retrieved from http://www.edletter.org/past/issues/2003-ma/noguera.shtml

Noori, K. (1995). Understanding others through stories. *Childhood Education, 71*(3), 134–136.

Paludi, M. (2002). *Human development in multicultural contexts: A book of readings.* Upper Saddle River, NJ: Prentice Hall.

Phinney, J., & Rotheram, M. (1987). Children's ethnic socialization: Themes and implications. In J. Phinney & M. Rotheram, (Eds.), *Children's ethnic socialization: Pluralism and development* (pp. 274–292). San Francisco: Sage.

Robles de Meléndez, W. (July 2000). Creating the multicultural environment. Paper presented at the annual conference of the Florida Department of Education, Tampa, FL.

Santrock, J. W. (2009). *Child development.* New York: McGraw Hill.

Shapiro, L. (1994). Guns and dolls. In L. Nunn & C. Boyatzis (Eds.), *Child growth and development, 94/95* (pp. 140–143). Guilford, CT: Dushkin.

Sheets, R., & Hollins, E. (1999). *Racial and ethnic identity in school practices: Aspects of human development.* Mahwah, NJ: Lawrence Erlbaum.

Streitmatter, J. (1994). *Toward gender equity in the classroom: Everyday teachers' beliefs and practices.* Albany, NY: State University of New York Press.

Super, C. M., & Harkness, S. (1995). *Parents' cultural belief systems: The origins, expressions, and consequences.* New York: Guilford Press.

Thorne, B. (1993). *Gender play: Girls and boys in school.* New Brunswick, NJ: Rutgers University Press.

Zigler, E., & Finn Stevenson, M. (1993). *Children in a changing world: Development and social issues* (2nd ed.). Pacific Grove, CA: Brooks/Cole.

PART II

Exploring the Roots
of Multicultural Education:
Issues and Directions

Recognizing that equality and equity are not the same thing, multicultural education attempts to offer all students an equitable educational opportunity, while at the same time, encouraging students to critique society in the interest of social justice.

National Association of Multicultural Education (2003)

CHAPTER 5

Tracing the Beginnings of Multicultural Education

But could I be heard by this great nation, I would call to mind the sublime and glorious truths with which at its birth, it saluted a listening world. . . . Put away your race prejudice. Banish the idea that one class must rule over another. Recognize . . . that the rights of the humblest citizen are as worthy of protection as are those of the highest, and . . . your Republic will stand and flourish forever.

—Frederick Douglass (1817–1895)

Wadsworth/Cengage Learning

CHAPTER OBJECTIVES

Upon reading this chapter and reflecting on its content, you will be able to analyze the struggle for equality in education and the foundation of multicultural education.

KEY CONCEPTS

- multicultural education
- equality
- inclusion
- Civil Rights movement

STANDARDS: THE FOLLOWING STANDARDS ARE ADDRESSED IN THIS CHAPTER:

naeyc Standard 6: Becoming a Professional

naeyc Standard 7: Early Childhood Field Experiences

InTASC Standard 9: Professional Learning and Ethical Practice

TEACHERS SHARE: THE NEW CLASSMATE

It was another morning at the center where Johanna had taught for the past four years.

As she entered the office, her director came over and said with a smile, "Johanna, what you did yesterday was great. Thank you. You really made Ms. Tanner feel comfortable."

"Oh, thank, you. I understood right away why she was so tense. I'm glad you think that everything went well," she replied.

The day before, just as Johanna greeted her 3-year-olds, she saw the center director at her door. With her was a woman holding the hand of a young girl. "A new arrival," she thought, as she signaled her assistant to continue the morning routines with her group. Approaching the door, she smiled at the little girl who shyly hid behind the woman.

"Good morning, Johanna, this is Ms. Tanner and this is Larissa," said the director.

143

"Larissa is a special child," Ms. Tanner said promptly, with apprehension in her voice.

Johanna knew what Ms. Tanner meant because Larissa appeared to be a child with Down Syndrome. "Just like Sammy," she thought to herself. "Every child is special," the teacher replied as she smiled at Larissa.

Curious, Ms. Tanner looked around the classroom. Gathered on the rug, she saw the group who was singing and doing some fingerplays. There was giggling and happy voices as the children followed the teacher-assistant. One of the children was in a wheel-chair and she noticed a little boy who looked very much like Larissa.

"Larissa, do you want to come in?" said Johanna, as she extended her hand to the child. "The children are always happy to meet a new friend." Smiling, Larissa was already waving to the children who were smiling back at her.

Ms. Tanner still stood by the door holding on to her daughter. "You see, since we moved here we haven't found a school for Larissa—one where they can really understand what she needs."

"Oh, you've come to the right place," the director quickly replied. "This is an inclusive classroom," the center director reassured the concerned mother.

"Ms. Tanner, you have nothing to worry about," Johanna said. "You see, I also have special needs." She pointed to the tiny hearing device on her right ear. "In this classroom, everyone is welcome. We work very closely with parents and the community to ensure that the needs of every child are met." At that moment, Larissa broke away from her mother and ran giggling toward her new friends.

"Thank you both. I see that this is the right place for my child."

EQUALITY FOR EVERY CHILD

Scenes like the one in the opening scenario would likely have never happened in the 1950s or even in the 1990s. Valuing and respect for the unique and diverse characteristics of individuals has been an ongoing quest that still continues today. In this chapter,

THINK AND REFLECT...

MULTICULTURAL EDUCATION AND ADVOCACY FOR CHILDREN

Children are the most precious resource because they represent the future. They are also the most vulnerable members of society. Children face many challenges both here and globally. Child advocates continue to act on behalf of children in the United States and around the world. Their efforts have resulted in many victories but the struggle continues. Some of the challenges faced by children range from basic needs for survival to educational and social services.

- How aware are you of the needs of children in your own community?
- What do you know about the needs of children in the global community?
- As an early educator, how can you become an advocate for children?

Multicultural education is grounded on the belief that all children deserve quality equitable experiences.

As early childhood educators we are advocates for the rights of every child to high quality and responsive education and services.

we take you to examine some of the events and factors that led to the formation of the multicultural education movement. As you explore them, keep in mind how they have also contributed to the sense of commitment and responsibility that early childhood educators have toward children and their families.

IN SEARCH OF EDUCATIONAL EQUALITY

> *In our globalized world, education and the fight against discrimination remains a major issue. Thus discriminatory practices still exist today despite the fact that discrimination has no justification in international law.*
> Convention Against Discrimination in Education (UNESCO, 2005)

Looking Back Through Time

> *. . . inequality of rights has been the cause of all disturbances, insurrections, and civil wars that ever happened.*
> Thomas Payne (1737–1809)

Inequality has existed since time began. Examples include the ancient civilizations of Egypt, Greece, and Rome that shared a system of slavery and gender bias. The opportunities for men and women across continents have been inequitable for centuries. Even today, in some, cultural, racial, gender and ideological differences continue to spark unfair and discriminatory practices.

Actions to correct inequities have been successful in some parts of the world, while in others progress has lagged due to culture, poverty, and prejudice. Around the world both men and women have played active roles in exposing and disclosing unfairness. Often, only a few benefited from the changes. However, the changes served to strengthen the quest for equitable service for all. This is the path that the struggle for equality has taken in our society.

EARLY EFFORTS TOWARD EQUALITY IN EDUCATION

As you recall from Chapter 2, multicultural education is based on establishing educational equality for all children. The concept of valuing the individual and respecting human diversity has evolved slowly over the years. Equality of educational opportunity may be a recent goal, but the notion of universal education has its roots in the distant past.

Historical Origins of Multicultural Education

Multicultural education is firmly rooted in the actions and events from the past as well as on those of today. Since its beginnings as a nation, education was recognized as a fundamental right of citizens in the United States. The public education system founded in the nineteenth century was based on what was then considered to be equal access to education. Unfortunately, this meant that educational opportunities were intended for mainstream citizens. There were very few provisions beyond primary grades for women and no provisions for the education of African Americans or others who did not belong to the mainstream culture of the nineteenth century United States. Modest efforts from early advocates led to creating schooling opportunities that promoted literacy among many otherwise excluded ethnic groups. Many of these efforts became the seed for current services and programs, some of which are discussed in this section.

LITERACY CONNECTIONS . . .

LEARNING ABOUT EQUALITY THROUGH CHILDREN'S BOOKS

- Hopkinson, D. (2003). *Sweet Clara and the Freedom Quilt*. New York: Knopf.
- Hopkinson, D. (2005). *Under the quilt of night*. New York: Atheneum.
- Ringgold, F. (2003). *If a bus could talk. The story of Rosa Parks*. New York: Simon and Schuster.
- Sisulu, E. (1999). *The day Gogo went to vote*. New York: Little, Brown & Company.
- Coles, R. (2004). *The story of Ruby Bridges*. New York: Scholastic.

PIONEERS OF EQUALITY FOR CHILDREN

The quest for equity and recognition of children's rights has been a long one. The voices of people who fought for children's rights have been resonating for centuries. They are a testimony to the undeniable rights of the youngest members of our society.

To learn about the evolution of multicultural education, let us look back at a few pioneers who raised their voices in the past in support of educational equity. Believing in their cause, these leaders fought for the welfare of the children of their times, often risking their own lives and personal safety. You will see how, despite the differences in time that separate them, these advocates of multicultural education parallel those of today by their:

- awareness of inequality in educational opportunities or services
- recognition of unfair treatment based on gender, social class, or ethnic origin
- proactive attitudes that led them to take action to resolve or modify the existing unfair conditions

We will briefly look at the work of selected pioneers who defended the rights of children to receive educational services and who established the importance of the early childhood years. Among the pioneers, we find John Amos Comenius (1592–1670), widely recognized as the father of modern education. He is best known as an educational reformer who strongly advocated for the rights of all people to be educated. Jean Jacques Rousseau (1712–1778), a philosopher and a political thinker, became best known for his works *The social contract* and *Emile*, where he called for reforms in education and politics. His ideas about the need to provide appropriate education to the child and his recognition of the inherent rights of people served as an inspiration to bring about changes in education in his times and today. Rousseau's ideas constitute the fundamental postulates of the multicultural education movement. Johann Pestalozzi, better known for the pedagogical method that bears his name, based his ideas on the essential principle that "all people, including the poor, could and should learn" (Smith & Smith, 1995, p. 190). Pestalozzi is credited with translating Rousseau's ideas into practice, devoting his life to education of the poor.

Maria Montessori's life's work on behalf of poor children and those with diverse characteristics was and continues to be inspirational. The first Italian woman to become a physician in 1907, Dr. Maria Montessori opened a school in one of Rome's poorest neighborhoods. A firm believer in social justice, it was at the school where she implemented her teaching ideas that addressed the educational needs of disadvantaged and underprivileged children in new and creative ways. Her method, known as the Montessori Method, evidenced that it was possible to provide quality educational experiences to children with special needs. Anchored in developmental practices, her teaching approach offered hope to an otherwise forgotten population. Today the Montessori Method is still widely used in education of young children.

Figure 5-1
Champions for
Educational Equality
in the Americas

Maestro Cordero's School for the Poor

Primary education, as we know it today, was a privilege of few during the nineteenth century. Illiteracy was rampant, especially among the poor, all over the world. In the nineteenth century, Rafael Cordero, the son of former slaves and a cigar maker by trade, opened a school where beyond social class lines he taught children of the poor and the rich on Luna street in San Juan, Puerto Rico (Gómez Tejera & Cruz López, 1970). In his spare time, the humble "Maestro Cordero" helped the children learn to read and write, turning his tobacco workshop into a school. At the time that he opened his school, there was no official elementary education in the then Spanish-ruled island of Puerto Rico.* Education was offered by private teachers who left out the children of the poor and the children of the blacks. Aware of their need, Cordero began offering classes in 1810, three decades before the Spanish government officially instituted elementary education (Ribes Tovar, 1973). Hundreds of children learned to read and write with Maestro Cordero, who never charged for his lessons. Today, he is remembered as the pioneer of elementary education for the humble in Puerto Rico.

Sarah Winnemucca, a champion for the rights of Native Americans

The daughter of a Paiute chief, Sarah Winnemucca left an invaluable legacy of tenacity and faith in the education of Native American children (Zanjiani, 2004). A writer and founder of the first school for Native Americans, she was described by her friend Elizabeth Peabody as the "Indian Joan of Arc." Early in life, Sarah learned about prejudice and discrimination. Her great desire to learn led her to enroll in a convent school in California. Because of opposition by white parents, she had to leave and move back to Nevada, where she worked as a domestic. Spending most of her salary on books, Sarah taught herself and became, years later, a translator and a spokesperson for the Paiutes (Zanjiani, 2004). Later, she became a school assistant and during her travels met Elizabeth Peabody, a leader in kindergarten education. Their friendship influenced her to organize a school for the Paiute children.

Booker T. Washington: A new beginning for African Americans

The education of African Americans was given a start with the abolition of slavery in the United States. Determined to become a productive part of U.S. society and to build a future, African Americans embraced education with great eagerness. The government formally undertook education for African Americans as part of the Reconstruction efforts after the Civil War. Under the auspices of the federal government, thousands of teachers arrived in the South, a result of the 51 voluntary Freedmen's Aid Societies that were formed (Smith & Smith, 1994a). A distinctive attitude towards learning to read and write characterized the former slaves who attended these schools (Watkins & Kelley, 2001). Few were too young, and none too old, to learn. This desire became the force that drove African Americans to give their strongest support to the schooling movement. In the latter part of the nineteenth century, higher education would also become a reality when many schools and colleges were opened for the now free African Americans.

   Booker T. Washington is one of the examples of African Americans' eagerness to learn. Historical accounts show that he learned he was a free person when "a Union officer appeared on his owner's porch and read the Emancipation Proclamation" (Smith & Smith, 1994, p. 335). This marked the beginning of a courageous and historic life for young Booker T. In 1872, Washington started his formal education at the Hampton Normal and Agricultural Institute. Overcoming humiliations and despite hard work and disappointments, he never lost hope and became a brilliant teacher. Today, Booker T. Washington is remembered as the founder of the prestigious Tuskegee University in Alabama.

Mary McLeod Bethune's legacy

Mary McLeod Bethune was a pioneer in establishing educational opportunities for young African Americans in Florida. With no formal school for black children in Daytona, she campaigned and called upon the generosity of people. In 1904, she opened The Daytona Normal and Industrial Institute for Girls with five students, aged 8 to 12 (Zrinyi Long, 2004). In the beginning years, students and teachers raised funds by selling ice cream and sweet potato pies. Mary's hard work and the support of many prominent Americans, such as John D. Rockefeller and James Gamble of Procter and Gamble, made her dream possible. Years later, her school, then a college, joined the Cookman Institute, becoming the now prestigious Bethune-Cookman College.

Wadsworth/Cengage Learning

Hull House, the work of Jane Addams

The founder of Hull House, Jane Addams, was born to a well-off family. Through her travels, she became aware of the needs of the poor and witnessed the efforts of some dedicated individuals to alleviate their problems. In 1889, she moved into a rented house on Halsted Street, in one of Chicago's poorest areas, opening it as a place with services for the poor. Before long, the Hull House became a haven for many immigrants in the Chicago area (Caravantes, 2004). Among Jane's first projects was a kindergarten that in less than a month had twenty-four children in attendance, with many more on the waiting list. Addams dedicated her entire life to social justice, struggling to open opportunities to families and children of the poor. Her philanthropic work was extended to serve people and children throughout the world and whose efforts were recognized when she was awarded the Nobel Peace Prize in 1931 (Caravantes, 2004). Today, the Hull House Association still serves needy children and adults in the Chicago area.

(Continued)

Figure 5-1
Continued

Miles Cary and the Poston School at the Relocation Camps
During the 1940s, another educator made a difference in the lives of others. Miles A. Cary organized educational services for thousands of Japanese American children in relocation camps. The magnitude of his accomplishment must be measured in the context of one of the most shameful periods of U.S. history. Relocation camps represent an injustice committed during World War II against one of our country's ethnic groups: the Japanese Americans. At the time of the Japanese attack in Pearl Harbor on December 7, 1941, there was a significant Japanese American minority population living in the U.S. Many of the members of this group had been born in the United States and had ancestors who had been citizens of this country for generations. Despite this fact, and fearing another attack and any anti-American activities from the Japanese immigrants, the government decided to confine this group to mass detention camps.

Camps were established to house nearly six million Japanese Americans, including more than 33,000 children. This experience forever marked the lives of those children who came to live behind barbed wire. In the midst of these unfortunate circumstances, educator Miles A. Cary became a voice that spoke against the unfair relocation of Japanese Americans. Cary, who believed relocation was an immoral act, accepted responsibility for organizing educational services in the Poston Relocation Center that housed more than 4,000 Japanese Americans (Smith & Smith, 1994). Poston, the school designed by Cary, became a spiritual oasis for hundreds of students who lived there. Today, many still remember that going to school at Poston was the best part of the years they spent behind the fences.

FOCUS
ON CLASSROOM PRACTICES

INTRODUCING CHILDREN TO THE CONCEPT OF INEQUALITY

An important step in teaching with a multicultural perspective is helping children develop an awareness of inequality. This is a topic that many times has been avoided in younger children's classrooms. Many consider inequality a concept that eludes the young child. However, because circumstances in the classroom and in the community demonstrate inequality, children are already exposed to it. Waiting until a child enters the upper grades to bring attention to this reality is not wise. Developmental research shows that it is during the early childhood years when the foundations for moral decisions are established. Fro this reason, it is important to incorporate experiences into the classroom curriculum where young children can gain a gradual awareness of their reality.

Teachers can use daily events to help children develop an awareness of inequality. Whether in the classroom or in the community, opportunities for designing such experiences abound.

Suggestions for Designing Curricular Content on Inequality

1. Substitute the term "inequality" for the concept of "what is fair and unfair." This is something most young children understand early in life and can relate to.

2. Identify the areas where the child is likely to experience situations of unfairness. This will define your content. You will find examples in events and places familiar to the child. For example, consider the following contexts and possible scenarios:

At home. Many chores are assigned to one family member whereas others do little or nothing; children leave their rooms disorganized and parents have to clean them up; one family member gets to choose all the TV programs; a child forgets to refill the pet's water dish which is already dry.

In the neighborhood. A group of children make fun of an older man because of the way he walks; people refuse to say hello to the new neighbors because they speak a language other than their own; people in the neighborhood want to close a shelter for the homeless; on a bus, people take the seats assigned for the elderly and those with disabilities who then have to stand.

In the classroom. A child refuses to let another child play with a set of manipulatives; girls in the housekeeping area send boys away; boys in the block center do not allow girls to play; some children refuse to wait their turn in the lunchroom; some children refuse to play with a child because she "speaks funny"; a child hides another child's pair of eyeglasses; children make fun of a family member because of the way she dresses; some children use racial epithets.

On television: Consider the kind of programs children watch. Make an effort to watch them as well. This will alert you to programs whose content is likely to impact the class. If you find they are talking about a special show or program, or if the parents bring it to your attention, plan to discuss it. Discussion about a specific show or program should only take place with the whole class if the majority of children show a reaction to it.

3. Make a list of those situations that could happen more frequently. Target those first. Periodically plan weekly activities to deal with the target situations. However, remember that when a situation happens, it must be dealt with immediately. Having the children's attention and interest is essential for exploration.

4. Aside from your planned activities, make use of teachable moments. Nothing proves more effective than the moment when we are trying to discover the whys behind an event.

5. Select appropriate literature. Using the list of areas and topics you chose in step 2, find related literature. Today, a wide variety of titles are available for initiating discussions on practically every topic.

6. Plan concrete, child-appropriate activities. Because unfairness is an abstract concept, design experiences in ways children can relate to literally. Remember to consider that children learn through their senses and use a variety of ways to present and foster interest in the topic.

7. Use puppets or *persona dolls* to introduce difficult topics particularly when they involve a child in your class (Derman-Sparks & A.B.C. Task Force, 1989). Persona dolls represent characters with specific ethnic and cultural traits. They help in conveying to children specific life experiences related to diversity. Also, use the dolls to discuss topics children may have seen on television that require clarification.

8. Become a perceptive observer. If you have good observational skills, you will see the curriculum sprouting all around you. Observe particularly what children do and say and the gestures they make during free-choice play. Listen to what they tell you while discussing a story. These comments will let you know how children react among themselves and what levels of awareness they exhibit.

THE LEGACY OF THE PAST

It is said that the past holds undeniable truths. The past also allows us to better focus the lens through which we look at life. Before continuing our search for the genesis of multicultural education, it is important to assess what we have learned from the past.

- Awareness of inequality has existed since ancient times. Educations for the poor and gender equity have been two areas of early awareness.

- Despite the awareness, actions by society to correct inequality have been delayed, or never taken.

- Both men and women played active roles in exposing and disclosing the existing inequities.

- Realization of unfairness in various aspects of life established the beginnings of the concept of *diversity* (gender, social class).

- Of the many cries for equality, only a few resulted in concrete deeds. Often, only a few benefited from the change. However, the changes served to strengthen the desire for fair service for all.

Wadsworth/Cengage Learning

According to many education scholars, in the U.S. multicultural education is a phenomenon of the 1960s. As pointed out earlier, little or no effort was made until then to accommodate the needs and particularities of children with culturally diverse backgrounds. Various factors responsible for this overdue awareness are briefly examined in the next section.

These children are and example of the diverse nature of society. They are also a testimony of the struggles of the past for equality in education.

Although slavery was abolished in 1865 after President Abraham Lincoln issued the Emancipation Proclamation, history shows that acceptance of free African Americans and their entry into society was a slow and painful process. Numerous accounts tell of unjust and unfair acts committed against former slaves through the decades following the Emancipation Proclamation. After a short lived period of freedom, court rulings lent legal validity to segregation and affirmed differences among people based on race. Among these rulings were the Supreme Court's 1883 declaration that the Civil Rights Act of 1875 was unconstitutional and the Court's approval of "separate but equal" facilities in *Plessy v. Ferguson* (1896). This case was the basis for numerous discriminatory practices including education that with time led to the momentous Civil Rights Movement.

THINK AND REFLECT...

PLESSY v. FERGUSON (1896)

In 1896, Homer Plessy, a 30-year-old African American, challenged the state of Louisiana's "Separate Car Act," arguing that requiring Blacks to ride in separate railroad cars violates the 13th and 14th Amendments. The U.S. Supreme Court upheld the Louisiana law stating in the majority opinion that the intent of the 14th Amendment "had not been intended to abolish distinctions based on color." Thus, the Supreme Court ruling in the case of *Plessy v. Ferguson* made "separate but equal" policies legal. It became a legal precedent used to justify many other segregation laws, including "separate but equal" education.

• How do you interpret the concept of "separate but equal" in education?

• Are there any vestiges of this ruling in present day society or within the global community? Share your findings.

Source: American Educational History Timeline, 2011.

THINK AND REFLECT...

IMPRESSIONS OF A CHILD

George Takei was four years old when he learned that his family could no longer live as free people. The following are his impressions of the moment when he and his family were forced to leave for the camp:

Then a terrible war had broken out, and my father's whole world was blown away. All people of Japanese ancestry in America were to be immediately removed to internment camps, leaving everything behind. So much was irretrievably lost. The business—abandoned. The rented house on Garnett Street—hurriedly vacated. The car sold for the best offer, five dollars—better to get something than leave it behind. But the new refrigerator got no offer. It nearly killed Mama to have to abandon it to the vultures. Everything other than what we were allowed to carry—all abandoned. All memories now. All fleeting as the sand blowing past the window. All gone.

- Reflect on the passage. Can you think about parallels that may be present in today's global society?

- What are the implications?

Source: Takei, G. (1994). To the stars. The autobiography of George Takei. New York: Pocket Books (p. 16).

During the late nineteenth and early twentieth centuries, while the United States was coping with the new societal role of African Americans, waves of immigrants were pouring into this country. The demographic changes presented new challenges. The fact that many new immigrants belonged to ethnic and racial groups different from those of the first settlers set in motion a new period of discrimination. Policies that accented the differences between specific ethnic groups and the majority were still enforced. Examples include the policy that led to the incarceration of Japanese Americans at the start of World War II, and the reaction against Mexican immigrants, which led to "Operation Wetback" in the 1950s.

BEGINNING OF MULTICULTURAL EDUCATION

One of the roles of the U.S. public education system was to assist waves of new immigrants to assimilate into society of *e pluribus unum*, where all become one. The system was rooted in the idea that all individuals would shed their cultures of origin and become "Americans." Today, we know that people can maintain their individual cultures while becoming proud members of society and upholding the principles of U.S. democracy. This new vision of pluralism is much closer to the basic principles of democracy that comprise the ideological foundations of this country. It is also what parallels the central goals of multicultural education.

Struggle for Equality and Civil Rights

The legacy of the Civil Rights movement which pursued the recognition of everyone is seen everyday in classrooms across the U.S.

The struggle for equal opportunities in the United States has a long history. Despite emancipation, African Americans continued to face legal and social obstacles. Their frustrated hopes and the feeling of powerlessness nurtured the spirit that ignited and sustained the Civil Rights movement of the 1960s. Two events in the 1950s fueled the beginning of this struggle for equality. The first was the landmark Supreme Court decision of *Brown v. the Board of Education of Topeka, Kansas*, in 1954, which ruled that segregated schools did not provide equal opportunities. The Brown decision reversed the view the Court had taken in *Plessy v. Ferguson*; separate but equal facilities were now considered unconstitutional. This decision marked the end of the legal segregation in U.S. schools and initiated equalization of education services. It also established the beginning of multiculturalization of our schools. The desegregation of schools that followed the 1954 Brown decision was enforced throughout the 1960s largely as a result of the work and the determination of the leaders of the Civil Rights movement.

IN ACTION . . .

THE IMPACT OF A COURT RULING

Here is James Fanner's description of the impact that *Brown v. the Board of Education* had upon the Civil Rights movement. While you read it, imagine how civil rights activists felt at the time. Think about how it relates to multicultural education.

The Brown decision set in motion boundless energies, spawned by the promise of Jeffersonian egalitarianism but penned up by the delay of fulfilling that promise. From Little Rock to Oxford, Mississippi, and throughout the South, children and youth of irrepressible and heroic dimensions rose and the barriers came down. There were other foci in the equality drive of the 1950s and 1960s. There were boycotts and freedom rides; sit-ins at lunch counters; voter registration drives; lynchings and killings; and admission of black students to all-white universities. Dr. Martin Luther King, who with his charismatic appeal succeeded in mobilizing as much as one-fourth of the entire black population, as well as millions of whites, led marches for across-the-board desegregation and for universal dignity of man. One of the most successful civil rights demonstrations was the march on Washington in 1963, which was conducted in support of the decision that segregation of educational facilities by race was unconstitutional.

Source: Turner-Sadler, J. (2006). African American history (An introduction). NY: Peter Lang Publishing.

The second event was the Rosa Parks incident, which took place on December 1, 1955, in Montgomery, Alabama. Ms. Parks refusal to move from the seat designated for "white" people, even though a white man was left standing, led to her arrest and trial for breaking the law (Turner-Sadle, 2006). The entire black community rose to her defense. The result was the famous Montgomery bus boycott. The entire black community refused to ride the public transportation system. After 381 days of boycott, the city capitulated ending the practice of segregation in buses, and blacks were free to sit anywhere they wanted on buses. The incident sparked the unification of African Americans across the South and marked the official beginning of the Civil Rights Movement. The Rosa Parks incident brought prominence to a young minister, Dr. Martin Luther King, Jr., who had similar aspirations for equality (McLemore and Romo; 2005). When the boycott to the buses was called, Dr. King became the spokesperson for the newly formed Montgomery movement. Addressing the community, he spoke about unity and nonviolence, which set the tone for the boycott.

The inability of many mainstream U.S. citizens to accept the decision to desegregate, and their efforts to set the fight for equality back, served to unite the African Americans and their supporters in the greatest struggle for freedom and equality known to this country. Civil rights became a major issue in national elections. Civil rights issues were also vigorously pursued by many black-led activist organizations. Among the most prominent were the National Association for the Advancement of Colored People (NAACP), formed

LITERACY CONNECTIONS . . .

LEARNING ABOUT THE MEN AND WOMEN WHO FOUGHT INEQUALITY

Children can increase their awareness of inequality when they learn what it actually does to real people in the context of daily life. Because literature has a special appeal for children, the use of biographical literature and historical fiction is particularly effective. One of the benefits of biographies is that they help children build a sense of the different kinds of inequalities real people have experienced. When concretely presented (using artifacts, role-playing), historical fiction is a "true voyage into time." A list of suggested titles is included here. Ask the school librarian and check your local library for additional and recent titles.

- Bains, R. (2005). *Harriet Tubman: The road to freedom.* New York: Troll.

- Boston Weatherford, C. (2007). *Freedom on the menu: The Greensboro sit-ins.* New York: Puffin Books.

- DeKay, J. (2001). *Meet Martin Luther King Jr.* New York: Random House.

- Greenfield, E. (1995). *Rosa Parks.* New York: Crowell.

- Krull, K. (2003). *Harvesting hope: The story or Cesar Chavez.* New York: Harcourt

- Levine, J. (2002). *Henry's freedom box.* New York: Scholastic.

- Monjo, F. (1999). *The drinking gourd.* New York: Harper & Row.

- Rockwell, A. (2002). *Only passing through. The story of Sojourner Truth.* New York: Dragonfly Books.

- Boston Weatherford, C. (2006). *Dear Mr. Rosenwald.* New York: Scholastic.

Although many of the titles are primarily for elementary-age children, teachers can retell these stories for young children. Retelling is a strategy that allows teachers to share a story in an abridged way, conveying the essential aspects and message of the story.

in 1909 by W. E. B. DuBois and a small group of African Americans and white supporters, and the Congress on Racial Equality founded in 1942. The social measures and programs accomplished during the Civil Rights movement in the 1960s were numerous. They contributed to establishing services and initiatives for people across racial lines. Yet, the fight for equality continues. Ensuring that the constitutional rights of all are protected and guaranteed to people regardless of their origin, race, or religious affiliation is still at the forefront of the agenda of national and state advocacy groups, especially those representing children and families from ethnic minorities.

Legacy of the Civil Rights Movement

I have a dream that my four little children will one day live in a nation where they will not be judged by the color of their skin but by the content of their character.

Dr. Martin Luther King (1963)

The Civil Rights movement was a major social force in the 1960s that survived tragedies, humiliations, and injustices to win many major battles fought for the dignity of the individual. Among these were battles for registration of black voters, desegregation of public facilities and private businesses, and desegregation in schools. The progress made in the area of equality in recent years can be traced to victories won by the supporters of the Civil Rights movement who continue their work today on behalf of all ethnic groups.

WHAT STARTED BROWN v. THE BOARD OF EDUCATION?

To many, the events that led to the landmark 1954 decision have faded from memory. Briefly, let us recall the incident that initiated this historic lawsuit.

During the 1940s, the unfair and unequal conditions of schools for African Americans had become obvious. During this time, the National Association for the Advancement of Colored People (NAACP) had brought the issue to local and national attention. It was 1947 when Esther Brown, a white woman, became concerned about the state of schools for African Americans in South Park, outside of Kansas City (Kelley, R.D.G., & Lewis, 2000). Initially, Brown tried to persuade the school board to improve the grade schools but failed. She then consulted about the situation with an attorney from Topeka, Elisha Scott, who found that there were legal grounds in the issue.

According to Kansas law, segregation was permitted in school districts larger than South Park (Kelley, R. D. G., & Lewis, 2000).

Determined to fight for what was right and equal for black children, Brown, along with the parents and children of South Park, boycotted the schools. The rest is history. With the support of the black community, Brown moved the case forward, achieving one of the major victories in the struggle for social justice.

- Reflect on the events that led to the landmark decision. From an advocacy perspective, what are some of the major implications of these actions?

Source: Kelley, R. D. G., & Lewis, E. (2000). To make our world anew: A history of African Americans. NY: Oxford University Press.

THE BIRTH OF MULTICULTURAL EDUCATION

Educators attribute the contemporary beginnings of multicultural education to the events and the social climate of the 1960s. According to Gollnick and Chinn (2006), interest in ethnic studies was brought to attention in the 1960s and early 1970s. Major sociopolitical events such as the assassinations of John F. Kennedy, Martin Luther King, Jr., and Robert Kennedy; the "hippie movement"; the changes in social values; and the new social culture created a climate of unprecedented change in U.S. society. In this atmosphere of uncertainty, tolerance and flux, multicultural education got its start.

War on Poverty Raises Awareness about Children

By the safeguard of health and the protection of childhood we further contribute to that equality of opportunity which is the unique basis of American civilization.

— President Herbert Hoover (1929) Excerpt from the Announcement of the White House Conference on Children.

The issue of inequality, central to many social and political movements of the 1960s, gave way to initiatives such as the War on Poverty of 1964. During this time, people realized that children of minorities were at a disadvantage with respect to the children of U.S. mainstream culture. Although this view of minorities led to misconceptions about the "culturally deprived," it acknowledged the existence of different cultural backgrounds. Concerted efforts made to bring people out of their "disadvantages" gave way to a number of important social and educational programs. Through these efforts, the government affirmed its interest in children. As a way to equalize opportunities for all, educators such as Jerome Brunner and Edward Zigler advocated the development of programs to serve the children of the poor and those of culturally different backgrounds.

Efforts Toward Equal Services for Children

The spirit of the 1960s was the perfect breeding medium for social reform. Thousands of people across the country, representing all the ethnic and cultural minorities, joined hands with African Americans to bring inequality to a stop. The constancy of their efforts for achieving equality was the force that rang the bell of action for children. With the understanding that children of the poor (who at the same time represented the ethnic minorities) would do better if offered additional educational services, the greatest revolution for young children began to unfold. Because people believed that *early intervention* was a way to ameliorate differences in social experiences, the public and the government took a decisive interest in young children (Dahlberg, Moss, & Pence, 2006). Growing out of the War on Poverty and the Civil Rights movement, the government decided to improve services for children living in poverty. It was estimated that

Collaboration of teachers and families in culturally diverse settings enhances opportunities and promotes positive outcomes for children.

40 million were living in poverty in the wealthiest country in the world (Dahlberg, Moss, & Pence, 2006). Recognizing that children from socially and economically disadvantaged environments were entering school less equipped for success, many initiatives were undertaken to serve the culturally diverse child. Targeting those from low socioeconomic communities across the nation, the government began focusing its efforts on children from the various ethnic minorities. Although many programs were designed during the 1960s to meet their needs, two in particular stand out: Head Start and Follow Through.

A Head Start for U.S. Children

Project Head Start began during the summer of 1965. At the time, approximately 2,500 Child Development Centers were established to serve more than 550,000 children across the nation (Osborn, 1996). The program was designed to provide learning experiences to children entering first grade in the fall of 1965 and who had not experienced kindergarten or preschool. Centers opened their doors to children in urban areas, on Indian reservations, and in places as far apart as Guam, Puerto Rico, and the Virgin Islands.

Head Start also proved that, to serve children, educators needed to involve the community and parents as partners. The experiences during the days and weeks of that memorable summer session in 1965 marked the first substantial efforts to reduce inequality. The program was a first effort to directly empower citizens by involving them in the educational decision-making process. Head Start programs opened and blossomed thanks to responsive communities everywhere. Knowing that this was an opportunity for their children to have a better education, people gave their full support to the project.

The need for parents and teachers to work as partners was realized through the concept of the *child development center*. Different from the classroom, the child development center affirmed the roles of parents and the community in a child's education. According to Osborn, "in concept it [the child development center] represents drawing together all the resources—family, community, and professionals—which can contribute to the child's total development" (1996, p. 298).

Designed as a comprehensive program for preschool children, Head Start was founded on the belief that a child's success was not to be defined only by intellectual growth but rather by a holistic perspective of the individual child. Consideration of the integral development of young children has since been the driving force behind Head Start services. Following this holistic view, interventions were planned to include a variety of direct and preventive services. Today, interventions take place through the following:

- *Developmental services*. Individualized developmental education services are offered.
- *Health services*. Comprehensive medical, dental, and mental health services are available to children. Preventive health is among its objectives.
- *Nutrition services*. Since its beginning, Head Start has emphasized the need for children to be well fed. Balanced meals (breakfast, snack, and lunch) are served family style, in what has become another trademark of this program. A strong nutrition program complements the meal services.
- *Family services*. A full range of social services is offered. Their purpose is to promote the best conditions for an improved quality of family life. A well-planned parenting skills empowerment program is also a part of the services. Here parents/families refine and acquire knowledge to enhance their child-parent relationships and interactions.

Currently, Head Start serves more than 900,000 children (infants to preschoolers) representing almost 40 percent of those eligible (Head Start Bureau, 2010). Of its enrollment, over 71 percent are ethnic minorities, with African Americans and Hispanics as the largest groups (Figure 5-2). Over 11 percent of those attending their programs are children with disabilities. The optimum "head start" for thousands of children is still the longest-lasting early childhood program, stemming from the 1964 War on Poverty.

Figure 5-2 Racial and Ethnic Composition for Head Start

Racial and Ethnic Groups	
White	40%
Black or African Americans	29%
Bi-racial or multi-racial	8%
Native Hawaiian, Asian, Pacific Islanders, Native American, Alaskan Native	6%
Unspecified	6%
Other	11%
Hispanic origin	36%
Non-Hispanic origin	64%

Source: National Head Start Organization (2010).

Head Start provides comprehensive services to meet the needs of children with disabilities.

Head Start and Children with Special Needs

Since 1972, Head Start has served children with special needs. Today, at least 10 percent of its enrollment must be allocated to children with disabilities (Head Start Bureau, 2004). Constant training and in-service activities prepare the staff of Head Start programs to offer quality services to children with disabilities. Comprehensive support services are offered to meet the needs children with disabilities and their families. Determination on appropriate placement and services follows the guidelines from IDEA for preschoolers. The goal is to provide developmentally appropriate experiences in the least restrictive environment that will best promote the child's development.

An Early Head Start, Services for the Very Young

During the 1990s, Head Start extended its services to infants and toddlers. This initiative is intended to prove that intervention begins at birth, something that most early educators have advocated for years. In 1994, Congress approved Early Head Start, a new program that provides services to infants, toddlers, and pregnant women. Based on research findings, the program acknowledges the value of early intervention and provides services to low-income families and young children during the prenatal and infant-toddler years. The program also offers support to pregnant women by providing parenting education classes. Today, Early Head Start provides services to thousands of infants and toddlers across the U.S.

Services for Young Children with Disabilities

VIDEO CASE 5.1 ▶‖

Go to the video library and watch *Bobby: Serving students with special needs.* Answer the following reflective questions:

- In what ways are Bobby's needs met in this classroom?

- What inclusion practices are observed in this classroom?

All children, including those with exceptionalities, have a right to quality educational experiences and services. Exceptionalities are one of the aspects of diversity found across society and ethnic lines (Paasha, Gorrill, & Strom, 2003). Yet, it is one that only in recent decades has been acknowledged. Before the 1970s, views about exceptionalities translated into discriminatory practices resulting in children being placed in isolated classrooms or special institutions. Responding to a Congressional disposition, in 1972 the Head Start Program allocated 10 percent of their enrollment to children with special needs. With the passing of legislation in the 1970s, services to these children formally initiated. The Education for all Handicapped Children Act of 1975, or P.L. 94-142, established the rights of young children with disabilities and exceptionalities to receive free education and services

IN ACTION . . .

LEARNING MORE ABOUT THE HEAD START PROGRAM

To appreciate the relevancy of the Head Start program, try the following:

- Interview someone who experienced Head Start during its beginning years. Ask about the kinds of activities and materials used and, especially, about the nature of the children enrolled.

- Visit your local Head Start office and find out about its services. Identify the populations being served.

- Interview a Head Start educator and inquire about his/her experiences working in the program. Find out about the services and accommodations to meet the needs of culturally diverse children.

- Search the Internet and read about the origins of the program and its successes.

VIDEO CASE 5.2 ▶❚❚

Bobby: Serving a student with special needs in an inclusive elementary classroom

Go to the website and watch the video. After watching the video, answer the following questions:

1. What evidence do you see in the video that Bobby's needs are being accommodated?

2. What role does the teacher play in an inclusive classroom?

in a least-restrictive environment. Backed by the law, the way was opened for children with special needs to participate in regular or mainstream classrooms.

During the 1980s, services for young preschoolers with special needs were mandated by the passing of P.L. 99-457. This legislation established the creation of the Federal Preschool Program and mandated states to offer services for infants and toddlers and their families. Furthermore, the law established the right to services of children with exceptionalities ages 3 to 5. Dispositions also included the development of an individual family service plan (IFSP) to better address the needs of both the child and the family.

Further steps toward equity were taken by the passing of the Americans with Disabilities Act of 1990. This important legislation established the right of young children to receive experiences in settings and environments especially designed with accommodations that meet their needs (Paasha & Gorrill, 2003). This legislation also acknowledged the children's rights to be included in regular classrooms. Thus, the concept of "inclusion" was created where children with disabilities join typically developing peers and participate in regular classroom experiences. Based on the diagnosed needs of the

THINK AND REFLECT...

SERVING YOUNG CHILDREN WITH SPECIAL NEEDS

Working with children with special needs requires the efforts of families, schools, and agencies.

- Talk with early childhood teachers and find out about current services available for young children in your community.

- Find out about how many of these services include parents and families.

- Plan to visit one of the programs in your local community and learn more about their goals and services.

child, accommodations are made to facilitate their full participation in daily activities. Inclusion practices brought about the need for better-trained early childhood educators that are able to respond to children with special needs and deliver to them quality experiences fundamental to equitable education. Although advocacy for the exceptional child continues, today, in classrooms around the country, young children with special needs share experiences and learn along with their less challenged peers. Together, they form a community that exemplifies the social diversity of our society.

EQUALITY FOR CHILDREN IN THE GLOBAL COMMUNITY

The search for equality in services and programs for children in our global community continues to be a concern. Numerous nongovernmental organizations (NGOs) have spearheaded efforts at the local, national, and world levels. Some have assisted children during and after natural disasters, disease epidemics, and rescue efforts in world conflict areas. Others provide continued medical care and fight against human trafficking and child labor exploitation.

Multicultural Education in the Global Context

"Children are the wealth of the nation"
                              —Tanzanian Proverb

There is a universal need to promote equality in services, programs, and attention to individuals with diverse characteristics. While multicultural education may be referred to as education for diversity, cultural pluralism, or pluricultural education, they all mean the same thing.

Although the social realities and efforts of many in the U.S. have provided a solid framework for the movement, the existence of inequities in other parts of the world has also made it into a global issue. The complex nature of global events from the past continues to create the need for social justice, a core element of multicultural education. Formal awareness about inequalities in education was raised by the Convention Against Discrimination in Education, which was declared in 1960 by the United Nations Educational Scientific and Cultural Organization (UNESCO). The convention denounced unequal practices by stating that, "of all forms of discrimination, those that occur in education are the most pernicious because they affect the very essence of the individual and society, namely the forming of the mind—and the most abhorrent—*because the victims are first and foremost children*" (emphasis added, Daudet and Eisemman, 2005, p. 1). Some of the world's continuing challenges that can be addressed through multicultural education are:

- Common challenges faced by immigrant families and their children in most parts of the globe.
- The discriminatory practices that continue to marginalize children by depriving and excluding them from quality educational experiences.

- Access to equitable services and the inclusion of children with special needs in developing countries.
- Gender equality issues that undermine life's opportunities for girls and women.

As early childhood educators we should remember that in some places in the world where demographic changes continue to transform the mainstream populations, awareness about the role of multicultural education in society may be at its beginnings, while in others it has been embraced as part of the social reality.

The Quest for the Rights of Children

Throughout the world, children are facing challenges daily, particularly in the developing countries. Their living conditions and the opportunities to develop to their fullest potential often barely exist or are hampered by the situations in their environments. In 1989, concerns about the violations against the rights of the children led to the enactment of the *Convention on the Rights of Children.* The vision of the convention is to protect the interest of children and to prevent them from being the victims of abuse, discrimination, lack of basic needs, and to promote the children's right to proper care and education. Guiding principles outline specific elements necessary to create environments that foster children's development and survival. The principles represent a detailed framework for action. Within the scope of the convention is the recognition of the undeniable human rights of children, such as the following:

- Survival and development
- Preservation of own identity
- Access to educational services
- Right to play
- Protection from violence and exploitation
- Right to preserve their own culture

Although the convention has been ratified by almost all countries, the struggle continues to enforce and protect the rights of children.

THINK AND REFLECT...

CONVENTION ON THE RIGHTS OF CHILDREN

- Research and find out about the countries that have not yet ratified the convention.
- Visit the UNICEF website and review the convention. Identify the principles that, in your consideration, are most relevant to the realities in your community.

UNICEF The Protector of World's Children

The best-known children's organization, the United Nations International Children's Emergency Fund (UNICEF), was created in 1946 at the end of World War II as a relief humanitarian organization with a central mission to provide care to children. With offices in over 150 countries, its mission today is still the same: to pursue the protection and well being of children throughout the world, especially in developing countries.

Through its efforts, UNICEF has brought attention to the most vulnerable members of society. Among its causes are reducing global child mortality rates and increasing survival rates for children under age 5. While there have been significant changes, in 2010 reports showed that 22,000 children a day were still dying of preventable diseases (World Health Organization & UNICEF, 2010). Violence and recent armed conflicts have prompted attention to safeguard and protect children in war torn areas. Efforts have also been directed to the rescue and rehabilitation of the "child soldiers," children forced to participate in armed conflicts. UNICEF strives to ensure all children's rights to grow in an environment that provides the necessary conditions to grow and develop.

Helping Hands: The Millennium Development Goals

> *We are determined to respect the dignity and to secure the well-being of all children.*
>
> —A World Fit for Children (United Nations, 2002)

 ## AROUND **THE WORLD**

TAKING ACTION: TRICK OR TREAT FOR UNICEF

It was over 60 years ago in Philadelphia that Mary Emma Allison started a program known today all around the world as "Trick or Treat for UNICEF.". Mary Emma, her husband Reverend Clyde Allison, and her family had been involved in post World War II relief efforts for children for some time and wanted to find other ways to continue their work. It was a few days after Halloween, when Mary Emma and her children followed a parade of youngsters dressed in their national costumes into a downtown department store in Philadelphia. There they noticed that the children and others were contributing money and candy to UNICEF to buy powdered milk for children. That gave Mary Emma an idea. Why not continue the efforts to collect for food, medicine, education, and other things children around the world required? She also thought that in the same way children collected candies on Halloween night they could instead collect money to support children in need. With the help of her husband, Mary Emma and her family put "trick or treat" for UNICEF into action. Through a network of churches soon they expanded the efforts nationwide, which resulted in UNICEF's adoption of "Trick or Treat for UNICEF." Today, the campaign begun by Mary Allison has raised nearly $160 million for programs for children in need.

Source: UNICEF USA Committee. (2010). Thank you, Mary Emma Allison. Retrieved http://fieldnotes.unicefusa.org/2010/10/mary-emma-allison.html

IN ACTION . . .

PROTECTING CHILDREN

- Find examples of national and global organizations that advocate for children and their families. Share your findings.

- What can you do personally to advocate for children's well being?

Within the global context, there are many different realities impacting people that still require action to be taken. Conscious of the existence of these challenges, leaders from around the world convened in 2000 and identified the most pressing concerns hampering the progress and well being of humankind. Their work led to what has been called the Millennium Development Goals (MDG) (United Nations, 2000). The MDG establish steps to achieve peace, security, and the reduction of poverty for the world's people. Their target is to achieve these by 2015.

The MDG are an action blueprint, with most of its priorities directly impacting children's development. Although all the MDG are relevant, the following bear special importance in achieving equality for children:

- Eradication of extreme poverty and hunger
- Achievement of universal primary education
- Promotion of gender equality and empowerment of women
- Reduction of child mortality rate
- Improvement of maternal health
- Reduction of the spread of diseases

The enthusiastic response to the MDG led in 2002 to the United Nations' Special session on children. The voice of children sounded strongly in the halls of the United Nations when leaders from the world and child advocates from non-governmental organizations concluded that addressing the needs of the young and most vulnerable was a priority. The outcomes of their discussions were captured in their declaration, *A World Fit for Children* (United Nations, 2002), that outlined specific goals for children's welfare. In *A World Fit for Children* they identified ten key principles and objectives (Figure 5-3) essential to the successful development of children. The impact of this landmark summit has led to the adoption of policies and practices that ensure the rights of children and the proper conditions that foster their development. Its progress continues to be monitored today.

AROUND THE WORLD

PROMOTING GENDER EQUITY IN AFRICA

Gender equity continues to be one of the challenges in current times. Across the world, the rights of girls and women are not equally regarded. In many developing countries girls continue to be deprived of their right to education while others are forced into early marriages or are the victims of humiliating abuse. The seriousness of this issue has been underlined by the United Nations' Millennium goals. Many organizations today work in an effort to raise awareness on the equal rights that girls and women have. Among these organizations is the Forum for African Women Educationalists (FAWE), a nongovernmental organization that spearheads the cause for women rights throughout the African continent.

FAWE was formed in 1993 by five African women ministers of education to advocate for equal education rights. Since its inception, their work has been aimed at closing the existing educational disparity between men and women in Africa. In 2009, more than half of the children in Sub-Saharan Africa reported as "out of school" were girls who had never been in a classroom. Their work has been directed at influencing policy changes leading to creating access to programs for girls and promoting the conditions for them to complete their education. They have also created models and gender-based practices to promote changes in school environments. Among their projects are their demonstration programs or Centers for Excellence promoting gender responsive environments to support the needs of girls and the *Tuseme* (Let's speak out) model, a program designed to empower girls and enhance their self-esteem. Through their advocacy and research efforts, FAWE is bringing attention to the need to establish parity, which will help to eliminate the gender gap.

Source: FAWE. (2010). Who we are. Retrieved http://www.fawe.org/about/index.php

Figure 5-3 Key Principles of the Declaration *"A World Fit for Children"* (United Nations, 2002)

1. Put children first.

2. Eradicate poverty: invest in children.

3. Leave no child behind.

4. Care for every child.

5. Educate every child.

6. Protect children from harm and exploitation.

7. Protect children from war.

8. Combat HIV/AIDS.

9. Listen to children and ensure their participation.

10. Protect the Earth for children.

Source: United Nations. (2002). Special session. A World Fit for Children. Retrieved from http://www.unicef.org/specialsession/docs_new/documents/A-RES-S27-2E.pdf

WHAT WE HAVE LEARNED—CHAPTER SUMMARY

Multicultural education has a rich history. In this chapter we learned about the contributions of many educators, philosophers, and activists such as Maestro Cordero, Sarah Winnemucca, Rosa Parks, Pestalozzi, Booker T. Washington, and others. We also learned that the struggles for educational equality, equity, and access have been a part of human history for hundreds of years. The multicultural education movement had its major impetus in the 1960s in the midst of political and social turmoil in our country. It was during this time that the Civil Rights movement facilitated major educational reforms and provided opportunities for equal education for the "disadvantaged." The multicultural education movement expanded globally as social and demographical characteristics of various societies evolved. In the past decades, organizations such as UNICEF and NGOs have had a major impact on the treatment and protection of children. Today, awareness of diversity has been raised in many countries due to the transformations in their population.

In the United States, one of the most effective programs created in response to the needs of children is Head Start, which to this day remains the longest running early childhood education program in the country. The passing in 1975 of the Education for all Handicapped Children Act, P.L. 94-142, established the rights to education for children with special needs. Additional support for children with special needs was sanctioned by the Americans with Disabilities Act of 1990. This chapter makes us aware of how much has been accomplished in the field of early childhood education and how much still needs to be done.

MAKING CONNECTIONS . . .

1. What are the main components of the multicultural education movement? Select three that you think are the most relevant.

2. Choose one of the advocates of equality from the individuals mentioned in this chapter. Do some library research to find at least two other characteristics that highlight his or her contributions.

3. Equality is a very difficult concept to define. To gain some insight as to how people see it, ask five people to define it. But first, write down your own definition. Begin your interviews and make sure to jot down their responses. Examine their responses to find the similarities and differences. Then, redefine equality to reflect what you learned. Share your findings with a classmate or colleague.

4. Equality is the catalyst for developing multicultural education. Do you think your school provides equal opportunities to all children? What areas do you think still require improvement? Explain.

5. The search for equality is a universal challenge. Efforts to achieve equality have been led by various organizations. Conduct a search and identify some of the leading non-governmental organizations that advocate for the rights of children and their families. Find out about those that operate at the national level.

6. Locate a copy of the *Millennium Development Goals* and identify those that in your consideration are also a priority in your community and at the state and national levels. Explain the reasons for your selection.

RECOMMENDED INTERNET RESOURCES

The following are selected organizations that promote equality in education. You are encouraged to learn more about their philosophy, programs, and resources available.

- Anti-Defamation League
  www.adl.org/default.htm

- National Association for Multicultural Education
  http://www.nameorg.org

- Early Head Start National Resource Center
  http://www.ehsnrc.org/

- National Head Start Association
  http://www.nhsa.org

- United Nations International Children's Emergency Fund (UNICEF)
  http://www.unicef.org/index.php

- United Nations Educational, Scientific and Cultural Organization (UNESCO)
  http://www.unesco.org/new/en/unesco/

YOUR STANDARDS PORTFOLIO

naeyc Standard 6: Becoming a Professional

naeyc Standard 7: Early Childhood Field Experiences

InTASC Standard 9: Professional Learning and Ethical Practice

Becoming a professional is an ongoing task. One of the aspects critical to building and strengthening your professional knowledge calls for learning about the challenges faced by children and families. Awareness about the social and diversity realities in the community both here and globally contributes to gaining new perspectives necessary for an early educator.

Here are some activities that will contribute to sharpening your skills as a professional early childhood educator:

1. Reflect on the topics discussed in this chapter and identify your position about the role of multicultural education in achieving equality for children.

2. Visit a local program providing services for children with special needs and interview one of their professionals. Find out about the services offered to children with disabilities and their families. Reflect on your findings from the visit and interview and comment on any challenges or issues that need attention.

3. Along with a classmate, review the goals of the declaration *A World Fit for Children* and select one that you consider most relevant. Draft a brief plan of actions you would take to address that need area.

4. Learn more about the work of early childhood national and international organizations that advocate for children with diverse characteristics. Select one and explore their goals, resources, and services. Investigate details about their membership.

REFERENCES

American Education History Timeline. (2011) Retrieved from http://www.cloudnet.com/~edrbsass/educationhistorytimeline.html

Caravantes, P. (2004). *Waging peace: The story of Jane Addams*. Greensboro, NC: Reynolds Publishing.

Dahlber, G., Moss, P., & Pence, A. (2006). *Beyond quality in early education and care: Postmodernist perspectives*. New York: Routledge Falmer.

Daudet, Y., & Eisemann, P. (2005). *Commentary on the Convention against discrimination in education*. Paris, France: UNESCO. Retrieved http://unesdoc.unesco.org/images/0014/001412/141286e.pdf

Derman-Sparks, L., & A.B.C. Task Force. (1989). *Anti-bias curriculum: Tools for empowering young children*. Washington, DC: National Association for the Education of Young Children.

Forum for African American Women Educationalists. (2010). Retrieved from http://fawe.org/about/index.php

Gollnick, D., & Chinn, P. (2006). *Multicultural education in a pluralistic society*. (7th ed.). New York: Prentice Hall.

Gómez Tejera, C., & Cruz López, D. (1970). *La escuela Puertorriqueña* [The Puerto Rican school]. Sharon, CT: Troutman.

Grant, C., & Sleeter, C. (2007). *Doing multicultural education for achievement of equity*. New York: Routledge.

Head Start Bureau. (2004). *Statement of purpose. Head Start Act. Section 636*. Washington, DC: U.S. Department of Health and Human Services.

Head Start Bureau. (2010). *Head Start facts*. Washington, DC: U.S. Department of Health and Human Services.

Kelley, R. D. G., & Lewis, E. (2000). *To make our world anew: A history of African Americans*. New York: Oxford University Press.

National Head Start Organization. (2010). *Basic Head Start Facts*. Retrieved from http://www.nhsa.org/files/static_page_files/48BADE30-1D09-3519-ADED347C39FA16A4/Basic_Head_Start_Facts_rev02212011.pdf

Osborn, K. (1996). *Project Head Start: An assessment*. In K. Paciorek & J. Munro (Eds.), *Sources. Notable selections in early childhood education*. Guilford, CT: Dushkin.

Paasha, C. L., Gorrill, L., & Strom, B. (2003). *Children with special needs in early childhood settings*. New York: Cengage Delmar Learning.

Sleeter, C., & Grant, C. (2006). *Making choices for multicultural education*. (5th ed.). New York: Prentice Hall.

Smith, L. G., & Smith, J. (1999). *Lives in education*: A narrative of people and ideas. (2nd ed.). New Jersey: Lawrence Erbaum.

Tabors, P. (1997). *One child, two languages. A guide for preschool educators of children learning English as a second language*. MD: Paul Brookes.

Takei, G. (1994). *The autobiography of George Takei*. New York: Pocket Books.

Tovar, R. F. (1973). *Chronological history of Puerto Rico*. New York: Plus Ultra Educaitonal Publishers.

Turner-Sadler, J. (2006). *African American History: An introduction*. New York: Peter Lang Publishing.

United Nations Educational Scientific and Cultural Organization (UNESCO). (2005). *Conventions against discrimination in education*. Retrieved from http://www.unesco.org/most/rr4educ.htm

U.S. Department of Health and Human Services. (2005). *Creating a 21st century Head Start: Final report of the Advisory Committee on Head Start Quality and Expansion*. Washington, DC: Author.

United Nations. (2000). *United Nations Millennium Declaration*. Retrieved from http://www.un.org/millennium/declaration/ares552e.htm

United Nations. (2002). *A World Fit for Children*. Retrieved from http://www.unicef.org/specialsession/docs_new/documents/A-RES-S27-2E.pdf

World Health Organization and UNICEF. (2010). Countdown to 2015. *Decade report 2000–2010. Taking stock of maternal, newborn and child survival*. Retrieved from http://www.childinfo.org/files/CountdownReport_2000–2010.pdf

Watkins, W. H., & Kelley, R. D. G. (2001). *The white architects of black education: Ideology and power in America, 1865–1954*. New York: Teachers College Press.

Zangiani, S. (2004). *Sarah Winnemucca*. Origor: Bison Press.

Zrinyi Long, N. A. (2004). *The life and legacy of Mary McLeod Bethune*. Florida: Florida Historical Society.

Approaches to Multicultural Education: From Frameworks to Action

Multicultural education is a vision of what education can be, should be, and must be for all students.
—Hilda Hernández (2001)

STANDARDS: THE FOLLOWING STANDARDS ARE ADDRESSED IN THIS CHAPTER:

naeyc **Standard 4:** Using Developmentally Effective Approaches to Connect with Children and Families

naeyc **Standard 6:** Becoming a Professional

naeyc **Standard 7:** Early Childhood Field Experiences

InTASC Standard 7: Planning for Instruction

InTASC Standard 9: Professional Learning and Ethical Practice

CHAPTER OBJECTIVE

Upon reading this chapter and reflecting on its content, you will be able to examine selected approaches and models for multicultural education and establish their applicability in the early childhood context.

KEY CONCEPTS

- approach
- model
- curriculum
- antibias
- typology
- multicultural curriculum

TEACHERS SHARE

Children in Ms. Rayda's kindergarten classroom were engaged in an interesting discussion. It all started after a boy asked why some people had no homes. Ms. Rayda decided that it was time to discuss homelessness with the group. She knew that there were several home-less children in the school. She also knew that some of them had been the focus of cruel comments by others. She saw the boy's question as an opportunity to address an important issue with her group.

Ms. Rayda read *Fly Away Home*, a book about a family that loses their home, and the children began to talk eagerly.

"My dad said some families live in their car," said Jordan.

"Yes, I saw a boy sleeping in one when my Mom was driving," commented Jessica.

"Sometimes that may happen but not always," answered Ms. Rayda. "Some people who don't have a home live in shelters, like the one at the church down the street."

Puzzled and curious, the children wanted to hear more about what it meant to be homeless and what life was like for those who did not have a home. Putting the book on the easel, the teacher prompted them by asking, "What would you do if you had a friend that was homeless?" She was happy to see how many little hands shot up right away.

"I would help him," said one of the children, while others nodded in agreement.

"What would you do if you heard someone saying bad things about your friend?" Ms. Rayda asked.

"You should always be nice to others," said one of the girls in the group.

"Can we do something for people who don't have a house?" asked another.

"What if we do what we did for the people after the floods?" suggested another child.

Pleased to see their reaction, Ms. Rayda said, "Of course. Let's see … what we can do?" A couple of days later, the children were busy writing signs to post in the school. One of them read, "Always be nice to your friends. We are all the same." In one of the corners in Ms. Rayda's classroom, there was also a sign on top of a large brown box holding a variety of items that read, "For our friends at the shelter."

GETTING TO WORK

Having examined some of the concepts and events that led to the origins of multicultural education, it is time to find ways to translate ideas into practice. Just like the teacher in the vignette that opens this chapter, you will also find that multicultural education provides ways to address issues related to the cultural and diverse nature of the communities where we live. Hopefully, by now you realize the importance of multiculturalism and are determined to make multicultural education integral to curricular activities for young children. These resolutions are part of the first action phase, "exploring and thinking," that is experienced by teachers when moving toward multicultural education. The next two phases, "making choices" and "activating ideas," are related to its implementation and practices (Figure 6-1).

The transition from believing in multicultural education to putting ideas into practice is an exciting process. However, many early childhood educators find themselves facing barriers. In recent years, whenever teachers were asked about major obstacles to translating multicultural education into practice, the responses have been the same: "What does it look like?" and "How can I do it?" Reflected in these questions are two major issues. The first reveals the problem of finding a practical model to follow. The second asks what guidelines to follow. There is always a need for both when engaging in innovation. The absence of both models and guidelines has often accounted for the inertia found in bringing about change. Lack of adequate knowledge is also a reason given by teachers when they are asked why multicultural education has not yet become a part of their school's curricula.

When teachers are empowered, the desire to effect change is heightened and their willingness to engage in change increases. This book is intended to empower you to

Figure 6-1 Phases of Multicultural Education

Moving into Multicultural Teaching	
Phase I:	*Exploring and thinking*
	Inquiring about the need and the supporting rationale. Reflecting upon your findings. Formulating a personal conviction. Establishing why multicultural education is considered important (both for the child and personally).
Phase II:	*Making choices*
	Selecting and deciding on the ways to design the program. Exploring the available models, approaches, practices, and materials. Reconfirming the decision to teach multiculturally.
Phase III:	*Activating ideas*
	Implementing the program. Constantly revising to redirect the efforts.

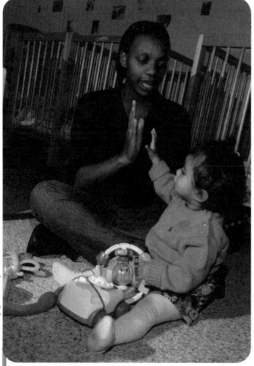

Wadsworth/Cengage Learning

Good planning and effective developmentally-based teaching go hand-in-hand.

transform those desires and aspirations into reality by providing you with the following:

1. Assistance in making a decision to teach in a multicultural way
2. Relevant knowledge that will help you implement a multicultural early childhood program

In this effort, we adhere to the principles drawn from Paulo Freire's ideas. Central to his concept of *critical pedagogy* is the importance of knowledge and the power it offers to those who possess it (Freire, 2000). Education in Freirean ideology is an instrument capable of eroding social inequalities by providing students with knowledge. In his view, effective and meaningful experiences take place when teachers recognize the role of the students' realities and cultures in shaping their identities. He also views learning as a dialogue where teachers engage students in exploring and critically discussing ideas and situations (Leystina, 2004; Merret, 2000). Well-informed teachers, within the context of Freire's thesis, can become effective participants and serve as leaders of the multicultural education movement.

EXPLORING APPROACHES AND MODELS

The purpose of learning about models and approaches of multicultural education is to assist practitioners in creating and implementing a meaningful curriculum for young children with diverse backgrounds. The terms *approach* and *model* are often used interchangeably in education. Essentially, they are proven frameworks for selecting, organizing, and delivering the curriculum. Most practitioners pick and choose among several to effectively address the needs of the children in their care.

Establishing Definitions

A model is a conceptual framework of sequential stages and processes designed to meet a specific purpose or to complete a process. Models can be structured or fluid. A structured model's procedures and ways to implement them are specified and must be followed. On the other hand, fluid models allow for modification as required by the target population. They are often named after or attributed to leading authorities in a special field or discipline. Bank Street (Goffin, 2001) and High/Scope (Schweinhart & Weikart, 1997) are examples of models.

An approach is a set of guidelines that defines an overall method used to implement a model. An approach dictates ways to present, develop, and select topics for classroom instruction. In the context of multicultural education, an approach describes techniques and practices for addressing with diversity issues. Whole language and collaborative learning are two examples of instructional approaches.

Another term that will be mentioned in connection with models and approaches is typology. Typology is a systemic structure or hierarchy in which approaches are placed. It is frequently organized in ascending order from least to most complex. This will become more evident as we discuss approaches and stages of models.

The Meaning of Curriculum

There are many ways to define *curriculum*. For Gordon and Browne (2007), curriculum includes practically all "that happens" at school. Williams (1999) notes that the term *curriculum* can have many different meanings. For some educators, curriculum is established by their school districts, whereas others consider it to be what they construct based on their experience and knowledge about children. However, Williams adds that most educators of children from birth to age 8 see the curriculum as centered and emerging from the whole child. This idea is in agreement with the essential parameters of developmental appropriateness and is relevant for teachers examining ways to bring multiculturalism into the early childhood classroom. We believe that the multicultural curriculum is what emerges after a careful analysis of the needs, individual and family characteristics, and interests of the child and also of the particular cultural and societal needs of the community. Teachers are instrumental in this process of creating a culturally responsive curriculum.

Like templates, curriculum models include directions for implementing educational programs (Figure 6-2). A curriculum also provides ways to organize the educational environment. Evans (quoted in Goffin, 2001) explains that a curriculum model also "refers to a conceptual framework for decision making about educational priorities, administrative policies, instructional methods, and evaluation criteria."

Figure 6-2 Early Childhood Curriculum Models

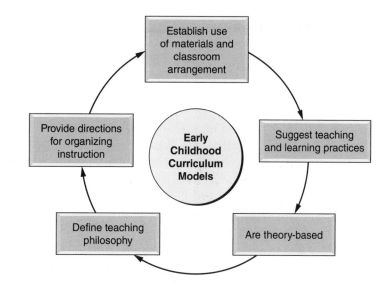

Appropriate Early Childhood Multicultural Curriculum

Multicultural curriculum is rooted and centered on the cultural reality of children with diverse backgrounds as well as their needs. An appropriate early childhood multicultural curriculum recognizes the following:

- Experiences during the early years contribute to shaping and influencing one's attitudes and ways to interpret reality.
- Opportunities for children to learn about themselves and about their own ways and heritages are essential for supporting positive social and emotional development.
- Classroom interactions with peers and adults with diverse characteristics prepare children to perceive differences as part of social reality and contribute to building an appreciation of others and their cultures.
- Responsive curricular experiences engage the child in meaningful learning about cultures and diversity issues. Exploration of real-life events and behaviors, such as occurrences of racism and other unfair practices, help children to recognize and talk about them and take action.
- Challenging and meaningful experiences for children promote knowledge about their own culture and those of their peers and environment.

MODELS OF MULTICULTURAL EDUCATION

Models of multicultural education are of two types: those developed through an analysis of existing experiences derived from classroom practices and those that are based on specific approaches or theories. A model consists of approaches which are often organized

Classroom experiences offer a variety of opportunities to explore diversity. Carefully selected and developmentally appropriate materials can engage the child in learning about his or her own cultural characteristics and those of peers.

in typologies or hierarchies. For example, Banks (1994) and Sleeter and Grant (1994) developed their implementation models through the analysis of existing practices. Among the theory-based models are those of Derman-Sparks (1989), Kendall (1996), and Derman-Sparks and Ramsey (2006). We have chosen to discuss James Banks's levels of integration for multicultural education (1994) and Christine Sleeter's and Carl Grant's (1994) typology for addressing human diversity. These models provide frameworks and recommendations for practice. Among the theory-based models we have selected Louise Derman-Sparks' (1989) antibias approach to multicultural education, with emphasis on fairness and equality, Derman-Sparks and Patricia Ramsey's (2006) antibias approach with emphasis on prevention of racial prejudice, the Head Start multicultural education framework, and Frances Kendall's developmental-interaction philosophy.

Proposed models for the implementation of multicultural education all have in common the fact that they evolved out of the efforts begun in the 1960s. They also share the belief that persistence in the use of a mainstream-centric curriculum does not facilitate the attainment of the *e pluribus unum* ("out of the many, one") ideal, which, according to Banks (1994), is the ultimate goal of education in the United States. Banks also says that insistence on following current mainstream-centric curricula is detrimental not only to children of diverse backgrounds but also to mainstream children. In his opinion, this type of curriculum is negative for mainstream students because it provides

. . . a misleading conception of their relationship with other racial and ethnic groups, and denies them the opportunity to benefit from the knowledge, perspectives, and frames of reference that can be gained from studying and experiencing other cultures and groups. A mainstream-centric curriculum also denies children . . . the opportunity to view their culture from the perspectives of other cultures and groups.

These models provide more opportunities for appropriately teaching young children and are also basic and open frameworks that allow practitioners to add their own elements or build their own curricula.

Banks's Levels of Integration of Multicultural Content

James Banks, one of the leaders in multicultural education in the United States, has studied the evolution of multiculturalism since its beginnings. For Banks (2006), multicultural education is an idea and a process based on the premise that all students, despite

Figure 6-3 Banks's
Levels of Integration

Source: Adapted from Banks, 2006.

their backgrounds, should have equal educational opportunities. That premise sustains the need to review and transform the curriculum to incorporate cultural diversity.

Banks proposes four levels of multicultural curricular integration. These levels are of ascending value, relating to both degree of complexity and degree of commitment to multicultural education (Figure 6-3). The common link in these levels is curricular change. In the next section, you will find a description of each of these levels with applications to the early childhood classroom.

Level 1—The Contributions Approach

Level 1 in Banks's typology is described as the Contributions Approach. At this level, topics about ethnic groups are added to the regular curriculum (2006). Occasionally, ethnic contributions are also presented through a selection of holidays and ethnic elements such as food and music. Banks warns that these insertions add to the existing curriculum but do not alter the already existing curricular goals and objectives. Including ethnic names and objects has basically the effect of "filling in" rather than promoting knowledge about the social reality of diverse groups present in society (Figure 6-4).

Level 1 can be seen as a beginning effort to integrate multicultural concepts into the curriculum. This level requires limited knowledge about the material that is added. Because these topics are presented as brief snapshots, relevant aspects of specific cultures are often not the focus. Actually, if teachers are not careful in their selection and presentation of the topics, concepts may be displayed in stereotypical ways. Some examples of topics are shown in Figure 6-5. Although well intentioned, this practice

Figure 6-4
Examples of Ethnic
Content in Level 1

Topics teachers include when using the contributions approach may include the following:

Heroes
- Eugenio M. de Hostos
- Benito Juárez
- Martin Luther King, Jr.
- Pocahontas

Artifacts
- food (eating tamales or sushi)
- dances (dancing a Venezuelan *joropo*)
- crafts (making an *ojo de Dios*)
- musical instruments (playing the ukulele)

Holidays
- October: Hispanic heritage month
- January: Chinese New Year
- February: Black history month
- May: Cinco de Mayo

Figure 6-5 Working
with the Additive
Approach

Applying the Additive Approach in the Classroom (4- to 5-year-olds)

Main theme: Things we like to eat at home and at school
Concept: Food
Integration: Social studies, science, math, literacy

Topics to explore:

1. Foods we like
2. Food we eat for breakfast
3. Food we eat at school
4. Food children eat in Japan and Mexico*

Literacy
Objectives: Learning new words, learning food words, learning words in other languages, comparing and contrasting, sequencing, retelling

Books to share and discuss with children:
1. Carle, E. (1970). *Pancakes, pancakes.*
2. Brown, M. (1947). *Stone soup.*
3. Brandenburg, A. (1976). *Corn is maize: The gift of the Indians.* *
4. Hitte, K. (1970). *Mexican soup.* *
5. Morris, A. (1989). *Bread, bread, bread.* *
6. Baer, E. (1995). *This the way we eat our lunch: A book about children around the world.* *

Social studies activities
Objectives: Identifying eating patterns, investigating the eating schedule in other countries, discussing how fruits and vegetables get to the grocery store, locating places where our food comes from, mapping
1. Preparing charts describing what children prefer for breakfast, dinner
2. Making a graph to show the class favorite fruits, vegetables, and so on

3. Taking a field trip to an ethnic grocery store to identify what they have*
4. Preparing a cooperative map to show the places/countries where our preferred food items come from
5. Learning the names of favorite dishes in another language*
6. Discussing the eating schedules in other countries*

Science/cooking experiences

Objectives: Observing changes in food (when mashed, ground, cooked), tasting, comparing flavors, identifying vegetables and fruits with similar colors

1. Making applesauce
2. Making Mexican quesadillas (cheese-filled tortillas)*
3. Making an Asian vegetable salad*
4. Tasting different types of cheeses
5. Comparing different types of breads (flat or unleavened, sweet, salty, crusty, and so on)*
6. Preparing a cooperative vegetable soup with vegetables from different countries (for instance, root vegetables, pumpkin, white sweet potatoes, plantains)*

Art experiences

Objectives: Using art to represent one's ideas, using common house items to create art, working cooperatively

1. Preparing a picture menu
2. Making "food mobiles"
3. Preparing a cooperative mural about food children eat in the United States, Japan, and Mexico*

* Indicates insertion of ethnic content.

communicates misleading information to the child. An example of commonly shown stereotypes is the use of "gauchos" to depict Argentineans or portraying calypso dancers as representative of all the people in the Caribbean. One of our students told us that her second-grade class doubted her Japanese heritage because she did not wear a kimono. These examples are but a few of the many instances in which children's ideas are influenced by their exposure to stereotypes either present in the media or learned from interactions with peers and adults.

We have a responsibility to remember the power that teachers exert over children. Information presented in class often remains with students through a lifetime. If cultural contributions are not carefully selected, students are likely to derive little from these experiences. An important point regarding the Level 1 approach is that it serves as an initial step for many early educators who decide to infuse perspectives of diversity into their curriculum. Such efforts deserve to be acknowledged and commended because the teachers are demonstrating a commitment to change classroom experiences. Providing teachers with support and opportunities for learning more about how to integrate ethnic topics into the curriculum is crucial at this point. This can help teachers continue the process of curricular change.

FOCUS
ON CLASSROOM PRACTICES

DEFINING A CONTRIBUTION

Perhaps you have already decided to follow the Contribution Approach. However, selecting what to include is sometimes difficult. Because you want to develop a good curriculum, it is important to begin defining what constitutes a cultural contribution. This will help you select appropriate themes.

Cultural contributions are those cultural details currently defining a culture and the events or actions that either made lasting changes or that dramatically affected the culture. The following example will help you identify and select key elements for your curriculum.

When identifying cultural contributions, look for the following:

- Events of lasting effect: independence of a country; abolition of slavery (in the United States and in other parts of the world; for instance, in Puerto Rico, the abolition of slavery is officially observed on March 22)

- Discoveries and inventions: geographical discoveries, such as the discovery of the Americas or of the Pacific Ocean by the Europeans; scientific discoveries, such as the botanical work of George Washington Carver; inventions such as the helicopter by Russian scientist Igor Sikorsky

- Foundations of leading organizations: for example, the Red Cross and the United Nations

- Heroes or people distinguished because of their contributions to society: Mahatma Gandhi, leader of the nonviolent movement that led to the independence of India; Harriet Tubman, an African American woman who risked her life for the cause of freedom; Eugenio M. de Hostos, a distinguished educator and philosopher who influenced educational practices in the Caribbean; African American poet Maya Angelou, who has been recognized as one of the most important contemporary U.S. poets and writers

- The Arts: music, dances, drama, literature and poetry, crafts, and decorative arts

- Beliefs and traditions: festivals, folklore, myths

Level 2—The Additive Approach

The Additive Approach, or Level 2, is based on the addition "of content, concepts, themes, and perspectives to the curriculum without changing its basic structures, purposes, and characteristics" (Banks, 2006). In this approach, teachers select an ethnic topic and plan activities around it. In Banks's opinion, this second level implies a first step toward the transformation of the curriculum. Success of this approach depends on how the teacher organizes the presentation of the concepts in accordance with the developmental characteristics of the children. Examples of how this level could be practiced in the early childhood classroom appear in Figure 6-5.

Level 3—The Transformation Approach

The third level, the Transformation Approach, represents a phase of substantial changes. At this level, teachers reconstruct the curriculum on the assumption that the content should address targeted situations involving social justice areas that children may be able to relate and explore. Content based on the Transformation Approach is designed to enable students to examine the issues from a variety of perspectives. As students look at a problem from a variety of angles, they gain an enhanced concept of the reality or of the time being studied. For example, while exploring how to reorganize the classroom, children can be led to consider how to facilitate access for peers that may have physical disabilities. Another example is presented in Figure 6-6.

Banks (2006) recommends that teachers applying the Transformation Approach remember that the key lies in the presentation of logically infused "perspectives, frames of reference, and content from various groups." He warns against adding topics to the already existing curriculum and recommends fusing the new with concepts already familiar to children. For the early childhood teacher, this means selecting materials that will not only respond to the developmental levels and interests of children but also be pertinent to the child. In this type of approach, considering the surrounding reality of the child is crucial to making the curriculum valid and culturally responsive. The term *responsive* is used because children are not only discovering their cultural identities but are also provided with opportunities to explore and learn about those of their peers.

Figure 6-6
Transformation
Approach—Let's Talk
About Ornaments

A kindergarten teacher who uses the Level-3 approach would make the following changes in the curriculum:

Theme: Things we wear and use

Topic: We all use personal ornaments

Concepts:

1. People are alike and different in many ways
2. People wear different objects
3. Personal ornaments have special meaning for people

Skills:

1. Looking for details
2. Observing and classifying
3. Identifying things that are alike and different

Goals:

1. To understand that most people use and wear personal ornaments (watches, bracelets, hair pins, scarves, necklaces, and so on)
2. To become aware of the different ornaments (earrings, Hindu dots [bindi], rings, African kente, and so on) that people in our community use
3. To realize that people with different cultural roots prefer different ornaments
4. To understand that ornaments have special meanings for people
5. To comment on the different occasions people use ornaments (weddings, birthdays, holidays, and so on)

(continued)

Figure 6-6
(continued)

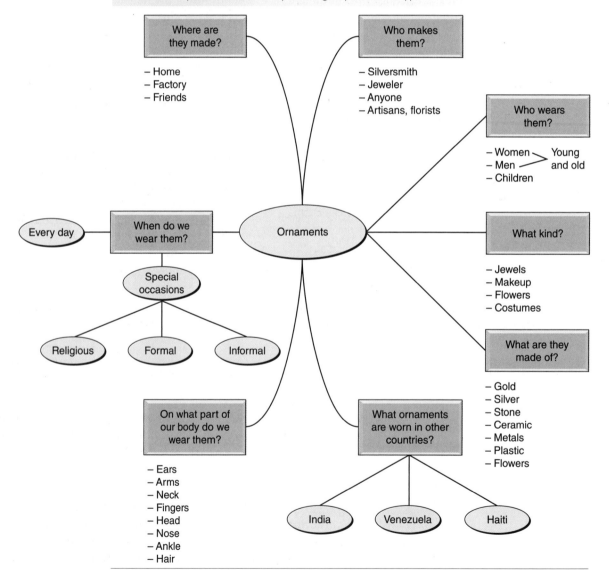

Learning centers:

1. Housekeeping area: A variety of clothing reflective of what people in the community wear; an assortment of clothing and accessories used by the target cultural groups.

2. Art/manipulatives: A variety of materials to create ornaments and crafts, including beads, coconut shells, dry leaves and flowers, and so on. Have materials used for women's makeup (for example, kohl pencils, blush, and so on). Do the makeup on paper plate faces for different occasions.

3. Math/science: Estimate how many pieces of coconut are needed to make a necklace. Taste raw coconut and coconut flakes to compare their taste.

4. Movement: Listen to music typically used during special occasions (weddings, birthdays, and so on). Respond to the music by creating steps. Learn a typical dance.

FOCUS
ON CLASSROOM PRACTICES

USING THEMATIC TEACHING TO CREATE THE LEVEL 3 CURRICULUM

Translating ideas into action is sometimes a hard thing to do. When some of our students began exploring how to apply the Transformation Approach, they felt overwhelmed by the task. As we talked with them, we discovered that they were trying to transform their entire program at once. We suggested that they start small by changing one small portion of the curriculum first. With that advice in mind, one of our students who teaches first grade chose to focus on the movement curriculum. Using thematic teaching as her strategy, she decided to target her activities on learning games from different cultures. She began by first selecting games played by people in the children's community (mainly European American) and then added games representing Asian and Hispanic cultures. Group games, musical games, dances were selected, providing opportunities for children to employ a wide variety of skills within the framework of play.

Using references such as *The Multicultural Game Book* by Louise Orlando (Scholastic, 1999) and *Children around the World* by Verna Wilkins (QED Publishing, 2004), our student began to compile ideas for her curriculum. The result was an appealing curriculum in which children were introduced to diversity through one of the best cultural artifacts: games. As she told us later, this initial trial with the Transformation Approach was the bridge she used to move into other areas of multiculturalism. In her words, once she "tasted" teaching in a different way, she just could not go back to her old curriculum.

Theme: It Is Playtime!

- Favorite games of our families
- Games from the African American tradition (hot butter beans; skelly; roly poly; tin can alley; hand soccer; four squares; jack rocks)
- Traditional games of European American families (hide and seek, hopscotch, tops)
- Games from the Hispanic tradition (arroz con leche; Doña Ana*)
- Games and dances from other countries
  1. Ghana: The clapping game**
  2. Zaire: Catching stars***
  3. Taiwan: Clapstick blind man's buff**
  4. China: 1, 2, 3 dragon***
  5. Haiti: Manee gogo**
  6. Jamaica: Sally water**
  7. Puerto Rico: Ambos a dos; Candela, candela
  8. Chile: Guessing game (Quién es?**)
  9. Mexico: La raspa
  10. Brazil: Bossa nova

*Delacre, L. (2002). *Rafi and Rosi: Carniv al. Popular songs and rhymes from latin America.* New York: Scholastic Books.
**Nelson, W., & Glass, B. (1992). *International playtime: Classroom games and dances from around the world.* Carthage, IL: Fearon Teachers' Aids.
***Orlando, L. (1999). *The multicultural game book: More than 70 traditional games from 30 countries.* New York: Scholastic Books.

Teachers working with Level 3 know that it requires constant planning and a great deal of flexibility to accommodate necessary changes. The flexibility gives teachers an opportunity to offer a pool of socially significant experiences for young children.

Level 4—The Decision-Making and Social Action Approach

The Social Action Approach is the highest level in Banks's typology and "includes all the elements of the Transformation Approach but adds components that require students to make decisions and take actions related to the concept, issue, or problem they have studied in the unit" (2006). Teachers using Level 4 have two major goals, both consistent with early childhood aspirations and practices (Bredekamp & Copple, 2009). They are the following:

1. To prepare children for social criticism (provide them with the ability to examine and analyze social situations and to originate and participate in the social change process)

2. To prepare children to become decision makers (help them learn decision-making skills)

Classroom instruction based on Level 4 is characterized by intense activity rather than the passive examination of issues and events from both the past and the present. Children operating in Level 4 are asked to analyze facts and practices closely. For example, a social analysis of a topic may be presented for the purpose of examining the issue of fairness. A goal of Level 4 is to confront children with situations describing unfair events for the purpose of leading them to take action. Expected behavior includes proposals of alternative views and suggestions of corrective measures for a situation. Teaching topics related to social realities provides valuable social learning experiences for children, who will discover that they can become agents for change.

FOCUS
ON CLASSROOM PRACTICES

Working with Banks's Level 4 requires careful preparation. It particularly requires effective selection of the issues children will explore. One of the ways to find sound and child-valid topics is to create a list of possible areas requiring social action both at the community level and at the national and international levels. To do this, you will need good observation and analytic skills. As you exercise them, you will find that there are plenty of areas to study. We have listed some suggestions to help you select themes for your classroom. When considering what topics or social issues to include, look for the following:

- *Issues arising from the classroom or school interaction patterns:* For example, an incident of name calling, cases of lack of acceptance of some children and adults because of their religious ideas, or reluctance to interact with adults based on their appearance.

- *Issues from the community:* For instance, cases of violent acts, situations of unfair practices against elderly people, loss of a recreational area, presence of

homeless people. Other cases include responses and actions taken after natural disasters such as hurricanes and floods (for example, hurricane Katrina, tsunami in Japan, or paralyzing snowstorms in the northeast).

- *Issues at the national and/or international level:* Possible topics are poverty, cases of unfairness because of people's status, loss of housing because of commercial expansion or construction, cases of violence against families, situations forcing people to leave their countries (immigrants and refugees), effects of epidemic diseases, and needs of communities after a natural disaster.

- *Issues from the past:* Examples include examining the life of African Americans during the years of slavery, emotions of Africans as they were taken away from their homeland, reactions of Native Americans as they were forced to abandon their land and lifestyles, heroic accomplishments for the cause of justice, children and the Holocaust, and the lives of immigrants.

Developing a curriculum based on Level 4 requires a careful selection of issues characterized by both relevancy and developmental pertinence. Lesson plans following the Social Action Approach have the four major components shown in Figure 6-7. An example of the Social Action Approach appears in the opening vignette to this chapter. In the vignette, the teacher engaged the class in taking action on behalf of homeless families, all stemming from a question posed by one child. Bringing community issues into the classroom and leading children to make decisions helps the young in becoming aware of the actions they can take to effect change.

Figure 6-7 Teaching Components of the Social Action Approach

1. *A decision problem or a question* (an issue or situation that requires attention)

   Example: Children are posed with the problem of a child who is being rejected by others because he speaks with an accent. Because of what is happening, the child does not want to come to school. Is there anything we can do? Is it right for others to make fun of him because of his accent?

2. *An inquiry that will provide children with data related to the problem* (questioning to discover the real cause of the problem, who is affected and how are they affected, and examples of the problem)

   Example: Lead children in the analysis of the situation with questions such as:
   - What do we know about the boy/girl who has the problem?
   - Is it wrong or bad to be different?
   - What happened to make the boy/girl feel bad?
   - Is he/she the only one who is different in our classroom/school?
   - If he/she is rejected, who else might feel rejected, too?

3. *A value inquiry and moral analysis* (discussions, role playing, presentation of different cases with the same issue)

   Example: Children will read and discuss selected readings to further illustrate that what happened was wrong and that it hurts people. For instance, they could discuss stories like *All Kinds: Who Cares about Race and Colour?* (Child's Play International, 1989) *The subway sparrow* (Torres, 1997) and *Crow Boy* (Yashima, 1955).

4. *A decision and a list of social actions to be taken* (a final determination of the case and a list of needed actions to correct the issue)

   Examples:
   - Working in small groups, children can prepare an action plan to avoid similar situations. Children can also create a slogan to help them reinforce their commitment to what they have decided to do. For example, declaring the classroom as a place where "Everyone is welcome because we are all the same."
   - Children can be prompted to take actions using questions such as:
     - What will this class do from now on?
     - If you find that someone is making a bad comment about another child, what should you do?
     - Can we help others understand what our beliefs are? How?

Source: Adapted from Banks, 2006.

Teaching with the Decision-Making and Social Action Approach provides ways of introducing children to topics that are not often studied in the classroom. While children can be introduced to topics such as social inequities, prejudice, and racism, these might be considered difficult or controversial by school colleagues and parents. Therefore, teachers who decide to teach about such issues must carefully select child-appropriate materials, experiences, and strategies, thus spending more time preparing to explore these in the classroom. Communication with families must be incorporated into the process if this approach is to be successful. A simple letter stating the topic and the purposes for studying it not only helps clarify them for those who have doubts but also allows families to see the need for the activities.

Creating a socially responsive curriculum in Level 4 is a challenging and exciting experience. This is a level that teachers can reach after they have gained experience and confidence dealing with the multicultural content. It is advisable to try the other levels before venturing into this highest one. Remember, moving toward reform takes time.

The Sleeter and Grant Typology for Multicultural Education

The model developed by Christine Sleeter and Carl Grant is a product of their extensive and continuous research in multicultural education. Their five approaches were constructed based on their experiences as educators and social scientists along with their extensive analyses of multicultural curricula in grades K–12 (Sleeter & Grant, 2008). The five approaches are structured around the social diversity issues of race, class, disability, and gender. The typology also serves as a way to observe how multicultural education has evolved since its inception. The typology offers an array of possibilities from which early childhood professionals can choose and adapt the one that best fits their needs. In Sleeter and Grant's typology, multicultural education is offered through the following approaches:

1. Teaching the exceptional and the culturally different
2. Human relations
3. Single-group studies
4. Multicultural education
5. Education that is multicultural and social reconstructionist

IN ACTION . . .

THINKING ABOUT BANKS'S APPROACHES

After learning about the levels or approaches that Banks proposes, take time to reflect and ask yourself the following questions:

- *Which one would I choose to use with children?*
- *Which one have I already experienced?*

- *Which one seems to be most developmentally appropriate for the children whom I teach? Why?*

LITERACY CONNECTIONS...

USING STORIES TO ENGAGE CHILDREN IN THE SOCIAL ACTION APPROACH (LEVEL 4)

Stories can spark interest for myriad topics related to social action in a culturally diverse society. In this section, you will find some of our age-appropriate favorites to share with young children.

Differences and racial issues

- Fresh, D. (2002). *Think again*. New York: Cartwheel. (primary-age)
- Igus, T. (2001). *Two Mrs. Gibsons*. San Francisco: Children's Book Press. (preschoolers–kindergartners)
- Katz, K. (2007). *The colors of us*. New York: Henry Holt. (preschoolers–kindergartners)
- Monk, I. (2004). *Hope*. Minneapolis, MN: Carolrhoda. (kindergartners and primary-age)
- Seuss, Dr. (2003). *The sneetches and other stories*. New York: Random House. (Original work published in 1961).

Homelessness

- Bunting, E. (2004). *Fly away home*. New York: Clarion. (preschoolers–primary)
- DySalvo, D. (1999). *Uncle Willie and the soup kitchen*. New York: Tandem Library. (preschoolers-primary)

- McGovern, A. (1999). *The lady in the box*. New York: Turtle Books. (primary)

Disabilities

- Fassler, J. (1974). *Howie helps himself*. New York: Albert Whitman. (preschoolers–primary)
- Shriver, M. (2001). *What's wrong with Timmy?* New York: Little, Brown. (preschoolers–primary)
- Thomas, P. (2005). *Don't call me special. A first look as disability*. New York: Barron's Education Series.

Social class and family issues

- Bartoletti, S. (2001). *The Christmas promise*. New York: Blue Sky Press/Scholastic. (preschoolers–primary)
- Loh, M. (1991). *Tucking Mommy in*. New York: Orchard Books. (preschoolers–kindergartners)
- Woodson, J. (2002). *Visiting day*. New York: Scholastic. (preschoolers–primary)

Gender

- Morrow, B. (2003). *A good night for freedom*. New York: Holiday House. (preschoolers–primary)
- Moss, M. (2001). *Brave Harriet*. New York: Silver Whistle. (preschoolers–primary)

Approach I: Teaching the Exceptional and the Culturally Different

Teaching the exceptional and the culturally different is based on the factors that make some students different from the mainstream. These include having a particular disability, being a part of a given social class or minority group, speaking a language other than English, or being a low-achieving female (Sleeter & Grant, 2008). These factors are also seen as areas that require actions. Actions are taken with the purpose of facilitating the child's entrance into the existing social structure of the United States. Providing the child with the necessary skills, knowledge, and language to effectively participate in society is the main goal of this approach.

Teachers following this approach adapt instruction to the students' skill levels and particular learning styles. Practices are based upon four important elements or bridges (Sleeter & Grant, 2008):

1. *Curriculum content:* This consists of challenging experiences that both engage and build necessary skills through meaningful content and relevant language.

    a. *Meaningful content:* The curriculum is designed around themes of interest to children and is related to their reality. Teachers need to have mastery of content (skills, concepts, and facts) as well as the ability to link the children's realities with what is being learned.

    b. *Language needs:* Strategies need to be carefully selected to support language learning for students with first languages other than English. Classroom activities must connect to the children's experiences "to make the content user friendly" (Sleeter & Grant, 2008). Teachers need to be aware of second language strategies and processes to plan experiences that support the children's learning. Teachers must keep in mind that acquiring another language takes time and that it happens as children learn the content.

2. *Instructional process:* Selection and use of age-appropriate and individualized pedagogical activities is essential. Adaptations must be made to respond to the children's learning styles and modalities. Practices need to be adapted to the characteristics of individuals and groups.

3. *Program structure:* There are several program formats for children who are culturally different or exceptional, such as inclusion, pullout, self-contained classes, after-school, and gifted enrichment programs. Typically, children with language differences may be served in bilingual classrooms, pullout programs, and ESL classrooms. Most schools also have compensatory education

Wadsworth/Cengage Learning

Culturally appropriate materials, visuals, and literacy resources and a well-designed classroom environment are effective ways to support second language learning.

programs that provide additional educational experiences and assistance (such as Title I, Head Start, Even Start, Early Head Start, and other readiness programs).

4. *Parent involvement*: Collaborations with parents and families of exceptional or culturally different children are essential. For such collaborations to be successful, teachers need to be aware of the cultural nuances of such relationships. Showing respect and consideration toward the parents and family members is essential for building effective alliances that benefit the children.

Examples of this approach can be found in the following types of programs:

- ESOL programs
- Title I programs
- Bilingual kindergarten programs
- Self-contained special education programs
- Programs for children at risk
- Head Start and Even Start programs

Commenting about the first approach, Sleeter and Grant (2006) say that it reflects the ideas of those who perceive our society "as the land of opportunity and as a good, technological society that is constantly improving itself." For this reason, the exceptional and culturally different child needs help to enter the U.S. mainstream.

Approach II: Human Relations

Founded on the idea of prosocial behavior, the concept of human relations evokes many ideas but essentially brings to mind the desire for positive interaction among people aside from their characteristics. Central to this approach is promoting positive feelings in children that lead them to a sense of unity, tolerance, and acceptance of social diversity within the existing framework of U.S. society. In essence, the following are the goals of this approach:

- To help students communicate with, accept, and get along with people who are different from them
- To reduce or eliminate stereotypes that students have (or might have) about people
- To help students feel good about themselves as individuals and as members of the group they belong to
- To prevent situations in which children offend others by putting them down because of their affiliations or characteristics (Sleeter & Grant, 2008)

Four basic principles define the human relations approach. First, this is a comprehensive approach, requiring infusion of its tenets throughout the entire curriculum. Sleeter and Grant recommend that this kind of program become school wide to avoid sending mixed messages to students. As a second principle, they recommend using a variety of teaching strategies that actively engage children. The third principle emphasizes the use of real-life and child-relevant experiences. Lastly, activities should be built around success for all children. Teachers should avoid competition and in its place should emphasize participation and involvement as end goals for classroom experiences. When using this approach in the curriculum, some of the themes could include the following:

- *We are friends*
- *We care for people*
- *Sharing with our friends*
- *I am important*
- *My family and yours*
- *We all have feelings*
- *Friends everywhere*
- *We can all play together*
- *We all live and work together in a community*
- *We are alike and we are different*

To effectively organize a human relations curriculum, teachers need to keep in mind that the emphasis is on the development of prosocial behavior as the vehicle to promote positive interactions among all. This is consistent with developmentally based practices. Topics and activities must be age-appropriate and culturally relevant. Teachers need to check materials constantly to verify that opportunities to develop a sense of fairness and equity are appropriately presented. In fact, use of this approach can provide relevant enabling experiences for teachers, preparing them to engage in more complex approaches to multicultural education.

Approach III: Single-Group Studies

This approach represents one of the three more complex methods of multicultural education. The term, coined by Sleeter and Grant, defines those programs in which a particular cultural group or element of diversity becomes the central focus of study. Promotion of social equality for a special group, as well as the recognition of that group, is the essence of the single-group studies approach. Advocates of this approach believe that exposing students to the realities of a specific group will result in the reduction of social stratification. Targets commonly chosen include women, ethnic groups such as Asian Americans, people with disabilities, or the working class (Sleeter & Grant, 2008). An important goal of this approach is to provide students with relevant knowledge that will encourage their willingness "to work toward social change that would benefit the identified group" (Sleeter & Grant, 2008).

PLANNING ACTIVITIES FOR THE HUMAN RELATIONS APPROACH

Structuring an effective human relation curriculum requires selection of child appropriate goals, objectives and strategies. Begin by establishing target goals similar to those proposed by Sleeter and Grant. Using them as guides, then select a number of basic concepts. Finally, in choosing a teaching strategy, opt for literature-based thematic teaching. The result, shown next, is a teaching framework easily adaptable to any age level. As you read it, think about ways to adapt it for your own classroom or target age group.

Sample Framework Using the Human Relations Approach

Goal I: To get along with people who are different from ourselves

Theme 1: We all have things that make us special

Concepts:

- Discovering ourselves: Finding that we all are special in some way
- Accepting differences in ourselves and others
- Becoming friends with all the children in our class

Goal II: To eliminate and fight against stereotypes about people

Theme 2: We are all alike and diverse

Concepts:

- Welcoming people as they are
- Clarifying our ideas about ourselves and others
- We listen and think: Learning to stop words that hurt

Goal III: To feel proud about one's identity

Theme 3: We are happy being what we are

Concepts:

- Valuing ourselves and our families
- Feeling proud of our identities: Learning who we are (ethnicity, religion, language, and so on)
- Accepting others

Goal IV: To become aware of unfairness and to take action

Theme 4: You and I can help make a better society!

Concepts:

- Working with everyone: Learning to be a good member of the classroom and school
- We can do it: Helping stop unfairness
- We can help make everyone feel accepted

When using this approach, early childhood teachers need to consider that effective teaching requires integration of subject areas. Topics taught in isolation may contribute little to the formation of ideas. Because children learn when concepts are presented in a holistic way, presentation of target topics must permeate all classroom activities. In designing curricular activities, remember that learning occurs as a result of the child's exposure to a continuum of logically interrelated experiences. Effective planning of the single-group approach resembles thematic teaching, in which children are immersed in the topic throughout the entire program. Opportunities for application are crucial in this approach, both for assessment purposes and as ways to provide the child with instances showing the actual need and importance of the concepts explored. Topics for single-group studies can be organized around investigative questions (Figure 6-8).

Figure 6-8 Topics for Single-Group Studies at the Primary Level (Ages 5–8)

- Homeless children and families
  (Who are the homeless? Who can become a homeless person? How does it feel when you do not have a home? Who helps the homeless? How can we help the homeless?)
- Learning about people with disabilities
  (What does it mean to have a disability? How do people with disabilities feel? How can we help?)
- Learning about refugees
  (Why do people leave their countries? How can we help?)
- Valuing our elders
  (Who are our elders? Why are they important to us? What can we learn from them? How can we show respect and appreciation toward our elders?)
- Learning about children in other neighborhoods
  (Where do they live? What activities do they do? What are their schools like? What games do they play? What do we have in common? In what ways are they unique?)

Classroom teaching structured around single-group studies requires careful preparation and knowledge about the chosen group. Sleeter and Grant (2006) recommend using authentic materials produced by and focused on members of the targeted group. This step is relevant if teachers want to demonstrate how people in that group perceive and feel about given events or facts. An accurate portrayal of the group's opinions and feelings will help students determine whether equality exists. These studies may also help children learn how each group interprets and views social reality. For example, children can examine the importance of knowing how to address a Hispanic adult (by his or her title rather than by the first name, if you are not a close friend). This will help them learn how social relationships are interpreted by that group.

Because of its empowering character, this approach is particularly valuable in helping children learn not only about themselves but also to begin gaining an appreciation about their own cultures. Effectively used, this approach is also valuable in helping the child develop a proactive awareness about social and cultural issues.

Wadsworth/Cengage Learning

Interactions among children are facilitated during playtime. These experiences prepare them to learn to see each one as part of the group. They also contribute to learning how to communicate with and accept others.

As with any other approach, caution should be used not only in the selection of topics but also in their treatment and presentation. Many times, in spite of the best teaching intentions, topics are presented in a trivial and stereotypical form. Taking time for good planning and reflection is the best way to infuse quality into our teaching experiences.

Approach IV: Multicultural Education

The multicultural education approach is based on the importance and value of cultural pluralism in U.S. society. A main tenet of this approach is that the United States is like a "tossed salad" made up of distinct parts to create a wonderful new whole (Sleeter & Grant, 2008). Rather than focusing on a specific curriculum topic, multicultural education is viewed as a comprehensive curriculum reform process affecting all aspects of schooling. Important to the organization of the curriculum are the social contextual realities and experiences pertinent to the classroom audience. This approach shares similar characteristics with Banks's Level 3. Basic to the multicultural approach are the ways in which students are led to analyze social issues involving bias, prejudice, and racism. The goals and parameters for this approach are described in Figure 6-9.

Nieto and Bode (2007) claim that effective multicultural education programs require modifications to the entire school "culture." Such changes encompass not only the materials but also the content, which should be drawn out of the cultural backgrounds of the students. Ability grouping, the behaviors and attitudes of teachers and staff, and the ways parents are involved in the school should be reviewed and changed. These changes reflect what several authors have agreed on: Multicultural education is a process of total education reform (Banks, 2006; Gollnick & Chinn, 2008; Kendall, 1996; Nieto & Bode, 2007).

Although, ideally, this is an approach for implementation at the school level, it also provides direction for the early childhood teacher. When implemented, this approach requires the following steps:

1. *Knowledge of the classroom cultural composition:* Essential to any successful activity is knowledge about the cultural identities of both the class and the community. This step requires a clear concept of the cultural setting where your teaching takes place. No responsive planning can be done without a realistic assessment of the

Figure 6-9
Parameters of the
Multicultural Education
Approach

1. To promote cultural values
2. To promote human rights and respect for those who are different from oneself
3. To promote alternative life choices for people
4. To promote social justice and equality for all people
5. To promote equity in the distribution of power and income among groups

Source: Gollnick & Chinn, 2005.

classrooms. Elements of diversity, such as religion and gender, are also considered cultures. The following are questions to consider:

- *What are the cultures or diversity found in my classroom?*
- *What are the cultures or diversity found in this community?*

2. *An appraisal of the existing curriculum:* Before you begin changing your curriculum, take time to analyze what you have. In other words, do not discard everything yet! In the process of determining the "fit," you will undoubtedly remove some topics and keep others. To expedite this analysis, review your curriculum framework or the list of topics planned for the year and check off those that correspond to the cultural and diverse characteristics reflective of children and the community. Reviewing the curricular expectations, consider the best ways to present those to children in ways that they can best relate to them.

3. *Establishing goals and selecting topics:* This step leads the teacher toward making specific curriculum decisions and creating the curriculum framework. Using the information gathered in Step 1, begin to outline your main targets or goals. Teachers following a mandated curriculum find it necessary to do some revisions to identify topics that match their targets. After your goals are established, begin to select your content, that is, the themes and topics you want to explore with the class. Instead of choosing the content for an entire year, begin by simply listing those you could develop in a month's time. Designing activities for only a month at a time proves to be easier. Remember that your activities should be age appropriate. Finally, implement the curriculum.

4. *Periodical review and assessment plan:* Taking time to review what actually happened is an important step. Having a simple assessment plan will help you identify the effective parts of the curriculum and alert you to the areas that need improvement. An assessment plan could actually consist of three simple questions:

- *How did children react to the activities/materials?*
- *Am I satisfied with the outcomes of the activities? Why?*
- *Were my goals/objectives met? How?*

Approach V: Education That Is Multicultural and Social Reconstructionist

This approach is the most complex one in the Sleeter and Grant typology. It is also the one they prefer. The name itself—education that is multicultural and social reconstructionist—indicates a higher level of sophistication. The goal of this approach is to foster a belief and a sense of social equality and cultural pluralism so that students will want to become actively engaged in achieving equality. A major expectation and a result of this approach is having students become active participants in the elimination of social oppression. In general, teachers find that this approach has many ideas in common with Banks's Level 4.

AROUND **THE WORLD**

CHILD FRIENDLY SCHOOLS

Responsive program models are guided by the goal of creating environments that meet the needs of children. Such is the intent that led to the development of the rights-based child friendly schools framework. Anchored in the Convention of the Rights of Children, the model developed by UNICEF acknowledges the rights that all children have to quality education. It is also aimed at "reducing educational inequities" UNICEF, 2011). Central to the model is establishing parameters to assist in building school supportive environments that foster learning and meet the needs of the whole child. Three main elements characterize child friendly schools:

1. *Inclusive:* Recognizing the rights of children, schools actively strive to provide experiences for those that may have been excluded from services. Equitable services are available for all children irrespective of gender, diverse needs, or cultural backgrounds. Responsive teaching and learning strategies integrate and reflect the diverse backgrounds of children and foster their fullest potential.

2. *Child-centered:* Schools are built around the children's best interest and are targeted at meeting their diverse needs. They are also centered on what is best to promote the child's development and potential.

3. *Democratic participation:* Schools engage the participation of families and communities in the school activities and decision-making process.

In practice, the model varies from country to country. Adaptable to the reality of any child, the model is reflective of the children and their families' culture and diverse characteristics. With a common overarching goal, child friendly schools are flexible and adapt to the needs of the community. Five key areas are defined by the goals of child friendly schools:

1. **Quality learners:** healthy, well-nourished, ready to learn, and supported by their family and community

2. **Quality content:** curricula and materials for literacy, numeracy, knowledge, attitudes, and skills for life

3. **Quality teaching-learning processes:** child-centered; (life) skills-based approaches, technology

4. **Quality learning environments:** policies and practices, facilities (classrooms, water, sanitation), services (safety, physical and psycho-social health)

5. **Quality outcomes:** knowledge, attitudes and skills; suitable assessment, at classroom and national levels

Since its inception over a decade ago, the model has been implemented throughout the world. Africa, Kenya, South Africa, and Mozambique are among those countries where child friendly schools are found. Others have been implemented in Cambodia, the Philippines, the Caribbean, and in Eastern Europe.

Source: UNICEF. (2011). Rolling out "child friendly schools" in Kenya. Retrieved February 10, 2011; UNICEF. (2010). Child friendly schools. Retrieved http://www.unicef.org/cfs/; UNICEF. (2009). Child friendly schools programming. Global evaluation report. New York: UNICEF.

Implementation of the multicultural and social reconstructionist approach presents two important challenges:

1. A need to redesign the total educational program to reflect the needs of diverse cultural groups

2. An openness to welcome children's questions, ideas, and proposals for dealing with current social issues

Sleeter and Grant (2006) present three advantages that support their selection of the multicultural and social reconstructionist approach. These same points become teaching guidelines when developing the classroom curriculum.

1. It targets issues and problems that have a current impact on some of the students.

    Classroom application: The curriculum developed addresses existent issues or problems at the classroom level or in the community. Activities and materials directly reflect issues currently faced by children.

2. It allows students "to take an active stance," offering opportunities to present alternatives to the existing situations.

    Classroom application: Curricular topics examine issues about unfairness. Activities are based on a participatory philosophy in which children take on the roles of active decision makers. By engaging children in a dialogue where they can express ideas and propose solutions, they have a leading voice in establishing a course of action to resolve situations of unfairness and discrimination. This approach is reflective of Freire's ideas on engaging the learner in a dialogue to critically examine situations with the goal of identifying actions to take (Freire, 2000).

3. It helps students participate and work as a group "to speak out, be heard, and effect change."

    Classroom application: Teaching activities are designed around the concept of the project approach and the group investigation model (Joyce, Weil, & Calhoun, 2003). Here, children work as a group in cooperative activities to find ways to resolve or to confront events and situations requiring action. Activities engage children in discussions to help them work out ideas together. A detailed description appears in the section Focus on Classroom Practices: "The group investigation model."

The multicultural and social reconstructionist approach represents a more direct way of dealing with social issues than the other models do. Given its complexity, educators are advised to carefully reflect on the requirements for its implementation (Sleeter & Grant, 2008).

FOCUS
ON CLASSROOM PRACTICES

THE GROUP INVESTIGATION MODEL

Aimed at offering children opportunities to develop skills needed to interact in a group and to become effective group members, the group investigation model (GIM) encourages the development of a sense of social life (Joyce, Weil, & Calhoun, 2003). Using the classroom as a model of the community or larger society, children are led through active participation to learn how to be group members and interact with others. Using cooperative inquiry, children are guided to problem solve or investigate specific situations. Properly used, the GIM is an effective and practical way for not only teaching children academic concepts but also providing experiences through which they can participate in the social process. Joyce, Weil, and Calhoun further emphasize that, besides the instructional effects, GIM also has relevant nurturing outcomes. They specifically identify the following significant nurturing effects, all relevant to multicultural teaching:

- To encourage a sense of respect for the dignity of all and a commitment to pluralism
- To instill a commitment to social inquiry
- To foster a sense of independence as learners
- Sharing elements with the project approach and cooperative learning, activities designed according to the GIM consist of the following phases:

Phase I: Children encounter a puzzling situation. The teacher, acting as a facilitator, describes and presents the problem to the class.

Phase II: Children are led to freely discuss and comment on the problem or situation. The teacher monitors the discussion, posing questions to help clarify any angles.

Phase III: With the help of the teacher, study areas are identified and groups are formed. Members of each group are democratically assigned tasks and roles.

Phase IV: Working in their groups, children look for resources and collect information.

Phase V: Each group takes time to examine what they have collected. Decisions are made as to what else needs to be investigated. The teacher acts as a facilitator during their meetings.

Phase VI: Children in each group present their findings. New areas of study are identified.

The Group Investigation Model

THINK AND REFLECT...

SELECTING A CHILD-APPROPRIATE APPROACH

Deciding what approach to use is a challenging task. The first step is to learn about the variety of choices that are available. After exploring the approaches described by both Banks and Sleeter and Grant, and, based on the realities of your community and of the children, which one would you choose? With your colleagues or classmates, comment on the reasons for your choice.

IN ACTION . . .

REFLECTING ON SLEETER AND GRANT

Having examined Sleeter and Grant's five approaches to multicultural education, answer the following questions:

- *Which of these approaches do you prefer? Why?*

- *Which approach is most appropriate for your classroom?*
- *What other choices can you use to implement multicultural education?*

EARLY CHILDHOOD MULTICULTURAL APPROACHES

After reviewing the generic multicultural models, we now take time to explore those designed for early childhood education. Three models will be discussed: the antibias approach, Kendall's model, and the Head Start Multicultural Principles framework.

The Antibias Approach

The antibias approach to early childhood curriculum centers on changing existing social inequalities. This approach proposes to eliminate the sources of stereotypes that lead individuals to form prejudices and cultural biases. The antibias approach is founded on the "practice of freedom" as defined by Paulo Freire. According to Freire (2000), people need to be able to face their social reality critically and propose ways to transform inequalities. Derman-Sparks (1989) asserts that this conceptual stance is "fundamental to anti-bias education." It has the potential to equip children to take action to stop injustice against themselves or others.

The antibias approach to multicultural education was developed to address diversity issues in the early childhood classroom. It is based on a belief that young children can be guided to develop positive attitudes toward social diversity. The antibias approach is grounded in cognitive theory and research on concept formation. Derman-Sparks contends that children will develop positive attitudes toward diversity and adopt a proactive stance against unfairness if the classroom offers experiences through which they can see people responding against unfair situations and accepting differences, and in which the children are encouraged to act in the same fashion.

Four central goals define the philosophy of the antibias approach; they also indicate the developmental appropriateness of the approach (see Figure 6-10). Structured within the parameters of DAP, curriculum in the antibias approach emerges from these four main sources (Derman-Sparks, 2003):

1. *Children's cultural realities, experiences, behaviors, and interests:* Observations and information about the individual children and their comments, questions, and developmental characteristics are the starting place for developing meaningful curricular experiences.

2. *The families' interests, beliefs, and concerns for children:* Awareness about the cultural beliefs and desires that families have for their young ones is a relevant and

Figure 6-10
Curriculum Goals of the Antibias Approach

Every child will be able to

• construct a knowledgeable, confident self-identity.
• develop comfortable, empathetic, and just interaction with diversity.
• develop critical thinking skills.
• develop the skills for standing up for oneself and others in the face of injustice.

Source: Derman-Sparks & the A.B.C. Task Force, 1989.

culturally valuable source for classroom experiences. It is also a way to demonstrate respect toward the child-rearing patterns followed by families. For instance, regard for a family's eating patterns based on faith (Hebrew) or custom (Chinese) is a way to show respect.

3. *Societal events, messages, and realities that surround children:* Most learning is contextual; thus, what happens in the children's environment is a fundamental source for building a curriculum. Social and cultural realities of the time need to be brought into the classroom in developmentally appropriate ways. For instance, incorporate discussion of diversity and cultural issues shown in the media. Addressing the children's questions helps to clarify their perceptions and avoids formation of erroneous views.

4. *Teachers' knowledge, beliefs, and values:* Classroom teachers are catalysts that transform the information gathered from children's families and society into meaningful and valuable learning experiences. How the curriculum is structured is largely influenced by the teachers' ideas and beliefs about diversity. Early childhood educators must have a clear understanding of their own views regarding diversity and multiculturalism.

Teachers following this approach find themselves eliminating the color-blind or color-denial position that "assumes that differences are insignificant" (Derman-Sparks & the A.B.C. Task Force, 1989). They find themselves dealing directly with prejudice, racism, and stereotypes as they arise. As teachers deal with unfair situations, children join them, learning how to take action to correct a given circumstance. The model is intended to assist children in acquiring attitudes and behavior modeled in the context of direct confrontations.

The Derman-Sparks antibias model presents and addresses cultural diversity content with an emphasis on promoting fairness and equality. It also refrains from using a tourist-like curriculum where the child "visits" a culture and usually learns about its more exotic details. Such curricula only offer glimpses of cultures, contributing little to development of awareness and knowledge about the daily life and problems people face in other cultures. Derman-Sparks provides specific guidelines for avoiding a tourist approach to curriculum (see Figure 6-11).

Wadsworth/Cengage Learning

The anti-bias approach promotes empathetic and fair interactions among diverse children.

1. Connect cultural activities to individual children and their families.
2. Remember that, although cultural patterns are real and affect all members of an ethnic group, families live their culture in their own individual ways.
3. Connect cultural activities to concrete, daily life.
4. Explore cultural diversity within the principle that everyone has a culture.
5. Have cultural diversity permeate the daily life of the classroom through frequent, concrete, hands-on experiences related to young children's interests.
6. Avoid the editorial "we" when talking to children ("we" implies homogeneity).
7. Explore the similarities among people through their differences.
8. Begin with the cultural diversity among the children and staff in your classroom, and then focus on the diversity of others.

Source: Derman-Sparks & the A.B.C. Task Force, 1989.

Two other important differences in the antibias approach are the inclusion of components of diversity appropriate for young children and the use of a developmental framework. Perhaps the best way to characterize the antibias approach is that it is targeted at preventing the formation of misconceptions about the individual and group. The approach offers a way to help children deal with the diversity embedded in our society through activities that are based on principles of child development. For that reason, it is an excellent strategy for the early childhood classroom.

Antibias/Multicultural Education

Derman-Sparks and Ramsey (2005) proposed an antibias/multicultural education approach focused on eradicating prejudice and racism. Their interest stems out of the need to provide the young with experiences that will guide the development of socially acceptable attitudes and ideas toward others, and they emphasize the need to prevent the formation of racist concepts and behavior (Derman-Sparks & Ramsey, 2006). Because, developmentally, racist behaviors begin to form very early in life and are influenced by interactions with adults and the environment, classroom experiences are central to building concepts of social equality. It is one of their goals to underline the role of purposefully designed experiences as a tool that helps children to see themselves and value people beyond racial lines.

The Head Start Multicultural Framework

As you learned earlier in the book, Head Start was established to improve the experiences and opportunities of young children with social and economic challenges. Reflective of the demographical changes in the U.S., its enrollment mirrors the intense diversity of communities across the nation.

Figure 6-12 Head Start Multicultural Principles

1. Every individual is rooted in culture.
2. The cultural groups represented in the communities and families of each Head Start program are the primary sources for culturally relevant programming.
3. Culturally relevant and diverse programming requires learning accurate information about the cultures of different groups and discarding stereotypes.
4. Addressing cultural relevance in making curriculum choices is a necessary, developmentally appropriate practice.
5. Every individual has the right to maintain his or her own identity while acquiring the skills required for functioning in our diverse society.
6. Effective programs for children with limited English speaking ability require continued development of the primary language while the acquisition of English is facilitated.
7. Culturally relevant programming requires staff who reflect the community and families served.
8. Multicultural programming for children enables children to develop an awareness of, respect for, and appreciation of individual cultural differences. It is beneficial to all children.
9. Culturally relevant and diverse programming examines and challenges institutional and personal biases.
10. Culturally relevant and diverse programming and practices are incorporated in all components and services.

Source: Head Start Bureau, 1992; 2010.

During the early part of the 1990s, Head Start proposed 10 multicultural principles as the framework for its programs. They were developed in response to the increasing ethnic and cultural diversity in our society. Reaffirmed in 2010, these principles provide guidance for program planning and delivery (see Figure 6-12). They also define expectations for services and classroom practices with attention to the role that culture and home language play for the young participants of the program (Office of Head Start, 2010).

Although developed for the Head Start program, the Multicultural Principles serve as a guide in designing all aspects of early childhood programs. They emphasize the role of culture in the lives of children and families and identify the responsibility of programs to acknowledge and integrate diversity into their practices. The principles set the goal for creating "appropriate multicultural programming that builds upon each child's culture and helps the child accept the many differences among individuals and eventually deal effectively with other cultures" (Head Start Bureau, 1992). Principles 3 and 9 describe the need for early childhood educators working with culturally diverse children and families to discard stereotypes and put aside biases. They also call for early educators to build relevant and "accurate information about the cultures" (Office of Head Start, 2010, p. 25). Equally relevant is the assertion regarding the child's cultural heritage made by Principle 5, which recognizes that "Every individual has the right to maintain his or her own identity while acquiring the skills required to function in our diverse society." This statement has implications on language diversity and directly establishes the need to value not only a child's culture but also language, which is recognized in Principle 6.

In general, the principles define what should be the nature of the overall program, based on diversity and multiculturalism, and stipulate the importance of addressing the needs

Wadsworth/Cengage Learning

Facilitating and making early experiences equitably available to all children is an essential tenet of multicultural education.

of all children and their families. The principles define best practices by emphasizing the importance of developing programs based on the realities of children, families, and the community. They affirm that successful multicultural experiences emerge and are related to the setting where children live. Also important is how they delineate developmental practices to effectively support the children's cultures and diverse needs. For teachers, the principles provide direction in organizing and establishing the quality of classroom experiences and interactions. They also describe the need to support first languages while children acquire English. More importantly, they task the teacher with a responsibility for creating a respectful and culturally sensitive environment that will help children be socially competent, proud of their own culture, and able to interact with others in positive ways.

Another Model for Early Childhood Education

Frances Kendall, an early childhood educator, sketched a model based on the framework of the developmental-interaction philosophy (the same model used by Bank Street) and the late curriculum expert Hilda Taba (Kendall, 1996). Kendall believes that existing racism can be overcome through education, and she aspires to help children learn to affirm their cultural differences and to respect those of other people. In her model, she bases the success and the attainment of these goals on the teacher as the pivotal element in the process of multicultural education. She believes that "teachers are models for children; therefore, they should show respect and concern for all people" (Kendall, 1996). In Kendall's view, the focus of any multicultural program begins with enabling teachers to, first, recognize their own beliefs and, second, to learn how to implement the program. Her ideas are relevant not only to the early childhood teacher but also to those aiming to initiate school wide diversity programs (see Figure 6-13).

TAKING A STANCE ON MULTICULTURAL EDUCATION FOR YOUNG CHILDREN

Through this chapter we have examined the variety of models and approaches available to deliver multicultural education. Developing our own stance regarding what is the best way to create an engaging and appropriate environment was not a simple process either.

Figure 6-13
Kendall's Goals for
Multicultural Education

1. To teach children to respect others' cultures and values as well as their own
2. To help all children learn to function successfully in a multicultural, multiracial society
3. To develop a positive self-concept in those children who are most affected by racism—children of color*
4. To help all children experience both their differences as culturally diverse people and their similarities as human beings in positive ways
5. To encourage children to experience people of diverse cultures working together as unique parts of a whole community

The term "children of color" refers to children of origins other than European American. In this book, we have excluded this term because it emphasizes not only a misleading human element but also one that has been responsible for many painful incidents.

Source: Kendall, 1996.

It came as a result of a careful analysis of what the literature presents (Banks & Banks, 2006; Derman-Sparks, 2003; Head Start, 2010) and through our continuous observations of teachers, children, and families in a variety of culturally diverse classrooms and communities. Their experiences are a living document and source of ideas and information on how to make learning meaningful for all. For us, the eclectic framework for teaching that is multicultural should be guided by an emphasis on providing experiences that are

THINK AND REFLECT...

REFLECTING ON MULTICULTURAL EDUCATION

As you prepare yourself to become a multicultural educator of the young, it is important that you take time to reflect on the kind of classroom environment you want to create. Ask yourself the following:

1. *Why do I want to teach in a multicultural way?*
2. *How do I define multicultural education?*
3. *What are my expectations of multicultural education?*
4. *What do my students need?*
5. *What are the cultural challenges present in my community?*

6. *Would my teaching be more developmentally appropriate if I infused a multicultural perspective?*

The more time you take to reflect on your convictions regarding multiculturalism, the more certain you will become of the direction you want to take. This will help guide you in planning the multicultural program you want to establish. Of all the decisions to make in multicultural education, the hardest one is resolving to change your teaching strategies. If you have resolved to do that (and we hope you have!), other decisions regarding teaching multiculturally will come more easily.

developmentally and culturally appropriate and intentionally planned to support learning. We also believe in teaching that is guided to promote pride in one's own heritage while recognizing that of others and that leads to the formation of a sense of social fairness and positive attitudes toward diversity (Figure 6-14).

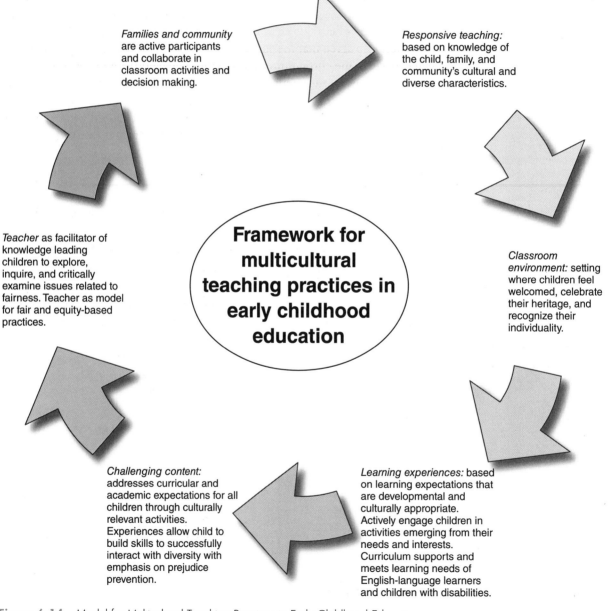

Families and community are active participants and collaborate in classroom activities and decision making.

Responsive teaching: based on knowledge of the child, family, and community's cultural and diverse characteristics.

Framework for multicultural teaching practices in early childhood education

Teacher as facilitator of knowledge leading children to explore, inquire, and critically examine issues related to fairness. Teacher as model for fair and equity-based practices.

Classroom environment: setting where children feel welcomed, celebrate their heritage, and recognize their individuality.

Challenging content: addresses curricular and academic expectations for all children through culturally relevant activities. Experiences allow child to build skills to successfully interact with diversity with emphasis on prejudice prevention.

Learning experiences: based on learning expectations that are developmental and culturally appropriate. Actively engage children in activities emerging from their needs and interests. Curriculum supports and meets learning needs of English-language learners and children with disabilities.

Figure 6-14   Model for Multicultural Teaching Practices in Early Childhood Education

WHAT WE HAVE LEARNED—CHAPTER SUMMARY

Multicultural education started in the 1960s. Since that time, many approaches and models have evolved through research and practice. In this chapter, we presented several major models and approaches created by the most important professionals in education and early childhood education: James Banks, Christine Sleeter and Carl Grant, and Louise Derman-Sparks. Each one has as its core the welfare of young children from diverse cultures. They share the belief that the child is the center of the educational process. All major researchers also agree that the success of every early childhood program depends on the degree to which the curriculum addresses the characteristics and needs of children with diverse backgrounds. Our intent for presenting the information in this chapter is to inform early childhood educators that goodwill and creativity in the classroom are important, but that they need to ground their teaching in proven models and approaches that will ensure the effectiveness of teaching efforts and positively affect the learning process.

MAKING CONNECTIONS . . .

1. Explain the following key concepts: *approach, model,* and *curriculum.*

2. Banks's and Sleeter and Grant's typologies have common points. Examine both carefully and find the common elements.

3. Define the antibias approach. Does this model have any points in common with the other approaches? Explain.

4. After exploring the different approaches to multicultural education, which one would you select? Why?

5. Some people have argued that many of the approaches to multicultural education are not suitable for the early childhood classroom. What is your opinion? Why?

6. Thinking about the multicultural approach you chose for activity #4, prepare a draft of the changes you would need to make in your classroom to implement it. After completing your draft, go back to it and find the following:
   - *the five major changes*
   - the three hardest changes
   - the five easiest things to change
   - *three initial changes*

RECOMMENDED INTERNET RESOURCES

- ESL standards for Grades Pre-K–3 (TESOL)
  www.tesol.org/s_tesol/sec_document.asp?CID=113&DID=314

- "Instructional Models for Early Childhood Education," from the Clearinghouse on Early Education and Parenting
  http://ceep.crc.uiuc.edu/eecearchive/digests/2002/golbeck02.pdf

- "The Role of Curriculum Models in Early Childhood Education," from the Clearinghouse on Early Education and Parenting
  http://ceep.crc.uiuc.edu/eecearchive/digests/2000/goffin00.html

YOUR STANDARDS PORTFOLIO

naeyc **Standard 4:** Using Developmentally Effective Approaches to Connect with Children and Families

naeyc **Standard 6:** Becoming a Professional

naeyc **Standard 7:** Early Childhood Field Experiences

InTASC Standard 7: Planning for Instruction

InTASC Standard 9: Professional Learning and Ethical Practice

Several models and approaches for teaching children with diverse backgrounds were discussed in this chapter. All of them are child centered and supportive of the diverse backgrounds and characteristics of children and their families. Reflect on the content and complete the following activities:

1. Conduct observations in two different classrooms serving culturally diverse preschoolers (such as Head Start or prekindergarten) and primary level children. Note the children's responses to materials and classroom activities. Observe how diverse elements are integrated into the daily experiences. Reflect on the observations and write a brief commentary describing your findings.

2. Interview two early childhood educators/practitioners and find out how the classroom activities they use promote an antibias environment. Based on the information, prepare a one-page summary of their comments. Add your reflections on what you learned.

3. Reflecting on the different approaches discussed in this chapter, write a brief description of what you think is the most effective multicultural approach for young children.

4. Select an approach or a model and write a short activity that is based on it. Explain in writing why you think the activity complies with the selected approach or model.

REFERENCES

Banks, J. (1994). Transforming the mainstream curriculum. *Education Leadership*, 5(8), 4–8.

Banks, J. (2006). Approaches to multicultural curriculum reform. In J. Banks & C. Banks (Eds.), *Multicultural education: Issues and perspectives* (6th ed., pp. 247–270). Needham Heights, MA: Allyn & Bacon.

Banks, J., & Banks, C. (2006). *Multicultural education: Issues and perspectives* (6th ed.). Needham Heights, MA: Allyn & Bacon.

Bredekamp, S. (1989). *Developmentally appropriate practice in early childhood programs serving children birth through age 8*. Washington, DC: National Association for the Education of Young Children.

Derman-Sparks, L. (2003). Developing antibias, multicultural curriculum. In C. Copple (Ed.), *A world of differences: Readings on teaching children in a diverse society* (pp. 173–178). Washington, DC: National Association for the Education of Young Children.

Derman-Sparks, L., & the A.B.C. Task Force. (1989). *Antibias curriculum tools for empowering young children.* Washington, DC: National Association for the Education of Young Children.

Derman-Sparks, L., & Ramsey, P. (2005). What if all the children in my class are white? *Young Children: Beyond the journal.* Retrieved September 28, 2008, from http://www.journal.naeyc.org/btj/200511/DermanSparksBTJ1105.asp.

Derman-Sparks, L., & Ramsey, P. (2006). *What if all the children in my class are white?* New York: Teachers College Press.

Freire, D. (2000). *Pedagogy of the oppressed.* New York: Continuum International Publishing.

Goffin, S. (2001). *Curriculum models and early childhood education: Appraising the relationship.* New York: Merrill.

Gollnick, D. M., & Chinn, P. C. (2005). *Multicultural education in a pluralistic society* (7th ed.). New York: Prentice Hall.

Gordon, A., & Browne, K. (2010). *Beginnings and beyond.* (8th ed.). Clifton Park, NY: Thomson Delmar Learning.

Head Start Bureau. (1992). *Multicultural principles for Head Start programs.* Washington, DC: U.S. Department of Health and Human Services.

Hernandez, H. (2001). *Multicultural Education: A teachers' guide to linking context, process and content.* (2nd ed.). New York: Allyn & Bacon.

Joyce, B., Weil, M., & Calhoun, E. (2008). *Models of teaching* (8th ed.). Englewood Cliffs, NJ: Prentice Hall.

Kendall, F. (1996). *Diversity in the classroom: A multicultural approach to the education of young children.* New York: Teachers College Press.

Leystina, P. (2004). Presence of mind in the process of learning and knowing: A dialogue with Paulo Freire. *Teacher Education Quarterly, 31*(1), 17–29.

Merret, C. (2000). Teaching social justice: Reviving geography's neglected tradition. *Journal of Geography, 99*(5), 207–218.

Nieto, S., & Bode, P. (2007). *Affirming diversity: The sociopolitical context of multicultural education.* Needham Heights, MA: Allyn & Bacon.

Office of Head Start. (2010). *Revisiting and updating the multicultural principles for Head Start programs serving children ages birth to five. Addressing culture and home language in Head Start program systems and services.* Washington, DC: Office of Head Start.

Schweinhart, L. J., & Weikart, D. P. (1997). The High/Scope preschool curriculum comparison study through age 23. *Early Childhood Research Quarterly, 12*(2), 117–143.

Sleeter, C. E., & Grant, C. (2005). *Making choices for multicultural education: Five approached to race, class and gender* (5th ed.). New York: Wiley & Sons.

Sleeter, C. E., & Grant, C. (2007). *Making choices for multicultural education: Five approaches to race, class, and gender* (6th ed.). New York: Wiley & Sons.

Southern Poverty Law Center & Gussin-Paley, V. (1997). *Starting small: Teaching tolerance in preschool and the early grades.* Montgomery, AL: Author.

Williams, L. (1999). *Determining the curriculum.* In C. Seefeldt (Ed.), *The early childhood curriculum* (3rd ed., pp. 1–12). New York: Teachers College Press.

PART III

Into Action: Implementing a Culturally Appropriate Program for All Children

Classrooms, Where Words Become Action

Curriculum respects and supports individual, cultural and linguistic diversity. Curriculum supports and encourages positive relationships with children's families.

—National Association for the Education of Young Children (NAEYC) and National Association of Early Childhood Specialists in State Departments of Education (NAEYC & NAECS/SDE) (2003)

Wadsworth/Cengage Learning

STANDARDS: THE FOLLOWING STANDARDS ARE ADDRESSED IN THIS CHAPTER:

naeyc Standard 1: Promoting Child Development and Learning

naeyc Standard 5: Using Content Knowledge to Build Meaningful Curriculum

InTASC Standard 6: Assessment

InTASC Standard 7: Planning for Instruction

TEACHERS SHARE

The first grade group was sitting on the rug and attentively listening to their teacher, Miss Mariana, read *Together,* one of the books she had selected for Black History Month. On the wall were pictures of people from diverse ethnic groups working together, and phrases from the story written in English, Spanish, and Creole. Listening to Miss Mariana was a group of young children, mostly Hispanics, Haitian, and African Americans. You could see the children's eyes sparkle as she read the story about two girls—one black and one white—and all the things they dream to do together. The children joined in repeating the phrase: *"Let's dream the same dream. Together!"* At the end of the story, Miss Mariana asked the children some questions related to the story. The discussion went on for a long time. The children were completely engaged in the conversation and interested in sharing their own dreams and experiences with friends and family. In addition to the discussion,

CHAPTER OBJECTIVE

Upon reading this chapter and reflecting on its content, you will be able to trace the development process of the multicultural curriculum.

KEY CONCEPTS

- assessment
- needs assessment
- curriculum
- multicultural curriculum
- curricular content
- planning

Miss Mariana had the children draw and act out their own stories of being "together." After a while, one of the boys suggested: "I'm dreaming of hearing the story again. Can we do it?" Happy to see the child's interest, Miss Mariana replied without any hesitation: "Of course! What a nice idea. Let's do it."

"That went really well, Mariana," said her assistant. "It's great to see that the children enjoyed the story so much that they wanted to hear it again."

"Yes, they really liked it," replied Mariana as she picked up some of the books from the tables.

"How do you do it? How do you get them to be so engaged? They were so enthusiastic."

"Lots of planning—there is no other way," the teacher replied with a smile. "It's knowing what the children need and planning with their needs in mind that makes classroom experiences a success."

CURRICULUM PLANNING IN THE MULTICULTURAL CLASSROOM

The classroom is the place where multicultural education becomes a reality. It is the setting where ideas to promote diversity move into action. Careful planning is an important step in implementing teaching practices with a multicultural focus. In order to be effective, it is necessary to have a sound knowledge about the process of planning as it relates to meeting the needs of each child. The process starts when teachers reflect on their own ideas and knowledge and ends with the implementation of meaningful and developmentally appropriate practices (DAP) in the classroom. Delivering engaging and responsive experiences like what you read in the opening vignette is the outcome of planning that is carefully done and aimed at meeting what each child needs. This chapter is devoted to reviewing ideas about the curriculum planning process and some of its essential elements: conducting a needs assessment, content selection, infusion of multicultural elements, and implementation. Together, they help in creating a framework for successful multicultural experiences.

Traits of an Effective Multicultural Early Childhood Educator

Teaching transforms lives, according to the old adage. Good teaching, as defined by leading educators and professional organizations, happens when teachers look for ways to reconcile the child's own needs with the aspirations of education. Some of these aspirations are grounded in the principles of developmentally and culturally appropriate practices (DAP). Teachers of young children need to incorporate both the perspectives of diversity and developmentally based practices into their instruction in an effort to respond to the whole child. This premise is at the core of multicultural education. Nieto and Bode (2007) consider that a true multicultural educator also believes in multiculturalism and diversity as an element of society at large. They believe that multicultural educators are characterized by very specific traits:

- *Thorough and strong knowledge:* Learning more about pluralism and how it is reflected in people and in our interactions
- *Honest assessment of our own biases:* Accepting that we all hold biases, sometimes very well hidden inside ourselves
- *Ability to view reality through countless perspectives:* Learning to approach reality from more than one angle

Additionally, a good multicultural teacher must believe in social justice and advancement of democracy. Social justice is the belief that guides professionals in ensuring that each child has the same opportunities to foster development and future success. The multicultural early childhood educator has an obligation to make certain that every child is treated fairly and has equal opportunity to develop to his or her full potential. The just and equitable treatment of children from all corners of the world benefits all those who inhabit the earth. Early childhood professionals must enhance their knowledge of *who* they are as educators and individuals, *who* the children and their families are in their classrooms and communities, *who* we are as members of a national and global society, and *why* as professionals they embrace social justice (Gallavan, cited in Romo, Bradfield, & Serrano, 2004).

Drawing upon the ideas of leading educators and the ideal traits defined by professional organizations such as the National Association for the Education of Young Children (NAEYC), the Association for Childhood Education International (ACEI), and the World Organization for Early Childhood Education [Organization Mondiale pour L'Education Prescolaire] (OMEP), we can now draw a profile of an early childhood multicultural educator.

An early childhood multicultural educator . . .

- has a sound knowledge about child development that he or she uses and applies in classroom teaching.
- believes that multiculturalism is an integral part of our society and that schools need to incorporate multiculturalism into their programs.

Teacher collaboration is an important element of multicultural education.

- is committed to helping the child learn and develop an appreciation for his or her own diverse characteristics and of our social diversity.

- is aware of and works to clarify his or her own ideas about diversity, biases, and beliefs, and recognizes and accepts his or her own diversity and that of children.

- holds high expectations equally for all children and helps all children to develop to their fullest.

- works and interacts in a respectful way with all families as partners and collaborators for the benefit of the child.

- is willing to try out new methods and materials to accommodate the needs of children.

- is constantly assessing his or her own teaching to guarantee its responsiveness to the children's needs.

- is constantly searching for new approaches and/or methods to improve multicultural teaching.

- creates a classroom environment where tolerance, respect, and openness to learn and understand others are its essential characteristics.

- keeps a positive, willing, and open attitude toward self and others as professionals.

- recognizes that reality is a composite of many different perspectives.

The characteristics in Figure 7-1 describe a classroom leader, the teacher, who will use skills and knowledge on behalf of children. This list of attributes also reflects a composite of knowledge and values, both personal and professional, that depict an educator who is personally and professionally willing to take action and set direction for children's success (Figure 7-1).

Figure 7-1
Multicultural Early Childhood Teachers are Leaders

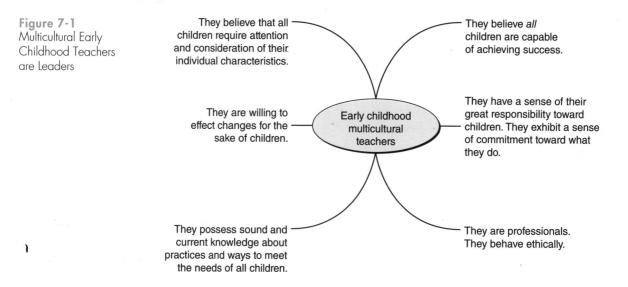

They believe that all children require attention and consideration of their individual characteristics.

They believe *all* children are capable of achieving success.

They are willing to effect changes for the sake of children.

Early childhood multicultural teachers

They have a sense of their great responsibility toward children. They exhibit a sense of commitment toward what they do.

They possess sound and current knowledge about practices and ways to meet the needs of all children.

They are professionals. They behave ethically.

Becoming a Good Multicultural Early Childhood Educator

Educators who commit to undertaking multicultural teaching often discover that they possess many more good teaching qualities than they had thought. This knowledge reassures them and acts as a catalyst for change. The change process is described in Figure 7-2. The first two steps are the focus of this chapter.

WHERE DO WE START?

Good and effective planning happens only when those involved in the process are knowledgeable about the children and the environment where the experiences are implemented. High-quality planning that is aimed at producing long-lasting transformations is based on sound knowledge of the children you teach. This common sense approach has been advocated by many educators and is at the core of developmentally based practices. John Dewey, who advocated for an active and child-based curriculum, argued that good curriculum was determined by its relationship to society. He thought that educational goals should emerge from the people and the societal context. Consideration of the social context, he felt, provides the appropriate basis for planning and designing school activities. Today, in the context of a diverse and continuously evolving society, his ideas resonate loudly. They also serve as a reminder to educators to learn more about the developmental needs of children and their settings.

Figure 7-2 Steps Toward Multicultural Teaching

1. *Knowing ourselves as teachers.* Who am I as a teacher? Self-assessment in which teachers examine their own teaching and beliefs.

2. *Assessing our present practices.* Where do I stand now? What kind of program do I offer my students? Analysis of current curriculum to determine the content and processes used. What is the school context like? What should my teaching be like? What do my students need?

3. *Designing the program.* Which goals and objectives will I have? What approach will I use? What materials and resources do I have and need?

4. *Implementing.* When will actions take place? How can I find out about their effects?

IN ACTION . . .

REFLECTING ON THE PROFILE OF THE EARLY CHILDHOOD MULTICULTURAL EDUCATOR

- Which of the characteristics of an early childhood multicultural educator mentioned here describe you?
- Which do you think are the most important ones?
- Which ones would you say are the hardest to achieve? Why?
- What other descriptors would you add to the list?

The Needs Assessment: Gaining a True Perspective of Appropriate Teaching Practices

A well-known principle in early childhood education is to never assume that you know what the child needs or knows. It behooves teachers to remain vigilant by constantly observing and checking what children do and say in the classroom. In the multicultural early childhood environment, verifying and checking what children bring into the classroom is crucial. Their prior knowledge and experiences are a valuable source of information when responsively planning learning activities. Time spent in assessment is as important as selecting materials and designing activities. The process whereby the teacher identifies the specific areas of concern from which the educator will later develop instructional goals and expectations is known as a needs assessment. In education, a needs assessment is a data collection process that is the first step in planning to implement changes that satisfy the needs of one or more constituencies. The process is structured and organized to permit the educators to determine the needs of the children through both formal and informal means.

The process of needs assessment can take place on many different levels in early childhood education. Needs identification should provide the teacher with a three-dimensional sense of the setting by providing information regarding the community where the school is located or which it serves (if children are bused in or come from different communities); the school itself as an entity formed by teachers and staff; and the children and their families. Getting a feel for the setting as seen from these perspectives provides information that contributes to designing an appropriate curriculum.

Multicultural education is a transformational process. It is also emerging in nature and takes hold gradually as educators continue to build effective knowledge about the realities of children. For this reason, it is essential for early childhood educators to constantly evaluate their practices to ascertain *what* needs to be changed and *why* it needs to be changed. This is one way to identify the strengths and challenges of the program and its instructional practices. By conducting an assessment (see Figure 7-3), educators gain a deeper understanding of their own approach and responses to young children with diverse and multicultural characteristics.

Assessing Practices from the Perspective of the Children's Experiences

Collecting information from the perspective of the child and families is an important step in a needs

How well do we know a child? The needs assessment is a way to learn about the child's strengths, needs and unique experiences.

Wadsworth/Cengage Learning

Figure 7-3
Conducting a Needs
Assessment: Informal
Activities

About teaching practices:

- Write down your own comments about classroom activities that support diversity. (I can support diversity by. . . .)
- Develop statements identifying the essential diverse characteristics of an early childhood classroom. (An early childhood classroom is diverse because it has . . . .)
- Do an appraisal of what you know or don't know regarding culture and diversity. (I know that . . . . . I need to learn more about . . . .)
- Check lesson plans to see if themes address diversity.
- Inspect your classroom to see if materials reflect diversity.
- Talk with other early childhood professionals about diversity practices.

About children and their families:

- Review information about families and children (culture, language, exceptionalities, and socioeconomic characteristics).
- Hold informal conversations with family members and parents to learn about their expectations from the school and from you.
- Talk with families about their traditions and special celebrations.

About the community:

- Visit the community to learn about its culture; that is, find out about languages spoken, religious groups, social rules and mores, and so on.
- Identify resources, ethnic-based organizations, and agencies serving families with diverse characteristics.

assessment. The process yields a truer picture of the child's unique characteristics, his or her social and cultural family environments, and of languages other than English spoken by children at home and in their community. It is equally relevant to gain a thorough understanding about the existing special needs and exceptionalities of the children.

Learning about the Children's Environment

The environment includes not only the classroom where learning takes place, but also the neighborhood and community where families and children live. Knowledge about the particular attributes of the community helps early childhood educators learn about the needs of the stakeholders in the child's life. These in turn assist in making decisions and determining the direction of the classroom experiences.

The family, school or center, classroom, and the community are the major contexts in which young children interact and learn. Assessing the elements and nature of these venues will help you plan experiences that appropriately reflect their cultural and social characteristics. There are many different ways to learn about the environment. Details about these environments can be gathered through informal interviews with children and adults (Figure 7-4 and 7-5). Visits to the home and

THINK AND REFLECT...

PLANNING WITH A DAP FOCUS

DAP planning for young children is based on a sound knowledge of the child and his/her reality. Considering that premise, what kind of information about the school and the community would you say is needed to plan developmentally-based multicultural experiences?

community are additional ways to learn about the children's realities. Getting to personally interact with the family provides invaluable insights. Use of purposefully designed instruments is also a helpful way to collect data. Figure 7-4 is a sample questionnaire you may want to use to obtain valuable information about the social and cultural reality of children, their families, and the community. Additional activities and ways to learn more about the families were discussed in Chapter 2 and others are found in Chapter 10.

Gathering Information About Children with Special Needs

Successful learning for special needs children happens in the context of an inclusive and supportive environment where experiences are geared to promote development. Awareness and an understanding of the children's specific conditions and disabilities are necessary for planning for their needs. In collecting information about the special needs child, consider the following:

- Has the child been screened and formally identified as having a disability? Does the child have an Instructional Evaluation Plan (IEP)?
- What is the nature of the child's disabilities?
- What accommodations are required?
- What are the recommendations in the IEP?

A review of the children's files will not only reveal those who have special needs but will also provide details about the nature of their disabilities and the required accommodations. Based on the children's needs, modifications may range from lesson planning to the use of special equipment and physical arrangement. Conversations with the child's former teachers, staff members, and special education service coordinators will also offer relevant information. Interviews with parents and family members along with your own observations will also contribute to building knowledge about the child's needs and how to best address these in your planning.

Figure 7-4
Learning About the
Children's Learning
Contexts

(Sample Questionnaire)

A. The Community

1. What is the cultural and ethnic makeup of the community?
2. What languages are spoken?
3. What are the immediate priorities of the community?
4. What are the main community issues?
5. How do the community members feel toward the school, toward my classroom?

B. The School

1. What is the cultural and ethnic makeup of the school?
2. What is the diversity profile of the school?
3. What attitudes do teachers and staff have toward diversity?
4. Is anyone engaged in a multicultural program? What approaches are they following?
5. Are multicultural programs among the school's priorities?
6. Would the faculty, administrators, and staff support my efforts?

C. Children and Families

1. What are the families like? Socioeconomically, how are they defined?
2. What elements of diversity are reflected in these families?
3. What are some of the essential needs of families?
4. What are their religious affiliations?
5. Can I address those needs in my classroom?
6. What are the traits that, ethnically and culturally, characterize children in my classroom?
7. What diversity issues are unclear to my students? (for example, language differences, equality, interracial relations)
8. How do children see me?

D. The Classroom

1. What are the ethnic and cultural origins of the children in this classroom?
2. What opportunities do they have for dealing with diversity at the school?
3. Generally, how do children interact in this classroom?
4. Have there been any incidents because of racial or cultural differences?
5. Are there children who tend to use racial slurs or pejorative terms against others?
6. How do they respond when a person with given cultural characteristics comes into the classroom?

Assessing Language Diversity: English Language Learners

Today, language diversity is one of the characteristics present in many classrooms. Projections indicate that by 2030 an estimated 40 percent of children in schools will have a primary language other than English. Nationally, census statistics already show that nearly 20 percent of children age five and older speak a language other than English (U.S. Census Bureau, 2010). Many young English language learners in Head Start and state prekindergarten programs were born in the U.S., while others immigrated with their families before entering preschool.

Information on children's language diversity is essential in order to design activities that will meet their linguistic needs. There are several ways to obtain linguistic information, which at all times must be conducted in a sensitive and respectful way. Some of these include the following:

1. *Interviews with parents and family members:* Parents and the family are a first-hand source of information on language preferences including those spoken at home. Through both informal and formal conversations with parents and family members we can learn about the primary language used at home.

2. *Classroom observations of linguistic interactions:* Anecdotal notes from observations of the children's language use during classroom activities yield valuable information about linguistic preference and level of proficiency. Individual conversations with children also provide relevant information on their ability to use English.

3. *Questionnaires and surveys:* A variety of informal and formal tools can be used to determine linguistic needs of young English language learners. Many centers and schools use questionnaires to collect information on English language learners.

LITERACY CONNECTIONS...

USING A LITERACY-BASED RESPONSIVE CHILD-CENTERED CURRICULUM

Literacy provides a way to design a developmentally and culturally relevant curriculum. The children's books in this section are a sample of stories that can be used to integrate diversity into the curriculum. Titles in this section address children and adults with disabilities and developmental differences. Selections on other aspects of diversity are found in every chapter.

- Bodeen, S. (2003). *Babu's song.* New York: Lee & Low. (relative with disabilities)

- Davis, P. (2000). *Brian's bird.* Morton Grove, IL: Whitman. (visual disabilities)

- DeBear, K. (2001). *Be quiet, Marina!* New York: Starbright. (Down syndrome and cerebral palsy)

- Dwight, L. (2005). *We can do it!* Long Island, NY: Star Bright Books. (variety of disabilities)

- Glenn, S. (2003). *Keeping up with Roo.* New York: Putnam. (relatives with developmental delays)

- Heyman, A. (2003). *The bicycle dog.* New York: Dutton. (physical disabilities)

- Millman, I. (1998). *Moses goes to a concert.* New York: Frances Foster Books. (hearing disabilities)

- Munsch, R. (2003). *Zoom!* New York: Cartwheel/Scholastic. (physical disabilities)

- Plucker, S. (2005). *Me, Hayley!* Hollidaysburg, PA: Jason and Nordic Publishers. (Down syndrome)

- Schaefer, L. (2001). *Some kids use wheelchairs.* Mankato, MN: Pebble Books. (physical disabilities)

- Thompson, L. (2007). *Ballerina dreams.* New York: Feiwel and Friends. (physical disabilities, cerebral palsy)

- Tildes, P. (2006). *The garden wall.* Watertown, MA: Charlesbridge. (hearing disabilities)

School districts and state Prekindergarten programs collect language data through the Home language survey. This information appears in the child's record.

More details and suggestions about working with young English language learners can be found in Chapter 8.

Focusing Our Lenses on Children's Needs

As we continue the journey into teaching with a multicultural perspective, there are several steps to follow. In order to plan appropriate experiences, consider the following:

1. Emphasis on diversity:
   - Does my current program reflect the diversity of my students' community?
   - Do I teach in ways that reflect the lives of my students, and does my teaching help them affirm their identities?
   - Am I providing all children with skills to deal and interact with people who are different from themselves?

2. Attention to special needs:
   - Is my planning inclusive and mindful of the needs of children with disabilities?
   - Are experiences planned to accommodate their needs while providing meaningful activities?
   - Based on the children's needs, are learning resources and materials appropriate?

3. Attention to linguistic differences:
   - Does my planning take into consideration the linguistic needs of young English language learners (ELL)?
   - Are materials appropriate based on the characteristics and needs of ELL children?

These questions will help in establishing practices that promote respect and appreciation for diversity.

Evaluating Curricular Practices

Before making any changes it is essential to determine the nature of the existing curricular practices. There are a variety of curricular assessment tools found in the professional literature which can assist in this process. Since they are readily available, they are good sources of information for educators to use them as they are, or to reference them in planning their own instruments. Among those found in the literature, Baruth and Manning (1992, 2004) propose a seven-point questionnaire, which we have adapted for the early childhood setting.

1. *Evidence of multicultural perspectives:* Are multicultural perspectives already incorporated throughout the entire school, the classroom curriculum, and the classroom environment?

2. *Attitudes toward diversity:* Do my attitudes and those of the rest of the teachers, administrators, and staff members indicate a willingness to accept and respect cultural diversity?

3. *Instructional materials/resources:* Do classroom materials—manipulatives, books, and other resources—reflect cultural diversity aspects such as language, gender, and social class differences?

4. *Teaching strategies/activities:* Do curricular activities and methods provide children with opportunities to work and play together in a cooperative fashion?

5. *Schoolwide activities:* Do general school activities reflect cultural diversity?

6. *Parent/community views:* Do curricular planning efforts reflect the reality (views and opinions) of families and the community?

7. *Language diversity:* Do curricular efforts include bilingual perspectives or provide assistance for students with limited English-speaking skills (when teaching children who are bilingual or who are learning English as a second language)?

Another tool is a questionnaire based on five dimensions needed for the implementation of multicultural teaching (Banks, 1994). The five dimensions include content integration, knowledge construction, prejudice reduction, equitable pedagogy, and an empowering classroom culture and structure. Questions to help teachers develop a detailed profile of their practices address each dimension. An adaptation of the questionnaire for early childhood education is found in Figure 7-5.

Using Your Own Multicultural Assessment Instrument

Use of data-gathering instruments is common practice in most schools where checklists and surveys designed at the district level, by teachers, or by multicultural specialists are utilized. You may want to informally assess practices in the classroom by creating your own questionnaire or checklist. Multicultural assessment instruments should always be closely reviewed before they are used. Before selecting a tool, check the questions, the kind of information requested, and how this is asked. A sample checklist appears on Figure 7-6.

Identifying "Things That Happen" in the Classroom

Analyzing the classroom experiences is easier when you think of it as "all" that happens in the classroom. The topics and themes the children explore and the materials they use represent the real curriculum. How these topics are presented and developed depends on the particular instructional strategies and processes employed by the individual teacher. To further analyze this, you may want to ask yourself: "What do I teach

Figure 7-5
Identifying Classroom
Practices

A. Content Integration
1. What is my curricular content? What topics do I explore with children?
2. Is diversity reflected in my classroom topics? How?
3. Are there opportunities for children to ponder similarities/differences?
4. Are materials and resources reflective of the children's/nation's diversity?
5. Are topics on diversity consistently included? How often?

B. Knowledge Construction
1. Are experiences offered for children to examine and discover likenesses/differences?
2. Are experiences at the cognitive developmental level of the child?
3. Are the classroom arrangement and materials exposing children to diversity?
4. Are questions used to guide the child as he or she ponders reality rather than providing the answers?

C. Prejudice Reduction
1. Is the classroom (materials, books) free of cultural stereotypes?
2. When they occur, are misconceptions examined and clarified?
3. Is the teacher proactive and not "color-blind" when situations arise?
4. Are positive attitudes toward diversity modeled and encouraged?
5. Does the classroom atmosphere inspire respect and tolerance?

D. Equitable Pedagogy
1. Are all children treated equally?
2. Are all children offered a sense of success?
3. Do I show to every child that I believe in what he or she can do?
4. Do I adapt/change the curriculum for the child?
5. Do I show children that I respect and value their cultural identities?

E. An Empowering Classroom/School Culture
1. Are my children screened/assessed in a developmental fashion?
2. Is the child's cultural identity acknowledged when planning/teaching?
3. Is my teaching mindful of the community's identity?
4. Is the classroom constantly acknowledging the children's identities?

Source: Robles de Meléndez, 2004.

and how do I teach it?" As you answer this question, three main aspects will emerge: *the content, the process,* and *the resources.* An honest answer to each of the following questions will help you identify the nature of the classroom experiences. In particular, consider how diversity is integrated in the classroom topics. The following questions can assist in analyzing the learning experiences:

- *The Content*: What are the themes or topics that children explore in this classroom? What are they learning? Is the content engaging and meaningful for every child? A way to keep track of this analysis is to jot down the diversity topics that are addressed. As you identify the topics, find out if the children's prior knowledge and experiences were taken into consideration. This contributes to making the content meaningful and, thus, promoting engagement. Also, write the dates when diversity related topics and experiences happen. This will help determine whether

Figure 7-6   Diversity Antibias Checklist

Goals: Program and Teacher

Do the program and the teacher	Yes	No
1. Foster multiculturalism, self-worth, a sense of dignity and unity, and understand that to be different is not to be inferior?		
2. Accept the uniqueness of each child and his or her cultural background and recognize that each has something valuable to contribute?		
3. Use the child's experiences to teach other children?		
4. Develop and encourage the teacher–learner model, where the teacher and the child learn from each other?		
5. Combine the teaching of skill with the teaching of multiculturalism and recognize that they do not need to be taught separately?		
6. Understand that all children bring with them valuable bases from which learning can occur, and understand the children's backgrounds to enhance the teacher–learner model?		
7. Develop an atmosphere in the classroom that encourages cooperation, unity, and the sharing of individual experiences?		
8. Present the children with objective materials about different cultures, instead of only those materials that have been prepared through the viewpoint of the dominant group? (They should include books, posters, and similar elements.)		
9. Help the teacher become aware of his or her own prejudices and biases?		
10. Understand that learning abilities, cognitive styles, and expectations vary among cultures and that these may have a significant impact on the teaching methods and curriculum plan?		

Goals: Children

Are children encouraged to	Yes	No
1. Become aware of their own uniqueness? (This may include body features, language, culture, and background.)		
2. Become familiar with their own historical roots as well as those of the group and the community?		
3. Accept the differences of others and realize that being different does not mean that someone is inferior?		
4. Promote equality between and respect for other cultures and arrest prejudices that breed ignorance?		
5. Encourage freedom of speech and a willingness to share without intimidation, both in their own and other cultural groups?		
6. Develop a sense of responsibility and belonging to the group and understand that unity is possible within a diverse group?		

Source: Elliot, 2002.

Wadsworth/Cengage Learning

Observations of daily activities and interactions provide rich information about the child's strengths and needs.

these instructional events only happen when observing holidays.

- *The Process:* How and what activities will help children learn about a theme? What things should they do? Are the activities mindful of the children's diverse learning styles, language differences, or special needs? Try to remember how all the children responded to the experiences. Be sure to find out if, at the end of each experience, all the children came away knowing that they were successful in their own way. This will help you know if the outcomes that you established are met.

- *Resources and Materials:* What do we use to support children's learning? Identifying the classroom materials and resources is a way of judging whether children are provided with things that either reflect their own background or that of others, or whether the materials are inappropriate or missing from the classroom. When listing your resources, recall how many times you have invited people of various cultures from the community to participate and share their experiences and knowledge in your class. Ask yourself if those times included only holidays or if they only happened during the "multicultural month." Best practices tell us that for teachers to establish a bias-free environment, children need to have their parents and other community members regularly involved in the classroom, not just on special occasions (Derman-Sparks & A.B.C. Task Force, 1989; Epstein et al., 2002).

The Classroom Environment: What the Child Sees

The classroom environment is another area to examine before making the change to multicultural teaching. Learning is not limited to what the teacher presents or says to the children. It also includes messages sent by the classroom environment. Therefore, it is necessary to detect the kinds of messages sent to the children through such media as pictures, manipulatives, and literature. Derman-Sparks (1989) believes that the environment is a powerful knowledge-building instrument. She recommends that teachers carefully analyze the environment as a first step toward change. She states: "What is in the environment also alerts children to what the teacher considers important or not important. Children are as vulnerable to omissions as they are to inaccuracies and

Wadsworth/Cengage Learning

The classroom environment is an active learning resource. What would you add to this classroom to acknowledge and validate the children's diverse cultures?

stereotypes: What isn't [seen] can be as powerful a contributor to attitudes as what is seen."

Your analysis should begin with what you have on the walls. After all, whatever you have hanging on the walls contributes to create the atmosphere in your classroom. Take time to list the kinds of pictures and decorations in your classroom that reflect diversity. This means finding out, for example, whether the pictures reflect a balance of ethnic backgrounds and include the cultures of your children. Determine whether pictures show activities commonly engaged in by your children's parents. You also need to see whether the manipulatives and other play materials, such as dolls, reflect diversity. Check the literacy area to see whether the books address a variety of multicultural themes and languages. A detailed listing of environmental elements to check appears in Figure 7-7.

Using the Findings to Plan Curricular Experiences

A thoughtful analysis of the data collected through the assessment of the children, community, and school environment is critical to the reform process entailed in multicultural education. The data will form the framework for future actions, assist in bringing reality into the classroom, and help determine and explain decisions and actions. More specifically, this information will help establish the appropriate instructional content and processes for children taking part in the multicultural program.

WHAT IS CURRICULUM CONTENT IN EARLY CHILDHOOD EDUCATION?

A curriculum framework is a dynamic system that should guide all aspects of a high quality program.

Division of Early Childhood (2007)

Teaching children with a multicultural perspective happens when educators use what they know about the children's learning, developmental needs, and diversity characteristics into their teaching and planning. What children should learn and what the curriculum content should be is a continuous process.

Figure 7-7 Assessing Diversity in the Early Childhood Classroom

Diversity Elements	Visuals (Pictures, Posters)	Literacy and Print Materials	Dramatic Area	Music	Art Materials	Classroom Arrangement	Manipulatives and Sensorial Materials
Language • Materials are available in English and in other languages • Library includes books and other print materials in languages other than English • Children use and are encouraged to use their first languages • Signs and labels are in languages spoken by children • There is singing in other languages							
Culture and ethnic groups • Materials include representation of a variety of ethnic and racial groups • Decorations and materials on display represent different cultural groups • Ethnic and culturally typical clothing is available in the dramatic area							

(continued)

Figure 7-7 (continued)

Diversity Elements	Visuals (Pictures, Posters)	Literacy and Print Materials	Dramatic Area	Music	Art Materials	Classroom Arrangement	Manipulatives and Sensorial Materials
• Materials (dolls, toys) include a variety of racial and ethnic groups • Artifacts from a variety of ethnic and cultural groups are integrated into play areas and available for children to manipulate • Listening environment includes selections representative of different cultural groups (music, rhymes)							
Exceptionalities and disabilities • Modifications are made to accommodate children with special needs (arrangement, equipment) • Materials include representation of children with disabilities							
Gender • Posters and visuals include nonstereotyped gender roles • Children's books include stories about people in nonstereotyped roles							

Faith • Visuals and images include people from all faith groups • Children's books include children and families from all faith groups		
Age • Pictures and visuals present positive images of people across age groups • Visuals include images of positive intergenerational familiar situations • Children's books include stories about successful and positive experiences of people across age groups, including children and elderly		
Social class • Images include a variety of social class groups • Visuals portray all social groups in positive and successful roles		

Reflecting on your findings and observations:

• *What messages about culture and diversity does the classroom convey?*
• *What will you change in the classroom as a result of the survey? Why?*

Curriculum content, according to general curriculum theory, is the body of knowledge that is taught in a specific grade level or developmental level. It becomes *what* is selected for children to learn. The content is considered appropriate whenever the concerns and the needs of the students and of society are addressed in ways that will provide opportunities for students to grow cognitively, psychologically, and socially (Bredekamp, 1987; Ornstein & Hunkins, 2004). Meaningful content acknowledges and incorporates the children's prior and current cultural knowledge and skills. Also, it is inclusive of the children's community and family experiences.

Factors to Consider When Choosing a Curriculum

Early childhood curriculum blends development with learning while focusing on the whole child; that is, "[t]he child is at the heart of the curriculum. All children are competent and their learning must be rooted in experiences appropriate to their developmental levels and cultures" (ACEI & OMEP, 2000). This position ensures that the physical, emotional, linguistic, cognitive, and social needs of young children are met. The curriculum provides opportunities to master knowledge and skills that are connected to valuable and real-world experiences. It is also important to allow young children to acquire positive values of both their cultural group and of the mainstream society to meet the expectations of families and communities.

Some schools may choose to adopt commercially produced learning materials. At times, these materials tend to be culturally inaccurate as well as developmentally inappropriate for young children. One way to avoid this is by applying guidelines or instruments specifically designed for curriculum selection. Our version was presented previously in Figure 7-6. Professional organizations such as OMEP, ACEI, and NAEYC are valuable resources for additional information regarding selection of curriculum content.

THINK AND REFLECT...

KNOWLEDGE ABOUT THE CONTENT AS A BASIS FOR APPROPRIATE PLANNING

Darling-Hammond (2004) states that what teachers know and do make the most difference in what children learn. Although early childhood education follows integrated curricular practices, sound knowledge of the content and teaching strategies provides direction and guides teachers in designing appropriate learning experiences.

As you reflect on these thoughts, consider the following questions:

• In what content areas are you the most knowledgeable?

• In what areas do you need to improve?

• What resources are available for you to further your knowledge?

FOCUS

ON CLASSROOM PRACTICES

SELECTION OF MULTICULTURAL CONTENT

Selecting child-appropriate concepts for your **multicultural curriculum** is not a simple task. It requires choosing what is meaningful for the child and what is valuable for building knowledge about a culture. Banks (1994) recommends choosing high-level key concepts that are interdisciplinary and organized around five main areas. Considering the developmental characteristics of young children, we adapted Banks's list, selecting those most appropriate. We also added some that seemed pertinent in a young child's classroom. The result is a master list of concepts teachers can use as a tool for content selection.

Key Multicultural Concepts

I. Main Concept: *Culture, ethnicity, identity*
- cultures of children in the classroom
- cultural beliefs
- cultural symbols
- cultural celebrations in the community
- ethnic groups in the United States/in my community
- characteristics of cultural diversity
- cultural groups in the classroom and community
- family and cultural identity
- children's languages

II. Main Concept: *Socialization and interaction*
- child-rearing patterns
- family patterns
- family values
- social interaction patterns
- racism
- prejudice and discrimination

III. Main Concept: *Intercultural communication and perception*
- languages in the community
- communication patterns
- nonverbal communication
- world/life view (how they see and interpret events)
- oral traditions
- literature and folklore (literary and musical)

IV. Main Concept: *Power and status*
- social classes
- poverty
- homelessness and children
- people with disabilities
- status of women, men, elders, and children

V. Main Concept: *The movement of ethnic groups*
- immigration
- purposes of migration and immigration
- immigrants in the community

Source: Adapted from Banks, 2008.

THINK AND REFLECT...

PLANNING WITH A DEVELOPMENTAL AND CULTURAL FOCUS

According to DAP guidelines, curriculum for children emerges from the blend of the children's needs, the teacher's knowledge, and the expectations of families and communities (Bredekamp & Copple, 2009).

Considering this statement, visit an early childhood classroom and interview teachers about what they consider the most important element of planning appropriate and relevant curricular experiences. Write a commentary of your findings.

FOCUS

ON CLASSROOM PRACTICES

PERSPECTIVES ABOUT ETHNICITY IN THE EARLY CHILDHOOD CURRICULUM

Educator James Banks shares some concerns about what the multicultural curriculum often presents. His remarks are particularly important for teachers who strive to create a responsive curriculum. According to Banks (2003), when planning multiethnic experiences, some educators assume that an ethnic group is monolithic and homogeneous or characterized by a single set of traits.

Nothing is further from reality than the presumption that all people from a cultural group possess identical qualities and views. Just as children from the same family have different characteristics, so do members of cultural groups.

Banks adds that another problem is that educators tend to believe that self-esteem and the academic achievement of youth from other cultures will be enhanced by teaching mostly about heroic characters and achievements of individuals of their cultural background, while demonstrating how their ethnic group has been victimized by the mainstream culture (Banks, 2003, 2008). The implications are clear. When the curriculum is built solely on the cultural past and a one-way description of a culture, despite the positive intentions of teachers, it will lack responsiveness and appropriateness.

Both of Banks's observations have relevance for the early childhood classroom educator. Designing curriculum while presuming that all members of a group have similar needs and reactions would result in a curriculum that risks not just finding stereotypical information about these groups but encouraging it, too. To avoid falling into this kind of curricular trap, answer and reflect on your responses to these questions:

- *Have I used more than one source to get information about the target cultural groups?*

- *Have I also considered and examined materials written by members of the cultures I am targeting?*

- *Have I included materials and activities based on assumptions or on what I believe about other cultures?*

- *Does the content offer a balanced view of the past and present realities of the target cultures?*

Towards Multicultural Teaching: Where You Are and Where You Want to Be

Today's social and diverse demographic nature of communities across the nation establishes the need for teaching with a multicultural focus. According to a statement presented jointly by the NAEYC and the NAECS/SDE (2003), multiculturalism should be embedded in every program for young children. More specifically, it states the following:

> The curriculum embraces the reality of multiculturalism in American society by providing a balance between learning the common core of dominant culture knowledge (for example, English language, democratic values) and knowledge of minority cultures. Curriculum accommodates children who have limited English proficiency. All cultures and primary languages of children are respectfully reflected in the curriculum.

Clearly, if schools remain mainstream-oriented and unresponsive to the pluralistic context of society, education will fail to provide the experiences that children and society require. Early childhood educators are urged to break away from school practices that perpetuate inequities and instead use their power to build nurturing classrooms where children will come to appreciate and value social diversity. The successful development and education of a child is a responsibility of all—families, teachers, caregivers, and communities. This reinforces the need to provide experiences at an early age to foment in children an appreciation and value for diversity, encouraging them to practice tolerance by recognizing differences and similarities among people. One of the most important lessons to be learned in that regard involves resisting biases. Parents and teachers need to join forces in shaping accepting attitudes and eliminating prejudice formation in young children. Position statements and materials from professional organizations (such as the NAEYC, ACEI, Southern Early Childhood Association, and Southern Poverty Law Center) about resisting biases and fostering a healthy self-esteem are sources of ideas and activities for effective curricular practices both in the classroom and beyond it.

Curriculum Process in Early Childhood Education

The curriculum process includes the methods and procedures teachers follow to deliver their content (Ornstein & Hunkins, 2004). The process entails the strategies, techniques, and overall methods used in the classroom to convey specific content and skills. The processes the teacher selects will influence the child as a learner. "The curriculum comes from the child" is a statement that reflects the nature of planning and curricular design in early childhood education. This is based on the premise that the best way to teach a child is always centered on what the child needs. To facilitate this process, special guidelines have been created to help practitioners

AROUND THE WORLD

CURRICULUM WITH A DIVERSITY FOCUS

Efforts of early childhood educators have led to the inclusion of diverse curricular experiences in many countries. Here are two examples of early childhood curricular programs where the children and families' culture serve as a framework for the learning experiences and instructional approaches.

- New Zealand

  Te Whariki is the name of the national bicultural education curriculum that encourages the transmission of New Zealand's diverse cultural values, languages, and customs. A framework for organizing early childhood experiences, it validates cultural belief systems with emphasis on respect and tolerance. Te Whariki is about providing a base that teaches one to respect oneself and ultimately others. Taught in Maori and English the program contains multicultural experiences of the indigenous people of New Zealand as well as its mainstream culture of English heritage. The bilingual curriculum also recognizes the language diversity of children and families and supports experiences that promote its preservation and learning.

- Peru

  Early experiences for infants and toddlers in Andahuaylas in Andean Peru, take place in the *Wawa Wasi* or house of children in Quechua, one of the languages spoken in Peru. These community-based programs are structured around the local culture and provide services to children 6-48 months old while their mothers are working. For families, the wawa wasi is a trusted place where their children receive attention following home-like practices. It is also a place where caregivers communicate and engage children in activities using their home language. "Using" with: With its culturally-based practices, the program has been successfully used throughout Peru.

Source: Brooker, L. and Woodhead, M. (2010). Culture and learning. Early childhood in focus 6. UK: Open University (With the support of the Bernard Van Leer Foundation). Ministry of Education. (1996). Te whariki, Early Childhood curriculum. Wellington, New Zealand: Author.

select appropriate teaching approaches and strategies. Among those particularly helpful are Bredekamp and Copple's (2009) guidelines for appropriate curricular practices. Grounded in the DAP concept, which introduced culture as an element for achieving equality, the guidelines provide clear directions regarding the nature of early childhood curricular activities and classroom experiences. More importantly, they uphold the need to follow the children's developmental needs, both universal and individual, to build a sound and fitting curriculum. At all times, good curricular practices should be guided by knowledge of the children's developmental and cultural strengths, needs, and individual characteristics.

Specific directions for designing curricular experiences are also found in the guidelines from the NAEYC and the NAECS/SDE (2003). They particularly define the need to ". . . implement curriculum that is thoughtfully planned, challenging, engaging, developmentally appropriate, culturally and linguistically responsive, comprehensive, and likely to promote positive outcomes for *all* young children" (emphasis added).

STANDARDS FOR TEACHING IN DIVERSE CLASSROOMS

Standards provide relevant direction to design appropriate curricular experiences in the multicultural classroom. Today many states have academic standards for early learning (NECTAC, 2009). Typically organized in five developmental dimensions—physical, social, emotional, cognitive, language, and literacy—they provide direction in designing the curriculum. They are another element that contributes to achieving quality in experiences for the young child. Early learning standards outline the age-level expectations on the concepts and skills that young children should master. In the curriculum, standards are also useful in identifying the children's expected learning outcomes. Valuable and relevant experiences in the multicultural classroom should be grounded and aligned to early learning academic standards. They are another way to ensure that children experience challenging and meaningful activities.

Standards for Culturally Responsive Pedagogical Practices

An important resource for early childhood educators is the document stating curricular standards for successful practice in classrooms serving children who are culturally and linguistically diverse, published by the Center for Research on Education, Diversity, and Excellence (CREDE). Funded by the Office of Educational Research and Improvement of the U.S. Department of Education, CREDE proposes five standards as a framework for teaching practices in programs serving children with diverse characteristics. Following the definition of pedagogy as an interactive experience between children and teachers and framed in the tenets of developmental and sociocultural theory, the CREDE standards identify specific pedagogical practices "proven successful with majority and minority at-risk students in a variety of teaching and learning settings over several decades" (Dalton, 1998). The five standards are described in Figure 7-8. In essence, the standards remind professionals working with

Figure 7-8 Five Standards for Effective Pedagogy (CREDE)

Standard I. Joint Productive Activity: Teacher and Students Producing Together
Facilitate learning through joint productive activity among teacher and students.

Standard II. Developing Language and Literacy across the Curriculum
Develop competence in the language and literacy of instruction across the curriculum.

Standard III. Making Meaning: Connecting School to Students' Lives
Connect teaching and curriculum with experiences and skills of students' home and community.

Standard IV. Teaching Complex Thinking
Challenge students toward cognitive complexity.

Standard V. Teaching Through Conversation
Engage students through dialogue, especially the instructional conversation.

Source: Dalton, 1998.

young children about the need to focus experiences on the strengths and knowledge of and about the individual child. Echoing the tenets of developmentally based practice, the standards also underline how important it is to meaningfully connect experiences with the child's prior knowledge.

Challenging Curriculum: Integrating Academic standards

Appropriate experiences for young children in diverse classrooms are also characterized by their relevancy. They are not only based on content that is relevant but also on ideas that contribute to concept formation. It is essential to choose content that is culturally and individually meaningful to the child but also that is worth learning. Time spent in selecting topics should be guided by the premise of how these will promote learning for children. While considerations of the child's needs may require specific accommodations (such as those needed for children with special needs) or modifications (as in the case of English-language learners) to facilitate understanding, it is important to remember that developmentally based experiences are based on what the child is able and capable of doing. CREDE's pedagogical standards remind educators that sound curriculum for culturally diverse children challenge them by presenting content that is valuable and that respects their ability to learn (CREDE, 2009).

MAKING DECISIONS FOR MULTICULTURAL TEACHING

Deciding on the best way to develop your multicultural program is not a simple task. Models, standards, and approaches provide guidance in determining how to organize and create learning experiences. Although all early childhood approaches are valid sources to develop and implement a multicultural program, some strategies are better for creating a focus on diversity. Some approaches that are considered especially appropriate are listed in this chapter (see "Focus on Classroom Practices: Recommended Curricular Approaches for Multicultural Teaching"). Making decisions happen when you:

- take time to consider the diverse needs of children and their families in your community;
- talk with experienced teachers;

IN ACTION . . .

CLASSROOM MESSAGES

Consider what messages your classroom environment conveys. With the eyes of a child, look and find ideas conveyed through your classroom environment. After your survey is over, write down what things made you feel "uncomfortable" and what made you "welcome," the way a child might.

- visit and observe classrooms where multicultural teaching takes place;
- engage in conversations with families of young children;
- read about curriculum for young children; and most importantly,
- reflect on what you read and learned through talking and observing what others do.

Infusing Diversity in the Content

Common questions asked by teachers are "How can I change what I teach?" or "How can I prepare a new content?" Behind their questions there is sometimes a reluctance and a realization that the task may be difficult. The teachers using prescribed or mandated curricula are often even more hesitant about the transition to multicultural teaching. Preparing and organizing new curriculum content is not only a difficult activity, but it also requires time and experience. We, therefore, recommend content infusion as a method to facilitate that process.

The multicultural content infusion is a strategy used to incorporate the perspective of a pluralistic society into the existing curriculum. It allows the teachers to continue using the existing curricula and, at the same time, incorporate new material. This also gives the teachers more confidence in the transformation process. In the approach recommended by James Banks (1992, 2005), the contributions and the additive levels represent examples of content infusion.

FOCUS
ON CLASSROOM PRACTICES

RECOMMENDED CURRICULAR APPROACHES FOR MULTICULTURAL TEACHING

Although multicultural experiences can be integrated into any teaching approach, some are particularly appropriate when working with young children. Remember that a DCAP orientation must prevail.

- *Antibias approach:* Developed by Louise Derman-Sparks and the A.B.C. Task Force (1989; 2010) at Pacific Oaks, this approach proposes strategies to organize experiences and classroom interactions to prevent the formation of bias. Experiences are designed to foster tolerance and fairness and to build a community in which all forms of diversity are acknowledged and valued as unique.

- *Thematic teaching:* This approach builds curricular experiences based on themes that appeal and are meaningful to young children. This approach provides for integration of multicultural content through theme selection. Themes emerge from those chosen together with children and by the teacher.

- *Cooperative learning:* This strategy and instructional approach allows children to work together on projects and explore challenging themes. The small-group format of this approach allows teachers to integrate children with linguistically and culturally diverse characteristics with mainstream children. Assigning and rotating children's roles provides minority and exceptional children with opportunities to assume responsibility and leadership within their group.

Teachers can infuse the curriculum by introducing appropriate views and ideas about diversity into the context of the curriculum. To accomplish that successfully, it is important to have a thorough knowledge of the embedded scope in diversity concepts.

Infusing diversity aspects in the curriculum begins with a careful analysis. This will reveal *how* the topics allow for the inclusion of diversity perspectives. The process will also show *where* and *what type* of multicultural views and ideas need to be included. Here are some steps that may help you in the analyzing the curriculum content:

1. Begin by reviewing your lesson plans and find the topics, or themes, you teach. List them. If you use a prescribed curriculum, check your guide and list all the topics/themes/units that you teach.

2. Review the profile of your students and look for the traits that are descriptive of cultural diversity (ethnicities, religion, languages, social class, exceptionalities).

3. From the list of topics/themes/units, circle or highlight those that you find lend themselves best to infusion of diversity. Begin first by considering how to incorporate those characteristics that are found in your classroom, and then consider those of others.

4. Next, brainstorm how you could incorporate diversity into the selected topics. Begin by asking yourself: What other views could help children expand their understanding of this topic? Write down all the ideas you think are plausible.

5. Gather all the ideas and rewrite your list of themes or units, including the additional diverse perspectives. The only way to know if your approach will work is to try it with your students. So, the next step is implementing your ideas!

6. Keep notes during the lessons on the children's reactions. This will help you assess the success of your venture and offer constructive information on aspects that may need revisions.

Avoiding Infusion of Trivial and Stereotypical Content

So many times, we find children involved in experiences that, while apparently fun, do little to expand their level of knowledge about human diversity. This commonly occurs when content without relevance is infused into the curriculum. The result is called *trivializing*.

The rule for avoiding trivializing is to first identify how a selected topic is consistent with the curriculum. Second, it is necessary to determine whether what is incorporated bears any valuable learning, particularly whether it will contribute to the understanding of life in our diverse society. To prevent choosing unimportant topics for infusion, ask yourself:

- *Is the topic presenting, elaborating, and/or expanding concepts on diversity that are commonly and currently found among the target groups?*
- *Does the topic fit logically into the child's learning/experiencing? Does it give a sense of real learning versus the unimportant?*
- *Can the topic be made to include the perspectives of how the people with diverse cultural views would behave or react to it?*

Is the topic reflective of issues that commonly happen to children in this classroom or to people in the community?

Does the topic offer an opportunity to present other positions that expose the children to divergent views or allow the children to respond to it?

Can the topic serve as a link to discuss emotions and feelings as perceived through the eyes of the children?

Can the topic facilitate clarification of stereotypes and biases? How?

WHAT IF MY CLASSROOM IS "MONOCULTURAL"?

Many times our students have asked us about how to infuse multicultural education in their classroom when these are mostly characterized by one main ethnic group. We always remind them that multicultural education encompasses all children and that no classroom is ever monocultural. The notion that diversity content is solely for children with a variety of diversity traits must be dispelled. The continuously diverse nature of society, whether local, national,

LITERACY CONNECTIONS . . .

PLANNING FOR DIVERSE CHILDREN

We chose the following children's books as an example of the different needs that children may bring to the multicultural classroom. With any of the titles that you read, think about how you would address their different needs. Think also about children that you already know and about how to best meet their expectations.

- Beaumont, K. (2002). *Being friends*. New York: Dial Books. (preschoolers—friendship among children with diverse characteristics)
- Cowen—Fletcher, J. (1993). *Mama zooms*. New York: Scholastic. (preschoolers—primary—parent with disabilities)
- Crowther, K. (2000). *Jack and Jim*. New York: Hyperion. (preschoolers—diversity and friendship)
- Girnis, M. (2000). *ABC for You and me*. Illinois: Albert Whitman & Company. (preschoolers—primary—ABC's using children with Down syndrome)
- Hudson, C. (1990). *Bright eyes, brown skin*. Just Us. (preschoolers—racial pride)

- Levine, E. (1995). *I hate English!* New York: Scholastic. (primary—experiences and feelings learning a new language and adapting to a new culture)
- Pak, S. (2002). *A place to grow*. New York: Levine Books. (preschoolers—primary—experiences about moving)
- Southwell, J. (2001). *Little country town*. New York: Holt & Co. (preschoolers—primary—culture and life in rural areas)
- Ransom, J. F. (2001). *I don't want to talk about it*. New York: Magination Press. (preschoolers—primary—children of divorced families)
- Thomas, P. (1999). *My family is changing*, Canada: Barron's Education Series. (preschoolers—primary—children of divorced families)
- Williams, V. (2001). *A chair for my mother*. New York: HarperTrophy. (preschoolers—family situations and caring for a parent with disabilities)

or global, serves as the best justification to bring multicultural education into action. In fact, even within the same ethnic group, diversity is still found. One of the relevant aspects of multicultural education is that it applies to all children. In fact, it is a way to offer students a sense about their own unique diverse characteristics while gaining a much wider view of diversity. So as to plan experiences that are meaningful to children, consider first their ethnic groups and cultures (Derman-Sparks, 1989). Then, think about other groups of children, whether in the community or not, that they should learn about. We emphasize this point because this is where most multicultural planning fails. Effective multicultural curricular planning requires early educators to consider not only the groups children represent, but also others not present in the classroom and in the community that they may be exposed to through other types of experiences. There are reasons to support this decision. First, with the high population mobility in our country, children have the potential of being exposed to many forms of cultural diversity. Second, the media (TV, movies, and so on) is a powerful source of cultural interaction for children, where the absence or token presence of many ethnic groups provides an unclear and sometimes distorted image about social diversity. Many times, exposure through other sources may lead to the formation of misleading ideas about people with diverse characteristics. For this reason, it is essential to provide activities in the classroom that lead children toward recognizing diversity as one of society's characteristics.

Learning opportunities that expand the children's scope of understanding about others should be integral to classroom planning. True "monocultural" classrooms are very unlikely to exist in our present society when we consider the comprehensiveness of diversity (Derman-Sparks and Ramsey, 2005). Remember that diversity includes not only ethnic differences, but also a wide range of other factors such as religion, social class, and physical disabilities that influence and determine people's behaviors and views about life. So, if your classroom happens to be characterized mostly by a single culture or diversity element, make sure to incorporate into the curriculum experiences about other groups the children would most likely interact with. Exposure to other ways and behaviors, abilities, or differences will help children in forming a more practical view about society. For instance, use of purposefully selected children's literature is an appropriate tool to introduce youth to people with disabilities or to activities from other groups. Suggested multicultural children's literature appears throughout this book in the *Literacy Connections* boxes. *Persona dolls* are another way to introduce children to other diversity aspects. Here, a doll character helps children in learning about the experiences of individuals with other social and cultural realities. What other cultural groups or aspects that might be included in the curriculum depend on the developmental level of your students as well as on their interests, needs of the school, and events in the community?

Building Experiences That Promote Respect and Appreciation for Diversity

One of the essential goals of curricular experiences in multicultural classrooms is to build a sense of appreciation for the diverse characteristics of people. This ongoing task begins in the early years. Supporting this aspiration calls for collaboration between the

AROUND THE WORLD

GLOBAL GUIDELINES FOR EARLY CHILDHOOD PROGRAMS

Developmentally appropriate and quality based experiences are essential for every child. There have always been concerns about the opportunities and nature of programs for children, not just in the United States but also in countries around the world. Given the numerous program guideposts and principles, the need for a common way to define quality expectations and characteristics of programs for children in the global community is evident. It was in response to this concern for the world's children that the Association for Childhood Education International (ACEI), along with OMEP, convened in the summer of 1999 an international symposium attended by representatives from childhood organizations. Delegates from various countries (including one of the authors of this book) gathered in Switzerland to find a way to ensure that programs for young children would adhere to similar expectations. The *Global Guidelines for Early Childhood Education and Care in the 21st Century* was the product of the intensive work of the group. The *Global Guidelines* identifies the essential principles defining appropriate children's program practices within a global context. Its core is built around five key philosophical points:

1. Children are both the present and the future of every nation, and they have needs, rights, and intrinsic worth that must be recognized and supported.

2. Every child should have the opportunity to grow up in a setting that values children, that provides conditions for a safe and secure environment, and that respects diversity.

3. Knowledge about human development is more substantial now than at any time in history. The new century offers opportunities to consolidate recent gains and respond to new challenges that lie ahead.

4. Children must receive appropriate nurturing and education within and outside their families from birth onward if they are to develop optimally.

5. Attention to the health, nutrition, education, and psychosocial development of children during their early years is essential for the future well-being of nations and the global community (ACEI, 1999).

Since its development, the *Global Guidelines* have been followed, adopted, and influenced the directions for early childhood programs in many countries. An assessment tool was later developed by ACEI in an effort to provide an instrument to assess the implementation of the Guidelines. The tool is available in nine languages other than English and has been used by programs in more than 35 different countries.

Source: ACEI. (2011). Global Guidelines for Early Childhood Education and Care in the 21st Century. Retrieved http://acei.org/education/guidelines/

classroom and the home. The following are things that teachers and parents can do to teach children how to resist biases.

- Counteract biases by voicing our opposition to them.
- Give children messages that deliberately contrast stereotypes.
- Show no bias in friends, doctors, teachers, or other service providers.
- Instill the notion that a person's appearance is never a true mark of his or her character.
- Talk positively about each person's physical characteristics and cultural heritage.

- Provide opportunities for children to interact with others who are culturally, racially, and religiously different from themselves and who have different abilities.
- Listen respectfully and answer all children's questions about themselves and others.
- Teach children how to handle biases about who they are.
- Use accurate and fair images instead of stereotypes and encourage children to talk about the differences and similarities.
- Teach children that unjust things can be changed. (Adapted from the NAEYC statement titled *Teaching Young Children to Resist Bias,* 1997.)

PUTTING THINGS TOGETHER

Identifying the children's diverse strengths and needs and analyzing curricular practices are essential tasks as you move into teaching with a multicultural focus. This information can be collected in a variety of formats. Because the findings will be for your own use, you should use the methods of collecting information you find most convenient and appropriate. What is important is to assess the program honestly and thoroughly so that the results of the inquiry present an accurate picture. This information is also the foundation for well-informed planning. Meaningful topics and experiences based on the children's developmental and cultural needs are essential to promoting effective learning in the multicultural classroom. Figure 7-9 identifies key aspects to consider when planning with a child-oriented focus.

Figure 7-9 Action Map

WHAT WE HAVE LEARNED—CHAPTER SUMMARY

This chapter addressed curriculum planning, a complex process that requires knowledge, planning, organization, and commitment on the part of every early childhood educator. Assessing the needs of the young children is an important starting point in the curriculum-planning process. Assessment also encompasses the classroom, family environment, and the composition of the community. Many early childhood organizations provide checklists, frameworks, and other tools for various needs assessments. Early childhood educators can also use these instruments and guidelines to develop their own surveys and checklists. Planning grounded in the data obtained through needs assessments establishes the framework for selection of the curriculum content and learning experiences implemented in the classroom. The most important element of an appropriate curriculum is its responsiveness to the needs of the diverse children it serves. This includes children with special needs who require unique accommodations in the classroom.

MAKING CONNECTIONS . . .

1. Examine a sample early childhood curriculum for a particular age group, such as preschool through third grade. Identify whether it reflects integration of diversity topics. See if the topics are integrated throughout the content or if they appear only when a special event or holiday is observed. Create a chart that provides a short analysis of your findings.

2. Visit three early childhood settings and assess the environment using the guidelines presented in Figure 7-8 in this chapter. Determine the areas that most frequently appear in need of change. Provide a summary of your findings.

3. Interview an early childhood educator and find out what steps are followed in planning experiences that address the children's individual needs. Reflect on the findings and provide your comments.

RECOMMENDED INTERNET RESOURCES

- "Promoting Positive Outcomes for Children with Disabilities," from the Division for Early Childhood of the Council for Exceptional Children
  www.dec-sped.org/pdf/positionpapers/Prmtg_Pos_Outcomes_Companion_Paper.pdf

- Rethinking Schools
  www.rethinkingschools.org/

- UNESCO Declaration *Education for All*
  http://www.unesco.org/education/efa/ed_for_all/background/jomtien_declaration.shtml

- Early learning standards for advocacy with agencies on behalf of young children.
  http://www.nectac.org/topics/quality/earlylearn.asp

YOUR STANDARDS PORTFOLIO

naeyc **Standard 1:** Promoting Child Development and Learning

naeyc **Standard 5:** Using Content Knowledge to Build Meaningful Curriculum

InTASC Standard 6: Assessment

InTASC Standard 7: Planning for Instruction

Planning is essential to high-quality learning. Getting ready to create a multicultural program calls for effective planning. Good planning requires teachers to use knowledge not only about the content but also about children, families, and the community's cultural and diverse characteristics. Having the child as the focus for what is planned is crucial for developing culturally responsive experiences. Complete the following activities to help you acquire experience in applying child-based planning skills to multicultural classroom teaching.

- The classroom environment is considered a pedagogical tool. To include appropriate elements in your classroom, create a web about the ethnic and social characteristics of the community. Based on the traits that you identified, articulate your vision about the elements that you would include in the design of a culturally responsive environment.

- Planning for each child requires knowledge about his or her strengths and needs. Using the DAP concept, describe the kind of developmental information you need to plan responsive experiences for young children.

- Visit an inclusion classroom and interview the teacher. Inquire about the Individualized Education Plan (IEP) and how it is used in the planning process.

- Obtain a copy of your state's academic standards and identify the sections addressing ways to meet the needs of culturally diverse children. Reflect on your findings and comment on how the analysis assists in planning responsive experiences.

REFERENCES

ACEI & OMEP. (2000). Partnership with families and communities. *Global guidelines for early childhood education and care in the 21st century.* Washington, DC: Author.

Banks, J. (2008). *Teaching strategies for ethnic studies* (8th ed.). Boston: Allyn & Bacon.

Banks, J. (1994). Transforming the mainstream curriculum. *Educational Leadership, 8,* 4–8.

Banks, J. (2003). *Teaching strategies for ethnic studies* (7th ed.). Boston: Allyn & Bacon.

Baruth, L. G., & Manning, M. L. (1992). *Multicultural education of children and adolescents.* Boston: Allyn & Bacon.

Baruth, L. G., & Manning, M. L. (2008). *Multicultural education of children and adolescents* (5th ed.). Needham Heights, MA: Allyn & Bacon.

Bredekamp, S. (Ed.). (1987). *Developmentally appropriate practice in early childhood programs serving children from birth through age 8.* Washington, DC: National Association for the Education of Young Children.

Bredekamp, S., & Copple, C. (2009). *Developmentally appropriate practice for programs serving young children from birth through age 8* (3rd ed.). Washington, DC: NAEYC.

Bredekamp, S., & Rosegrant, T. (Eds.). (2001). *Reaching potentials: Appropriate curriculum and assessment for young children, 1.* Washington, DC: National Association for the Education of Young Children.

Dalton, S. (1998). *Pedagogy matters: Standards for effective practice.* Washington, DC: Center for Research on Education, Diversity, and Excellence (CREDE).

Darling-Hammond, L. (2004). Inequality and the right to learn: Access to qualified teachers in California's public schools. *Teachers College Record, 106*(10), 1936–1966.

Derman-Sparks, L., & the A.B.C. Task Force. (1989). *Antibias curriculum tools for empowering young children.* Washington, DC: National Association for the Education of Young Children.

Division of Early Childhood. (2007). *Promoting positive outcomes for children with disabilities: Recommendations for curriculum, assessment, and program evaluation.* Missoula, MT: Author.

Elliot, E. (2002). *Measuring performance.* CA: Wadsworth.

Epstein, J. L., Sanders, M. G., Simon, B. S., Salinas, K. C., Jansorn, N. R., & Van Voorhis, F. L. (2002). *School, community, and community partnerships: Your handbook for action* (2nd ed.). Thousand Oaks, CA: Corwin Press.

Hill, H. D. (1989). *Effective strategies for teaching minority students.* Bloomington, IN: National Association of Early Childhood Specialists in State Departments of Education (NAECS/SDE).

National Association for the Education of Young Children. (1997). Teaching young children to resist bias. Retrieved September 30, 2008, from http://www.naeyc.org/ece/1997/10.asp.

National Association for the Education of Young Children & National Association of Early Childhood Specialists in State Departments of Education (NAEYC & NAECS/SDE). (2003). *Guidelines for appropriate curriculum and assessment in programs serving children ages 3 through 8.* Washington, DC: NAEYC.

Nieto, S., & Bode, P. (2007). *Affirming diversity: The sociopolitical context of multicultural education.* Boston: Allyn & Bacon.

Ornstein, A., & Hunkins, F. (2004). *Curriculum: Foundations, principles, and theory* (4th ed.). Boston: Allyn & Bacon.

Robles de Meléndez, W. (2004). *Theory and practice in early childhood education* (study guide). Fort Lauderdale, FL: Nova Southeastern University.

Romo, J. J., Bradfield, P., & Serrano, R. (2004). *Reclaiming democracy: Multicultural educators' journeys toward transformative teaching.* Upper Saddle River, NY: Pearson.

Language Diversity in the Classroom: Working with Young English Language Learners

"Recognize that all children are cognitively, linguistically, and emotionally connected to the language and culture of their home"
—NAEYC Position Statement. Responding to Linguistic and Cultural Diversity (1995)

STANDARDS: THE FOLLOWING STANDARDS ARE ADDRESSED IN THIS CHAPTER:

naeyc Standard 1: Promoting Child Development and Learning

naeyc Standard 2: Building Family and Community Relations

naeyc Standard 4: Using Developmentally Effective Approaches to Connect with Children and Families

naeyc Standard 7: Early Childhood Field Experiences

InTASC Standard 2: Learning Differences

InTASC Standard 7: Planning for Instruction

CHAPTER OBJECTIVE

Upon reading this chapter and reflecting on its content, you will be able to identify appropriate ways to support the learning needs of young English language learners.

KEY CONCEPTS

- English language learners
- heritage languages
- second language acquisition

TEACHERS SHARE

Miss Mendoza was with her young students on the playground and overhearing them actively talk with each other in English. She remembered how a few months ago many of them spoke only Spanish and smiled to herself, thinking how much they had learned. There had been a time she thought she would not be able to help the young English language learners at all, but then one of her colleagues had approached her with an idea. "I have the same challenge, so let's talk," said Miss Harris, another pre-K teacher. "I recently attended a wonderful workshop about a bilingual model that might work for us."

"I would love to learn more about it. When do we start?" said a much relieved Miss Mendoza.

Miss Mendoza recalled how she and her colleague started to plan their collaboration on the bilingual classroom model. The main

247

concept was to have both of them teach the same group of children. Miss Mendoza would teach in Spanish and Miss Harris in English. The collaboration began by both teachers learning about second language acquisition. They also talked to the school curriculum specialist and got some very good ideas. She even volunteered to work with them. For the next few weeks, Ms. Mendoza and Miss Harris transformed Miss Mendoza's classroom, created new materials, and planned a variety of new activities. They also identified a few parents who were willing to help. The greatest challenge was working as a team, with Miss Harris teaching in English and Miss Mendoza in Spanish. At first, it was a demanding adjustment for both, but as time went on they came to enjoy it. One of the most gratifying things was not just to see that the young ELLs were learning English but to see that the English-speaking children were beginning to use Spanish in their interactions. The word started to go around and soon some parents who heard about this new teaching model came to the school asking to have their native English-speaking children moved to Ms. Harris and Mendoza's.

On the playground, the voices of the young ELL children clearly showed they have made progress, as evidenced by their more frequent use of English. As she listened to them, Ms. Mendoza said to herself, "Yes, I would do it again."

THE LANDSCAPE OF LANGUAGE DIVERSITY

Today, the voices of young children in classrooms across the United States resound in a variety of languages, a reminder of the linguistic diversity of the nation. Statistics show that during the last 30 years the number of speakers of languages other than English has increased considerably (Shin and Kominsky, 2010). Reports from the U.S. Bureau of the Census show that almost 20 percent of the population age five and older speaks a language "other than English at home" (see Figure 8.1). The current immigration trends also show the majority of immigrants arriving to the U.S. come from Latin America and Asia.

Projections indicate that language diversity will continue to grow and that by 2030 almost 40 percent of students in the U.S. will speak a language at home other than English (Thomas & Collier, 2002). In 2008, 55 percent of all schools both public and private reported having at least one student who was a speaker of a language other than English (National Center for Education Statistics, 2009). Education reports show that in 2006, programs for English language learners in the country's largest school districts provided services to almost 14 percent of students enrolled in grades K-12 (National Center for Education Statistics, 2008).

A Nation of Many Languages

Language diversity has always been an important element of U.S. society. Just like in the past, today new immigrants continue to bring with them their home languages. Today it is common to hear their voices mingled with speakers of English in every corner of the

Figure 8-1
Percentage of the
Population Who
Spoke a Language
Other Than English at
Home by State: 2007
(U.S. Bureau of the
Census)

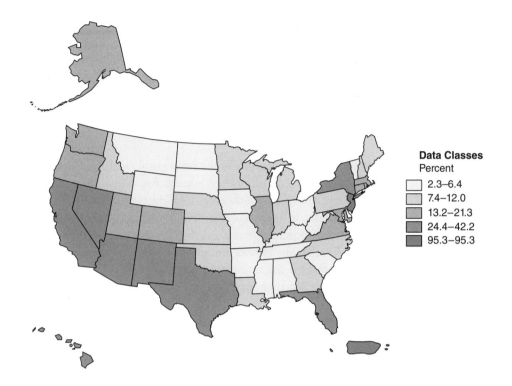

Data Classes
Percent

- 2.3–6.4
- 7.4–12.0
- 13.2–21.3
- 24.4–42.2
- 95.3–95.3

nation. Television and radio programs, newspapers, and commercial advertisements in different languages are common in many communities. What has then changed? What may be different is that in the past diverse languages were spoken mostly at home. Many second-generation immigrants remember being told not to speak their home language outside the home. Others felt a sense of embarrassment when trying to communicate in a language that was not English. In this kind of cultural atmosphere, with their voices quiet, in many cases the home language of immigrants gradually faded as they learned the language of their newly adopted country.

THINK
AND
REFLECT...

LANGUAGE DIVERSITY

Becoming aware of language diversity in your community is a step toward understanding the multicultural reality of children. Take time to answer the following questions and to share your thoughts with colleagues or classmates:

- Do you think that everyone should preserve their native language?

- Should learning English be the first priority for those arriving to the United States?

Today, with rapidly changing demographics, educators are recognizing the importance of learning English along with other languages. Many agree that the ability to speak more than one language is necessary for future success in an already global society. Yet, despite this growing awareness, language diversity continues to be a controversial issue in U.S. society.

Language Diversity in the Classroom

Linguistic diversity is one of the most visible distinguishing characteristics in the United States society. The number of households where languages other than English are spoken are counted in the thousands (Figure 8-2). This phenomenon is reflected in classrooms across the country. Statistics show that in many school districts, children speak as many as 40 different languages. In some states like Florida schools report over 100 languages spoken by children enrolled in their programs. Nationally, enrollment of English language learners (ELLs) showed a growth of almost 57 percent in grades Pre-K–12 (National Clearinghouse for English Language Acquisition and Language Instruction Educational Program [NCELA], 2006). While over 76 percent of ELLs speak Spanish, there is a wide variety of languages other than English spoken by children attending schools across the United States (National Council of Teachers of English, 2006) (see Figure 8-3).

Programs serving young children such as Head Start have also seen a rise in the number of children and families with home languages other than English. The Office of

Figure 8-2
Percentage of Children Speaking Languages Other than English at Home and Difficulty Speaking English

	2003	2008
Children ages 5–17 who speak a language other than English at home	19%	21%
Children who speak a language other than English at home and have difficulty speaking English	5%	5.1%

Source: *Forum on child and family statistics. (2010). America's Children: Key indicators of Well-Being (2010).*

Figure 8-3
Home Languages of ELL Students in U.S. Classrooms (2001–2002)

Languages	Percentage (%)
Spanish	76.9
Vietnamese	2.4
Hmong	1.8
Korean	1.2
Arabic	1.1
Haitian-Creole	1.1

Source: *Hopstock & Stephenson (2003)*

Programs like Head Start where children experience developmentally based activities facilitate second language learning.

Head Start reported that in the 2006-2007 period, 30 percent of families served spoke a language that was not English (Office of Head Start, 2008). Almost 85 percent of families in this group spoke Spanish followed by East Asian languages and Middle Eastern/South Asian languages as the three most spoken language groups of Head Start families (see Figure 8-4). They also found "a significant number of programs" serving families that spoke as many as eight or more different languages. Many of the families had varying levels of proficiency in English that range from speaking very well to those considered as linguistically isolated (households where the primary language used is their home language and where adults or siblings age 13 or older do not speak English well) (Office of Head Start, 2008).

Linguistic Diversity: Another Descriptor of Multiculturalism

Language is one characteristic that defines human diversity. Whether it is Spanish, Arabic, Russian, Creole, or French, many languages spoken throughout U.S. communities evidence the ever-increasing cultural diversity of U.S. society. The importance of language goes beyond communication and is fundamental to the individual's appropriate

Figure 8-4 Ranking of Language Groups Spoken by Families and Children Attending Head Start Programs (2007–2008)

Language groups
1. Spanish
2. East Asian languages
3. Middle Eastern/South Asian
4. European/Slavic
5. African
6. Native Central/South American and Native Mexican languages
7. Caribbean languages
8. Pacific Island languages
9. Native North American/Alaska Native languages.

Source: Office of Head Start (2008).

MORE THAN JUST LANGUAGE

- In what way is your language a part of your identity?
- Do you speak a language other than English?
- What are the repercussions for children in your community who do not speak English?

- What is your personal view of people who live in the United States who do not learn to speak English?

development. It is also one of the essential tools of cultural acquisition and a part of a child's cultural identity. Earlier in this book (see Chapters 2 and 4) we discussed how through language children build a sense of who they are as members of a family and of a social group. You will recall that language is also what helps us learn and understand the culturally accepted behaviors that guide the actions of a social group. As children become more competent in using a language, they are able to better understand the meanings and ideas of their cultural group.

Terms that Describe Speakers of Languages Other than English

You may have noticed a variety of terms used to refer to individuals who do not speak English. *Limited English Proficient* (LEP) is one of the terms commonly used to designate the child who has a primary language that is not English. *Second language learner* and *English as a second language* (ESL) are also used to designate this population. *English language learner* (ELL) is currently more commonly used in the literature and schools when discussing children who are non-native speakers and who are learning English. In this chapter and throughout this book, the term ELL is used to address the needs and issues of linguistically diverse children acquiring English. Whichever term is used, they all describe the realities and challenges faced by children every day in classrooms across the country.

Using folk songs and other oral language traditions helps preserve heritage languages.

Wadsworth/Cengage Learning

AROUND **THE WORLD**

LANGUAGES AT RISK: PRESERVING THE WORLD'S HERITAGE

"Everyone loses if one language is lost because then a nation and culture lose their memory and so does the complex tapestry from which the world is woven and which makes the world an exciting place."

Vigdis Finnbogadottir (2004)

It is estimated that nearly 6000 to 7000 languages are spoken by people in the global community (UNESCO, 2003). In some places, like Papua New Guinea, close to 800 different languages are spoken. Wherever they are practiced, they define and represent the individual group's identity and wisdom. It can be said that the world's cultural heritage lies within this panorama of linguistic diversity.

Unfortunately, many languages today are facing extinction. It is estimated that about half of the world's languages are facing the possibility of disappearing (Malone, 2008). Among those that are in peril most are the many languages of the Pacific, Africa, as well as North America and Europe.

Why are languages at risk? There are many reasons. In some cases, the members of a language group are becoming extinct. This was the case of Eyak, an

indigenous language of people in Alaska (United States), when the last person who spoke it died in 2008. Another reason is that globalization has made it more expedient and practical to replace the heritage languages with those spoken by the mainstream cultures. Social and cultural factors including the perceived devaluing of a language may also lead to its gradual loss. All over the world, many families are no longer using or passing on to the young their heritage language.

The perils of the world languages led UNESCO to create the *Endangered languages program*. The program is aimed at assisting communities with technical support and resources to advocate for language preservation and strengthen language diversity. Through its efforts, UNESCO hopes to build greater awareness about the importance of language in preserving the world's traditions and knowledge.

Source: Malone, E. (2008). Endangered languages. Special Report. In National Science Foundation. Retrieved from http://www.nsf.gov/news/special_reports/linguistics/endangered.jsp; Woodbury, A. (2002). Endangered languages. In Linguistic Society of America. Retrieved from http://www.lsadc.org/info/ling-fields-endanger.cfm; UNESCO. (2003). Language and Multilingualism. Endangered languages. Retrieved from http://www.unesco.org/new/en/unesco/themes/languages-and-multilingualism/endangered-languages/

WHO IS THE ENGLISH LANGUAGE LEARNER?

"English language learners (ELL), like all children, bring a range of experiences and instructional needs into the classroom."
—The Center for Public Education (2009)

"Who is the English language learner?" is a question asked by many. *English language learner* is the term used to generally designate children "whose first language is not English and who are in the process of learning English" (NCELA, 2008). More than 14 million children attending school in the U.S. speak a first language other than English (August & Shanahan, 2006). Today, it is estimated that one or more out of five children under age six live in a home where a language other than English is spoken (Capp, Fix, Ost, Reardon-Anderson, & Passel, 2006).

Wadsworth/Cengage Learning

ELL children are a very diverse group and come from a variety of cultures from the U.S and around the world.

There are several characteristics that define ELL children. Some are newly arrived while others have been living in the U.S. for a period of time. Both groups live in environments where the language spoken is something other than English. Census data show that the majority of English language learners are U.S. born. In 2004, 93 percent of children of immigrants were U.S. born (Capps et al., 2006). Statistics also show that many ELL children have at least one foreign-born parent. Linguistically, most ELL children are Spanish speakers, followed by Asians and Pacific Islanders, with Hmong, Tagalog, and Chinese among the languages spoken by this ethnic group. Geographically, ELL children are found in every state in the nation. Several states house the majority of speakers of other languages. Among them are California, Florida, Texas, Nevada, New Mexico, Illinois, New York, and New Jersey. Immigrant populations are now found in states like Georgia, Maine, Arkansas, North Dakota, and North Carolina where the percentage of ELL has grown significantly in recent years.

ELL, a Very Diverse Group

Those who work with English language learners know that one of the characteristics that defines this group is its own diversity. Saying that ELL children are those with different home languages is not an accurate description. Overall, English language learners in our classrooms possess a variety of language characteristics and proficiency levels. Differences in their proficiency are not only limited to English but are also evident in their own home languages. Experiences at home and in the community along with social and economic factors are among the elements that influence the ability of ELL children to become competent speakers of their home languages. Demographically, some ELL children live in neighborhoods and environments where only their home language is spoken. In some cases, their parents and older siblings are characteristically ELL as well and have limited or no proficiency in English. In other instances, some children may already come with the ability to speak several different languages. This is due to the fact that in some parts of the world, it is expected for individuals to acquire more than one language in the early years of life. For example, Swiss children generally speak German, French, and Italian, and often are taught English as well. Children from India may already speak their regional language along with Hindi and have knowledge of English as well.

Language diversity also exists within an ethnic group. Examples of this are found among Hispanic children and their families from Central and South America as well as

IN ACTION . . .

ELL CHILDREN IN YOUR COMMUNITY

Today English language learners are enrolled in classrooms in most communities around the U.S. In many states, the number of ELL has significantly increased over the past five years. Even states that traditionally had few immigrants, like Utah, Nebraska, and Montana, today have classrooms with ELL children. Learning about children and families in your community that are speakers of other languages helps in becoming informed about their needs and reality. Are you aware if ELL children attend programs in your community?

- Do you know any ELL children?
- What are some of the characteristics that define them? What language (or languages) do they speak?

from some parts of Mexico where many continue to speak their indigenous languages. Some may actually be fluent in both. For instance, in addition to Spanish, in some of the Mexican regions people continue to speak Mayan, Huichol, Mixtec, Huasteco among other indigenous languages.

Language Learning during the Early Years

Learning a language is a developmental process that begins during the early childhood years. It is one of the major milestones of early childhood. All children are born with the ability to learn languages. In fact, it could be said that we are all born multilingual. Which language is learned is determined and influenced by the family and the environment. Exposure to language and interactions with family members and adults play a leading role in how and what language the child acquires. In fact, "… the language one speaks and the variation of the language spoken are not the products of biology. They are products of environment" (Hulit, Howard, & Fahey, 2011, p. 333).

IN ACTION . . .

FACTORS THAT INFLUENCE LANGUAGE ACQUISITION

Linguistic experts identify seven factors that influence language acquisition (Taylor, 1990, as cited by Hulit, Howard & Fahey, 2011):

- Race and ethnic group
- Social class, educational level, and occupation
- Geographical region
- Gender
- Situation or context
- Peer group association or identification
- First language of a community or culture

Considering these factors, which one(s) do you think influenced you to acquire the language or languages that you speak?

We all have a need to communicate. Communication is the principal factor that leads individuals to acquire language. As active participants in the social context of their families or classroom children gain interest and become motivated in learning how to communicate. The desire to communicate, in turn, helps and leads children in learning the language spoken by those in their environment. Language is built as children engage in a context rich in linguistic interactions (Otto, 2009). Whether at home, in the preschool, or in the neighborhood, children are influenced by those with whom they interact. Informal conversations, singing, and verbal exchanges between the child and his/her family and caregivers are the seeds that promotes language learning. Acquiring a language is a gradual process. As children engage in more and frequent language experiences, they become able to understand the language used by those in their context and thus acquire it as well.

Learning More Than One Language

Because children are born with the capacity to learn languages, this ability predisposes them to acquire more than just one language. Nowadays, many children are exposed very early on to not only their home or heritage language but to many others in their environments as well. Through encounters with individuals from diverse cultures, children are coming into contact with languages other than their own. Many of them are actively engaged in learning additional languages and using them to communicate with others. This is particularly evident in large metropolitan areas where most new immigrants tend to settle. Both at home and in school, children are prompted to learn how to communicate in the languages spoken to them by others who live in their environments. This also includes interactions with media and entertainment that are prevalent elements of life in our modern society. Such exposure favors building skills in more than one language. Examples of young children who at an early age are able to understand two languages are not uncommon. In the case of one of the authors' families, her nephews living in Canada spoke French, English, and Serbian from the time they were born. Many of us have also observed how a child holding a conversation in English transitions to Spanish with no difficulty when her *abuela*, grandmother approaches her. Observations also reveal that children develop the capacity to switch with ease between languages according to the situation or the individual with whom they are speaking. Bilingual development, the process when the child learns more than one language, has many benefits.

Developmental Benefits of Learning a Second Language

Many ELL families are concerned about having their children learn a second language other than English or continuing to speak the home language. Some believe that practicing another language may interfere with successful learning of English. There are many cases where ELL families even decide to avoid speaking their home language with their children fearful that it may lessen their opportunities to acquire English. The fact

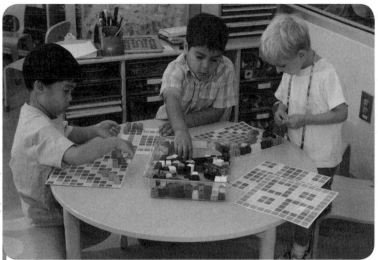

ELL children benefit from working cooperatively with English speaking peers. It promotes participation and invites children to engage in conversations which stimulates language acquisition.

is that having a home language does not inhibit learning a second language (Collier, 1995). In reality, it has several developmental benefits for children.

One of the benefits of learning languages is enhanced brain development. Studies have shown that learning two languages promotes neurological activity. Linguistic interactions with a child such as talking, singing, or reading stories, stimulates brain growth particularly in the areas of language processing and memory (Genesee, 2000; Owens, 2012; Espinosa, 2008). Being able to speak more than one language is not just an additional communication skill, but rather a cognitive and social boost to the overall development of the child.

Experts agree that the ability to use language is a cognitive event. Before a word is uttered, the child engages in highly sophisticated cognitive work: processing the inputs from his environment, connecting those to what he/she already knows, applying the ideas from own culture, and finally deciding on what makes sense. For children this mental exercise provides ways to continue building a range of ideas and concepts that define their own reality. Because they are able to understand and communicate with others using a home or second language, they also expand the variety of opportunities they have to experience their environment. With a wider variety of experiences, the ability to increase their knowledge about their immediate reality is heightened.

Socially, learning a second language also has many advantages. From being able to interact with others to being able to understand their ideas and culture, the ability to speak more than one language is a social asset. According to Vygostky, language is a tool that facilitates interactions in one's social and cultural context. With language as their tool, children are able to interact with people in their environment—parents, family members, caregivers, adults, and peers. In general, this extends their circle of individuals with whom they interact and from whom they come to learn the social ideas and ways of their group. Through language they also gain the ability to enter into the dimensions of ideas and values allowing them to connect with their own group and to understand others. This is a major benefit, underlining the importance of language as a key to learning and understanding one's culture and those of others.

Looking at the future, it is relevant to remember that the goal of early childhood education and education in general is to prepare children appropriately to meet the needs of society. Beyond facilitating understanding and communicating with speakers

THINK AND REFLECT...

IT'S ALL IN THE ENVIRONMENT

Imagine that you were present when the following incident happened:

Three-year-old Eric was visiting from a Spanish-speaking country. He had been visiting for almost a week. One afternoon, he was with his family at a restaurant. They were reading the menus and getting ready to order. Young Eric also had a menu, which he was reading with great interest. Looking at the illustrations, he was excited to place his order. "Yo quiero un burger/I want a burger," he kept saying. When the waiter approached Eric in English, his father quickly told him that Eric only spoke Spanish. Asking his son what he wanted to eat, he was surprised to hear the child say: "Yo puedo/I know how to order." Without any hesitation,

Eric opened the menu and started to "order" in English, or at least in what he thought was English. Using a combination of words in English and English-like sounds, he proudly ordered his meal. Everyone looked at him with disbelief. His awareness of English was evident to all. In his very own way, the three year-old had been capturing the language and was happy to show that he could also communicate with it.

- *What do you think influenced young Eric's awareness of a different language?*
- *What implications does this incident have for teachers of young ELL children?*

of languages other than English, additional languages prepare the child for future successful participation as member of a diverse society. Within the context of the global society, learning a second language provides more job and professional opportunities when the child matures into an adult.

Second Language Acquisition

The time when a child becomes exposed to learning languages defines the type of second language acquisition process he or she will follow. For many children, acquiring a second language happens along with their first language. When a second language is learned at the same time as they learn their first language, children experience what is called *simultaneous acquisition*. This is what describes children who from birth grow up in environments where both a home language and another language are spoken by family members, caregivers, or they interact with adults. Some children learned a home language before being exposed to a second language. In this case, they are learning the second language in what is defined as *sequential acquisition*, that is, after already having acquired a first language. Many language experts consider that children who already have a first language are familiar with the use and role of language. This knowledge assists them in the process of learning a second language (Espinosa, 2008; Garcia, 2005).

ACQUIRING ANOTHER LANGUAGE

Developmentally, the time when a child begins to learn a language other than English defines the type of acquisition process he or she will experience. Share your answers with others.

- If you speak a language other than English, do you remember at what time in your life you learned it and why you learned it? What were some challenges you experienced during the process?

- If you are an adult who has not acquired another language, discuss with peers what has prevented you from doing so.

Stages of Second Language Acquisition

Experts agree that language acquisition is a process that occurs in stages over time. Similar to the acquisition of the first language, when children build a new or second language they also go through a series of steps.

Typically, the following steps are observed (Owens, 2001; Tabors, 2008; Otto, 2009):

- *Discovery:* During this stage, children become aware that a language different from their own is used. When faced with the need to talk they will try to use their home language. These experiences will lead the child to discover that her first language is different from the one used in the setting.

- *Silent stage:* In this stage, children typically abstain from using verbal language. Many have described this apparently "silent" period as a time when they are actively engaged in listening and experiencing the new language. Although little or no verbalizations may occur, during this time children are becoming aware of the language learning key phrases, words, and expressions.

- *Single word/short sentence:* During this period children begin to venture into using English. They will verbalize ideas using a single word or in short sentences. As they continue to experiment and try out the newly acquired language forms, they gain both experience and become more confident in using them.

Routinely sharing culturally based stories validates ELL children's heritage. It also provides valuable language models (vocabulary, expressions, voice intonation, and others) for the young child.

Wadsworth/Cengage Learning

LITERACY CONNECTIONS...

USING CULTURALLY BASED STORIES TO CELEBRATE CHILDREN'S LANGUAGES

In every culture children's stories are a way to learn about their rich heritage. They are also a way to foster language development. Here are some selected stories that can be shared with children to celebrate their heritage languages. Some of the stories are bilingual while others include words in other languages.

- Christian, C. (2005). *Where is the kitten?/Kote ti chat la ye?* New York: Star Bright Books. (English/Haitian Creole)
- Hyechong, C. (2008). *K is for Korea.* London, UK: Frances Lincoln Books. (Korean alphabet book)
- Mendoza, L. (2005). *Lola.* New York: me+mi. (bilingual)

- Montes, M. (2000). *Juan bobo goes to work.* New York: Rayo.
- Mora, P. (2009). *Gracias/Thanks.* New York: Lee and Low. (bilingual)
- Park, (2008). *Bee-bim-bop!* New York: Sandpiper. (with phrase in Korean)
- McSween, M. (2009). *Gordon and Li Li. Words for everyday.* China: McWong Ink. (Mandarin)
- Tafolla, C. (2009). *What can you do with a paleta?* New York: Trycicle Books. (with words in Spanish)

- *Early understanding of grammatical rules*: At this stage, the child begins to apply the rules of grammar which is first evidenced through their oral interactions.

As with any language, support from adults, teachers, and peers is vital through all stages of English language acquisition. These significant individuals serve as language models for the child and provide a sense of need for learning the new language. Equally relevant is having sensitive early childhood educators who will be able to encourage and celebrate the child's attempts as he/she becomes confident in using English.

Recognizing the Role of Home Languages, a Child's Right

For decades, the preservation of the heritage or home language and learning of English as a second language have been debatable issues. In the past, policies and teaching practices concerning non-speakers of English were created from the perspective of deficiency. Children who spoke their heritage languages only and were not proficient in English were perceived as lacking until they acquired English language skills. No value was placed on the retention of the children's native languages. The result of these policies was that too many children grew up thinking that it was an embarrassment to speak a language other than English. Parents and families wanting to carve a future in U.S. society thought that it was best for their children to give up their home language and become "Americans" as soon as possible. The result was the erosion of native languages, many of which disappeared and many more of which are still at risk of vanishing forever. As a result, many adults who once had different heritage languages have either completely or partially lost the ability to use them.

Due to the efforts of families, educators, language scholars, multicultural researchers, and concerned leaders, today attitudes have started to change acknowledging the

Figure 8-5
What We Know
about Second
Language Learners

The need to support the child's cultural heritage while acquiring English language skills has been recognized as an important aspect of the child's development. Research in second language development has revealed the following (Garcia, 2005; Tabors, 2008):

- Language acquisition and development is best facilitated during the early years. Although the ability to acquire a new language remains, during early childhood children tend to acquire languages in a more native-like way.

- Young children are capable of learning more than one language. Becoming bilingual is a task that brings valuable developmental benefits to the child.

- Second language learning happens most effectively in familiar, natural contexts.

- The first language scaffolds and contributes to the acquisition of a second language, in this case, English.

- There are ample developmental gains (cognitive, social, and emotional) for the young child through the acquisition of another language.

- Learning another language fosters understanding of more than one cultural reality, a necessary characteristic in a multicultural society.

- Knowing another language fosters empathy and tolerance by facilitating an understanding of the values and frames of reference of others.

- Maintaining the home language contributes to the family's sense of connection. It facilitates communication with family members and links children to gaining an understanding of their family's heritage.

importance of the home language (see Figure 8-5). Programs like Head Start recognize the role and value of home languages as part of the overall development of the child. This is expressed in Principle 6 of the *Head Start Multicultural Principles* (2010), which establishes that "effective programs for children who speak languages other than English require continued development of the first language while the acquisition of English is facilitated" (p. 45). In its position statement, *Responding to linguistic and cultural diversity*, NAEYC (1995) addressed the role of first languages and provided recommendations for early childhood educators to support the children's home languages. It particularly set as direction to encourage families to continue using and fostering development of their home language.

Supporting young ELLs while preserving their home languages is considered today the appropriate educational practice that adheres to DAP

Wadsworth/Cengage Learning

Developmentally based experiences lead ELL children to feel a sense of accomplishment.

IN ACTION . . .

PRESERVING HOME LANGUAGES

Today, many languages are at risk of disappearing. It is estimated that about 182 languages are at risk just in North America with many of those in the United States. Data from the Census shows that while speakers of other languages have increased, there are others from various ethnic groups that have significantly decreased.

- Did your family have a home language? Are you still a speaker of that home language? If not, what

are some of the reasons that led to losing that language? What are some of the consequences of not having that home language?

- Find out if any of your neighbors or classmates had a home language that they no longer speak.
- What is your position regarding the preservation of the home language?

THINK AND REFLECT...

INCREASING DEMOGRAPHICAL DIVERSITY

According to the Bureau of the Census, in 2009 nearly 24 percent of children age 0-17 had a foreign-born parent. Considering this fact, what implications does this statistic have in terms of language diversity of children in classroom across the country? With such large numbers, can you project into the future what could happen to the acquisition of English as a second language?

principles. It is also a critical element in classrooms serving multicultural children. Careful planning must occur to assist each child who is learning English while facilitating the preservation of the first language. With the national emphasis on reading and literacy development, it is particularly important to consider the selection of materials, strategies, and assessment practices to use with young ELLs. Keeping in mind that the environment is one of the elements that promotes language learning, it is essential to create a classroom atmosphere that both supports learning English and respects and values the child's first language. When selecting strategies, educators should be mindful of the children's needs and learning styles as well as appropriate practices. Necessary accommodations must be made to meet the development needs of ELL children.

IN THE CLASSROOM: DAP PRACTICES TO MEET THE NEEDS OF YOUNG ELL CHILDREN

What works best with young ELLs depends on their developmental and cultural needs, experiences, and characteristics. Working with ELLs requires careful and thoughtful application of developmentally based practices. Six key aspects should be considered when planning experiences to support the needs of young children who are English

ENCOURAGING PRESERVATION OF HOME LANGUAGES

Knowledge about the benefits of acquiring a second language also has implications on practices to promote the preservation of home languages. Many children who are in classrooms across the nation already speak a first language other than English. Awareness of the advantages that knowing more than one language should guide teaching experiences to support a child's language while learning English. In some cases, educators eager to have children build English proficiency may not want them to use their home languages in the classroom. Yet, it has been shown that use of one's language may assist in acquiring a second one.

Some of the steps to take in support of first language preservation include:

- Clarifying and demystifying views about first languages and becoming cognizant of the second language acquisition process.

- Visibly supporting children's home languages in the classroom through acknowledgment of these (for example, integrating materials and resources in the children's home languages to demonstrate and validate these as important).

- Routinely including selections such as books in the literacy area, songs, fingerplays, and others in the children's home language.

- Being accepting of the children's home language by letting them use them when they are communicating with peers.

- Helping parents and families to understand that maintaining a first language does not prevent or interfere with successfully acquiring English.

language learners: knowledge about the child, appropriate environment, engaging experiences, appropriate assessment, collaboration with families, teacher's knowledge base.

Knowing the Child Who is an English Language Learner

Getting ready to work with ELL children begins with a good knowledge about them. Before considering what to plan or selecting materials, taking time to learn who they are helps in planning what best meets their needs. Each child, as we know, follows an own developmental pathway. The same principle applies to ELL children. Because each child brings unique experiences, it is important to carefully gather information about their developmental characteristics and needs. Observations of ELL children have revealed that not all children who are learning a second language share the same linguistic experiences. In some cases, ELL children come from rich language environments while others may bring limited experiences with their home language or with English. Others may bring experiences from environments where more than one language is spoken. Awareness about the diverse experiences of ELL with both their home language and English yields a more precise view about the child as a speaker of language. Conversations with families also provide additional information about the child and his/her experiences with language. For example, interactions with the family will yield data about the languages regularly spoken at home including both home language and English. You can also learn who and what languages family members use.

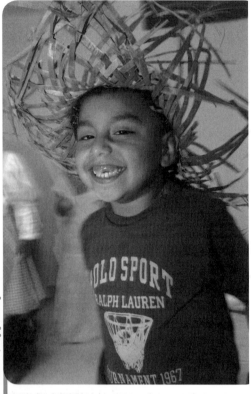

Each child brings unique language experiences which underlines the need to learn about their developmental characteristics.

Identifying if children are actually speakers of languages other than English is a first step in gaining knowledge about the child. The *home language survey* is commonly used to identify children who are English language learners. This informal screening tool consists of key questions that assist educators to recognize who is the child that is exposed or speaks a language other than English. In the U.S., the survey is used at the school district level and includes questions such as the following:

- *Tell us about the language most frequently spoken at home.*
- *Which language did your child learn when he/she first began to talk?*
- *Does your child most frequently speak a language other than English at home?*
- *What language do you most frequently speak to your child?*

Responses to the survey provide information about both the language experiences of the family and the child. They are also used in determining educational services for children. Other sources to learn about the ELL child include the following:

- Informal conversations with children during classroom experiences
- Observations about language interactions with peers and with other adults
- Results from formal language assessment activities

THINK AND REFLECT...

THE FLORIDA CONSENT DECREE

A court decision in August 1990 recognized the rights of children with languages other than English to receive appropriate and equitable educational experiences. The landmark case was brought about by a group of concerned citizens and organizations that advocated for the civil rights of ELL students against the Florida Board of Education. As a result of the favorable decision, an agreement was reached. The Consent Decree today serves as the legal framework to provide services to ELL children in the State of Florida.

- Considering this decision, what role does advocacy play in supporting the rights of ELL children? As an early educator, what are the implications of this ruling?
- What similar efforts that guarantee the rights of ELL children are in place in your community?

Creating a Welcoming Literacy Learning Environment for ELLs

The environment is a powerful tool in fostering language learning. It also plays an important role in motivating and engaging children in learning a second language. Preparing the classroom for language acquisition and preservation of first languages requires effective use of materials and resources. It also includes selecting appropriate literacy materials in both English and the first languages of the children such as the following:

- Age-appropriate children's books in English and the children's home languages
- Abundance of printed materials such as newspapers, flyers, and others for children's use
- Posters, signs in both English and the children's home languages
- Labeling materials in English and the children's home languages
- Music, both instrumental and vocal, representative of diverse cultures and in English and the first languages of the children
- Listening materials in both English and the children's home languages
- Child-appropriate language and literacy software
- Manipulatives to support concept formation
- Ethnic and cultural regalia reflective of the children's cultures

Use of materials in the children's home languages welcomes the child and provides validation to their heritage. It also creates interest and motivates children to engage in experiences aimed at helping them to acquire English.

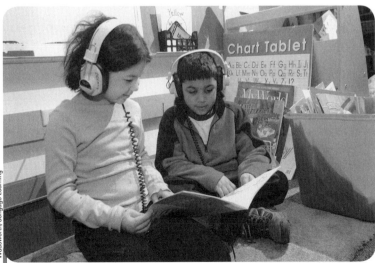

Listening to age-appropriate materials is another way to foster language acquisition. A listening center can also engage ELL children in activities with peers.

Planning Experiences

Appropriate experiences begin with planning based on the developmental needs of children. In the ELL classroom, planning should focus on language needs and acquisition ability of each child. The process begins by assessing the children to identify their level of language proficiency.

Relevant and meaningful activities are developed with expectations set at levels that children can meet. Best practices in early childhood and second language learning point out that meaningful classroom experiences

FOCUS
ON CLASSROOM PRACTICES

USING TRADITIONAL FOLKLORE TO SUPPORT
SECOND LANGUAGE LEARNING

Use of songs, rhymes, riddles, tongue twisters, and others from Latino oral traditions in the children's first language contributes to building a strong framework for oral language and phonological development. This learning has been shown to be a key predictor of successful acquisition of a second language. Children's folklore provides a wealth of culturally related songs, tongue twisters, and fingerplays. These can be used in the classroom to support language acquisition with young ELL children. Traditional Latino children's songs also provide opportunities to support oral language skills while supporting children's heritage. Some suggestions to include these in the classroom are the following:

- *Promote oral expression through singing.* Integrate traditional songs during transitions. Consider the following:
  - *Mi escuelita* [*My school*] for morning meetings or circle time
  - *Al ánimo*, to signal time for outdoor activities
  - *Las vocales*, [*The vowels*] for storytelling time
  - *El coquí* [Little frog] to signal quiet time

- *Use lyrics to build vocabulary.* Special words from the lyrics of their favorite songs can be added to a word wall. Explore the meaning of selected words and create a web with synonyms.
- *Explore rhyming words.* Engage children in exploring rhyming with their favorite songs. Some that especially promote rhyming are: *El coquí, Aserrín.*
- *Clapping syllables* while singing favorite traditional songs.
- *Singing nursery rhymes*: learning and singing those learned at home. Some of these include: *La Linda manita* [the pretty little hand], *El coquí [Little flog]*, *Aserrín, Duérmete mi niño* [Sleep my baby] among so many others.
- *Word segmentation*: songs such as *El barquito* [Little boat] and la *Señorita Elena* [Miss Elena] offer opportunities for children to emphasize letter sounds by stretching out words and names.

Reference: W. Robles de Meléndez & M. Valdés-Díaz (2008). Preserving children's oral traditions. *Presentation at the Annual Conference of the National Association for the Education of Young Children. Dallas, TX.*

connecting the child to his or her reality are central to successful learning. Planning needs to be soundly anchored to what is relevant to the child and intentionally designed to build language skills. It is important to remember that successful learning activities relate to the child's culture and experiences, that is, are connected to their *funds of knowledge*. Central to effective planning is considering that children benefit from content that is both age-appropriate and developmentally challenging. While considerations on how to facilitate understanding for the ELL child guide planning, selection of the content should always be cognitively challenging.

Selection of appropriate teaching strategies and incorporation of necessary modifications to lessons and materials to facilitate learning are also critical. Among the strategies use of thematic teaching and cooperative learning experiences provide a variety of ways to engage young ELL children in gaining knowledge about English. Use of themes familiar to children creates interest in the experiences and motivates them to

Working together in cooperative learning experiences with native speakers benefits ELL children. It provides ways to foster oral interactions while supporting their sense of being part of the group.

participate. Use of thematic units helps ELL children to connect with their own cultural and language experiences, facilitating acquisition of new concepts and language. The content also needs to uphold expectations appropriate to the age group that reflect the standards while challenging the child to learn. Integrating experiences that tie into the children's prior knowledge also provide opportunities for them to share what they know about the topics. Allowing the child to use words and terms in their home language to describe related experiences or activities not only engage their interest but also serve to validate their culture. This is an aspect that developmentally supports the child's social and emotional needs. Considerations to the individual social and emotional needs should always guide the planning of learning experiences for ELL children as well as for every child.

Planning cooperative learning opportunities is also an effective way to support the ELL child. When children work together with native speakers, they learn expressions and words that support their growing communication in English. A sense of belonging is also fostered as they participate along with others.

Some suggested practices to consider during your planning include the following:

- Plan experiences that build and promote language development. For example, regularly integrating related read aloud activities and singing. These provide opportunities to hear and practice language. They are also a source to build vocabulary.
- Connect themes with what is familiar to children and related to their prior experiences.
- Use concrete objects and photographs to enhance and support understanding and concept development.
- Aside from fostering social and conversational language, provide opportunities that support academic language, which is the language typically used in classroom discourse (for example, using appropriate vocabulary, expressions, phrases, and terminology to present and describe experiences).
- Plan and include on a regular basis songs, chants, poems as part of transitions that provide opportunities to practice language and learn vocabulary.

VIDEO CASE 8.1 ▶❚❚

Bilingual education: An elementary two-way immersion program

Watch the video and answer the following questions:

1. What are the benefits of the two-way immersion program for the ELL child and for native English speakers?

2. What is the goal of the two-way immersion program?

Wadsworth/Cengage Learning

Time to plan and discuss how to address the needs of young ELL children is essential. It contributes to effectively supporting learning expectations.

- Include and provide a variety of hands-on activities to support concept building.
- Use and display concept organizers to facilitate understanding. They provide a visual way to connect ideas and language.
- Integrate teacher-made materials purposely created to address specific topics and concepts.

Using Appropriate Assessment

Continuous observation and use of alternative ways of assessment practices are necessary to document progress. Authentic assessment describes the use of procedures that include multiple sources reflective of what the children do including what is initiated by them and as well as planned teacher assessments. Experiences show that when authentic assessment is used to evaluate progress, a more realistic view about the child's needs and strengths is gathered. One of these activities is the use of portfolios. There are a number of ways to collect information about the child's learning gains in language and in all other areas. Some sample artifacts to include in a children's portfolio that demonstrate language progress may include anecdotal notes gathered during observations; recordings of children's utterances; videotapes of children's interactions; journal writing; and story writing.

Use of standardized instruments must be carefully decided upon to avoid any testing bias that may unfairly depict the child's performance level. Fair assessment practices for ELL children is one of the aspects that continues to challenge educators. Taking time to examine and discuss the purposes and use of any formal assessment tool is essential to ensure appropriate use and administration.

A warm environment communicates to families that their culture and home language are welcome.

Families of ELL children play a vital role in their successful language development and learning. How would you engage them and support them?

Collaboration with families

Maintaining open communication and interaction with the child's parents and families is vital. This is particularly important for the preservation of the first language as the second language is learned. Providing materials, giving suggestions, responding to questions about language learning, and asking families to share materials and favorite stories that can be incorporated into experiences all set a positive tone and build a strong relationship between the home and the classroom. Suggestions to help preserve the first language may include activities such as encouraging family members to read and share stories with their children, to take time to sing songs meaningful to their culture, and to talk to their children in the first language. Perhaps the most important suggestion is to show your sincere interest in learning more about the culture of families. Families will value your desire to know more about their heritage. Additional suggestions are discussed in Chapter 10.

In many cases, the parents and family members of ELL children are themselves learning English. If communication with parents is challenging, educators should seek help from their program agency or school district in obtaining appropriate interpreters and other resources that will enhance communication.

Enhancing the Teacher's Knowledge Base

Your knowledge about early childhood practices is the foundation for child appropriate practices. Supporting the needs of young ELL children depends and comes from knowledge about the following aspects:

- *Cultural ideas.* Language is a vital cultural element and a learning tool. For that reason, the early childhood educator must understand the role that language plays in the life of a child. Becoming aware and learning about traditional literary works written in the children's home languages, children's folk songs, and other oral traditions helps in gaining an appreciation about the role that language plays in a culture.

- *Knowledge about developmentally appropriate practices (DAP).* It is important to understand that DAP applies to working with all children. This includes the ELL child. DAP is anchored in developmental principles and provides a framework for designing experiences that meet the needs of every child. Culture and language

Wadsworth/Cengage Learning

are relevant elements that influence the developmental process and guide the planning of learning activities.

- *Knowledge about practices of second language acquisition.* Having knowledge regarding the acquisition of a second language and first language preservation practices is essential. This is an area where many studies are being conducted. It is important to keep up with current research and use the findings for developing your own ideas about the role of the educator in first and second language learning. Every day, researchers are learning more about the intricacies of second language acquisition, which adds to one's knowledge base and impacts teaching practices. This knowledge assists in selecting DAP teaching strategies.

WHAT WE HAVE LEARNED—CHAPTER SUMMARY

This chapter addressed teaching and working with children whose first languages are ones other than English. This group, commonly referred to as English language learners (ELL), is rapidly growing as a result of an increasing number of immigrants coming to the United States. ELL children come from every corner of the world. Demographical data show that most ELL children are Spanish speakers, followed by Asian and Pacific Islanders ethnic groups. Children and their families bring a variety of language experiences including various proficiency levels in both their home and second languages. Research has shown that acquiring a second language has many developmental benefits, particularly in the areas of social and cognitive development. Current teaching practices advocate for the preservation of heritage languages while supporting the acquisition of English. Similar to acquiring a first language, second-language acquisition is a process that occurs in stages. Well-designed and intentionally developed classroom activities support the process. A welcoming classroom environment and close collaboration with families are other important elements that play a major role in supporting ELL children's language acquisition experiences.

MAKING CONNECTIONS . . .

1. Visit a preschool serving English language learners (ELL) and observe one of the children. Using as a reference the stages of second language acquisition, observe the communication strategies that the child uses. Note the use of either home language or English.

2. Develop a sample lesson plan for the group of ELL children where you conducted your observations. Reflect on the experience of planning for ELL children and comment about what was more challenging.

3. Interview an early childhood educator about ways to facilitate communication with ELL families. Using the findings from the interview, create a list of appropriate strategies to foster communication with children who are speakers of languages other than English.

RECOMMENDED INTERNET RESOURCES

- Center for Applied Linguistics
  www.cal.org/topics/ell/

- Information about researched-based practices to meet the needs of English language learners
  Colorin, Colorado
  www.colorincolorado.org
  This is a bilingual site with numerous ideas and resources for educators and parents

- *Responding to cultural and linguistic diversity*
  www.naeyc.org
  This is a Position statement from NAEYC.

- *How to make every child feel value*
  http://www.aplaceofourown.org/downloads/tip_makechildvalued_07.pdf
  A *Place of our own* is a PBS program. The website provides a variety of ideas and suggestions to make culturally and linguistically diverse children feel welcome.

- *Safeguarding the intangible cultural heritage*
  http://www.unesco.org/culture/ich/index.php?lg=EN&pg=home
  A valuable site describing efforts to preserve aspects of culture such as language, architecture, and art works that represent the world's culture.

YOUR STANDARDS PORTFOLIO

naeyc Standard 1: Promoting Child Development and Learning

naeyc Standard 2: Building Family and Community Relations

naeyc Standard 4: Using Developmentally Effective Approaches to Connect with Children and Families

naeyc Standard 7: Early Childhood Field Experiences

InTASC Standard 2: Learning Differences

InTASC Standard 7: Planning for Instruction

Successfully meeting the needs of young ELL children begins with a thorough knowledge of the role of language and culture in the child's development. It also depends on carefully planned and child-oriented activities. The following activities are intended to help meet the NAEYC and INTASC standards that will help you appropriately support ELL children.

1. Plan a visit to the multicultural or ELL program coordinator of your local school district. Find out about the materials used with ELL children. Inquire about services available for typically developing children with diverse and linguistic differences as well as those with special needs.

2. Create a linguistic profile of your community. Consult the data from the Census for your community and identify the main languages that are spoken. You could also obtain information about languages from the local school district. Based on your findings, reflect on the implications that your findings have on addressing the needs of children and families.

3. Considering the languages spoken by families in your community, design a sample bulletin board to share materials and information.

4. Conduct observations in two classrooms with young ELL children (preschoolers, kindergarten, or primary-age children). Hold informal conversations with children. Note how they utilize language to communicate ideas, note the terms used to describe experiences, and ways in which they communicate with peers and adults. With preschoolers, observe them while at learning

centers. Take note about their use of language and record any instances where you see them 'sharing their culture' (phrases, names of objects, ways they are dressed, etc.).

5. Reflect on the observations and write a commentary describing how you would use the information from observations to plan classroom activities for ELL children.

6. Plan a read-aloud session for a group of ELL children. Create a set of materials to facilitate comprehension and promote vocabulary development. Implement your activity if possible.

REFERENCES

August, D., & Shanahan, T. (Eds.). (2006). *Developing literacy in second language learners: Report of the national literacy panel on language minority youth and children*. Mahwah, NJ: Erlbaum.

Bodrova, E. & Leong, D. (2006). *Tools of the mind: The Vygostkian approach to early childhood education.* (2nd ed.). NJ: Prentice Hall.

Capps, R., Fix, M., Ost, J., Reardon-Anderson, J., & Passel, J. (2006). *The health and well-being of young children of immigrants*. Washington, DC: The Urban Institute.

Collier, V. (Fall, 1995). Acquiring a Second Language for School. *Directions in Language & Education*, vol. 1, no. 4. National Clearinghouse for Bilingual Education.

Early Head Start National Resource Center and Office of Head Start. (2010). *Revisiting and updating the multicultural principles for Head Start programs serving children ages birth to five*. Washington, DC: Author.

Espinosa, L. (2008). *Challenging common myths about teaching English language learners.* FCD Policy Brief no. 8. Advancing PK-3. Retrieve from https://www. claytonearlylearning.org/files/espinosaarticle.pdf.

García, E. (2005). *Teaching and learning in two languages: Bilingualism and schooling in the United States*. New York, NY: Teachers College Press

Genesee, F. (2000). Brain development: Implications for second language learning. *ERIC Digest.* ERIC Clearinghouse on Languages and Linguistics. ED 447727

Hulit, L. Howard, M. & Fahey, K. . (2011). *Born to talk. An introduction to speech and language development.* (5th ed.). Boston, MA: Pearson.

Malone, E. (2008). *Endangering languages. Special Report.* Retrieved from http://www.nsf.gov/news/special_reports/linguistics/endangered.jsp

National Center for Education Statistics. (2009). *Characteristics of public, private and Bureau of Indian education elementary and secondary schools in the United States: Results from the 2007-2008 schools and staffing survey.* Retrieved from http://nces.ed.gov/pubs2009/2009321/

National Association for the Education of Young Children. (1995). *Position Statement. Responding to linguistic and cultural diversity. Recommendations for effective early childhood education.* Washington, DC: Author.

National Clearinghouse for English Language Acquisition and Language Instruction Educational Programs (NCELA). (2006). Urbana, IL: Author.

National Council of Teachers of English. (2006). Washington, DC: Author.

Office of Head Start. (2008). *Dual language learning. What does it take? Head Start dual language report.* Washington, DC: Author.

Otto, B. (2009). *Language development in early childhood.* (3rd ed.). NJ: Prentice Hall.

Owens, R. (2012). *Language development. An introduction.* (6th ed.). Boston, MA: Allyn and Bacon.

Robles de Meléndez, W. & Valdés, M. (2008). *Preserving children's oral traditions.* Presentation at the Annual Conference of the National Association for the Education of Young Children. Dallas, TX.

Shin, H. & Kominsky, R. (2010). *Language use in the United States 2007.* United States Bureau of Census. Retrieved from http://www.census.gov/prod/2010pubs/acs-12.pdf

Tabors, P. (2008). One child, two languages. A *Guide for Early Childhood Educators of Children Learning English as a Second Language* (2nd ed.) Baltimore, MD: Paul Brookes.

Thomas, W. & Collier, V. (2002). A *national study of school effectiveness for language minority students' long-term academic achievement*. Washington, DC: Office of Educational Research and Improvement.

UNESCO. (2003). *Education in a multilingual world. UNESCO Position paper.* Retrieved from http://unesdoc.unesco.org/images/0012/001297/129728e.pdf

Activities and Resources for Multicultural Teaching: A World of Possibilities!

An environment that is rich in possibilities for exploring gender, race/ethnicity, and different ableness sets the scene for practicing anti-bias [and multicultural] curriculum.

—Louise Derman-Sparks (1989)

Wadsworth/Cengage Learning

STANDARDS: THE FOLLOWING STANDARDS ARE ADDRESSED IN THIS CHAPTER:

naeyc **Standard 4:** Using Developmentally Effective Approaches to Connect with Children and Families

naeyc **Standard 5:** Using Content Knowledge to Build Meaningful Curriculum

naeyc **Standard 6:** Becoming a Professional

InTASC Standard 3: Learning Environment

InTASC Standard 4: Content Knowledge

InTASC Standard 9: Professional Learning and Ethical Practice

TEACHERS SHARE

Mr. Herman, a student intern at a local prekindergarten, looked very excited as he came into the classroom. He was holding a large bag which caught the eye of his cooperating teacher who came over curious to know what he had.

"Good morning, Ms. Morris," he said laying the bag on one of the round tables.

"Indeed it is a good morning, Herman. I see that you bring a lot of goodies," remarked his cooperating teacher.

"Oh yes," he replied as he started to get things out of the bag. "Remember when we talked about making the dramatic area more appealing for children? Well, look at what I brought," he said showing her an array of artifacts. Among them were a variety of kitchen utensils

CHAPTER OBJECTIVE

Upon reading this chapter and reflecting on its content, you will be able to plan an appropriate environment that included, resources, and varied activities for a multicultural classroom.

KEY CONCEPTS

- behaviors
- attitudes
- creativity
- instructional experiences
- instructional materials
- learning encounters
- classroom environment

including some that Ms. Morris have never seen before, small dishes, pots, several empty food boxes and canned products, and even a couple of cookbooks.

"This is great. Where did you find them?" his cooperating teacher asked.

"One of my neighbors is moving and was giving them away. And I thought they would be perfect for the classroom," said Mr. Herman.

"They surely are," replied Ms. Morris.

A couple of days later, Mr. Herman was sitting at the table in the socio-dramatic play area. Open on the table was one of the cookbooks he had brought. A four year-old came over with a *greca*, a typical Latino espresso maker. She carefully pretended to pour something in the cup in front of him. "Here is your coffee," the little girl said.

"*Está caliente*," she said with emphasis looking at him. "Yes, it's hot," Mr. Herman replied as he pretended to sip the "coffee." "Hot" repeated the expressive four year-old turning to the toy cupboard where she started to sort some of the empty food boxes. A boy and girl joined them and sat at the table while the busy four year-old came over to talk with the "visitors."

From a corner in the room, Ms. Morris smiled at Mr. Herman, while the children continued playing very actively engaged in a lively conversation.

BUILDING A CLASSROOM FOR OUR MULTICULTURAL SOCIETY

You learned in the previous chapters that the classroom is a very important place of learning for young students. The classroom is where the microcosm of reality is encountered in forms of the new ideas, concepts, and social interactions the students experience. Similar to the opening scenario, in this chapter we will discuss how to design appropriate activities and use materials and resources that will support the children's culture and help them learn about diversity. You will see how the ideas discussed throughout the book become classroom practices.

THE MANY ENVIRONMENTS OF A CLASSROOM

The classroom environment is an important teaching vehicle in early childhood education. The classroom is not only a place where the teacher and the students meet but also a part of the teaching process as a learning and communication medium. It is important to consider the impressions and messages conveyed to the children through the classroom environment.

The organized and informal activities that take place in the classroom include complex intellectual and social actions that represent a microcosm of the real world. Individuals, young and old, who find themselves in classroom settings create ideas, make discoveries, exchange views, and rehearse ways to interact in a larger social context. Changes in personal views, positions, and attitudes are often derived from classroom activities.

Figure 9-1
Classroom
Environments

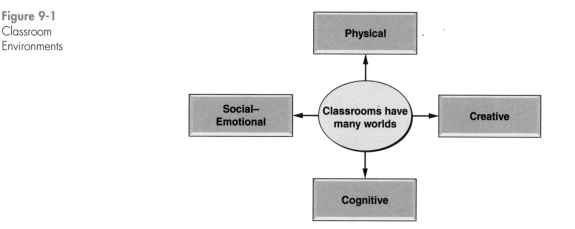

Classroom activities and events can be classified into four major worlds or environments: the physical, the cognitive, the social–emotional, and the creative (Figure 9-1). These four environments need to be both developmentally based and child centered.

The Physical Environment

The physical environment—defined by all the objects found within an identified space—is considered the most overt of the four classroom worlds. The space itself is something over which the teacher usually has little or no control because it is assigned by the center or school administrators. Adequate classroom space is frequently a problem in early childhood programs. According to the accreditation criteria from the National Association for the Education of Young Children (NAEYC), space should be allocated according to the number of children enrolled. It also indicates that the physical environment must be of high quality because it affects the behavior and development of children.

The physical environment also encompasses the equipment, furniture, and teaching materials located in the classroom. The adequate and developmentally based combination of all these elements makes a good classroom for each child.

Research in classroom practice shows that the classroom environment impacts the behavior, knowledge acquisition, and emotional state of the child. Curtis and

IN ACTION . . .

• What do you remember about the classrooms of the schools you attended?

• If you are currently teaching, what does your classroom say to those who enter?

Wadsworth/Cengage Learning

Learning about their heritage is important to young children.

Carter (2003) indicate that young children's learning spaces should be inviting, warm, and colorful. Such stimulating environments contribute to the development of appropriate behaviors and attitudes as well as support the major goals of multiculturalism.

The efforts of many early childhood educators have been hindered by the disregard for the physical setting as a determining element for success of children. John Holt (cited by Ornstein & Hunkins, 2008) once pointed out the value of the physical setting as being an effective motivator of students. He also stated that if the role of the learning setting were more seriously considered in the teaching-learning process, teachers would achieve more success.

AROUND **THE WORLD**

CLASSROOMS

Not all classrooms are the same. Just like culture, they reflect the ideas and values of their people. Among those things that children coming to the United States remember are early childhood settings in their native countries. Some were much different than those they experience in this country. Sometimes the differences in the physical environment are the most distinct.

Rosales (1992), who came to the United States from Puerto Rico, recalls her impressions of the first U.S. classroom she encountered:

"My eyes were fixed on the door. It was closed and it remained closed *all the time*! I couldn't help but miss the classrooms in my island where the doors were always open, where I could always see the sky and hear the world outside. And, we had windows from which we could see the mountains and hear the noises of the airplanes ready to

land. This room has those high windows that don't let you see anything. Here, the noise of the air conditioner never stops. And it's cold. One feels trapped inside the classroom."

Although the physical elements may vary, each culture organizes the classroom environment to provide optimum learning conditions for children. Conversations with children and families about previous experiences help educators learn about the children themselves. This also helps educators become more familiar with the children's current realities and previous experiences. The *Global Guidelines for Early Childhood Education and Care in the 21st Century* is a valuable document that provides expectations for organizing learning environments for children that are applicable in any part of the world (ACEI, 2000).

A carefully designed classroom arrangement can facilitate children's interactions.

The Cognitive Environment

A classroom is a place of continuous intellectual activity. Intellectual or cognitive activity is the process of forming and acquiring ideas and concepts. Cognition thrives in young children when they are given opportunities to experience and discover realities on their own. A good cognitive environment facilitates experiences that challenge and allow the children to discover and make sense of their reality. They are expected to make errors during the process. For Piaget, this stage of error making is as important as that of discovering the truth. Teachers act as facilitators and companions for the children as they work around the challenges. Questions rather than answers abound because the intention is to lead the children into self-discovery.

The Social–Emotional Environment

The social–emotional environment can be perceived by the "feeling" a child gets from being in the classroom. Social interactions in the classroom between the teacher and the students, as well as among the students themselves, can clearly convey a sense of welcome and acceptance or of something quite the opposite, such as fear and rejection. Because the early childhood years are a formative period, attention to social–emotional development is fundamental. Much of the children's time is dedicated to further development of this domain. The emerging social experience of the child underlines the need for making social–emotional development a major focus of the teacher's efforts.

Every area of the classroom presents opportunities for children to explore and discover their culture and those of others.

Figure 9-2 Words Can Reveal the Emotional Atmosphere of the Classroom

Comments can send strong messages to a child. Think about the impressions that the following make:

1. "He can't do it. He does not know English."
2. "They can't understand the story. In their country, they don't have those things."
3. "Oh, well. She *is* LD, you know."
4. "It doesn't look like food to me." (referring to an ethnic snack)
5. "I learned to read already. If you don't want to learn, that's up to you."
6. "Here we use utensils, not our hands."

Behaviors are actions exhibited by individuals in response to certain situations or stimuli. Attitudes are the dispositions people have toward others and/or to a circumstance that guide their overt and covert behavior. The behaviors and attitudes of adults and of other children convey messages that a child can use to construct his or her own responses and ideas. Classrooms and homes are among the ideal settings for acquiring the responses and behaviors commonly related to multicultural education, such as tolerance, understanding, and acceptance of the cultural differences present in society (Figure 9-2).

The Creative Environment

Creativity can be defined as the special ability to see things in unusual or unconventional ways (Cropley, 1992). Creativity is an important resource in multicultural education and an essential element of the classrooms where teaching about diversity takes place. A classroom where nontraditional ideas and views are fostered is an ideal setting for promoting creativity. An environment that is open and flexible serves as a vehicle for growth and development, especially if the children are encouraged to find alternative ways to approach realities. For example, children are encouraged to find solutions to situations presenting unfair treatment of others.

MAKING THE BEST USE OF TEACHING ENVIRONMENTS

For years, educators have focused attention on the intellectual content while little attention has been paid to the setting, or the physical space, where instruction takes place. Comments about procedures, goals, and objectives abound in curriculum materials, but directions on how to organize the stage—that is, the classroom—are much more difficult to locate. In teaching for diversity, the role of the physical context is as important as what is discussed and shared. An educator of young children knows that imagination and ability to conceptualize are sparked when children are surrounded by an environment that is visually and emotionally inviting. To maximize the power of the classrooms, let us examine how they can be turned into powerful instruments of education about diversity.

A CLASSROOM FOR TEACHING AND LEARNING ABOUT DIVERSITY

The multicultural classroom is a place where the teacher attempts to guide young children through the process of learning to live with diversity. This process of social transformation requires a special setting conducive to the children's dreaming, fantasizing, skill building, and socialization. Such classrooms already exist in many schools across the United States; however, many more need to be transformed into the learning settings that children deserve and need.

ORGANIZING THE CLASSROOM

Arranging the classroom goes beyond moving furniture and having work areas. Creating an appropriate multicultural classroom requires the knowledge about classroom elements. Three elements make up the classroom: the space, the interest areas, and the instructional resources. In addition to these, there is the classroom's arrangement. Awareness of these elements will help the early childhood educator with any change efforts (Figure 9-3).

A Flexible Space Where Objects Are Carefully Arranged

An early childhood classroom should be a space especially designed for young children. Equipment and furniture are selected according to the developmental needs of the children and are multifunctional. This gives each classroom its own character. For

Figure 9-3 Multicultural Early Childhood Classroom Arrangement

Space	Interest areas	Arrangement	Instructional resources
– Flexible, well ventilated and lighted. – Meets DCAP criteria for physical space. – Includes access to a DCAP playground.	– Includes the following: housekeeping, art, dramatic play, blocks, literacy, language, discovery, and manipulatives. – Includes rotating areas. Areas can be converted to accommodate new interests or topics. – Interest areas are periodically rotated or modified to replicate organization in other cultural groups (i.e., the dramatic area, the housekeeping area).	– Equipment is flexibly arranged and periodically modified. – Children use arrangement freely. – Display of objects and materials are child-oriented and reflect a learning target. – Needs of exceptional children are reflected in the arrangement.	– A variety of nonbiased, nonsexist, multicultural materials exists. – Resources reflect the characteristics of children, their families, and the community. – Labeling in more than one language is observed. – Pictures, posters, and other visual aids reflect diversity. – Emphasis on what is actual practice or typically current is depicted in the resources. – A balance between what is current and what is traditional is found in the materials.

example, tables and chairs are not just for children to sit on but also to use for other purposes. A rocker in the infant room is not just a place to soothe the child but also a place where lullabies and stories are shared. In the preschool classroom, a table turned on its side can become a puppet theater, or it can serve as a workplace for arts and crafts. Because of the classroom's flexible use, teachers need to ensure that the arrangements correspond not only to the age level of the group but also to their needs. This is especially true of children with exceptionalities who may require specific furniture, equipment, or materials to accommodate their needs.

The Interest Areas

The space in early childhood classrooms is best organized into learning or interest areas. Terms such as *learning area, center,* or *station* refer to those spaces where specific activities take place and related materials are provided for children's use. A major portion of what the child learns occurs in learning centers.

Learning areas offer a variety of instructional experiences. Each learning center is usually organized around a specific developmental area or topic and is intended to promote acquisition of concepts and skills. Careful selection of age-appropriate materials, how these are displayed, and opportunities to engage in their use will influence the children's responses and learning. What to include for diversity will be described later on in this chapter.

Classroom Arrangement

The *arrangement* refers to the classroom space targeted at supporting the children's abilities. It is essential that there be flexibility and accommodation when using the classroom and all within it. For example, objects in the center of the room and on the walls should be easily movable and appropriately sized so that the children are able to manipulate them. Images on the walls should be placed at eye level so that the children can easily see and enjoy them. Any arrangements for children with disabilities need to be flexible and accommodating of their needs. An appropriately arranged classroom allows for good flow and makes it easy for the teacher to see what the children are doing.

Instructional Materials

Didactic or instructional materials are the common denominator of all classrooms. Instructional materials include a broad category of objects ranging from commercially produced resources to teacher-made classroom materials, real objects, objects on the wall and hanging from the ceiling, the costumes in the play chest, and any item that promotes learning.

All objects that comprise the classroom environment have the potential of influencing children. Consider, for instance, the impact of a poster of community helpers in which all the professionals, such as the physician, the lawyer, and the engineer, are portrayed as European Americans, whereas the custodian and the sanitation employee are depicted as minorities. Take, for example, a classroom with children with special needs but where no images convey the idea that they are part of the group. The message sent is a subtle but an influential one for the children, who are just beginning to form ideas about the world.

GUIDELINES FOR A MULTICULTURAL CLASSROOM ENVIRONMENT

Central to effectively planning and organizing the space for multicultural teaching is answering the following question: What characteristics of the classroom make it suitable for teaching about diversity?

There are many sources of valuable ideas for creating the ideal classroom environment for teaching about diversity. For many years, experts in the field and professional organizations have shared their visions about an ideal multicultural classroom (Banks, 2007; Byrnes & Kiger, 2005; Davidman & Davidman, 2000; Derman-Sparks & the A.B.C. Task Force, 1989; Hernandez, 2000; Neugebauer, 1992; Nieto & Bode, 2008; Peck & Shores, 1994). Although some recommendations were not particular to early childhood classrooms, their insights provide relevant ideas (e.g., Banks, 2007; Davidman & Davidman, 2000; Hernandez, 2000; Nieto & Bode, 2008). Through this analysis of the findings, we identified the following seven areas of emphasis:

- learning materials, including all manipulatives, books, toys, props, classroom decorations, and everything written
- art
- literature
- music and movement
- games and play activities
- attitudes and behavior
- activities

We will focus our attention on the first five areas. The remaining areas, *attitudes and behavior* and *activities*, will be discussed in another section of this chapter.

To better understand the multicultural classroom environment, it is important to consider the following questions about the first five elements:

- How do they contribute to a successful multicultural education program?
- How do they meet the needs of young children?
- What should each one be like in a multicultural classroom?
- What does each one consist of?

These are the questions that we plan to answer as we "walk through" the multicultural early childhood classroom environment.

Learning Materials

Children use learning materials to experience, ponder, produce, and process ideas. Instructional materials are necessary resources that help children acquire and shape knowledge. The Piagetian approach suggests that materials are an important resource to provoke cognitive construction in the child. Because they incite interest and learning, careful and intentional planning is essential. As a first step, ask yourself: *Are these resources developmentally appropriate? Do they match the age and individual characteristics of the children?* Guidelines to help early childhood educators answer these questions are presented in Focus on Classroom Practices, in which we summarize ideas and suggestions for selecting classroom materials with a developmental focus. These suggestions offer ways to choose resources that are appropriate and cognitively challenging, a pertinent aspect in multicultural education for young children.

Bias-free Classroom Resources

Good multicultural classroom materials need to be free of biases, stereotypes, and misrepresentations of cultural groups. As a practice, never rely on the title or content of a resource. Instead, take time to verify the nature of learning materials by asking the

FOCUS
ON CLASSROOM PRACTICES

USING A DEVELOPMENTAL FOCUS TO SELECT INSTRUCTIONAL MATERIALS

Selection of learning materials is a task that requires time and caution. Here are some helpful tips for selecting materials for the early childhood multicultural classroom:

1. Before selecting materials, keep in mind the age levels and needs of children in your classroom or care.

2. Be mindful about what is meaningful and relevant for children to learn. Make sure that materials match the content and the needs of children (special needs, linguistic differences, cultural differences).

3. Always take time to carefully examine materials or resources before they are selected. Check the instructions, if any, and identify the purpose and goals. Verify

that these connect with the curricular experiences and expected learning outcomes.

4. Consider materials that provide opportunities for all intellectual levels and that may be used to promote a variety of skills and concept learning.

5. Select materials that intrigue children and promote exploration and inquiry. For example, consider real and unconventional items that will spark the children's curiosity. Remember that interest guides learning, which becomes the foundation for knowledge.

6. Consider the physical needs of children, including those with disabilities. Choose materials that are appropriate and safe to manipulate by all children.

following: Do these materials present an accurate, bias-free, and stereotype-free picture of the group?

Karen Matsumoto-Grah (in Byrnes & Kiger, 1992) establishes seven guidelines for selecting materials that include all the aspects of diversity. She recommends observing to determine whether the materials do the following:

1. Present the contributions of groups other than European Americans; reflect a cross-cultural perspective of what women have contributed

2. Portray people, including women, without stereotypes (for instance, European Americans portrayed as professionals and minorities portrayed as poor) across socioeconomic classes and religions

3. Depict religious issues appropriately "when religion is integral to the context of the subject"

4. Give socially balanced views of famous people; that is, include outstanding people from both the privileged and working classes

5. Reflect the cultures and ethnicities of the classroom children and of their community

6. Exhibit and include the native languages present in the class (for example, if the class has children who speak Spanish and French-Creole, materials in those languages should be available)

7. Are at the developmental level of the children and offer challenges with opportunities to experience success

Both Kendall (1996) and Derman-Sparks (1989) call attention to the need for teachers to ensure that classroom resources are totally bias-free. In their opinion, during the formative years, it is of utmost importance to make the classroom a place where the child will experience and encounter human and social differences as an aspect that characterizes people. Targeting unbiased representations should be one of the first aspects to emphasize when choosing materials. This means scrutinizing what and how the content is presented in resources (see Figure 9-4).

Avoiding "Token Diversity"

Many times, classrooms exhibit what is called *token diversity* (Derman-Sparks & the A.B.C. Task Force, 1989). Tokenism happens, for instance, when there is just one doll or artifact of a given ethnic group. While it may seem a way to evidence representation, it minimizes the existence of certain cultures and groups, such as women and the elderly. Token representation reduces the importance and significance of the contributions and roles of a group (King, Chipman, & Cruz-Janzen, 1994). More importantly, a minimal inclusion of the elements of diversity will not transform your classroom into a culturally responsive setting.

Figure 9-4 Ways
to Appropriately
Depict a Cultural
Group

What is presented shows

- A variety of gender roles and racial and cultural backgrounds
- A variety of occupations
- A variety of ages
- A variety of abilities (includes special-needs individuals from different backgrounds)
- A variety in time (past and present) and place (local, national, international)

How it is presented portrays

- An assortment of social contexts
- Contrasting lifestyles and configurations
- A variety of languages (those of the children must be acknowledged first, and then others as chosen by the teacher)
- An assortment of representations or symbols to depict a given event or fact
- Different social and racial groups
- An accurate portrayal of racial characteristics (pictures do not use the Caucasian facial traits to depict different races/ethnic groups)

Two main reasons for tokenism are the lack of awareness among teachers about the importance and the need to establish appropriate settings for diversity and insufficient time to transform the classroom environment. In examining the first reason, many new and experienced teachers throughout this country still refuse to acknowledge the importance of teaching multiculturally. Some of them still argue that in the past, children learned fine without any special materials "about the others." Others still cling to the traditional phrase: "Children don't see colors. They only see children." Research does not support either one of these positions. Allocating time to choose good, child-appropriate materials for adapting the classroom environment is essential to effectively plan and design an environment that promotes multiculturalism.

The best way for teachers to avoid tokenism is to not display the single item, such as a doll, from a specific culture and to save it until other items are acquired. Some early childhood teachers have found that families and staff members are a good source for obtaining images that more accurately convey diversity. For example, in a migrant program, teachers took digital images of parents, family members, and staff. With the help of a computer photograph program, these were reproduced and printed as classroom posters. Another solution, as observed in some classrooms, is to use pictures along with the dolls or real objects. Teachers in a classroom of 3-year-olds visited by one of the writers, for example, selected magazine and catalog pictures of ethnic dolls, pasted them on pieces of cardboard, and laminated them. The pictures were placed among the real dolls. The children used the paper dolls in much the same way as they used the real ones because of the magic of "pretend play."

When to Keep and When to Remove Materials

You may find that some of your multicultural materials may not meet the criteria for appropriate classroom resources. Decisions to remove a given item should be based only on the character of the stereotypic or misleading information that it contains. Even materials depicting stereotypes can serve as teaching resources (Derman-Sparks & the A.B.C. Task Force, 1989). Used only by the teacher, and not available to the class, they can be kept as part of the materials.

Two things can be done before making the determination to remove any inappropriate resources from the classroom. One, incorporate the cultural elements into the existing material; and two, consider the possibility of altering or transforming the materials. Start by checking how the resource could be altered or modified (Derman-Sparks & the A.B.C. Task Force, 1989). For example, a set of manipulatives depicting people can be altered by adding figures with different ethnic characteristics. The dramatic area can be enhanced by including dresses representing different ethnicities. Artifacts common to specific cultures and a balance of gender objects can also be included. In the case of pictures and posters, collages can be prepared with pictures portraying other cultures. You can also paste pictures over those in posters or even in books (Derman-Sparks & the A.B.C. Task Force, 1989). This will visually change and broaden the resources. For the manipulatives area, puzzles reflecting different elements of diversity can be easily made by teachers or volunteers. Curtis and Carter (2003) suggest preparing flash cards and other manipulatives with pictures that depict characteristics of the various cultures represented by the children in the classroom.

Art as a Source of Awareness about Diversity

The arts are humanity's expression of life itself.

Merryl Goldberg (2006)

The art center is another important place in the classroom. Art serves the purpose of offering children the opportunities to explore ways to use the materials to represent what they perceive through their senses. Art is a powerful source for learning that can also facilitate learning about diversity.

The colors of the paints are the first art objects that should be expanded. Adding more browns, tans, and black will allow the children to play with various skin color tones inducing the children to notice their own skin color and those of their classmates. Creative ways of developing these tones include using chocolate or coffee, which can be diluted to create various shades of brown.

Art can help young children dispel the most damaging of myths: that people are divided by the color of their skins (Allport, 1986). Tempera paints, crayons, and markers can be selected to include more colors reflecting the range of skin tones. There are effective multicultural art materials, such as the multicultural crayons that contain many varieties of skin shades. Another very useful item is the multicultural modeling clay.

IN ACTION . . .

"I'M NOT THAT DOLL!"

A student visiting a mostly European American kindergarten classroom overheard a discussion among three girls. Two of the girls were European Americans and one was an African American. The girls were working in the dramatic area. One of the girls was holding a black doll. Everything had been going well until one of the girls called the black doll "Elissa," the name of the African American child. "That's not me. I told you the last time. Give her another name!" said the child, clearly upset. Judging by Elissa's reaction, this was not the first time this had happened. The two girls continued calling the doll by the same name. "Oh, yes, see, it has her face and her hair. It is Elissa," said the younger one, while her friend gave an affirmative nod. This time, Elissa snatched the doll away and threw it into the trash can. At that point, the teacher intervened and took the opportunity to talk about what happened. While talking with the children, she realized that the African American doll was the only ethnic doll in the classroom. The teacher understood the negative effect "tokenism" can have on children.

- How would you handle this situation?
- What kind of a class lesson can emerge from this experience?

Teachers can also shade play dough to produce various skin shades using powdered tempera and even cocoa powder (see Figure 9-5). Whether teacher-made or commercially produced, multicultural art supplies should be available in the classroom at all times.

Felt, art paper, and construction paper in shades of brown and black are other important materials to include in the art center. Traditionally, only white paper has been used. However, when children are drawing pictures of themselves, family, and friends, they should find paper in shades that more accurately reflect their reality. The shades of tan and natural are more appropriate than the plain white paper. An inexpensive source is the packing paper that comes in a natural shade. Also useful are brown grocery bags. Manila folders and a roll of manila paper are additional sources of art materials.

Figure 9-5
Easy-to-Make
Multicultural Play
Dough

You will need the following ingredients:

    4 cups corn starch
    1 cup salt
    1 1/2 cups water
    powdered tempera (brown, red) or cocoa
    2 1/2 cups water

Mix all the ingredients. The amount of tempera or cocoa to add will depend on the skin colors you want to make. Place on medium heat for 5 minutes, until it thickens. Remove from heat. Cover the pot with a wet paper towel. When cool, knead for about 5 minutes, working on a surface covered with waxed paper. When making objects, allow them to dry before painting.

FOCUS
ON CLASSROOM PRACTICES

DISCOVERING THE COLORS OF PEOPLE

The first-grade class was working on a project, "Friends Across the Border," when the teacher discovered that most of the children thought the people in the countries neighboring the United States were "not white." This incited an argument among some fair-skin Hispanics who refused to be described as "not white," arguing that their skin was as light as that of others in the class. Everything reached a climax when several members of the class agreed: "They can't be white because they speak Spanish." The teacher understood that the children were using not only race but also language to define others. She decided to do something immediately to correct the misconceptions.

The teacher proceeded to divide the class into teams of five. Then, using white play dough as well as different shades of play dough that resembled the various colors of the skin, she asked the children to match the play dough to the colors of the skin of their group members.

The results were recorded on a graph. Upon completing the survey, the teacher entered the names of the colors the children chose during the discussion. The colors ranged from peachy, rose, and dark peach to tan, burnt brown, and "kind of creamy vanilla." All names were accepted and entered. Then, the groups began to share their findings. At the end, the column that read "white" was empty, while the rest of the entries appeared in all the other categories. "What do we see in this graph?" "Where do we have most of the names? Where do we have the least names, or no names?" Without hesitation, the answers began to show the truth. Entries of colors with a variety of fancy names were entered in the graph. At the end, no entries were made for the category depicting "white." "No one is really white," said a child of very fair skin, who described himself as being "golden vanilla." "Why do they say that people are white or black? They lied to us," said one girl.

The teacher, by using self-discovery, helped the children to clarify their ways of looking at others and ensured the continuous harmony in the class.

Arts and crafts activities contribute to the holistic development of the child by providing opportunities for "actively solving problems, thinking critically, becoming visually literate, making aesthetic decisions, weighing and measuring, expressing themselves, using their imaginations, communicating with peers, and developing motor skills" (Gómez, 1999). Children need to have access to the materials used in handicrafts to explore and experiment. Part of the classroom art area should include selected art forms and handicrafts from the children's own cultural groups as well as from other groups they will learn about. A sample of the materials listed in Figure 9-6 can enhance the

Figure 9-6
Common Art Materials Used by Different Cultures

- dry gourds, dry coconut shells, beans, seeds, leaves (Caribbeans, Africans, Native American groups)
- feathers, clay, colored beads, strings (Latin Americans, Native American groups)
- yarn, scraps of fabric, sequins, glitter, watercolors (Asians, Europeans, Latin Americans)
- straw, sticks, twigs, raffia (Latin Americans, Native American groups, Africans, Asians)
- sea shells, dry fish scales, coral rocks (Caribbeans, Asians)

FOCUS
ON CLASSROOM PRACTICES

TEACHERS ARE ALWAYS RESOURCEFUL!

A first-grade teacher ran out of art paper one day. She found some brown boxes that had been discarded and had an idea. She cut the boxes into pieces of various sizes, placed them on the art table, and waited for the reactions. When children asked what they were, she said they were "special art canvases for pictures they could easily hang after they finished them." The result was a lot of "artistic canvases" the children displayed around the classroom. The experience was so successful that the teacher decided to make corrugated cardboard a permanent part of the art supplies.

---

child's perspective of other people. In parentheses, we have indicated the cultural groups that more frequently use these art materials. You may add some others. A preschool teacher shared another interesting source for materials, described in Focus on Classroom Practices.

The colors white and black have been ascribed with the symbolism of good and evil in Western society. Unfortunately, this concept has been extended into the racial context that children encounter very early in life. Classroom activities can be designed to disperse and correct these unfounded views. Teachers can set aside specific days when the only art items to be used are those of less frequently used colors, such as blacks and browns. This is a way of helping children overcome their socially based fear of these colors. For instance, a preschool or kindergarten class can take a field trip around their neighborhood to see all the things that are the various shades of brown or black. We can already anticipate a long list of items! The realization that these colors are part of our daily life is a start for children to see that there is nothing mysterious or malicious about them.

Carefully selected materials promote interest and encourage interactions among children.

Wadsworth/Cengage Learning

Using Artwork to Promote Diversity

The arts as an aspect of culture provide insights into various groups. For example, artwork representative of different ethnic groups is a valuable source that brings cultures and diverse images into the classroom. It also engages the child in appreciating the artistic work of famous masterpieces and of local artists.

Artwork also connects children with tangible aspects of their own culture and those of peers and adults. Use of color, choice of materials, and representations all provide ways to learn more about the traditions and ideas of a group. There are many sources of artwork that can be used in the classroom. Some of these include the following:

- *Visits to local art museums:* Your local museum is one of the best sources. Contact the museum education department and find out about current and upcoming exhibits. Plan a field trip to the museum and have a guided visit. After the visit, engage children in a discussion about what they saw.

- *Posters and reproductions:* Posters of many well-known masterpieces are usually available from museums, bookstores, and teacher supply stores. Choose those that represent the work of different artists and different cultures.

- *Picture books:* Aside from the literary content, children's picture books are an excellent way to create awareness about how life events are interpreted and represented by different cultural groups. For example, Carmen Lomas Garza's *Cuadros de Familia/Family Pictures* (1990), Arthur Dorros's *Por Fin es Carnival* (1995), Demi's *One Grain of Rice* (1997), and Faith Ringgold's *Tar Beach* (1996) are among those that also introduce children to cultural artistic representations.

- *Photographs:* Photo collections are an excellent medium to expose children to the arts. Using a digital camera, create your own collection by taking pictures of artwork in the community and from local fairs.

- *Art fairs:* Local art fairs are one of the best sources for crafts typical to the community and representative of various cultures. Information on local activities can be found in newspapers, on public radio, and from community centers.

The Literacy Area

Literature is one of the most powerful sources of ideas, personal values, and wisdom. Donna Norton (1995) says that literature plays an important role in helping people learn and appreciate their cultural heritages. She further maintains its critical relevance in a multicultural society like ours:

> Carefully selected literature can illustrate the contributions and values of the many cultures and is especially critical to fostering an appreciation of the heritage of the minorities in U.S. society. A positive self-concept is not possible unless we respect others as well as ourselves; literature *can contribute considerably* [emphasis added] toward our understanding and thus our respect.

Some of the impressions, fantasies, and words many of us still cherish are from the stories, rhymes, and poems we heard or read as children. Our favorite books made us dream of unknown places and people. The benefits of literature go beyond the pleasure

VIDEO CASE 9.1 ▶️❚❚

Video Case Activity Using the Arts to Welcome Children's Culture

Go to the Cengage website and watch the video *Diversity: Teaching in a Multiethnic Classroom.* After watching the video, respond to the following questions:

1. What are some of the goals of using traditional art in this classroom?

2. How does it enhance the children's knowledge about their own culture and that of their peers?

and enchantment they provide. Literature is a complementary developmental element for the young child. Joan Glazer (cited by Norton, 2003) has listed four ways that literature promotes good emotional development. According to Glazer, a good selection of books in the classroom can (1) help children see that other people have the same emotions and feelings they do; (2) facilitate the exploration of feelings and emotions from a variety of perspectives; (3) show different ways to deal with emotions and feelings; and (4) demonstrate that, at times, what we feel might be in conflict with our own emotions (Norton, 2003).

Literature is one of those common denominators found across cultures. You can learn about the ideas, beliefs, values, and struggles of daily life in any country around the world through literature. Because of its powerful character for cultural transmission, literature is an ideal resource for multicultural education (Figure 9.7). In the opinion of Tway (cited by Norton, 2003), "[i]n a country of multicultural heritage, children require books that reflect and illuminate that varied heritage."

Figure 9-7 Using Literature to Develop Multicultural Awareness: Sample Planning Web

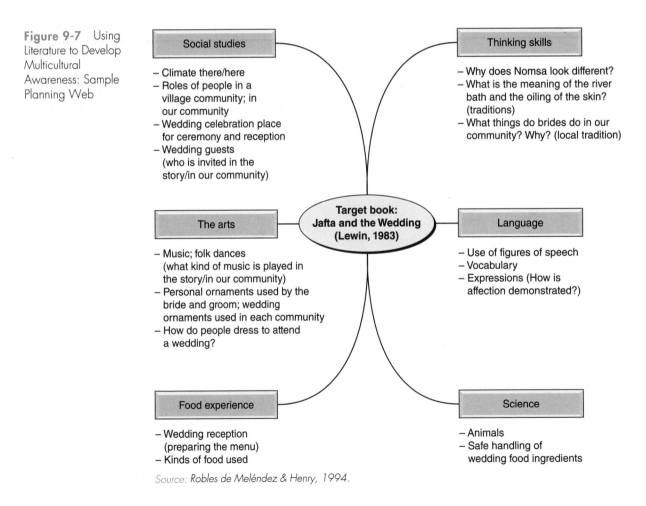

Social studies
– Climate there/here
– Roles of people in a village community; in our community
– Wedding celebration place for ceremony and reception
– Wedding guests (who is invited in the story/in our community)

Thinking skills
– Why does Nomsa look different?
– What is the meaning of the river bath and the oiling of the skin? (traditions)
– What things do brides do in our community? Why? (local tradition)

The arts
– Music; folk dances (what kind of music is played in the story/in our community)
– Personal ornaments used by the bride and groom; wedding ornaments used in each community
– How do people dress to attend a wedding?

Target book: Jafta and the Wedding (Lewin, 1983)

Language
– Use of figures of speech
– Vocabulary
– Expressions (How is affection demonstrated?)

Food experience
– Wedding reception (preparing the menu)
– Kinds of food used

Science
– Animals
– Safe handling of wedding food ingredients

Source: Robles de Meléndez & Henry, 1994.

The arts provide a source for children to express their feelings and to show pride about themselves.

Artwork like this painting from artist Nicoll Nicoll, which provides glimpses into her family and childhood traditions, can lead children to discuss their own families.

The emphasis on literacy development has opened the door to more quality literature for children. With it, a profusion of ethnic literature has also emerged because of the recognition given to the absence and misrepresentation of cultural groups. Today, most classrooms have a good supply of multicultural books. Discovering what kinds of books are in the classroom is important because of the power literature has for young children. Bonnie Neugebauer (1992) recommends assessing the classroom library corner to determine (1) how the books portray the characters; (2) the types of situations they present; (3) the value, accuracy, and appropriateness of the illustrations; (4) the nature of the messages conveyed in the stories; (5) the credibility of the author and illustrator to tell the story and portray the characters; and (6) whether the stories depict the ethnic groups and the diversity of the class and community.

Sources of good multicultural literature have significantly increased. Many book publishers have begun to include titles covering all aspects of diversity. Several book publishers and distributors specialize in the distribution of ethnic literature. Most local libraries also include multicultural books in their children's sections. A visit to the local library will lead teachers to find a wealth of literary resources appropriate for young children.

Using Journals, Magazines, and Newspapers

Journals, magazines, and newspapers are considered part of literature that can be used to enhance the children's learning process. They are excellent sources of pictures children can view while learning about their world and the worlds of others in our society. Periodicals and newspapers in different languages should be included in the classroom literature areas. They provide unique opportunities for the children to explore the linguistic symbols of other languages. Analyses of the various sections, such as the advertising section, found in foreign papers can turn into interesting activities for the children. Teachers can

LITERACY CONNECTIONS...

BOOKS ABOUT ANIMAL CHARACTERS THAT ADDRESS DIVERSITY ISSUES

- Best, C. (2009). *Goose's story*. New York: Farrar, Straus and Giroux.
  This is the true story of a goose with one foot and how he managed. It is very appropriate for discussing exceptionalities.

- Brett, J. (2003). *Town mouse, country mouse*. New York: G.P. Putnam Juvenile.
  The book is about two distinct cultures of city and country. The story is a classic that has many opportunities for discussion.

- Brett, J. (2010). *Three little Dessies*. New York: Puttman Juvenile.
  This is a South African adaptation of *Three little pigs*. The Dessies live in the desert and are harassed by the fierce eagle. The story can be used to discuss similarities between cultures. The book depicts the color-rich African setting complete with vegetation and animals.

  Hadithi, M. (2004). *The crafty chameleon*. New York: Hodder & Stoughton.
  This is a beautifully illustrated book that teaches children about how to cope with being different.

- Jenkins, S., & Page, R. (2003). *What do you do with a tail like this?* Boston: Houghton Mifflin.
  This is a fantastically illustrated book showing animals with different kinds of eyes, noses, tails, and other body parts. The differences allow for discussion about those with diverse characteristics and abilities.

- Kirk, D. (2000). *Little Miss Spider: Sunny Patch School*. New York: Scholastic Press Callaway.
  This is a rhyming tale of a spider that goes to school with other bugs. All the bugs seem to be able to do something special except for Miss Spider. Finally, she discovers her special ability.

- Lowell, S. (2009). *The three javelinas*. New York: Scholastic.
  The story is a version of *The three little pigs*. This book is great for comparing cultural similarities and differences.

  Nieman C. (2008). *The pet dragon: A story about adventure, friendship and Chinese characters*. New York: Green Willow Books.
  This is a book that introduces children to the Chinese characters. The story is about a little girl who has a pet dragon.

  Parkinson, J. (2010). *Pequeña the burro*. (Kindle ed.) Amazon Digital Services.
  This is a story of Pequeña the donkey who is unhappy to be "just a burro." A friend reminds Pequeña that being a "burro" is very important. The book promotes appreciation of diversity and bonds that unite people.

- Tsai, I. Y. (2008). *The frog in the well*. New York: CE Bilingual Books.
  This is a Chinese and English bilingual book that tells the story of the frog that lives happily in a well until a sea turtle tells him about the vast ocean.

obtain international papers and journals from local bookstores, newspaper stands, and, in some cases, from local ethnic stores. Other sources are the donations made by children's parents or by staff members who buy ethnic publications. Teachers are advised to examine the donated literature materials carefully to verify the appropriateness and the quality of the content. Figure 9.8 provides criteria for proper selection.

Many journals can also be added to the book center. For example, *National Geographic* and *World* (both from the National Geographic Society); *Faces: The Magazine About People* (Cobblestone Publishing); and *Smithsonian* (from the

Artistic expression is an important part of the development of young children.

Smithsonian Institution) make good additions to the classroom literature corner. They can be found in most public and school libraries.

Newspapers are an inexpensive source of rich cultural materials. They offer glimpses into the realities of other individuals and groups. A newspaper also reports on current views, attitudes, conflicts, and values of different ethnicities. Newspapers can help the child discern a variety of human characteristics through the racial and physical portrayals of people living in our communities.

We know a second-grade teacher who developed a project about people solely from newspapers. During an entire year, her students saved the pictures they thought best portrayed different people. More than 800 pictures pasted on tag board

Figure 9-8
Selecting Authentic Multicultural Literature: Evaluation Criteria

When selecting children's multicultural books, take time to find out if the story meets the following criteria:

- The story and characters present an accurate portrayal of a specific culture.
- The story is free of any historical distortions or stereotypes. Messages about the cultural group, including race and social class, are free of any biases.
- Characters are portrayed according to the time and setting. If set in contemporary times, characters reflect current lifestyles.
- Characters reflect a variety of physical diversities.
- Story presents people with disabilities in a positive, nonstereotypical way.
- Female and male characters are presented in a variety of roles that exemplify nonstereotypical tasks. Roles of females and males are consistent with those in their cultural groups.
- Elderly people are presented in respectful and culturally accurate ways.
- Roles and importance of families are reflective of views held by the cultural group.
- People from diverse groups are portrayed in positive and leadership roles.
- Illustrations depict the culture and people in culturally accurate ways.
- Language representative of the cultural group is used to enhance the message. Linguistic expressions of the cultural group reflect their oral traditions.
- Authors and illustrators are members of the cultural group or have firsthand knowledge about the culture.

Source: Adapted from Cullinan and Galda (2009); Kasten, Kristo, and McClure (2005); Norton (2003); and Robles de Meléndez (2004).

Figure 9-9
Ways to Organize
Pictures and Postcards

Sample theme topics in postcards	
• How we dress (clothing)	• Celebrations/festivals
• Things to eat	• Houses and buildings
• Flowers and trees	• People everywhere
• Faces	• Colors and decorations
• Places to visit	• Natural landscapes
• People's hats	• Fun places
• Musical instruments	

became a permanent picture file that captivated the children's imagination throughout the year.

Pictures are an important element of any literature corner. Journals, newspapers, and magazines are good sources of provocative illustrations. Postcards are an inexpensive source of good pictures, as well. Most people who travel are tempted to bring home cards that end up not being used. They can become an excellent resource in the classroom. Robles de Meléndez (2001) recommends that professionals use their "teacher's eye" in selecting postcards when traveling. The good "eye" alerts us to the images children will enjoy and savor in their imaginations. Postcards can easily be used to make picture books that will expand the literacy resources. A world map or globe should always be close to the literature area for easy consultation. The notion of "here and there" gives appropriate opportunities to compare and contrast for the purpose of finding out what makes us so alike.

Postcards have been successfully used by many educators at all levels to teach about communities and local history. Postcards were organized into thematic areas (architecture and historical scenes; major industry scenes, agriculture, and transportation; environment and tourist sites) that provided a wealth of perspectives for children. Teachers can either file them by topic or make picture books with them. A list of themes commonly found in postcards is given in Figure 9-9.

Ways to Enhance the Literature Area

An optimal literature area can be built by using some of the resources common to all schools: the stories of children and families. Grandparents and senior volunteers are invaluable sources of information and anecdotes about traditions and

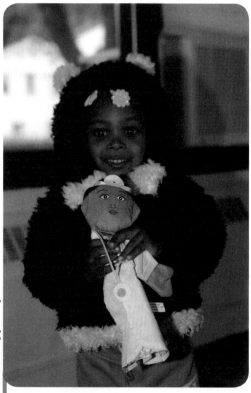

Objects reflective of the children's backgrounds can contribute to building a positive image about their heritage and ethnic groups.

Wadsworth/Cengage Learning

FOCUS
ON CLASSROOM PRACTICES

CINDERELLA, A TRADITIONAL LITERATURE CHARACTER CONNECTING CULTURES

Literature is one of the elements that link us in our multicultural and global community. Around the world, some story characters are common to many cultures. Such is the case of Cinderella. We selected a list of Cinderella stories to get you started in exploring more about how this character is seen through the lenses of people from other cultures. You may want to try some of the following activities. They include the key multicultural concepts for each activity.

- *Cultural heritage:* Using a map, locate the settings of the stories read. Talk about the locations and find out if anyone is familiar with the place. Identify whether any of the children or their families are natives of those countries.
- *Linguistic diversity:* Talk about the names of the Cinderella character in each of the stories. Highlight any words in other languages and have a discussion about the importance of languages. Prepare a Cinderella word chart and write down words in other languages learned from the stories.
- *Cultural patterns:* Using a Venn diagram, compare and contrast the stories (characters, name of the main character, setting, ways they are dressed, problem, and problem resolution). Have children draw their favorite scene and talk about what they liked best.
- *Gender issues:* Share with children any of the Cinderella stories with male characters (for example, *Sumorella: A Hawai'i Cinderella story* or *Joe Cinders*). Discuss how the situation applies to both boys and girls. Have children talk about and draw pictures of activities that can be performed across gender lines.

African:
- Climo, S. (1992). *The Egyptian Cinderella.* New York: HarperCollins.
- Steptoe, J. (2003). *Mufaro's beautiful daughters: An African tale.* New York: Viking Books.

Native American:
- Chenkie, B. (1999). *Naya, the Inuit Cinderella.* Green Bay, WI: Raven Tree Press.
- Pollock, P. (1996). *The turkey girl: A Zuni Cinderella story.* New York: Little, Brown.
- San Souci, R. (1997). *Sootface: An Ojibwa Cinderella story.* New York: Dell.

Appalachian:
- Compton, J. (2004). *Ashpet: An Appalachian Tale.* New York: Holiday.
- Schroeder, A., & Sneed, B. (2000). *Smoky Mountain Rose.* New York: Penguin Books.

Cajun:
- Hebert, S. (1998). *Cendrillon: A Cajun Cinderella.* New York: Pelican.

Hawaiian:
- Takayama, S. (1997). *Sumorella: A Hawai'i Cinderella story.* Honolulu, HI: Bess Press. (boy Cinderella)

Southwest and Western United States:
- Mitchell (2002). *Joe Cinders.* New York: Henry Holt. (boy Cinderella)

Caribbean:
- San Souci, R. (1998). *Cendrillon: A Caribbean Cinderella.* New York: Simon and Schuster.

Latino/Hispanic:
- DePaola, T. (2004). *Adelita: A Mexican Cinderella story.* New York: Putnam.
- Reinhart, J. (2000). *Domitila: A Cinderella tale from the Mexican tradition.* San Diego, CA: Shen.

(continued)

Middle East:

- Climo, S. (1999). *The Persian Cinderella*. New York: HarperCollins.
- Hickox, R. (1999). *The golden sandal*. New York: Holiday House.

Asian:

- Climo, S. (1996). *The Korean Cinderella*. New York: HarperCollins.
- de la Paz, M. (2001). *Abadeha: The Philippine Cinderella*. San Diego, CA: Shen.
- Louie, A. (1996). *Ye-Shen: A Cinderella story from China*. New York: Philomel.

- Sierra, J. (2000). *The gift of the crocodile: A Cinderella story*. New York: Simon and Schuster. (Indonesia)

European:

- Climo, S. (2000). *The Irish Cinderland*. New York: HarperTrophy.
- Huck, C. (1994). *Princess furball*. New York: Greenwillow Books.

With thanks to Audrey Henry, EdD, professor of Reading Education, for providing the list of recommended Cinderella stories.

lifestyles. Teachers can have them as guest "tellers" and record their stories to form a "story bank" for later enjoyment. This is also a way to save the wisdom of the past for future generations and to develop an appreciation for the elderly, a diversity group frequently overlooked. Recordings of stories special to each family are also a valuable addition to the listening center. You may want to select a theme or topic and invite parents and family members to share their favorite stories or songs typical of their cultural group. Reasonably priced and easily available, blank tapes or CDs can be sent home for families to tape their stories, which will then become part of the listening library.

Persona Dolls as a Literacy Resource

All of us have enjoyed the stories told by puppets at one time in our lives, largely because we believed they were real. That is precisely why the persona doll is another child-appropriate resource (Figure 9-10). A persona doll is a vehicle for telling stories about the lives of children and their families in a method developed by Kay Taus (cited in Derman-Sparks & the A.B.C. Task Force, 1989). According to Taus, persona dolls also bring into the classroom the lives of people who have "differences that do not exist within one classroom." Each doll acquires a "persona" from a character it represents in a story. A script accompanies the doll, which periodically visits the classroom and becomes a part of it. Because they are intended to serve as a teacher resource, persona dolls should be kept in the teacher's area. However, they can be available to children whenever they ask for them. Stories with persona dolls are created from four main sources:

1. Issues emerging from the children's lives and experiences
2. Current world and community events
3. Relevant information that the children should learn
4. Significant historical events (Derman-Sparks & the A.B.C. Task Force, 1989)

Figure 9-10
Sample Persona Doll Story

Using Persona Dolls

One way to establish a diversity-responsive classroom environment is by incorporating characters that reflect the cultural nature of your group and of the community. Teachers know that puppets, dolls, and masks are good developmental resources that spur the child's imagination. They also serve to stimulate the child to talk, revealing feelings and emotions otherwise known only to the inner self. When addressing issues of diversity, a persona doll (Derman-Sparks & the A.B.C. Task Force, 1989) helps teachers to focus on a variety of situations suitable for discussion.

But, what is a persona doll? Basically, it is any resource used to personify a given character. What makes it different is that the doll is given a specific personality that will reflect any of the variables that define the concept of diversity (i.e., ethnicity, religion, social class, gender, special needs, race). The object receives personal attributes that establish a very distinguishable identity; that is, it becomes a "person."

The goal behind each doll is to provide teachers with a resource they can use to help children face situations that are typical for people of diversity. Using the principles of storytelling, the doll is then used as the key character in teacher-made stories that are shared with the children. They can become permanent "members" of the classroom, helping children to learn how "they view" different circumstances as they arise. When dolls are placed in the housekeeping area or in the "guest visitor" corner, children can reflect and reenact their problems.

Designs of persona dolls are as varied as classrooms are. The basic rule is to frame them according to the diversity parameters characteristic of the community and children. In this way, they become a device to help teachers address issues before or as they arise. Also, they will serve to expose children to aspects of diversity that are not part of their environment. For example, in a school with a predominantly upper-middle class student population, a teacher might use the persona dolls to expose children to issues such as homelessness.

Another use would be to have children share specific problems faced by persons with special needs. Issues of race and ethnicity are equally feasible to be displayed through the "personas."

If you are planning to use the dolls, here are three key suggestions to remember:

1. Have a clear purpose for each "personality" that will enter into your classroom. Ask yourself: *"Why is _____ in our classroom? What will the children derive from or learn through _____?"*

2. Create a believable story about the character. Dolls must present daily life situations faced by people of those same characteristics. Remember, children are to construct ideas through their stories, thus, stories must be faithful to the diversity circumstance that is being personified. Avoid unreal, hard-to-believe personalities. Select situations you are familiar with that will also be at the child's level. Ask yourself: *"Is the character an example of a real person? What makes the character authentic?"*

3. Use appropriate artifacts or materials to design and prepare the persona dolls. Avoid objects that would misrepresent the character. Remember, you are dealing with very sensitive issues! Ask yourself: *"Is the characteristic an accurate portrayal? Is it realistic?"*

Stories to Enhance the Child's Perception of Social Differences

Topic:
  Learning about the contribution and role of farm workers in our society.

Goal:
  To enhance the social value of migrant workers.
  To learn about family life in a migrant worker community.

(continued)

Figure 9-10
Sample Persona Doll
Story (Continued)

Concepts:

- Work as a valuable activity
- Interdependence
- Migrant/farm worker
- Pride in one's social world

Focus on Diversity:

Social class; ethnicity

Materials:

- Map of Florida; world map
- Persona dolls
- Pictures of flowers, live flowers and ferns

Procedure:

Using a persona doll, the teacher will introduce " Guillermo," a child whose parents are migrant farm workers.

Guillermo came to Crescent City, Florida, two months ago. His father works in a fern farm. He likes this town because it is less warm than Homestead where they lived before. Guillermo also enjoys the new apartment where he lives with his family. Now, after losing everything they owned during the *huracán Andrés*, he finally has new clothes and, in particular, a new pair of tennis shoes that shine at night!

His father works all day long. With his little sister, he goes to school while his mother stays at home taking care of Lalito, his baby brother. In the afternoon, when he comes back home, he likes the *pupusas* that his mom prepares.

Today he feels very proud. He just learned that the ferns that his father helps to grow are highly valued in countries far away from Florida. Yesterday, when he went to the packing house, he saw how they prepared the ferns for their long trips. He saw the farm owner and a man from an airline making all the shipping arrangements. With a lot of care, every fern was carefully wrapped and placed in special boxes.

Guillermo was going to ask where they were being sent when he heard the *capataz*, his father's boss, saying, "Those ferns are going to Amsterdam." "There they are used to make all the finest bouquets," said the person from the airline. He talked about the huge flower market in Amsterdam where ferns are sold and distributed all over.

Guillermo felt proud to hear that those plants that his father grows are so important. This morning, during circle time, he told his kindergarten teacher about the ferns. And he also said that there is something else he wants to learn: where is Amsterdam?

To think and do . . .

1. If you were Guillermo's teacher, what would you do with his question?
2. What activities would you design to involve the rest of the children?
3. In what ways could you use this opportunity to enhance the child's self-esteem?
4. Think about other circumstances or stories that define the daily lives of children with diverse cultural backgrounds. Select one and describe how you can address their situations to make the rest of the class aware of the things that they all have in common.

Wadsworth/Cengage Learning

Movement and dance are young children's favorite activities.

Music and Movement Experiences

Another of the universal traits that characterize human cultures is music, along with its counterpart, movement. They are considered important because they provide avenues to becoming culturally literate. Children seem to have a natural inclination toward anything involving rhythm and body movement. They are constantly exposed to a variety of experiences in the classroom, such as listening to music, singing, performing, and movement, that contribute to their holistic development. Singing and dancing should be incorporated into many daily activities such as story time, circle time, outdoor play, and so on. Because of the appeal these activities have for the child, they also serve as an avenue of learning about themselves and about others.

Wadsworth/Cengage Learning

Traditional games provide a source of learning about one's culture and the cultures of peers.

Folk songs and ethnic music need to be incorporated into the regular curriculum to initiate an appreciation for these art forms. They should not be limited to whenever a given holiday approaches. Reserving music representative of different cultures and dancing for specific dates only serves to reinforce a sense of cultural remoteness of a particular group. Typical ethnic musical instruments like a *güiro* (a percussion instrument made out of a gourd) and a *quena* (Andean flute) could be included in the music and listening center. Figure 9-11 presents a list of selected musical instruments that can be added to the classroom. When integrated into the regular plan of experiences, children learn to hear and sing the music of other countries as logical expressive representations of human beings.

Music is also known for conveying emotional feelings, which children seem to emulate easily (Haines & Gerber, 2000). This affective characteristic of music offers an opportunity for learning about the similarity of feelings people express through music. An effective strategy is to organize your musical selections as well as dances according to the many emotions that originate from life events and that are shared by a group of people. Children can listen to the tone and rhythm

Figure 9-11
Suggested Ethnic Musical Instruments for the Classroom

- Native American: drums, horns, conch shells
- Caribbean; African: guitars, maracas, güiros (gourds), percussion instruments
- Latin American: guitars, tambourines, wind instruments (for example, the Andean *quena*), xylophones (to represent the marimba), maracas
- Asian: string instruments, percussion instruments

Figure 9-12
Suggested Themes to Select and Incorporate Ethnic Music into the Curriculum

Life events
- happiness (marriage, births, successes, holidays)
- sadness (death, losses)
- solemnity (graduations, patriotic events, some cultural celebrations)

Daily life
- home and family
- nature
- motherhood/fatherhood
- children
- games

Which other ones can you name?

used to describe the different feelings and emotions and form body movements to accompany their interpretations. Introducing some of the typical dances can also occur as part of the learning about things people share. For example, dances commonly performed during weddings or other festivities provide an understanding of the existing multiple views.

Music of different cultural groups is easily obtainable through most local public libraries. Many libraries even include examples of typical musical instruments as well as recordings from various cultural groups. Performers such as Ella Jenkins, Raffi, José Luis Orozco, and Hap Palmer have recorded multicultural music appropriate for young children. Most music stores now have an ethnic music section where teachers can also find adequate instrumental and vocal pieces. When making selections, remember to look first for the musical representations of those cultural groups present in your classroom, and then look for others. Integration of music into classroom experiences provides not only a source to meet the children's developmental needs but also another way to explore cultural expressions (see Figure 9-12).

Games and Play: The Medium of All Cultures

Jean Piaget defines play as a natural and inherent characteristic of individuals found across cultures. He established that children respond spontaneously to any game-like activity. This inclination facilitates the acquisition of knowledge across cultures. Piaget's

FOCUS
ON CLASSROOM PRACTICES

USING MUSIC TO BUILD CULTURAL AWARENESS

Music is a universal element of cultures that is integral to early childhood development. In the classroom, music offers a developmentally sound opportunity for building awareness about self and other cultures. From infancy to the primary age, music provides young children with opportunities to express themselves, learn about their own heritage, and discover the cultures of others. Here are some suggestions for activities that involve music:

- Recess and quiet time: Using as background music selections representative of children's cultures, provides opportunities for children to become familiar with the musical tradition of other groups. In a classroom with 3-year olds, we observed teachers interchangeably using classical music along with soft popular music representative of children's cultures. The experience served the purposes of both exposing the youngsters to other rhythms and validating the musical traditions represented in the class.

- Transitions: Multicultural chants and songs with short lyrics are ideal to signal and prepare children for activities to come. Select those with simple lyrics so that children can learn and follow. For example, in a classroom we visited, teachers used "El Coquí [Little Frog]," a lullaby from Puerto Rico as the children prepare for their naptime.

- Morning circle time: Singing songs in other languages is a good way to both help children become aware of linguistic diversity and engage them in learning words in other languages. Several teachers we visited told us that while they sang bilingual morning songs, others even included the use of sign language as they sang. One of our graduate students uses a repertoire of children's folk music to start the day's activities. She adapts the songs to the season, making it a versatile learning experience for the children.

theory stresses the role of play as a common learning strategy and a central channel for knowledge formation about the world. Aside from their recreational aspects, play and games are found to keep their power throughout our lives.

Educator Frances Kendall (1996) believes play "enables children to grow out of their egocentric and ethnocentric picture of the world." Play and the games children learn offer an excellent foundation for developing and increasing the awareness about human diversity. Kendall contends that despite their differences, children around the world share the culture of childhood through play, another universal characteristic. Attributes of play make it a vital resource for teaching about diversity. Kendall (1996) contends that culture influences the meaning and interpretation of play. For some, play is seen as a solitary or interactive creative and spontaneous process. For others, play is structured and rule-driven, such as ballet or tennis lessons. In today's society, watching television and DVDs, playing video games, reading aloud, and listening to stories are all considered to be play. Two theorists, Jean Piaget and Lev Vygotsky, have dominated the research and theories about play. Piaget believed that play evolves "from practice play, to symbolic play, to play with rules. In other words play is carried out as part of the individual child's development growth. Vygotsky, on the other hand, believes that the child's

LITERACY CONNECTIONS...

RECOMMENDED MULTICULTURAL MUSIC RESOURCES

Many multicultural music books provide valuable literacy learning opportunities while exploring diverse musical traditions. Some of those we have used and found especially relevant are listed here:

- Cohn, A. (1996). *From sea to shining sea: A treasury of American folklore and folk songs.* New York: Scholastic.
- Delacre, L. (2006). *Rufi and Rosi: Carnival!* New York: Scholastic.
- Fox, D. (2003). *A treasury of children's songs: Forty favorites: songs to play and sing.* New York: Henry Holt.
- Goode, D. (1998). *The Diane Goode Book: A treasury of American folk tales and songs.* New York: Puffin.
- Grand-Bernier, C. (2002). *Shake it, Morena! And other folklore from Puerto Rico.* New York: Millbrook Press.
- Kantor, S. (2003). *An illustrated treasury of African American read-aloud stories.* New York: Black Dog & Leventhal Publishers.
- Orozco, J. (1999). *Diez deditos: Ten little fingers & other play rhymes and action songs from Latin America.* New York: Dutton.
- Orozco, J. (2002). *Fiestas: A year of Latin American celebrations.* New York: Dutton.
- Sullivan, K. (2005). *The best Hawaiian style Mother Goose ever!* Honolulu, HI: Hawaya.
- Yolen, J. (2000). *Sleep rhymes around the world.* Honesdale, PA: Boyds Mills Press.

primary purpose for play is not individual but social" (Kendall, 1996). Since Piaget and Vygotsky, many other experts on play have put forth their theories. No matter what model a teacher adopts, it is essential that she or he recognize that play is an important element of positive social, emotional, and physical development of all young children. Play is

- *voluntary and intrinsically motivated:* It is initiated by things that present challenges and where children find an interest.
- *symbolic and meaningful:* Children will assign meanings to their play items as they serve to bridge realities.
- *active and pleasurable:* The child's social context will determine the kind and type of activities.
- *rule-governed:* Rules established by children reflect the cultural values they know. Encountering different views is a way to learn about the ideas of others.
- *episodic:* Experiences shape the roles and purposes of play (Jalongo & Isenberg, 2008).

Observing what the child does when playing in the learning centers offers a window into the cultural ideas and values the child is acquiring. Some classroom areas are especially conducive to revealing the role culture plays in the child's interactions. For example, the block and dramatic centers serve as stages for young preschoolers to

IN ACTION . . .

PLAY IN THE CLASSROOM

Play is another universal element of culture. Taking into account the role of play in child development, think about the multicultural learning opportunities that it presents in the context of the classroom.

- Visit a classroom and observe children while at play.

- Consider the types of play taking place in the classroom. Think about ways to enhance them for the purpose of multiculturalism.

- To encourage learning about others, what items would you add to the block area or to the dramatic area? Why?

practice and apply their social and cultural ideas. Attention to what takes place there helps the teachers follow the dynamic lives of their students.

Games from the students' cultures should be the first ones to consider when teaching about diversity. Information about traditional game activities can be located in libraries and through the physical education specialists in the schools. A good way to begin is by inviting parents to share some of their favorite childhood games with the children. Learning games enjoyed by significant adults helps children to value their experiences. Fingerplays, rhymes, and songs accompany many of the ethnic and folk games, which make them a source of integrated learning. Lulu Delacre's *Arroz con leche: Popular Songs and Rhymes from Latin America* (1989) and *Rafi and Rosi: Carnival!* (2006) are examples of traditional children's folklore that are good sources for integrated learning.

IDEAS INTO ACTION—DESIGNING CLASSROOM ACTIVITIES

The time to bring ideas into practice has come. This is your opportunity to use and apply all the information about multicultural education as well as all the ideas presented in the previous chapters. This is the most exciting part of your journey into multicultural education. Your desire to create the best learning environment for children, your professional knowledge, and your sense of commitment to the young will guide you as you design and create your program. We have already defined the ideal multicultural classroom and taken inventory to find out what is available and needed to create an environment conducive to learning about diversity. Now let's think about appropriate activities that will transform ideas into action.

What Are Our Goals?

A primary goal of education for diversity is teaching children to be productive members of a culturally eclectic society. An appropriate classroom environment, where considerations for multiculturalism are followed, constitutes an ideal place for children

VIDEO CASE 9.2 ▶❙❙

Planning a Multicultural Curriculum

Go to the Cengage website and view *"Multicultural lessons: Embracing similarities and differences in preschool education.* After viewing the video, answer the following questions:

1. In what ways is this classroom addressing the needs of children with culturally diverse characteristics?

2. What is the teacher's philosophy about planning for diverse children?

to develop the appropriate social cognition. Social cognition allows the child to perceive life from the perspectives of others. Perspective taking, or the ability to see and understand one's position and the positions of others, is developed by growing up in a supportive environment (Berns, 1994). Early childhood classrooms must become such places that promote learning about diversity. The classroom activities lead children in discovering diversity as a normal part of life and, at the same time, adhere to the principles of cognitive development. In the next section, we will examine what cognitive and developmental characteristics teachers must consider as they prepare the classroom experiences. We will also examine the steps in lesson planning that will help us achieve instructional goals.

Planning for Multiple-Perspective Learning

Teaching is defined as developmentally appropriate when it provides children with *accurate* and legitimate views about our contemporary society that help build social knowledge and a *valid* assortment of interaction skills that are reflective of contemporary society. Both are acquired and developed through the quality experiences the child encounters. But what are the attributes that characterize those activities or encounters? What is the framework that will help the professional to organize them?

Defining the Elements of Developmentally Appropriate Learning Encounters

The whole philosophy of developmentally appropriate practice (DAP) is based on the belief that the child follows a process of growth and development that defines what the child needs to learn to grow. Education for diversity is solidly founded in this DAP principle. Its aim is not to expose children to the pluralistic society because "it is fun," but because it is necessary.

An Environment for Active Learning

Piaget's research on how children learn revealed that knowledge building is a process resulting from the dynamic interaction of the child with the environment. Piaget also found that the child's active learning depends on the stage of the child's cognitive development. Both the concept of active learning and the existence of cognitive stages are relevant for designing classroom activities. He defined four cognitive stages (see Figure 9-13), spanning birth to adolescence.

Active learning in children occurs when the child forms concepts about the world from direct experiences or "hands-on" learning. Because of the need for appropriate active learning, teachers need to carefully structure the child's learning encounters (Forman & Kushner, 1987). This term refers to the child's experiences that occur in the environment *purposefully* set and organized by the teacher. Learning encounters are emphasized in a program based on DAP. The classroom where the children are able "to encounter" denotes an active involvement and obvious participation of the environment

Figure 9-13
Piaget's Stages
of Cognitive
Development

Sensorimotor Stage (Birth-2 years)*: Learning occurs mostly via the senses and via motor activity, which facilitates the child's interactions with the environment.

Preoperational (2–7 years): Learning happens through the senses and via language, which gives the child access to communicate interests and ideas and to inquire. Play is used as a means to "play out," or represent, actions from reality.

Concrete Operations (7–11 years): Learning occurs as a result of reasoning and direct experiences. Child still requires direct experiences (hands-on).

Formal Operations (11–15+): Learning is based on reasoning of abstract ideas and suppositions about reality.

*Ages do not indicate rigid age periods but rather when the particular reasoning ability is most characteristically observed.

with the children. This requires that the activities be interesting to children to promote the acquisition of meaningful knowledge.

Traits of Quality Learning Experiences

An organized environment is an integral part of multicultural education, in which the classroom prepared to facilitate experiences is based on diversity. Quality experiences should include special traits, such as the following:

- active involvement
- child participation
- age appropriateness
- cognitive appropriateness
- developmental relevance to the child
- holistic learning

A Framework for Planning: The Cycle of Teaching and Learning

The possibilities for learning encounters in a multicultural classroom are endless. Translating many opportunities into action requires a child-appropriate framework for planning. Bredekamp and Rosegrant (1992) refer to this framework as "the cycle of learning and teaching." The cycle, consisting of four major levels, represents a practical and meaningful approach for implementing what Bredekamp and Rosegrant call a "mindful curriculum." A mindful curriculum should be meaningful, integrated, and based on the realities of the classroom. This is also the most appropriate curriculum for teaching about diversity issues.

The four levels of the cycle of learning are awareness, exploration, inquiry, and utilization (Figure 9-14). Like building blocks, the experiences at each level are built upon the previous ones. This kind of planning and teaching strategy is considered to

Figure 9-14 Cycle of Learning and Teaching

	What Children Do	What Teachers Do
Awareness	Experience Acquire an interest Recognize broad parameters Attend Perceive	Create the environment Provide opportunities by introducing new objects, events, people Invite interest by posing a problem or question Respond to child's interest or shared experience Show interest, enthusiasm
Exploration	Observe Explore materials Collect information Discover Create Figure out components Construct own understanding Apply own rules Create personal meaning Represent own meaning	Facilitate Support and enhance exploration Provide opportunities for active exploration Extend play Describe child's activity Ask open-ended questions—"What else could you do?" Respect child's thinking and rule systems Allow for constructive error
Inquiry	Examine Investigate Propose explanations Focus Compare own thinking with that of others Generalize Relate to prior learning Adjust to conventional rule systems	Help children refine understanding Guide children, focus attention Ask more focused questions—"What else works like this?" "What happens if . . . ?" Provide information when requested—"How do you spell . . . ?" Help children make connections
Utilization	Use the learning in many ways; learning becomes functional Represent learning in various ways Apply learning to new situations Formulate new hypotheses and repeat cycle	Create vehicles for application in real world Help children apply learning to new situations Provide meaningful situations in which to use learning

Source: Bredekamp & Rosegrant, 1992.

be constructivist in nature. Let us examine more closely how the circle of learning and teaching can be used to set up your classroom scenario.

The learning process described in the cycle has two distinctive levels. The first level consists of the **awareness** and **exploration** phases. At this stage, the child is presented with what is new or different. The novelty or the "intrigue" of the new experience triggers the child's interest to learn more about it.

1. *Awareness:* The child becomes familiarized, or apprised of the existence of an idea or an issue. The following questions can be used to guide the teacher's planning in this phase:
   - How can the child become cognizant about this issue or idea?
   - In what ways can the environment be set up to engage the child's interest as related to the selected issue or idea?

2. *Exploration:* The child begins to search for the elements that define the issue or idea that captured his or her attention. In the process, the child will process information according to his or her own experiences. The child is actively using his or her cultural knowledge to filter what is meaningful. The following questions guide the teacher's planning:
   - How can I facilitate and support the children's investigation?
   - What activities and materials can help the children in the process?
   - What questions should I ask the children to verify their progress and understanding?

Level 2 is more advanced and requires careful planning. In this level, the child, who already has acquired an individual understanding and is cognizant about the issues or concept, begins to reformulate the existing knowledge. During this reformulation, children discover the views of others as well as ways to apply the acquired knowledge. This is what happens when the child enters into the **inquiry** and **utilization** phases.

1. *Inquiry:* Child begins to reexamine and compare the acquired knowledge. The child begins to consider his or her own beliefs while comparing them to the beliefs of others. The outcome of this process is a refined view of the issue or concept where common points are ascertained. The following questions can be used to guide your planning:
   - What are the additional experiences that will help the child see the idea from the point of view of others?
   - What questions can I pose to the child that will help him or her focus on other aspects of the topic?
   - What other areas, information, or resources would the child need to examine the acquired knowledge?

2. *Utilization:* The child begins to bring things into a functional reality. Activities and opportunities are offered to help the child apply what has been learned. This validation of knowledge occurs as the child finds its usefulness in daily life. The following questions will help you plan this phase:
   - What opportunities can I create in the classroom for the child to apply or demonstrate what was learned?
   - What real-life situations can I use to illustrate the applicability of the knowledge learned?

SUCCESSFUL PLANNING

Early childhood professionals who want to create successful experiences for young children must engage in many planning steps. Reflection is a very important step in the planning process. You should learn to reflect on daily events in the classroom and determine the high and low points of the day and what worked and what did not. One of the ways to do that is to keep a daily journal. Find out about other ways that are also effective.

Ask experienced teachers to share their ideas about how they use reflection in their classrooms. Find out what strategies experienced teachers use to help them reflect on the day's events. Based on their comments, decide on the one that you feel best suits you.

A learning cycle implies a series of events that will lead to the re-initiation of the process. After a child learns a concept, it can be applied to other contexts that lead the child to examine new ideas. In teaching about diversity, leading the child to examine the perspectives of others will create endless situations where the cycle of learning will be repeated over and over again. As that happens, you will see how the children's consciousness about diversity grows and becomes more concrete.

Using the Cycle of Teaching and Learning: An Example

The Cycle of Teaching and Learning is a useful planning tool. Here is an example of how it can be applied using families as the topic. Exploring the concept of families provides a good opportunity for children to learn about diversity in their own families and in that of their peers.

Group: Kindergarten
Topic: Learning that my peers' families can be different from my own

I. Awareness/What they seem to know

1. Read and discuss Taylor's story *All Kinds of Families* (Delacorte, 2005).
2. Draw our families and display them on our "classroom mural."
3. Have posters about families displayed around the classroom. Ask the children to bring pictures of their families and display them in the classroom.
4. Include family sets in the block area.

II. Exploration/Investigating

1. Make paper bag puppets of our families. Have the children present "families."
2. Prepare family trees. Make a list of terms used to describe family relationships.

3. Invite family members to the classroom to talk about their families.

4. Have persona dolls talk about their families (single parent, foster).

5. Include pictures of different families in the literacy area.

6. Find and learn lullabies or *canciones de cuna*.

7. Have a grandparent or any other relative come to sing to the students.

8. Use play dough or paints to make representations of our families. Present them during circle time.

9. Make a graph about the sizes of families and types of family members.

10. Prepare a chart about things families do. Search for pictures in old magazines. Do a Venn diagram to compare and contrast children's families.

11. Include baby and toddler items from other countries, such as India and Haiti, in the housekeeping area. Observe reactions and ask questions.

12. Talk about the roles and tasks done by family members. Make stories about what we do at home. Role-play some of those stories. Share Gary Soto's story *Too Many Tamales* (Scholastic, 1996).

III. Inquiry/Self-Investigation

1. Bring family prop boxes. Have the children examine the contents. Ask them to infer what families they represent. Draw or make with play dough the family members they think each box represents. Guide children to describe their inferences. (*Why do you think there are _____ in this family? How did you discover that?*)

2. Using art materials make or draw families based on the characters in favorite stories. Discuss and compare them with the families of the children. Ask: *Why do you think we have families?*

3. Read stories about grandparents (such as *Song and Dance Man* by Karen Ackerman [Dragonfly, 1992]). Discuss other relatives in our families.

IV. Utilization/Applying What We Know

1. Read and discuss Sol Gordon's *All Families are Different* (Prometheus, 2000). Have children talk about what keeps families strong even when they live apart or when a parent works until late at night. Discuss how children can help parents (What can I do at home?). Role-play some of the suggestions.

2. Display pictures of families from other countries (these can be made into a book and placed in the literacy area). Add and read stories such as Ifeoma Onyefulu's *Welcome Dede! An African Naming Ceremony* (Frances Lincoln Children's, 2004).

3. Add family figures to the manipulatives in the block and manipulatives areas.

4. Make game cards showing different family configurations as well as configurations of other kinds of groups. Ask the children to identify what family configurations the cards depict.

5. Have children create their own persona doll story. Have the dolls tell the class about their families.

6. Make a collective chart about "things in common and things that make families different." Refer to it whenever needed.

7. Have the children make a picture vocabulary depicting the different family configurations. Reinforce the terminology that defines them. Keep it available as a reference.

8. Take children on a field trip to observe how many families they see. Have them take a small note pad to jot down their findings.

Sources for Planning the Content and the Experiences

Developmentally appropriate content is characterized by being child-centered and integrated (Morrison, 2008). The content in early childhood is derived from the children's interests and needs. It can also originate from what the teacher considers to be relevant for the children. The content identified by the teacher usually targets the needs and aims of families, the school, and the community in relationship to the children. Issues relevant to the community need to be targeted because children are members of and interact with the communities in which they live. Meaningful issues identified by the particular groups of which the children are members, and of the society at large, should be integrated into the instructional content as well. Content based on the interests of the child, the needs of society, and the concerns of the teacher is considered child-centered and integrated (Figure 9-15).

Appropriate content presents topics as parts of a whole, not in isolation. When examining a theme, the child is led to view it holistically by providing opportunities to examine the theme from all angles and never in isolation. This integrated approach facilitates valid learning that occurs when the child knows how an idea relates and applies to a general context (Figure 9-16).

This same rule applies to selecting topics for teaching about diversity.

Two things are important for teachers who are trying to define the content of the multicultural curriculum:

1. First, accurately observe the actions and interactions of children in the learning areas.

2. Second, become a proactive teacher and bring the multicultural issues into the classroom. Throw away your "color-blindness" and seek ways to prevent the behaviors and beliefs that act against diversity and equity. Discard any misleading and

Figure 9-15
Sources of Child-Appropriate Content for Multicultural Classrooms

inaccurate views about children and consider them individuals capable of facing situations when appropriately presented.

You also can define the content when you are alert to the following:

- Comments made about other children in the class because of their race, language, or disability; about other children in the school; about adults and staff members; about story or TV characters; about stories read; about pictures; and about visitors
- Use of pejorative words and terms to describe or allude to others; use of intentional name calling
- Nonverbal expressions (puzzled faces, frowns, nuances) made in a response to a person, an incident, or a story
- Open rejection or being upset about others
- Fear and distress when in front of other people (Derman-Sparks & the A.B.C. Task Force, 1989; Robles de Meléndez, 2004)

Figure 9-16 Web of Integrated Topics

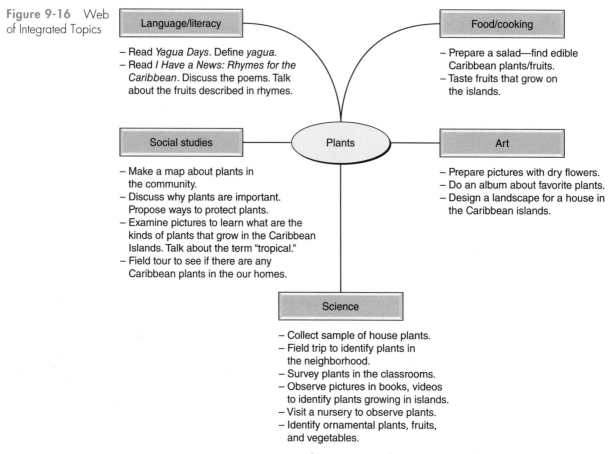

Language/literacy
- Read *Yagua Days*. Define *yagua*.
- Read *I Have a News: Rhymes for the Caribbean*. Discuss the poems. Talk about the fruits described in rhymes.

Food/cooking
- Prepare a salad—find edible Caribbean plants/fruits.
- Taste fruits that grow on the islands.

Social studies
- Make a map about plants in the community.
- Discuss why plants are important. Propose ways to protect plants.
- Examine pictures to learn what are the kinds of plants that grow in the Caribbean Islands. Talk about the term "tropical."
- Field tour to see if there are any Caribbean plants in the our homes.

Plants

Art
- Prepare pictures with dry flowers.
- Do an album about favorite plants.
- Design a landscape for a house in the Caribbean islands.

Science
- Collect sample of house plants.
- Field trip to identify plants in the neighborhood.
- Survey plants in the classrooms.
- Observe pictures in books, videos to identify plants growing in islands.
- Visit a nursery to observe plants.
- Identify ornamental plants, fruits, and vegetables.

Creating Your Own Curriculum Using Thematic Teaching

Thematic teaching is a DAP strategy that facilitates integrated teaching. Introduced by Dewey and Kilpatrick (cited in Katz & Chard, 2000) in the early part of the twentieth century, it is a popular classroom strategy. It is also an appropriate way to develop a classroom curriculum for diversity. Theme teaching is a holistic approach to a broad content area that includes many different related topics. The thematic approach is child centered and rooted in problem-based learning and inquiry. It is a discovery method that facilitates meaningful experiences for children. Developed around the topics that are of interest to children, theme studies present an opportunity to create a curriculum that addresses the reality of the classroom. The flexible nature of theme studies allows teachers to incorporate issues as they arise in the classroom. Several other characteristics define the appropriateness of theme teaching. We suggest the following guidelines for theme teaching.

1. Select a theme because of its relevance to children and their ability to assimilate it based on their developmental characteristics.

2. Emphasize development of skills and acquisition of knowledge, not the accumulation of facts.

IN ACTION . . .

FORMULATING THE CONTENT

What additional elements should teachers observe that may serve as a basis for multicultural instructional content? What other factors should be taken into consideration for child-appropriate planning?

3. Place balanced attention on both the content and the process by providing developmentally sequential ideas and skills that are similar to building blocks.

4. Encourage group work, collaboration, and social interaction that promote tolerance, compromise, and coping skills.

5. Instill in children responsibility for their own learning by guiding them to solutions through finding sources, examining information, and arriving at conclusions.

Many times, theme-based studies take the form of projects. Also called the project approach (originally called the project method by Dewey and Kilpatrick), theme-based studies are actually active investigations. The approach also offers an opportunity to have more than one topic "investigated" at one time. Theme teaching, or project work, in early childhood education for diversity is centered on four goals: knowledge, skills, dispositions, and feelings (Katz & Chard, 2000). According to Katz and Chard, in an early childhood classroom, each of these goals indicates different types of learning.

1. *Knowledge:* describes concepts, ideas, facts, information (for example, learning correct names to designate ethnic groups or the significance of a given cultural celebration)

2. *Skills:* refers to specific discrete units of behavior, such as social skills and thinking skills (for example, acquiring the ability to participate in a group or to make friends)

3. *Dispositions:* describes the patterns or habits of mind that characterize the individual's ways of responding to experiences (for example, curiosity, desire to learn about others, desire to share with others, and unbiased responses)

4. *Feelings:* indicates the emotional or affective stances exhibited during and because of a given circumstance (for example, a positive attitude, tolerance, and acceptance of others)

Areas of study in thematic teaching originate from the children's interests. However, the teacher can also introduce topics when they are based on the children's needs identified through the teacher's observations. Topics chosen by the teacher should guide the children to recognize the universal cultural traits shared with other groups first. Emphasizing what makes us alike reduces the possibilities of children distancing themselves even further from the group. Consider, for example, a classroom where there are children of different Caribbean ethnicities who are the subject of name calling by their classmates,

Figure 9-17
Sample Concept
Web

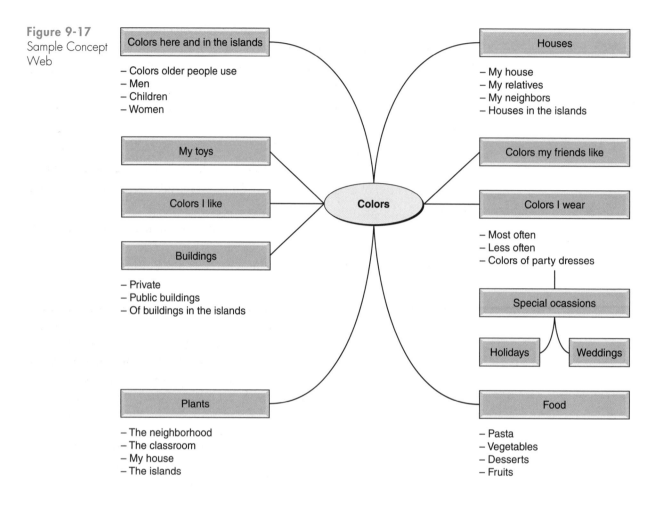

probably because their peers have limited exposure to members of those cultures. The teacher who observes such a confrontation is presented with an opportunity to introduce a very relevant and timely project. Possible topics that offer an initial awareness about Caribbean children could be "colors" and "decorations." Both topics depict universal concepts found in every culture that permit children to discover and establish the similarities among people. A description of the possible areas of investigation appears in Figure 9-16 and Figure 9-17.

Selecting Topics for Teaching

According to some educators, it is advisable to observe the following rules when selecting topics for classroom exploration (Katz & Chard, 2000):

- The topic is based on things of direct interest to the child. It leads to information or skills readily applicable to the child's reality. Teachers can generate the appropriate topics based on their knowledge of individuals and groups in their classrooms and based on classroom observations.

- The chosen topics are feasible to investigate and allow for the child's involvement for a minimum of one week.
- Topics should be interdisciplinary in nature. Integration into several areas should be possible.
- Children work on topics for which there are sufficient resources at the school.
- Appropriate concrete and print materials are available for the investigation of the topic.
- The investigation of a topic will provide for the acquisition and enhancement of knowledge, feelings, and dispositions.
- Opportunities for parent, family, and community collaboration are possible through the investigation.
- Outcomes will have validity and usefulness in the child's current and future life.

A group-specific curriculum framework, developed around the concept of islanders, has also been proposed by Robles de Meléndez (1999). This model provides sample ways to create experiences aimed to help children develop an appreciation and an understanding about a particular cultural group. Rationale for the curriculum emerged from two facts: (1) The islanders are an underrepresented minority across the curriculum that infrequently defines them in common and real-life settings, and (2) the islanders constitute a cultural entity demographically significant in the United States. Using social studies as a key organizer, Robles de Meléndez suggests a series of themes, all leading to develop an understanding about this ethnic group. Focus is on similarities, and it serves as a way of discovering and establishing the aspects that make the identity of the islanders so unique. The model for the curriculum is founded on a developmental framework in which the tenets of education for diversity were incorporated (Figure 9-18).

Suggestions for Culturally Appropriate Planning

Creating curricular experiences based on the ideas of diversity is a difficult task that will not be accomplished overnight. The progress for some teachers may be slow if they are required to follow a state or district curriculum. Whatever the reason for moving into multicultural change, to implement an optimum program, it is important to focus on what is culturally and developmentally valuable for all children. This belief is central and must guide the design, implementation, and modification of an effective and relevant program for the children you teach. As one begins to develop a multicultural education program, there are some points to remember that will facilitate the transition from current practices to teaching from a multicultural perspective. These points are equally helpful when following a prescribed curriculum:

- Begin by knowing the expected learning outcomes for the age level you teach. Check and be mindful about the learning standards. Look at these as opportunities to validate the meaningfulness of planned experiences.

Figure 9-18   Framework for the "Children of the Islands" Curriculum

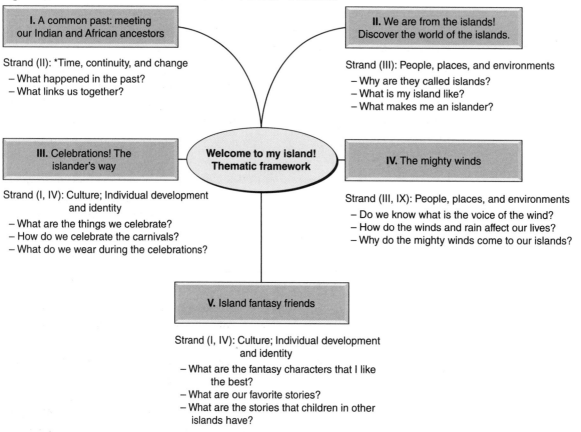

- Review your present content to determine what was successful and what felt comfortable.

- Go through your lesson plan book and identify the topics developed in class.

- Find in your curriculum *where* you could add or expand the children's views by including another perspective. Determine *what* other perspective you can add. Begin with only one additional perspective; then, as you gain confidence, add others.

- Adopt a flexible thematic teaching approach. It facilitates the integration of topics and views and helps guide children into examining things they like or in which they have shown an interest.

- When including a second perspective, think about the ways in which it relates to the children's own cultural experiences. Remind yourself to always center your selections first on what is connected to the lives of your students.

- Include as many concrete experiences as possible. Children need things to do, things to touch and manipulate, if they are to construct new knowledge. In dealing with views and perceptions about others, present common daily-life situations where they can see the meaningfulness and the impact of the behavior.
- Make sure the experiences offer accurate portrayals and not stereotypes. Avoid the exotic and include what defines the current lifestyles and realities. When presenting the folklore and traditional dresses or customs, clarify that they may describe what happens during a holiday or a festivity, not everyday life.
- If uncertain about a detail from a particular group, postpone the experience until you have clarified it. Remember that children see you as an authority.
- Present perspectives in time frames that define the present first and then move into comparisons of the present with the past. Bring in ideas in terms of place (here/there) where there are elements children can relate to, such as common climate, topography, and so on.

Helpful Planning Sources

Several reference sources can help teachers select the curriculum content. Consider having copies of resource materials like Bredekamp and Copple's (2009) book on developmental practices, which includes the guide to DAP teaching. Talk with colleagues and visit the library, where you may find relevant and helpful sources describing a variety of activities teachers can use as they launch their multicultural programs. Include multicultural literature as well as materials from professional journals such as *Childhood Education, Teaching Tolerance, Children Our Concern, Dimensions,* and *Young Children.* When using activities from manuals or books, be sure to adapt or modify them in accordance with the realities of your students.

As you get yourself ready to design and experience your curriculum, make sure that you keep good notes during your implementation. Prepare yourself to jot down the reactions and comments children make after and during the activities. Discussions and comments from colleagues also provide valuable insights and ideas to improve your planning. Altogether, these will be your sources for future adaptations and continuous improvements.

WHAT WE HAVE LEARNED—CHAPTER SUMMARY

In this chapter, we discussed the importance of the classroom environment as well as instructional materials and learning experiences. The classroom is intended to foster the cognitive, social, and emotional development of all children. Such a place must be very special. It must be safe, inviting, and welcoming, and, at the same time, it must be a place of learning where everyone is valued and treated with equal care and respect. The early childhood classroom has to have many different learning environments, which, in a multicultural classroom, presents additional challenges. The various centers in the room must contain materials that are developmentally appropriate and accommodate children from different cultures and with various physical, emotional, and linguistic abilities. The early childhood educator is tasked with providing a wide range of rich learning materials from many different sources and ensuring that, through play and other more structured experiences, the children are afforded the best opportunities to further their development. This chapter also contains specific suggestions for activities using literature, music, and art.

MAKING CONNECTIONS . . .

1. Visit a local teacher supply store and examine its multicultural materials. Make a wish list of those you would like to have. Use the multicultural evaluation guidelines presented in this chapter to determine whether or not they are developmentally appropriate. If you find any that are not DAP, describe what made them inappropriate.

2. Select two topics that are commonly taught in a multicultural classroom. Research the local school library, resource center, or a public library and find 10 resources for each topic that will help you develop two new perspectives about them.

3. Select three learning centers found in classrooms for children of the age level of your preference. Assess them and determine what needs to be added or replaced. Make a plan of the things you would incorporate to make them suitable for learning about diversity.

4. Select an area of diversity and prepare your own persona doll story. Share it with your colleagues.

5. Visit a local ethnic store and see which of its items you could include in your learning centers. List them and describe the learning areas where you would include them.

6. Examine the sample curricular topics that appear here. Determine *what* you would incorporate and *where* in order to transform them into content for learning about diversity. Do the same with your own current curriculum.

Grade: Prekindergarten
Topics:

1. Who am I?
2. This is my family
3. My friends in the classroom
4. My favorite games
5. Special places in the community

RECOMMENDED INTERNET RESOURCES

Book awards:

- Coretta Scott King Book Award
  http://www.teachingbooks.net/crc.cgi?id=1

- Pura Belpré Medal
  http://www.ala.org/ala/mgrps/divs/alsc/awardsgrants/bookmedia/belpremedal/index.cfm

- Sydney Taylor Book Award for Jewish children's literature
  www.jewishlibraries.org/ajlweb/awards/st_books.htm

- Caldecott Medal and Honor Books 1938-Present
  http://www.ala.org/ala/mgrps/divs/alsc/awardsgrants/bookmedia/caldecottmedal/caldecotthonors/caldecottmedal.cfm

Children's books on selected diverse groups:

- African Americans
  http://www.multiculturalchildrenslit.com/africanwel.
  html New site.

- Appalachian culture
  www.carolhurst.com/subjects/appalachia.html

- Japanese Americans
  www.multiculturalchildrenslit.com/japaneseameri-cans.html

- Women in history
  www.carolhurst.com/subjects/history/women.html

YOUR STANDARDS PORTFOLIO

naeyc **Standard 4:** Using Developmentally Effective Approaches to Connect with Children and Families

naeyc **Standard 5:** Using Content Knowledge to Build Meaningful Curriculum

naeyc **Standard 6:** Becoming a Professional

InTASC Standard 3: Learning Environment

InTASC Standard 4: Content Knowledge

InTASC Standard 9: Professional Learning and Ethical Practice

Successful classroom experiences are child-oriented and culturally appropriate. Additionally, an emotionally positive, supportive, and sensitive atmosphere makes children and adults feel welcome and respected. In this kind of classroom environment, learning is enhanced through a variety of well-planned activities. Complete the following activities to demonstrate your understanding of the following standards:

- Select a concept related to diversity to teach to a group of first graders. Using the sample concept web in chapter (Figure 9.17), design a classroom activity. Be sure to include the objective of the activity, teaching strategies, required resources, and end-of-activity assessment. Be sure to include an activity to extend learning at home. Present your activity to your peers.

- Think about the cultural and ethnic characteristics of your community. Meet with colleagues or classmates and discuss the characteristics of a classroom environment that would be culturally sensitive to both children and their families. Identify the elements that the group considers most important and describe each one in writing.

- Personal dispositions are behaviors that affect how we approach and respond to working with children and their families. Reflect on your personal dispositions and behaviors that could help you build respectful and sensitive relationships with children and their families. Write a list of those that you feel are your strongest assets. Ponder your challenges as well.

REFERENCES

Allport, G. (1986). *The nature of prejudice.* New York: Anti Defamation League of Benai.

Banks, J. (2007). *Multicultural education* (7th ed.). Newton, MA: Allyn & Bacon.

Berns, R. M. (1994). *Topical child development.* Clifton Park, NY: Thomson Delmar Learning.

Bredekamp, S., & Copple, C. (2009). *Developmentally appropriate practice in early childhood programs* (3rd ed.). Washington, DC: National Association for the Education of Young Children.

Bredekamp, S., & Rosegrant, T. (Eds.). (1992). *Reaching potentials: Appropriate curriculum and assessment for young children*, *Vol. 1*. Washington, DC: National Association for the Education of Young Children.

Byrnes, D., & Kiger, C. (Eds.). (2005). *Anti-bias teaching in a diverse society*. Wheaton, MD: Association for Childhood Education International.

Cropley, A. (1992). *More ways than one: Fostering creativity*. Norwood, NJ: Ablex.

Cullinan, B., & Galda, L. (2009). *Literature and the child* (7th ed.). New York: Wadsworth.

Curtis, D., & Carter, M. (2003). *Designs for living and learning environments*. Saint Paul, MN: Red Leaf Press.

Davidman, L., & Davidman, P. T. (2000). *Teaching with a multicultural perspective* (3rd ed.). Needham Heights, MA: Allyn & Bacon.

Derman-Sparks, L., & the A.B.C. Task Force (1989). *Anti-bias curriculum: Tools for empowering young children*. Washington, DC: National Association for the Education of Young Children.

Forman, G., & Kuschner, D. (1987). *The child's construction of knowledge: Piaget for teaching children*. Washington, DC: National Association for the Education of Young Children.

Goldberg, M. (2006). *Integrating the arts: An approach to teaching and learning in multicultural and multilingual settings* (3rd ed.). Boston: Allyn & Bacon.

Gómez, A. (1999). *Crafts of many cultures: Thirty authentic craft projects from around the world*. New York: Scholastic.

Haines, J. B., & Gerber, L. L. (2000). *Leading young children to music*. (6th ed.) New York: Merrill/Macmillan.

Hernandez, H. (2000). *Multicultural education: A teacher's guide to content and process* (2nd ed.). New York: Prentice Hall.

Jalongo, M. R., & Isenberg, J. (2008). *Exploring your role: An introduction to early childhood education* (3rd ed.). Upper Saddle River, NJ: Merrill.

Kasten, W., Kristo, J. V., & McClure, A. (2005). *Living literature: Using children's literature to support reading and language arts*. Upper Saddle River, NJ: Pearson Merrill Prentice Hall.

Katz, L., & Chard, S. (2000). *Engaging children's minds: The project approach* (2nd ed.). Norwood, NJ: Ablex.

Kendall, F. (1996). *Diversity in the classroom: A multicultural approach to the education of young children* (2nd ed.). New York: Teachers College Press.

King, E. W., Chipman, M., & Cruz-Janzen, M. (1994). *Educating young children in a diverse society*. Needham Heights, MA: Allyn & Bacon.

Morrison, G. S. (2008). *Early childhood education today* (11th ed.). Englewood Cliffs, NJ: Merrill.

National Association for the Education of Young Children. (2005). *NAEYC Early childhood program standards and accreditation criteria: The mark of quality in early childhood education*. Washington, DC: NAEYC.

Neugebauer, B. (1992). *Alike and different: Exploring our humanity with children* (Rev. ed.). Washington, DC: NAEYC.

Nieto, S., & Bode, P. (2008). *Affirming diversity: The sociopolitical context of multicultural education* (5th ed.). New York: Pearson/Allyn & Bacon.

Norton, D. (2003). *Through the eyes of a child: An introduction to children's literature* (6th ed.). Englewood Cliffs, NJ: Merrill.

Norton, D. & Norton, S. (2008). *Through the eyes of a child: An introduction to children's literature* (8th ed.). New York: Pearson Custom Education.

Ornstein, A. C., & Hunkins, F. (2008). *Curriculum foundations, principles, and theory* (5th ed.). Boston: Allyn & Bacon.

Peck, N., & Shores, E. (1994). *Checklist for diversity in early childhood education and care*. Little Rock, AR: Southern Early Childhood Association.

Robles de Meléndez, W. (1999). *Vocesillas de los niños de las islas: Un modelo multicultural para el nivel Pre-K–2 (Voices of the children of the islands: A multicultural model for the pre-K–2 level)*. Unpublished document.

Robles de Meléndez, W. (2001). Creating the multicultural environment. Paper presented at the annual conference of the Early Childhood Association of Florida. Orlando, FL.

Robles de Meléndez, W. (December 2004). Using multicultural literature to learn about families. Paper presented at Blue Ribbon Schools Conference. Biloxi, MS.

Robles de Meléndez, W., & Henry, A. (October 1994). Using constructivism to develop literacy skills. Paper presented at Florida Reading Association Annual Conference. Orlando, FL.

Rosales, L. (1992). *Listen to the heart*. Unpublished manuscript.

A World of Resources: Engaging Families, Friends, and the Community

All men [individuals] know their children mean more than life.
—Euripides (480–406 B.C.)

Wadsworth/Cengage Learning

STANDARDS: THE FOLLOWING STANDARDS ARE ADDRESSED IN THIS CHAPTER:

naeyc Standard 2: Building Family and Community Relationships
InTASC Standard 10: Leadership and Collaboration

TEACHERS SHARE

It was another day at the local center and Miss Esther, an experienced toddler teacher, was greeting the parents who were bringing their children to school. In the toddler room, the children's photos on the walls seemed to say "hello" everywhere you looked. Right next to the door, a colorful bulletin board in English and Spanish read: *"Things to Share with Our Families/ Cosas para compartir con nuestras familias."* Today, a new sign with Chinese words saying *"welcome"* was there as well. That was because Miss Esther was waiting for a new child to join the group. It was a little past nine when she saw the child and her mother coming. Along with them, an older lady was carefully tying the ribbon in the little girl's hair.

"Ni hao [Hello], Mrs. Chang!" said Miss Esther with a smile as the three stepped into the classroom. As the little girl smiled shyly, the surprised Mrs. Chang quickly replied, "Zao an! [Good morning!]" It was clear that all three newcomers were pleased with the teacher's greeting. Miss Esther did not hesitate to tell Mrs. Chang the greeting was all the Chinese she knew.

"Miss Esther, this is Lian's grandmother," Mrs. Chang continued, "and this is my daughter, Lian."

It was then that the grandmother pointed to the bulletin board that read: *Welcome Lian and your family to our classroom.*

CHAPTER OBJECTIVE

Upon reading this chapter and reflecting on its content, you will be able to design learning activities that include families and the community of early childhood students.

KEY CONCEPTS

- involvement
- intervention
- collaborative efforts
- community resources
- families

321

"Thank you, Miss Esther," a smiling Mrs. Chang said. "My mother and I are very happy to see this."

"We are happy that you are part of our classroom," said Miss Esther.

"I am, too," replied Mrs. Chang in a tone that revealed how comfortable she felt knowing that her daughter and her family were in the right place.

WORKING TOGETHER: THE ESSENCE OF A CHILD'S SUCCESS

The old adage "No man is an island" reminds us that we all need and depend on each other. The same is true of schools and families. Classroom practices reveal that when parents work together with their children's teachers, there are positive emotional and intellectual gains. This partnership becomes even more important in contemporary society, where family patterns and routines have drastically changed, forcing parents and children to depend more and more on the schools (Figure 10-1). Furthermore, the need for collaboration among teachers and families of young children is most critical because the parents and the family are the child's first and most influential teachers. Welcoming families and engaging them in the classroom is integral to creating an environment geared toward meeting the children's needs. When families bring their children to the classroom, they also bring their hopes for the children's success. Just like in our opening scenario, all it takes is to genuinely show the parents and families that we welcome them as partners in our classrooms.

CHANGING COMMUNITIES, CHANGING REALITIES

Not only have families changed as you saw in Chapter 3, but neighborhoods have also become different. Today, across the United States, neighborhoods are experiencing high population mobility, which lessens the possibilities of establishing any stable, long-lasting relationships. Serious economic pressures have caused the deterioration of many neighborhoods, forcing their character to change (Children's Defense Fund, 2005). These events have eroded the social relationships and changed the lifestyles and practices in our neighborhoods. More impersonal and less caring, they are no longer the safe havens our children and families need. As a result of this transformation, schools have taken over more of the social responsibilities that parents and neighbors used to

Figure 10-1 Family Configurations and Living Arrangements of Children

Family Structure	Percentage of Children
Two-parent families	69%
Living with mothers only	22%
Living with fathers only	4%
Living with neither parent	4%

Source: *Federal Interagency Forum on Child and Family Statistics, 2005.*

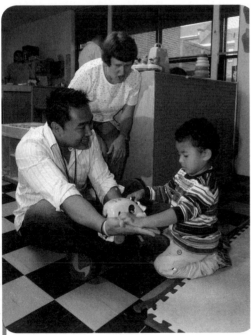

Including parents and family members in early childhood multicultural programs ensures success. We believe that. Do you agree?

have. Thus, more and more families and children now depend on schools as one of their main sources of social support.

The transformation of the U.S. family and the neighborhood have resulted in the need for closer collaboration among the key players—schools, families, relatives, and the community. The purpose of this alliance is perceived as a way of solving problems of students in schools that also impact the society at large. Offering children a better and more responsive education has become a priority in the United States, because it has been recognized that without an effective education system the future of our society may be in jeopardy. Educators recognize that one of the keys to the successful schooling experience can be found in the close collaboration between teachers and families. This collaboration is the basis for developmentally appropriate practices (DAP) that recommend creating classrooms where the child's needs are being met, the child's individuality as a cultural entity is respected and strengthened, and all efforts are made to enable the child to become a successful person. This kind of a DAP environment cannot be established without the joint efforts of teachers and families. Failure to bring parents closer to their children's school causes even the best of interventions to fail (Swick, 2004). Intervention is defined as any special effort made to assist a child in performing at an established standard.

Evidence abounds throughout the literature regarding the impact of parent and family involvement in their children's successful performance (Barrera & Warner, 2006; Berger, 2007; Jung-Sook & Bowen, 2006). Creating the atmosphere for learning both in the classroom and at home is a necessary component of effective education. Goals 2000, which define the national standards of education, speak to such learning environments for our children. Educator Ernest Boyer (1994) eloquently explained this idea in his interpretation of what "ready to learn," addressed in Goal 1, actually means.

HOME IS THE FIRST CLASSROOM [capitalized in the original]. Parents are the first school and most essential teacher. . . . [We] recommend that preschool PTAs be organized to give support to parents and build a bridge between home and school.

Our classrooms can become the best kind of bridge between home and school. To build it, educators need to reaffirm their commitment to children and families. The social web that teachers and families can form together will nurture the child and guide development.

DEFINING FAMILY INVOLVEMENT

To develop relationships of mutual trust and create partnerships with the families we serve.

NAEYC Code of Ethical Conduct, Ideal 2.2 (2005)

Research in early childhood education has shown that family and parental involvement are central to successful schooling experiences (Berger, 2004; Moles, 1996). Findings from studies reveal that children exhibit higher achievement when parents are directly involved in the children's school activities (Henderson & Mapp, 2002; Pelletier & Brent, 2002). Although there is no best way to successfully engage parents and families, concerted efforts by early educators will usually make involvement possible. Examples of successful involvement abound in Head Start, which is the model program dedicated to serving families and children. The pioneer work of Ira Gordon with Head Start programs set the tone for many of today's parent and family engagement strategies. Gordon's parental model was focused on interventions directed to address the characteristics and needs of individual families. His seminal work evidenced the impact of parent participation in classroom activities on children's performance (Berger, 2004).

A Definition of Family Involvement

Family involvement consists of efforts aimed at providing parents and families with opportunities to participate in the children's classroom and school activities. A review of the literature shows that family involvement is characterized by the following beliefs and areas of service (Berger, 2004; Children's Defense Fund, 2005; Garbarino & Garbarino, 1992; Swick, 2004):

- A holistic vision of those who are the sources of influence in the lives of children
- Consideration of the entire family as the target client for services
- An inclusive approach that considers *all* individuals (including the extended family and those without blood relationship) in the family unit as important when deciding on an intervention strategy (see Figure 10-2)

Figure 10-2
Families Have a
Myriad of Structures

Cross-Cultural Configurations of Families	
Nuclear:	The unit where parents and children live together. It is the more commonly found unit in countries where life expectancy is high. Includes such configurations as —Biological —Social (cohabitation) —One-parent —Adoptive —In vitro
Extended:	A combination of several family members who together form an extended family. It does not imply size. It can be, for example, a grandparent and grandchild living together. Includes configurations such as —Three generations —Kinship —Tribal
Reorganized:	A unit that happens through marriage, remarriage, or cohabitation of persons who had children by former partners. Some of the causes are —Remarriage (step-parenthood) —Community living due to migration, exile, economics —Same gender

Source: United Nations, 1994.

- A systems perspective to deal with the reality of the child and to determine all the elements the school looks into that may affect an influence
- A realization that any attempts to plan and establish services without the whole family would prove unsuccessful

There are many benefits for children when parents and families participate in classroom activities. Such involvement influences student performance and individual development. Among the outcomes noted are successful schooling and higher retention levels (Broussard, 2003).

Planning activities to engage parents and family members begins with a good knowledge of the families. Learning about the families, who they are, and what problems and issues they face will provide ways to initiate appropriate actions. This is especially important when working with families from diverse cultural backgrounds.

Overcoming Barriers to Successful Family Involvement

Working with families with diverse characteristics calls for early childhood educators to examine their views about what it means to "be involved." One's ideas about participation and involvement may reflect points of view that differ from those held by families. Many times family involvement efforts are challenged because of these differences. Each cultural group holds its own views about the role of education in

FOCUS
ON CLASSROOM PRACTICES

ENGAGING FATHERS IN EARLY EDUCATION: THE FATHERHOOD INITIATIVE

Fathers, like all family members, play a leading role in children's development. Research reveals that their participation can positively influence children's school achievement, self-esteem, and social competence. However, statistical data show a high incidence of children living without a father figure. It is estimated that 60 percent of children born during the 1990s will spend an important part of their lives growing up away from or without their fathers (U.S. Government, 2001). Divorce, death, estrangement, and incarceration are the main reasons. According to the Department of Justice, 7.4 million children under the age of 18 have incarcerated fathers, with 21 percent of those children being under the age of 5 (Stahl, Kan, & MacKay, 2008). In response to this

situation, a national initiative was created with the goal of increasing awareness among fathers about their role and their participation in their children's activities during the early years. Sponsored by the U.S. Department of Health and Human Services, the initiative Promoting Responsible Fatherhood is aimed at fostering responsibility and engagement of fathers in raising their children and becoming their role models. A variety of activities are delivered through community agencies and Head Start programs.

For more details about activities in your community, contact your local community action agency or Head Start program. Information can also be obtained on the Internet at http://fatherhood.hhs.gov/index.shtml.

Relationships between the young child and family members are essential for positive development.

the lives of their children. Some believe that education is the sole responsibility of the school and therefore rely on the teacher's knowledge and experience to guide the child. Many hesitate to differ or argue with the teacher because they see him or her as an authority figure. Family members' negative personal experiences with the education system may also account for a lack of involvement. Lack of knowledge about how the education system works is yet another factor that prevents families from being involved in the education of their children. Realities of family life, such as economic pressures, illnesses, and presence of disabilities, also influence how family members may balance time and how they set priorities. Social class differences may account for contrasting ideas about participation and classroom involvement.

Beyond the factors that may hinder school involvement, it is important to consider that at home, families may provide valuable support to children by passing on stories and traditions, sharing ideas about the importance of education, helping with learning tasks, and being aware of their children's performance. All these play a leading role in the children's overall success (Epstein, Sanders, Simon, & Salina, 2002).

Collaboration, Also a Goal of Education for Diversity

Every school and home will engage in partnerships that will increase parental involvement and participation in promoting the social, emotional, and academic growth of children.

Goals 2000, Educate America Act of 1994

Education for diversity cannot exist without including and considering families as a fundamental element in the lives of children. The process of teaching and learning is enriched by bringing parents and entire families into the classroom as our partners. One of the main objectives of multicultural education is to have parents sharing with teachers the miracle of the children's learning. The proper development of any program about diversity must include the issues and needs of the families. Combining the ideas and concerns of parents and families improves the quality of the service provided to the child and increases the responsiveness of the program to the child's needs. Quality and responsiveness are vital elements that must be considered by teachers as they transform their teaching.

LITERACY CONNECTIONS...

BOOKS ABOUT FAMILIES AND CHILDREN

Stories are a special way to learn about families in your classroom and community. Sharing these with children or during a parent and family meeting can lead to a very interesting discussion that facilitates everyone learning more about families. These are some of our favorite titles:

- DiSalvo-Ryan, R. (2000). *Grandpa's corner store.* New York: HarperCollins.
- Frasier, D. (2005). *On the day you were born.* New York: Harcourt.
- Greenfield, E. (1991). *My daddy and I.* New York: Writers and Readers Publishing.
- Kaksa, K. (1996). *A mother for Choco.* New York: Putnam.
- Krisnawahmi, U. (2006). *Bringing Asha home.* New York: Lee & Low Books.
- McCaughrean, G. (2002). *My grandfather's clock.* New York: Clarion Books.
- Newman, L. (2009). *Heather has two mommies: 20th Anniversary Edition.* New York: Alyson Wonderland.
- Polacco, P. (2000). *The trees of the dancing goats.* New York: Aladdin.
- Ryland, C. (2005). *The relatives came.* New York: Aladdin.
- Simmons, J. (2004). *Daisy and the egg.* New York: Little, Brown.
- Smith, W. (2005). *Just the two of us.* New York: Scholastic.
- Valentine, J. (2004). *One dad, two dads, brown dad, blue dads.* New York: Alyson.

WHAT DOES COLLABORATION MEAN?

Collaboration, identified by some as a current buzzword in the field of early childhood education, refers to the quest to remedy the inequalities and sparse existence of social programs and services (Couchenour & Chrisman, 2004). In schools, collaboration calls for the concerted efforts of educators, families, and communities. A kind of joint work ambition, collaboration is based on "a vision of better society" (National Commission on Children, 1991). A better society, where equity exists for all individuals regardless of their characteristics, is the principle on which education for diversity is founded.

We envision a nation of strong and stable families, where every child has an equal opportunity to reach his or her full potential and where public policies and personal values give highest priority to healthy, whole children (National Commission on Children, 1991). Educators Sharon Kagan and Ann Rivera (1991) define collaboration as "those efforts that unite and empower individuals and organizations to accomplish collectively what they could not accomplish individually." Applying their definition to what multicultural educators advocate implies the need for establishing collaborative efforts (Figure 10-3). Multicultural programs cannot exist without the support and constant sharing with the children's families. Attempts to do so would be fruitless. Pretending to separate our classrooms from the families can only produce fragmented, if not isolated, views of the children's realities. When our programs are linked to the children's and families' realities, the programs acquire a sense of valid connectedness. Collaboration begins when we learn more about the wealth of ideas and potential for learning that families bring to classrooms.

Figure 10-3   Sample Questionnaire for Family Collaboration

Can you help us in our classroom?

Our class wants to count you among its collaborators. Please tell us in what ways you would like to participate. Just enter check marks to indicate your preferences. Any kind of collaboration is always welcome!

_____ 1. I can serve as a room parent. I am available during (please indicate weekdays and times) _____.

_____ 2. I can help prepare materials for the class.

_____ 3. I can help organize activities.

_____ 4. I can help collect materials for the students.

_____ 5. I can accompany a group during field trips.

_____ 6. I can share my knowledge about (please indicate) _____ .

_____ 7. I can serve as an interpreter of _____ (indicate language).

_____ 8. I can be a member of the PTA.

_____ 9. I cannot volunteer in the classroom; however, this is what I can do at home: (for example, preparing materials, evaluating materials, contacting other parents, recording songs and music) _____.

ON CLASSROOM PRACTICES

FAMILIES IN THE CLASSROOM

Learning about the family configurations in our classroom is an important step. The first days of school present a particularly opportune occasion to do so. For instance, as family members come to bring the children, you might want to try a more personal registration form for those very first days. Instead of just having the official school list where they will sign in the child, have a piece of butcher paper (size 14"x17") or poster board and a basket with markers in different colors. As they come in, ask family members to draw their families. Having your own family drawing conspicuously displayed will help to encourage family members to share theirs. Make sure each work is labeled with the child's name. The result will be a graphic depiction of the family configurations. Take time to carefully examine each one and make notes about the patterns in your classroom. Of course, display them in your classroom for children and family members to enjoy. They will draw many good discussions and will be a good starter for a thematic study you could title "This Is Who We Are."

Consider the Community as Your Partner, Too

Successful collaboration also includes the community. Now more than ever, public agencies and the private sector are willing to offer their support to schools. Consider them as partners and as a part of your team for multicultural education. Every community is the hub for a variety of agencies, civic organizations, services, and programs that can greatly contribute to what we do for families in our classroom. Whether through services, enhancement of existing resources, or community members sharing their expertise, schools can find countless resources right in their communities (Olivos, 2006). Take the time to learn about existing programs and organizations and you may find that you have a treasure trove waiting for you. You may find that resources like the two community initiatives described in the next Think and Reflect are available in your community.

Wadsworth/Cengage Learning

Collaboration with significant adults shapes the futures of young children.

FOCUS ON CLASSROOM PRACTICES

WELCOMING FAMILIES

Nothing makes a better start for positive relationships with families than making them feel important and welcome in the classrooms. Professionals know that showing our sincere respect for and interest in them and their children will open many doors. Here are two simple tips to make families feel welcome in your classroom, especially during the beginning of the year.

- During the first days of school, have a basket of simple treats right next to the sign-in sheet. A simple sign reading "Have a good and sweet day!/¡Que tenga un buen y muy dulce día!" could be placed next to the treats. Choose healthy treats such as fruits (grapes, apples, and bananas are especially good), granola

bars, and low-sugar hard candies. Even those family members who rush in and out will enjoy taking a sweet bite as they leave their children.

- Send welcome notes. A simple message presented in a creative and colorful manner is another way of reaffirming the desire to work together with the children's families. If some families speak languages other than English, write the message in both languages. Your school or the school district probably has resource people to help you with the translation. To make families remember your note, try rolling or attaching a sweet or lollipop to the note. They will certainly remember the detail!

IN ACTION . . .

COMMUNITY SUPPORT

Have you considered the community agencies that could support your program? Make a list of possible groups to contact. Use the local phone directory and look for the agencies you think may be willing to help. Begin a list titled "Community Resources for My Program."

HOME: A PLACE WHERE WE BECOME

To properly appraise the important role of families and the need for their involvement, it is important to remember how critical they are in the life of the developing child. Also central is the need to understand that families bring valuable knowledge and skills, or "funds of knowledge," that can become the best resource for multicultural education. It is impossible to know who each child really is based on official school information. It is equally hard to anticipate the children's needs. The secret to knowing who they really are and what the children need rests with their families. Families are the children's primary source of care and contact, having firsthand and intimate knowledge about their young. Good multicultural early childhood educators know that and strive to work

THINK AND REFLECT...

SUPPORTING FAMILIES AND CHILDREN THROUGH LITERACY: THE *LEE Y SERÁS* AND *READ AND RISE* INITIATIVES

There are many examples of national initiatives sponsored by communities and corporations. Among those aimed at promoting literacy success we find *Lee y Serás* (Read and You Will Be) and *Read and Rise*. These two initiatives were developed under the sponsorship of Scholastic and in collaboration with national organizations with the goal of providing support while responding to the cultural needs of both Latino and African American children and their families.

Lee y Serás was designed to support and enhance early literacy development for Latino families, children, and child-care teachers. The initiative began as a response of the corporate community to close the gap in reading development for Latino children by promoting early literacy skills. Scholastic, in collaboration with Verizon and the National Council of La Raza (NCLR), developed curricula for families and child-care providers and an institute for community leaders. Available in

English and Spanish, each curriculum is embedded in Latino values and traditions. Free literacy workshops for families and child-care teachers are offered by NCLR affiliates, local nonprofit agencies, and school districts in communities across various states including Texas, Florida, California, Illinois, New York, Connecticut, and Georgia. Through its website, *Lee y Serás* also provides suggestions for families, child-care teachers, and communities.

Read and Rise was developed in collaboration with the National Urban League with the goal of helping African American children and their families improve literacy skills. The initiative provides a guide for parents, a monthly *Read and Rise* magazine, and reading tips available on the Internet. To this date, over a million *Read and Rise* guides have been distributed, offering families ideas and suggestions for promoting their children's reading development.

closely with the children's families. As they join hands with parents, they come to know their students. This partnership also facilitates new directions for the curriculum.

We are all products of our families and our home environments. In Chapter 3, you saw how your family and relatives influence your ways and behaviors. You examined their roles in transmitting ideas and beliefs. From our families, we even learned the gestures and nuances that characterize each of us.

When trying to "read" a child, one comes to understand that the key to deciphering some of the behaviors and attitudes lies in the family. The more we know about the values, culture, and ways of the families, the better equipped we are to provide a setting that is responsive to the children's needs.

A Positive Approach toward Children's Families

An early childhood professional is an advocate for young children. He or she is expected to be open and tolerant toward children's and families' diverse characteristics. This facilitates success in building strong relationships with families and promoting positive

Family routines contribute to the passage of cultural values and heritage.

communication and interactions. As a person who believes in equity and in the rights of all families and children, your attitudes and behaviors affirm your aspiration and desire to engage in practices geared to meeting the needs of culturally and linguistically diverse children. This positive attitude should also extend to the families of children in the classrooms. We ask you to set aside your own notions of what families should be or how they should act. By putting aside personal biases, you will see your children's realities clearly, without blurring them with your value judgments.

Working with families of different ethnic and cultural backgrounds brings the early childhood teacher in contact with value systems not necessarily consistent with those held by the educators. We base many of our opinions on our particular value systems. Our own perceptions and reactions are many times the hardest roadblock to overcome.

Because we all rely on our own values when meeting and communicating with others, it is important to realize that a difference in ideas will affect our communication and interaction with the family members of the children we teach. Sadly, a lack of awareness about the interference of our own ideas often hinders even the best-intended efforts.

To say that the solution lies in educators becoming more aware of their attitudes is overly simplistic (Turnbull & Turnbull, 2004). Although evidence exists that attitudes are modified over time, central to successful multicultural education is the need to demonstrate our commitment to children by exhibiting a positive, nonjudgmental attitude about their families. This reaffirmation needs to be shared in visible ways such as written communications, statements posted in the classroom, daily activities, and, more importantly, through our interactions with parents and family members. Let's remember that our belief in those we work with establishes the emotional tone of any involvement efforts and that successful programs are built by people who believe in the individuals with whom they work.

Building Trust with Families

Developing and achieving a sense of trust among families and early educators is essential to a successful program. It is important to remember that families will trust us when they see that they are respected as individuals. They will also believe in teachers when they find that we are safeguarding the information about them and the children. Because early childhood teachers gather a lot of details about the families they work with, it is necessary to emphasize the need for confidentiality.

This is essential to establishing a relationship of mutual trust between the family and the teacher.

There are two relevant points that underscore confidentiality. First, families are not required to give information about what happens inside the family unit; it is their choice to do so. Second, any information a family member gives to the teacher furthers the understanding of the child and the child's reality. Even the simplest detail offered by families must be used professionally and treated confidentially. Professionals need to remember that protecting data about children defines ethical practices in early childhood education. Section II of the NAEYC Code of Ethical Conduct and Statement of Commitment (2005) specifically addresses responsibilities and practices with families.

FOCUS
ON CLASSROOM PRACTICES

SURNAMES, LIKE LOOKS, CAN BE DECEIVING

Have you ever attempted to use your students' surnames to identify their families' cultural backgrounds? Or, have you tried to use them to learn who is a non-English speaker? We hope your answer is "NO" to both questions, because names can often prove deceiving. Because today we have a more open level of acceptance for social interaction, which has resulted in more frequent interethnic marriages, chances are a family surname might not necessarily reflect that a person belongs to a specific cultural or language group. Also, remember that many families might not be recent immigrants but possibly second and third generations or groups who have historically inhabited a given region. In both cases, the child and his or her family might be proficient English language speakers. Unfortunately, there are occasions in which children have been assigned to special groups because they are presumed to be non-English proficient. So the moral here is to never assume children with names such as Perez, Takeshita, and Singh cannot speak English. (Also, do not assume that they speak the languages of the ethnicities their names suggest!) Always wait until you meet the child and the family. Decisions should always be made based on concrete evidence and never on assumptions or stereotypes.

IN ACTION . . .

FAMILY INFLUENCES

- Have you ever thought about where you learned some of the gestures and phrases you use or where you acquired the tastes you have? Try to identify one of them, and explain its origin.

- Observe the children at the housekeeping area. What adult-like behaviors do they show while role-playing at the center?

Developing a Philosophy About Families

What will be your philosophy about families? Which of your beliefs will you share with the families of your children? Take time to outline your beliefs about the concept of family as a social unit. Have them posted in a place where parents and families can see them. Here are some ideas that may be shared:

> All families are important in this classroom.
> Families are the child's richest source of nurturance.
> Families want the best for their children.
> All families and family members can help in this classroom.
> Here, we learn about children through their families.

Learning More About the Families in Our Classrooms

Knowledge about the families and planning for their participation have increased in importance as a result of continuous changes in our communities. Experts in parent and

FOCUS

ON CLASSROOM PRACTICES

LEARNING ABOUT THE FAMILIES IN OUR CLASSROOM

The more you know about the families in your classroom, the better prepared you will be to effectively work together. Because culture influences the raising of children, learning about child-rearing patterns opens doors to an understanding of the family's and the child's behaviors. A favorite unit in most early childhood classrooms is learning about ourselves when we were babies. This important theme is a source of cultural data for teachers that also helps children to explore the concepts of time, change, and cause and effect. Three aspects in particular yield interesting details about child-rearing practices: food, nursery rhymes and songs, and infant toys.

1. Food: A thematic unit titled "What We Used to Eat as Babies" could offer good opportunities to explore the variety and kinds of foods considered appropriate for infants. Ask families to share what they served children during the first year of life. You may want to ask families to share what children's favorite foods were and which ones they disliked.

2. Nursery Rhymes/Songs: A unit titled "Our Favorite Baby Songs and Rhymes" could lead to many creative experiences. For example, the opportunity to compare how babies react to music and rhymes and how the class reacts now (concept of change) presents an excellent way to explore traditions and movement.

3. Toys: One of cultures' common denominators is toys. Exploring what the class enjoyed during infancy gives children an opportunity to discover how their preferences have changed. A unit titled "Toys We Used to Like" can also provide chances to explore materials used to build toys and could introduce children to view toys in a nonsexist way.

If you work in a community of high cultural diversity, do not be surprised to find that families have more in common than you expected. Remember that not all families are recent immigrants and that social status and the level of ethnic identity also influence their behaviors.

IN ACTION . . .

EXAMINING OUR POSITION ABOUT FAMILIES

- What can you say about the families in your community and in your classroom?

- If you were to create statements affirming your views about families, what would they be?

- What is your views regarding the role of parents and families in the classroom?

Wadsworth/Cengage Learning

Building relationships with parents and family members helps promote understanding about the child's strengths and challenges.

family involvement agree that in order to plan effective involvement activities, it is necessary to learn about families (Berger, 2007; Coleman, 1991). This is an ongoing process. One can never get to know everything about a family from the answers on a questionnaire or from a parent conference. Such strategies only emphasize the need to find additional ways to learn more, formally or informally. Formal sources include the following:

1. Information included in the child's file
2. Formal interviews
3. Parent questionnaires, surveys, or checklists administered by the school or district
4. Interviews with other professionals, such as a guidance counselor or social worker
5. Reports of formal home visits

Data obtained through formal sources provide necessary documentation to support program decisions and services for the child and the family. Analysis of the data provides an initial insight into the children's families, particularly in terms of the home culture. Learning about the home cultures of the children will help readdress curricular planning and guide parent involvement activities. Additional data can be collected through informal means. Actually, many relevant details can only be gathered through more informal methods. Some of those methods teachers can use are the following:

1. Meeting and talking to parents or family members as they bring their children to school

2. Holding unscheduled parent–teacher interviews

3. Establishing periodic telephone contacts

4. Doing informal interviews and surveys

5. Inviting parents and family members to share morning "coffee/tea"

6. Using a "pony-bag" (a plastic bag in which teachers periodically send a note asking about a particular detail about the family, such as things they like to eat, things they do together, and so on)

7. Using a classroom "family sharing tree" (a collection of interesting details that identify each family and that are shared on a weekly or monthly basis in the classroom)

Using Surveys and Checklists

There are many instruments teachers can develop to use in acquiring more information about the families of their students. They can create their own surveys and checklists structured to the unique needs of their families. When deciding to use a teacher-made tool, there are some rules to remember:

1. *Purpose:* To create a good instrument, first identify its purpose and goal. Knowing what information you want and need to obtain defines the questions to be asked.

2. *Missing data:* A way to begin learning about the families is to review the children's files and see what relevant data are missing. What is not included, and what you consider important, should be incorporated into your instruments. Among the information to be considered could be details such as nicknames used at home, the meaning of the child's name, the correct pronunciation of the child's name, holidays that are more important for the family, and so on.

3. *Data relevant for curricular planning:* Information that is relevant to the curriculum also needs to be included in the instrument. For example, data that will help teachers know more about the cultural ways of the family can clarify what should be emphasized in the classroom. Remember, the more you know about families, the better prepared you will be to organize your teaching.

4. *Family needs and interests:* When teachers are aware of the family's needs, issues, and interests, actions can be taken to provide the support or assistance at the classroom level. The information concerning the diversity variables that characterize particular families is most important for establishing an effective classroom curriculum. This knowledge also establishes a foundation for a sound collaboration between the school and the family.

A teacher-made instrument is not only to be used for "writing in" answers. It can also be used as a guide during a parent interview. Instruments should not be too lengthy, and they need to be clear and simple in language and format. Some samples are included in Figure 10-4.

Figure 10-4   Survey of a Family

SURVEY OF THE FAMILY—PART A

Sample Letter to the Family

Dear Parent/Family Members:

In this classroom, we believe families are an important part of the child's life. We also believe that to create a good program for your child, we need to know more about your family. For that reason, we are asking you to share some information about your family by answering this questionnaire. Answering this questionnaire is optional; however, it will help us to better know your family and your child. As we learn more about the students and families, we will discover more ways to make your child succeed in school. Please know that all information will be kept confidential and that it will be used only for planning purposes. Thanks!

Sincerely,
(classroom teacher)

Sample Questionnaire

Dear family of _____ (child's name):

Please read each question carefully and write your answer in the space provided.

1. Who are the members of your family?
2. Does your family use any language other than English? Is the child encouraged to use that language?
3. Who is the family member we should contact in case of an emergency? Please give name and relationship to the child.
4. What is your family's favorite TV program?
5. Does your family have pets?
6. What are some of the activities that your family enjoys doing together?
7. What are the holidays that your family celebrates?
8. Are there any religious or cultural traditions your family considers very important?
9. What expectations does your family have of this school/classroom?
10. We would like to know in what ways we can collaborate with you. From the list below, please check all those areas that represent areas of **interest** or **concern** for your family. If the point is of interest, write an *I*; if a concern, write a *C*.

    _____ Understanding my child

    _____ Learning more about my child's behavior

    _____ Planning activities at home for my child

    _____ Locating good materials for my child

    _____ Learning more about my child's development

    _____ Dealing with nutrition (appropriate feeding)

    _____ Obtaining after-school care services

    _____ Dealing with health problems in the family

    _____ Locating health services for the child

    _____ Learning more about what the community offers for my child (for example: parks, library, and others)

    _____ Obtaining information about housing, food stamps, county services

    _____ Other: (please comment)

(continued)

Figure 10-4 (continued)

SURVEY OF THE FAMILY—PART B

Name of the child: _____ Age: _____ Gender: F _____ M _____

Directions to the teacher:

(This part is to be administered in the classroom. After a motivational experience, have the child draw his or her family. Provide crayons and/or markers.) After the child has finished, ask the following questions:

1. Can you tell me what this drawing shows?
2. Can you tell me who are the people in your drawing?
3. Are you in this drawing? Show me where.
4. What is the family doing in this drawing?
5. Can you tell me what you like most about your family?

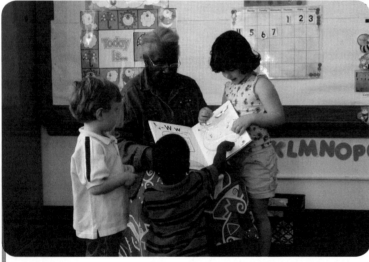

Wadsworth/Cengage Learning

Volunteering is one of the many ways in which family members collaborate in the classroom.

Working with children from a variety of cultural and ethnic backgrounds underlines the need to know more about their families' cultures. This is especially important when teachers may be unfamiliar with some of the cultural groups. A good way to initiate positive interaction with family members is by showing interest in learning more about their cultures.

One helpful way to learn more about families' cultures is the questionnaire developed by Saville-Troike (1978). Teachers can use it as a guide when trying to learn more about the culture of the family. The questions provide a way to profile the cultural life of an individual and an opportunity to depict the family in a non-stereotypical way. Questions are categorized by different areas that are commonly impacted by culture. Very comprehensive in nature, the questions cover points including the life cycle, roles, religion, communication, and food and can be used selectively to obtain information from the family whenever teachers feel that a particular aspect requires more clarification (Figure 10-5).

Figure 10-5   Culture Questionnaire

Selected sections from Saville-Troike's questions about culture

- Family
  a. Who is in the 'family'? Who among these (or others) lives in one house?
  b. What is the line of authority in the family?
  c. What are the rights and responsibilities of each family member? Do children have an obligation to work to help the family?
  d. What are the functions and obligations of the family to the larger social unit? To the school? To its individual members?
  e. How close together does the family appear to be? Is there a degree of solidarity among its members?
- The life cycle
  a. How do they refer to or define the different stages, periods, or transitions in life? (i.e., before X was born, after the divorce, etc.)
  b. What are the attitudes, behaviors, and expectations held by the family members during different life stages?
  c. What behaviors are deemed acceptable or inappropriate for children? Are they in conflict with the expectations of the school?
  d. How is language related to the life cycle?
- Roles
  a. What roles exist in the family or group? Who holds those roles? Do they consider education an important requirement to hold any of those roles?
  b. What knowledge or perception does the child or the family have about the roles found in their cultural group?
  c. Does the group consider the use of language as an important characteristic or social marking of roles?
  d. Do expectations about children's attainment differ according to class status? Are expectations realistic?
- Interpersonal relationships
  a. How do people greet each other? What are the forms of address used between people? Are there differences because of status held (age, position)?
  b. What are the expectations held for interaction between girls and boys? Do these differ from what is expected in school?
  c. When and how is consideration or deference shown? What are the social courtesies expected by and from the family?
  d. What constitutes an insult or an offense? How are these expressed?
  e. Who is allowed to disagree and with whom? When are individuals allowed to disagree?
- Communication
  a. What are the languages and language varieties used by the family? In the community? When? Who uses what? For what purposes? Are children expected to know these varieties?
  b. Which varieties of the language are written? Is there a widespread knowledge of the written form? Does the family use it?
  c. How does the family define "speaking well"? How does it relate to age, gender, social context?
  d. What is the acceptable speech behavior? What roles, attitudes, and personal characteristics are commonly associated with particular ways of speaking?
  e. What is the current level of functionality of the native language in the house? In the community?
  f. What are the gestures or postures considered socially objectionable? What are their meanings? What meaning is ascribed to direct eye contact? To eye contact avoidance?
  g. What are some of the terms or words that are socially unacceptable? Why?
  h. Who is allowed to talk to whom? Under what circumstances? What topics are acceptable for discussion?
- Food
  a. What do the family members eat? How often?
  b. What foods are favorites, taboos, typical?
  c. What rules are observed during meals regarding age and sex roles within the family (order of serving, seating, appropriate verbal formulas)? What social rules are individuals expected to observe during meals? What utensils are used during meals?

(continued)

Figure 10-5   (continued)

  d. What social obligations are there in regard to food preparation? In regard to food giving, reciprocity, and honoring people?
  e. What medicinal uses are made of some categories of food?
  f. What rules exist regarding food handling, offering, or discarding?
- Dress and personal appearance
  a. What type of clothing is considered "typical"?
  b. What clothes are worn for special occasions? What seasonal differences are considered appropriate?
  c. How does dress differ for age, gender, and social class?
  d. What restrictions are imposed for modesty?
  e. How is beauty or attractiveness defined? What characteristics are most valued?
  f. What are the acceptable verbal compliments?
  g. What symbolic value, if any, is given to color of dress?
- Education
  a. What are the family's ideas about the purpose of education?
  b. What methods of teaching are used at home (for example, direct verbal instruction, modeling, proverbs, didactic stories)?
  c. Do teaching methods vary according to class, setting, or depending on what is taught?
  d. Is it acceptable for the child to ask questions or volunteer information?
  e. What is accepted as a positive response by teachers to students? By students to teachers?
  f. How many years are children expected to normally attend school? Does it differ by gender?
- Work and play
  a. What range of behaviors are considered as "work" and as "play"?
  b. What kind of work is considered prestigious, and why?
  c. Do they hold any stereotypes regarding the occupations of particular groups?
  d. What is the purpose of "play"? Who is allowed to participate?

Source: Adapted from Saville-Troike, 1978.

Saville-Troike (1978) suggests that educators use this set of questions to accomplish the following:

- *Reflect on one's culture:* By answering some of the questions, teachers can clarify some of their own views about cultures. Through this introspection, teachers can appreciate and understand the similarities and differences found in the views held by their students and families.

- *Serve as a guide for observations:* Because of their comprehensiveness, questions can be used to guide teachers' observations in the classroom or in any other setting. For instance, questions regarding communication can help teachers identify the appropriate and acceptable patterns in a family's or child's culture.

Recording What We Know about Families: The Family Folder

Throughout the school year, you will learn many interesting details that are worth saving. Usually, teachers keep this information in the child's portfolio, where it is often lost amid all the work samples and drawings. We recommend that teachers

THINK
AND
REFLECT...

FAMILIES, SCHOOLS, AND COMMUNITIES MAKING A DIFFERENCE IN THE LIVES OF CHILDREN

Programs for children and their families have dramatically grown in the past decade. Let's sample a few that have made a difference in the lives of children.

• *CentroNía, Washington, DC:* Established more than 20 years ago, CentroNía (formerly known as Calvary Bilingual Multicultural Learning Center) serves a multicultural and bilingual community in the District of Columbia. The name reflects the program's commitment to serve the culturally diverse community of the area: Centro means "center" in Spanish; Nía means "our" in Esperanto and "purpose" in Swahili. CentroNía has evolved from a child-care center to become a comprehensive family support organization offering education, parent services, and community leadership. The center is accredited by the NAEYC, and it is nationally known for its quality programs for young children and their families. CentroNía provides early childhood education programs along with professional development for caregivers. Through the Family Institute program, the center provides social services, consultation, referrals, and workshops for parents and families of children. They also house the DC Bilingual Public Charter School, the first of its kind in the area, which services children ages 3 through 5. Plans are to add grades one through five.

CentroNía's dedication to young children and their families, the community, and continuous commitment to provide quality and equitable services sets an example in the field of early childhood education.

The Redlands Christian Migrant Association (RCMA) Child Development Program, Florida: Serving children in Florida, the RCMA is an organization that provides services to children of migrant and low-income families. Established in 1965 in the Redlands agricultural area in South Florida, today RCMA offers services to more than 8,000 children and families through more than 75 centers and two charter schools. At their centers throughout the state of Florida, children from six months to age 12 attend their programs.

Central to their mission is their belief that parents and families want to help and are capable of helping their children. The continued success of the program is the best acknowledgment of what families and parents can do. Having an active voice in the program's decision-making process, farm workers, individuals from various cultural groups, local community members, and committed educators participate as members of the State Board of Directors. Today, RCMA is considered a model in the delivery of services to young children who are culturally and linguistically diverse.

keep a separate file for family information. Like the children's portfolios, the family folder is open to families to incorporate samples of activities done or pictures and information about important family events. As an ongoing project, it serves as another way to bring families into your classroom. Confidentiality of the information kept in the folder is essential. Early childhood teachers need to guarantee families that the data saved in the folders are to be used only to plan and design activities for both children and their families. Information can also be kept in a

IN ACTION . . .

THE FAMILY FOLDER

- What other items would you include in a family folder?
- Who would be allowed to read the family folder?

- How would you ensure that the child's next teacher understands the information in the folder?
- Regarding the issue of confidentiality, what do you suggest to protect the contents of the family folder?

VIDEO CASE 10.2 ▶❚❚

Using a family journal to XXX

Go to the Cengage Education video case website and watch the video *Using a family journal to XXX*. Then, respond to the following questions:

1. In what ways does the family journal foster communication with families?

2. If you were to use a family journal like the one described in the video, what would be your purposes?

large envelope within the portfolio. Information that teachers might want to save includes the following:

- Data about the family (surveys, checklists)
- Written communications from and between the family and teacher
- Photographs of home, school, and classroom activities
- Notes from telephone conferences
- Family referrals
- Samples of projects done by families

In some ways, the family folder lays the foundation for the development of the individual family service plan (IFSP), used in programs serving exceptional students and in many early education programs. The IFSP was initially introduced as a result of the statements established in Part H of the Education of the Handicapped Act Amendments (PL 99-457). Experiences in the field have shown that programs for the culturally diverse child are significantly improved when they assume a family-centered approach, especially when the family is also included in the services offered.

THE SCHOOL, THE NEIGHBORHOOD, AND THE COMMUNITY

Planning a multicultural program cannot take place devoid of the community. The community has relevant qualities and characteristics that are just as important for the children's learning as the knowledge about the families.

According to Garbarino, Galambos, Plantz, and Kostelny (1992), the neighborhood is the child's territory, and it plays a leading role in the child's process of socialization. The neighborhood is the playground where the child is initiated into the community life (Garbarino, Galambos, Plantz, & Kostelny, 1992). What a neighborhood or a community offers to the child and to the family will affect

Responsibilities to Families According to the NAEYC Code of Ethical Conduct and Statement of Commitment

Section II: Ethical responsibilities to families

Families are of primary importance in children's development. Because the family and the early childhood practitioner have a common interest in the child's well-being, we acknowledge a primary responsibility to bring about communication, cooperation, and collaboration between the home and early childhood program in ways that enhance the child's development.

Ideals

I-2.1—To be familiar with the knowledge base related to working effectively with families and to stay informed through continuing education and training.

I-2.2—To develop relationships of mutual trust and create partnerships with the families we serve.

I-2.3—To welcome all family members and encourage them to participate in the program.

I-2.4—To listen to families, acknowledge and build upon their strengths and competencies, and learn from families as we support them in their task of nurturing children.

I-2.5—To respect the dignity and preferences of each family and to make an effort to learn about its structure, culture, language, customs, and beliefs.

I-2.6—To acknowledge families' childrearing values and their right to make decisions for their children.

I-2.7—To share information about each child's education and development with families and to help them understand and appreciate the current knowledge base of the early childhood profession.

I-2.8—To help family members enhance their understanding of their children and support the continuing development of their skills as parents.

I-2.9—To participate in building support networks for families by providing them with opportunities to interact with program staff, other families, community resources, and professional services.

Source: NAEYC, 2005.

their experiences and their abilities to cope with life. The characteristics that define a community even affect the internal life of its families. The following factors in the neighborhood directly influence the lives of the family (Garbarino, Galambos, Plantz, & Kostelny, 1992):

- neighborhood safety
- recreational facilities

FOCUS ON CLASSROOM PRACTICES

SHARING THE CODE OF ETHICS WITH FAMILIES

The purpose of the NAEYC Code of Ethical Behavior and Statement of Commitment is to help early childhood teachers define their work professionally. It also serves as a tool for parents to understand that what we do for children and for parents is guided by ethical beliefs. For that reason, the Code should be shared with parents and other professionals. It will help underline our commitment to work together. There are many ways to share the code. Some suggestions are listed here:

• Display it permanently on the classroom bulletin board. A good place is by the door or next to the sign-up sheet.

• Share copies during parent meetings and conferences. This is a good opportunity to discuss some of its vital points.

• Leave copies or segments as part of home visits.

• Share segments. Include a section in the classroom newsletter to bring attention to it at a specific point in time.

• Have copies available as part of the center/school registration/information packet.

• health and social services
• schools
• economic conditions
• opportunities to develop supportive relationships

Building Knowledge About the Community

The success of school programs is influenced by the level of awareness we have about the nature and the characteristics of the community. Discovering the cultures of our communities helps teachers obtain an accurate portrayal of the communities' expectations. This knowledge facilitates the planning of activities that will propel the collaboration between the school and the community. The fact that many educators commute to their workplaces and are not members of the local cultural and/or ethnic groups makes the need to learn about the community in which the families and the children live even more important.

Learning about the community can be accomplished in a variety of ways. You can begin by checking the school reports in which general data are found. You may "tour" the community with a local resident who can point out the various relevant places. Another way to learn is by going on a field visit on your own. When visiting the community, observe the following:

• Physical appearance (general impression)
• Types of residential areas (public housing, private developments)

- Available recreational areas and kinds of recreation offered (parks, playgrounds, stadiums, theaters, community centers)
- Public and private services (hospitals, libraries, churches, banks, public service agencies, transportation, police stations, fire stations, other educational institutions)
- Existence of religious institutions and types of denominations
- Types of businesses (grocery stores, craft shops, repair shops, etc.)
- Languages used in signs, advertisements, and in anything posted or on the walls
- Decorations and symbols found throughout the community
- Activities people do (what they are engaged in during your observation)

You can also gather information about the community by finding the answers to the following questions:

- What is defined as the perimeter or what are the different parts of the community?
- How do children define their community?
- How do residents describe their community?
- What social classes do the families represent?
- What specific services are available for families?
- What community agencies are found in the community?
- What issues or problems are present in the community?

AROUND THE WORLD

IT TAKES A VILLAGE: RECOLLECTIONS

My name is Mira (Mee-rah). I was a child in Kosovo during the war and I was raised by a village. My parents died during the war, as were the parents of five other children in the small village outside of Pristina where we lived. I had an aunt who also lived on our street in the village who took me home with her after losing my parents. A few days after the tragedy, the village council decided that "everyone" would raise the six of us. This was not as strange as it may sound to others, because in Kosovo the children in our village were the responsibility of the entire community. I lived with my aunt, but the neighbor across the street took all six of us who lost our parents to her house to help us with our homework. On Saturdays, two of the "village uncles" would take us to play soccer. My aunt taught us to make bread and how to use a needle and thread. We even had several grandmothers who read to us and told us stories at bed time.

Thanks to the entire community, all six of us ended up being loved and taken care of until we were adopted. I was lucky to come to America and have a wonderful new life, but I have never forgotten my childhood in Kosovo. In my case, the saying "it takes a village" was the truth about my life.

Many communities have their own newsletters and newspapers, which are usually available in local stores. Reading them can give you an idea about current events and what is considered socially important. Local news publications will also tell you about community organizations, activities they sponsor, and who their leaders are.

Using What We Know About Families

There are so many different ways of engaging families in our classrooms. An analysis of information collected informally and formally by the school and teachers will provide information about the families' interests, traits, concerns, and talents. Together, these will serve as a foundation for building a strong family–teacher partnership.

All information yielded from surveys, checklists, and notes is important. There are some aspects, such as the following, that will be particularly relevant:

- *Family configurations:* What are the different family patterns (single-parent, extended, etc.)?
- *Social class:* What particular social and economic characteristics define the families of your students?
- *Expectations:* What do families expect from you? From the school?
- *Diversity:* What elements of diversity are descriptive of the families (language, exceptionalities, ethnicities, religion)?
- *Concerns/issues:* What are the problems and situations faced by parents?
- *Possible resources for the classroom:* What abilities and characteristics of the families can become a resource for the class? Include those parents who expressed a desire to help.

Information highlighted through such an analysis will help you refocus your efforts and decide on more effective ways to link families to your classroom. Knowing who our families are will also contribute to making decisions to help our activities become more sensitive and realistic for both the child and the families.

IN ACTION . . .

A VISIT TO YOUR OWN NEIGHBORHOOD

Take time to visit your own neighborhood. Using the guidelines mentioned in this section, describe what you discovered about your own community.

FOCUS
ON CLASSROOM PRACTICES

IDENTIFYING CLASSROOM COLLABORATORS

The first source of classroom collaborators is found among the families themselves. Doing a simple survey early in the year will help to identify them. Here is a sample survey you can use to create one that is customized to fit your classroom needs.

Dear Parents and Families,

We are happy that your child is in our program. We also know that parents and families always have so many things to share and contribute to the classroom. There are many different ways in which you can collaborate. We would appreciate it if you would take a few minutes to answer this survey.

Thanks so much,

_____

Teacher

1. Would you like to collaborate as a volunteer in our classroom?

   _____ Yes, I am interested in collaborating.

   _____ No, I am unable to help at this time.

2. If you answered "yes," how would you like to collaborate with our classroom? Please enter a check mark to indicate how:

_____ I can help as a classroom volunteer. Please call me to discuss times and days.

_____ I can prepare materials at home.

_____ I can share my expertise in: _____.

_____ I can collaborate sharing resources _____.

_____ I can help by serving in the PTA.

After you get your surveys back, remember to tabulate the answers. An easy way to make good use of what you discovered is to classify answers according to the following categories:

1. In-classroom volunteers (those interested in coming to the classroom)

2. Resources (those interested in doing things from home and those who can collaborate for specific activities such as craft making, music and dancing, speaking, etc.)

3. Translators (important if you have children and families who speak languages other than English!)

4. Storytellers (essential because they add interest to literacy activities)

5. Community services/network (those who can provide information or help with community agencies)

Planning Successful Family Involvement Activities

Have you ever considered how richly talented the families in your classroom are? The more we get to know them, the more we come to appreciate their skills, knowledge, and experiences. Because each family has unique characteristics and circumstances, we cannot assume that they will all be ready to collaborate or participate in the children's education at the same level. Being mindful of the families' needs and expectations will help in planning activities that foster partnerships. The following guidelines will help us plan appropriate and culturally respectful experiences for parents and families.

- *Be mindful of the social and cultural characteristics of families.* The key to successful activities is to always respond to the needs of the participants. Keep in mind that a program that is successful in one community may not be suitable for families in your community. Use the information about the families to select the type of activities and programs you offer. Engagement occurs when activities are related to the parents' and families' realities.

- *Consider language differences.* If your classroom includes parents and families who speak languages other than English, it is important to provide translators and to have materials available in their languages. This will facilitate communication and increase their participation and involvement in the classroom.

- *Use your knowledge about families to select and present the content.* Your knowledge about the family's social and cultural characteristics is instrumental in planning successful meetings. Consider the cultural values of families and carefully select content and presentation strategies. If addressing any sensitive issues, be mindful of their cultures and present the information in culturally respectful ways.

- *Plan activities with all parents and families in mind.* Always consider what you know about the characteristics (such as educational levels and cultures), special skills, and interests of parents and families and plan events that will promote their participation. Keep in mind the importance of the extended family and plan experiences that facilitate their participation.

- *Plan activities with a purpose.* Be considerate of the parents' time and plan activities and meetings that have a clear goal and purpose. Remember that time is very precious for all, so make sure that you carefully plan any meetings and activities. Always ask yourself, what is the purpose of the meeting? What will parents and families learn or gain from the meeting?

- *Be creative and provide a variety of activities.* Use your creativity and plan different types of activities that will build interest in attending classroom events. Consider the purpose of the meeting or activity and select appropriate delivery strategies.

- *Consider the parents' schedules in planning activities.* Planning responsive activities always begins by taking into consideration the time factor. Find out from parents and families about times that are more convenient to attend. Be flexible and try scheduling activities at different times during the day in order to increase participation. Also, plan activities of reasonable length to avoid imposing a long time commitment.

- *Show your appreciation.* Always take time to express your sincere appreciation for the family members' attendance and participation. Before ending the meeting or activity, sincerely show how much you value their presence. Be ready to say "thank you" to all who come. Try learning or having signs reading "thank you" in all families' languages.

Joyce Epstein's six roles of parent involvement are another relevant guidepost that promotes successful collaboration with families. Her research focuses on the various ways to promote participation and engagement of parents and family members. As you review in Figure 10-6 the six roles that she proposes, consider those that may fit the needs and reality of families in your classroom.

Figure 10-6
Epstein's Six Types
of Roles of Parent
Involvement

1. *Parenting:* Providing support to families to build a supportive home environment that promotes development and meets the needs of children

2. *Communicating:* Creating and maintaining appropriate and effective communication between the classroom and homes

3. *Volunteering:* Establishing a group of volunteers to collaborate in classroom and school activities

4. *Learning at home:* Providing information, ideas, and resources to extend and support classroom-related learning at home

5. *Decision making:* Creating opportunities for active participation of families in classroom and school decisions

6. *Collaboration with the community:* Locating, coordinating, and integrating community resources and services that support the families, children, and classroom activities

Source: Epstein, Sanders, Simon, & Salina, 2002.

COMMUNICATION: THE ROAD TO POSITIVE RELATIONSHIPS

Good communication is the key to any successful relationship. Teachers are in a position to establish the foundation for a productive and lasting relationship the very first time parents come to the school. Everything you say from the very first time you meet the families counts! What can you do to develop good communication with them? To begin, be open-minded and assume a nonjudgmental attitude regarding the family members. This will contribute to the establishment of a successful and effective multicultural program.

Communication is a process that involves sending and receiving messages. Good communication begins when the messages are not just received but actually understood by the receiver. There are many times in our schools when we fail to complete this process. For example, parents receive our notes and letters; however, they may not grasp our intentions. The chance of this happening is much greater when working with families whose ethnicities or languages differ from our own. Therefore, it is important to verify that the messages we send are received and understood

Teachers and parents have the best interests of the child at heart.

IN ACTION . . .

PARENT–TEACHER RELATIONSHIPS

In the following quote, educator James Hymes describes how parent–teacher relationships can become positive or negative.

> Show your interest in a child, and parents are on your side. Be casual, off-handed, be cold toward the child and parents can never work closely with you . . . To praise the child is to praise the parent. To criticize the child is to hit the parent. The two are two, but the two are one.

- Do you agree with what Hymes says? Why?
- How else could you express the relationship between the child and the parent?
- How do your personal experiences support or deny his premise?

Source: Berger, 2004.

by the recipients. In a study done with parents of children with disabilities, Beth Harry (1997) found that in cases of parents with different cultural backgrounds, written communication was usually received but failed to convey any messages. Harry found that miscommunication was not just restricted to what was written. She found that even during personal interviews, the school personnel failed to communicate effectively with parents. Three important points influencing communication with those with cultural differences are derived from Harry's study:

1. Language used in written communications should be explicit and free of professional jargon. Even when letters are written in the parents' native language, professional jargon should be avoided. If any such terms are used, they should be explained.

2. A bureaucratic tone might fail to convey the message. The tone of written communication should be personal and not intimidating. The message should indicate the school's concern and desire for success for the child and the parent.

3. Communication should not be limited to what is sent in writing. Opportunities for participation in open conversations should be encouraged. A person whom parents can trust should serve as a liaison during meetings.

Opening Doors to Collaboration with Parents and Families

Positive communication in diverse settings is built when teachers show their honest desire to help families. Your frank intent to collaborate with them and the children, accompanied by a friendly smile, opens doors to many opportunities. Those opportunities also arise when you invite the families for a closer look at your classrooms. But, how will they know they are welcome and that their help is wanted in our schools? This is where skillful communication works like magic.

Effective communication requires a combination of one- and two-way methods. One-way communication happens when parents receive letters, handbooks, memorandums, or printed materials aimed at *informing* them about the school plans. On the other hand, two-way communication occurs when schools and families *interact by sharing* views and ideas. In two-way situations, each part gains from each other's knowledge and experience (Berger, 2004). Teachers working in multicultural settings will find many opportunities to share ideas and communicate with families. Let's examine some of the strategies you can use to establish better communication.

Sharing Ideas in Writing

Perhaps one of the things that parents value most is being informed about the events and activities in their children's schools. Good and appropriate written communication is important to keep parents well apprised of what occurs in the school. It can be either periodic or incidental. Whether formal or informal, written communication sent home should be clear and simple. Newsletters, reports, and notes with curriculum information are examples of periodic communication. Forms of incidental communication include notes, letters, and flyers about special events. Here are a few points to guide your written communications:

- Use simple and clear language. When there is a language difference, write your messages in that language, if possible. When writing in a language you do not have mastery in, ask someone fluent in the language to edit your materials. Remember, you represent the school.
- Avoid using figurative language in communications to parents who have limited English language proficiency. Figurative language is usually culturally based and not easily understood by those who do not share that culture. Remember that sometimes it is difficult for a nonnative speaker to grasp the meanings of metaphors and analogies.
- Communications should be attractive and appealing to the reader. For newsletters, Berger (2004) recommends using colorful paper and clear headlines, using samples of children's work, and including practical suggestions for the families.
- Communications should have something relevant to tell. Make sure that the message is important to the reader.
- Include topics that relate to the families' cultures. Try to incorporate ideas or points that recognize the value of the cultural groups in your classroom.
- When writing notes or letters, always include something positive about the child.

Classroom News

Families enjoy receiving materials that are both informative and fun to read. A good practice that enhances a constant flow of communication is to have a classroom newsletter. Simple and not difficult to prepare, teachers can send home one-page weekly or

WHAT COMES FIRST: COMPLIANCE OR COMMUNICATION?

A study done by Harry with parents of exceptional students of culturally different origins revealed that many schools often seek and achieve compliance with the law while failing to establish positive communication with parents. In her study, Harry examined the incidents and perceptions held by a group of Puerto Rican parents of children with disabilities regarding the educational system. She found that communication styles due to language differences, not the experiences and expectations between parents and schools, were found to be the leading cause of miscommunication. Although parents wanted to trust the school, the impersonal approach used by the school personnel only served to widen the distance between the groups. Harry documented various instances where use of educational jargon and the bureaucratic tone, even when written communications were in the parents' language, failed to convey the urgency or importance of the situation. In one of the cases studied, a parent realized after a year that her son had been placed in an exceptional student self-contained classroom. Although the parent had received a letter, she was unable to comprehend its meaning. When the parent visited the school, she received oversimplified information about what the school intended to do with her son. Told by a social worker that the boy was going to receive "extra help in English and math," and not that the boy was being assigned to a self-contained classroom for exceptional students, the parent accepted the school's decision. Her trust in the school made her accept the decision without knowing the implications of her child's placement. A year later, during a meeting with the teacher, the parent discovered not only what the self-contained classroom was, but also that her child was classified as emotionally disabled in accordance with PL 94-142.

Harry found that to develop an appropriate level of communication with culturally diverse parents, schools need to use a more personal tone as well as a more open-ended type of communication. Although compliance with the law is important, it should not be done at the expense of the clients, especially when they are not being properly informed.

Source: Harry, 1997.

semi-monthly news briefs. Decide on an appealing name, which can be suggested by your class, and get ready to become an editor. If your students' families are linguistically diverse, having a bilingual edition is a great help. A parent can volunteer to serve as a translator if you do not have mastery of the other language. The next step is to select your content. For example, teachers can include notes about topics studied, a list of songs learned, highlights about children's accomplishments, and a schedule of upcoming events. When working with a multicultural curriculum, this kind of communication is important because it allows parents to learn and know what is happening in the classroom.

Another useful technique is regularly sending a list of suggested activities for parents to do at home with their children. This not only allows families to participate in extending the curriculum into the home, but it also provides parents with good activities to share with their children. Including a section for parents to provide feedback about the activities they like the most is a way to invite their participation.

Planning Meetings and Conversations

Nothing takes the place of personal interactions. What is shared through personal contacts carries a totally different meaning from any other kind of communication. The opportunity to share an actual moment in time with another person enhances the quality of the experience. You probably know of many instances where the impression you had about someone drastically changed after meeting the individual in person. Whether face-to-face or by telephone, personal contact should be established with families and parents. Personal interaction requires attention to such communication elements as the tone of voice, voice inflections, and body language. All convey messages that can never be transmitted by a letter or a note. Results from research done by Miller Wackman, Nunnaly, and Miller (cited in Berger, 2007) confirm that in an interpersonal communication, many more things are "said" through our gestures and movements and our tone of voice than by words alone: "Oral, verbal messages (the spoken word) account for only 7 percent of the input; vocal and tonal messages (the way in which the word is spoken) account for 38 percent; visual messages account for 55 percent." Conversations need to be carefully planned because they provide the perfect opportunities to initiate real partnerships. Effective interactions involve consideration of several factors. The first thing to understand is that the impression you leave on a parent is not solely conveyed through your words but also through the context and the manner in which they are spoken. The place and time chosen for a conversation also play an important part in creating effective communication. Working with families who have cultures and languages different from yours requires even more careful planning. Always remember that in some cases, the parents' views of education may be very different from yours. Their perceptions and knowledge about the philosophical concepts and systemic issues of education are grounded in their cultural heritage. That alone establishes how they will approach and react toward "a meeting with the teacher." Try to be sensitive to this by just considering how you would feel in a setting where your values and ideas might be distinctively dissimilar from those of the school.

When planning to talk with parents, consider the following:

- Select a pleasant environment. If the conversation takes place in the classroom, have adult seats available.
- When planning a telephone conversation, make sure the time you plan to call is convenient. Know in advance how much time you have. However, avoid long telephone conversations. A series of short, specific ones are usually more productive than very long ones.
- Whether on the telephone or in person, always treat parents with respect and courtesy. Even if your values and ideas are not in harmony with theirs, show your professionalism by respecting their ways.

- Be aware of your own body gestures and avoid any nuances that might send a distorting message. For instance, if the parent or adult dresses in a different way or wears a particular personal decoration, avoid staring at it.

- Remain focused on the conversation. Avoid looking around, which sends a message of "I'm not interested."

- When meeting the parent or family for the first time, introduce yourself in a friendly manner. Avoid giving the impression of being a "know-it-all" kind of person (Eliason & Jenkins, 2002). Show that you are a professional through your work with children and not by presenting yourself as the "power person."

- To maximize your meeting, it is important to send a note in advance describing in simple terms the purpose of the meeting. Providing a brief description is especially convenient for those families who are linguistically different because it prepares them to have a more productive conversation (Lee, 1995). Some parents have said that before coming to school, they would ask a friend or consult a dictionary for how to say given words and phrases. A note sent in advance explaining the objective of the meeting will avoid misinterpretations. For some cultures, being called by the teacher means the child has misbehaved. Some parents have reported punishing their children in advance because of what they "might have done" (Robles de Meléndez, 2006).

- Keep your conversation friendly and professional. Avoid asking very personal questions about the family. People of some cultures might find it offensive to be asked certain personal details. Accept what they are disclosing. Remember that by establishing a positive relationship, you will encourage families to continue sharing ideas.

- When meeting parents, always refer to them as "Ms. _____, Mrs. _____, or Mr. _____" and never by their first name. In many cultures, people would feel offended if called their first name by someone who is not a close friend or relative. Using a title not only shows your respect but also establishes a professional tone. If elders are present, show deference and acknowledge their presence. Although you may prefer that parents call you by your first name, remember that in some cultures this is not customary.

- Avoid addressing your conversation to the mother alone if her husband, or the child's father, is also present. In some cultures, such as Hispanic and Middle Eastern, males play a strong role in the family. Acknowledge their participation and input.

- Talk in a courteous, not patronizing, way. Talking slowly and clearly can be accomplished without using a patronizing tone.

- Avoid using "teacher jargon" to show your knowledge when describing a situation. Speak in simple and clear terms. This is especially important to facilitate communication.

- Be patient. Do not rush to say a lot because you have limited time. Also, be patient with parents who are linguistically different and for whom communicating in English is difficult. Most cultural groups show a lot of patience toward English speakers when they try to communicate in other languages. Imagine yourself trying to speak in the languages of your children's families!

- When parents or relatives are not fluent in English, have an interpreter. Always check with your school or program about selecting an interpreter. They may have a list of recommended interpreters. If you use interpreters, give them a summary or a description of the purposes of the meeting. This will help them to become aware of the content and context of a conference in advance.

- If parents or family members speak a language different from English, try to learn a few words in that language. It is always a good opener and also demonstrates that you are interested in learning more about them and their child.

- When parents are accompanied by other family members, relatives, or friends, acknowledge their presence. Find out who they are and what their relationship is to the family. Many cultural groups include relatives and some close friends among those responsible for the well-being of the child (Lynch & Hanson, 2004).

- Be a good listener. Don't monopolize the conversation. Remember that we all have very busy lives, and time is very precious to everyone. Select topics that can be feasibly discussed in the time you have.

- Show you care and want to help their children. Be positive and show your warm feelings. Always have something positive to say about the child. Share an anecdote or a sample of the child's work.

- Try to end your conversations with a positive outlook.

Using Modern Technology to Enhance Collaboration

Because technology is an important part of our world, we need to consider using it as part of our communication system. Best practices in early childhood education today recognize the role and need for technology as a means to improve and maintain communication between families and classrooms. What technology early childhood educators use depends upon the resources available in the school.

Voice mail is among today's commonly used technology-based communication tools. Many people rely on voice mail to keep them informed and organized. Voice mail enables teachers to establish information lines parents can access at any time. Details about activities, descriptions of the classroom events, or things children need to bring to school can be recorded in advance (Eliason & Jenkins, 2002). Families may also appreciate voice mail suggestions for possible activities during weekends and holidays. Having information in the languages spoken by the students' families is an excellent way to link them to the classroom.

FOSTERING COMMUNICATION USING TECHNOLOGY

Attending a meeting or conference is, at times, a challenge to many parents and family members because of their work schedules. Conversations with parents have revealed that many wanting to attend are unable to due to conflicts with their schedules and also because of transportation obstacles.

Think about the ways you could use technology to help parents participate in a meeting and to keep them informed about their children's progress and success.

In many places, schools operate a homework hotline. Parents can easily access daily assignments that have been taped by teachers. Some schools also have bilingual specialists available for consultations during specific evening hours. Often, these specialists are parents and community members who donate their time. This service helps parents clarify their children's homework, which benefits the child. Children whose parents work evening hours can call to verify and check on the next day's assignments.

If available, include e-mail among your communication tools. Many schools now have messages offered regularly to parents through e-mail. This opens another channel of interaction particularly suitable for working family members with full schedules.

The Internet has opened doors to a wealth of information for parents and families. Access to the Internet has also contributed to fostering communication with parents and families. One of the most popular methods is through school websites, which provide information to parents and the community. Accessible at any time of the day, a website makes it possible for working parents and family members to learn about school activities. By offering resources and information in languages other than English, web pages may also facilitate dissemination of school events and program news to families from diverse linguistic groups.

IDEAS FOR PLANNING ACTIVITIES WITH FAMILIES

What you know about the families and children in your classroom will help you plan a wide variety of activities. The innumerable differences families exhibit become your best source of ideas for learning experiences. Families can literally energize the whole school program.

Curriculum Activities

Consider how families can enhance the curriculum. Examine your projected curriculum experiences and identify those areas where families can help with demonstrations, telling stories, teaching a song or a dance, bringing specific resources, or serving as speakers.

For instance, parents and family members can help by demonstrating how to use a given ethnic instrument or how to wear a typical piece of clothing. Make a list of the instances where their collaboration is needed. If told in advance, families are usually willing to share their knowledge and their resources. Notes can be sent home asking for help with specific topics children will study. An example of this kind of note appears in Figure 10-7.

Keeping a file of resources that parents have and are willing to share is a convenient way to know what is available to support your curriculum. Include the parents

Figure 10-7   Notes (Bilingual) Can Be Sent to Parents to Ask for Their Participation in the Classroom

---

Can you help us? Our class needs your help!

Soon our class will be studying _____. Can you share some of your ideas? We know that sharing what you know will benefit our students. Please let us know how you can help by completing the included form.

Thanks!

_____

The family of (child's name) _____ can:
_____ bring the following: _____
_____ demonstrate a dance or a song.
_____ talk about my experiences.
_____ describe some of the traditions.
_____ other: _____

(Spanish Translation)

¿Nos puede ayudar? ¡Nuestro salón necesita su colaboración!

Estimada familia:

Muy pronto estaremos estudiando _____. Es posible que ustedes sepan mucho sobre este tema. Sabemos que al compartir algo de lo que ustedes saben nuestros niños aprenderán mucho más. Contamos con su ayuda. Si puede colaborar, déjenoslo saber completando el volante que incluímos.

¡Gracias!

_____

La familia de (nombre del estudiante) _____ puede:
_____ traer lo siguiente: _____
_____ demostrar un baile o enseñarles una canción.
_____ hablar sobre nuestras experiencias.
_____ leer algún cuento sobre el tema.
_____ describir algunas de las tradiciones y costumbres.
_____ demostrar como preparar algún plato típico.
_____ Otros: _____

---

as resources as well by creating a "special resources" file of materials and information shared by parents. To facilitate identification, include a note about those areas of diversity the families represent (i.e., cultures or exceptionalities). Even if you no longer teach their child, parents can always be contacted to share their knowledge with your current class. They will feel flattered to serve as your "special resources."

Parents and families are also valuable resources when planning the curriculum. Their participation is one of those required components of developmentally appropriate teaching. Considering them partners while developing units and experiences can bring in fresh and relevant ideas. Parents and family members can provide valuable suggestions when trying to determine how to address a topic from a variety of perspectives. They can also be considered a source of support and affirmation for your activities.

Supporting and Involving Families in School

Activities can provide opportunities for parents and families to interact with the school and with other families. This way they can learn more about other families and build their sense of identification with the school. The list of possible activities can be as long as your creativity allows. Here are some suggestions.

1. *Family of the month/week*: Prepare a display presenting the special characteristics and uniqueness of families. All families have something special and particular that you can highlight. You can either use a bulletin board or the classroom door to exhibit your display. Make sure it is located in a prominent place.

2. *Families' get-together*: Times can be arranged to have families come to the classroom to be together and to get to know each other (Berger, 2007). The traditional potluck meal is a good idea when parents are able to come in during evenings or on a Saturday. Parents can bring something to share with others. Ask them to write the names of their dishes so that everyone can remember them. Early morning coffee can be organized for families who work. Midday or afternoon refreshments and cookies are other activities for those whose schedules are more flexible. Some centers hold mid-morning meetings and offer a light "merienda" or snack for parents and families with flexible schedules. The *merienda* meetings are short with very focused goals lasting no more than 45 minutes.

3. *The classroom mural family album*: A mural album of activities carried out by families and their children can be prepared and displayed in the classroom. Things to include are important events, celebrations, and participation in classroom activities. Parents can share pictures, and children can make drawings of the special times spent with their families.

4. *Classroom "experts"*: Identify those areas where families are definite experts. For example, a family can become your expert for craft making or for learning typical dances. Recognition of their qualities affirms their importance.

5. *Family/parent networks:* With the collaboration of families in your classroom, you can organize a support network. Families new to the neighborhood or those with limited English language skills can benefit from the support that other parents may offer. A list with names and telephone numbers of the support persons can be made available to those in need (Berger, 2007).

6. *Storytellers' club:* Invite families and family members to share their stories. They can also read stories from their cultural groups. A pool of volunteer storytellers can add variety to your classroom activities while reinforcing to parents that their collaboration is wanted.

7. *Special multicultural events committee:* Families are the best source of ideas about what and how to celebrate cultural events. Invite families from different cultural backgrounds to form a committee. Together they will advise how to appropriately celebrate special dates.

8. *Meetings:* Good topics that are of interest to the families are always attractive. Periodic meetings can bring families together to discuss and share ideas while learning about other views.

9. *Welcome committee:* Parents from different cultural groups can form a "welcome" group for other parents. They can prepare handouts with key places in the community, recreational services, and other important information that a newcomer always appreciates. This is a particularly effective resource for families who have recently immigrated and may need resources to cope with their new reality.

10. *Educational packets:* With the help of the teacher, a group of volunteers can prepare home-learning materials. Parents and volunteers can duplicate materials to be sent home and prepare calendars of activities. With the guidance of the teacher, parents can locate resources in the school library or even develop their own set of references.

11. *Special projects:* All classrooms have special projects for which parents and community volunteers are essential resources. Call on the parents whenever you and your class plan to begin a project. They are the best resources to ensure that experiential activities are designed to define the realistic and not the idealized ways of cultures.

Counting on the Community as a Resource

There is a wealth of resources in every community. Communities are important sources of materials, information, and support for early childhood programs. Agencies, sites, organizations, businesses, and, especially, people all represent resources. You may want to create an inventory of your community to help you learn more about its exciting resources. For example, find out if your community includes any of the following:

- public library
- local civic organizations
- public agencies
- community center
- programs and activities for children and their families
- art activities sponsored by community or civic groups
- type of businesses
- local newspaper
- public places (parks, museums, sports complex)

Using community resources facilitates establishing collaborative experiences and promotes partnerships. It also creates appreciation of the community's heritage and diversity. This is especially relevant for families and for children. By being involved with the community, children will not only develop a greater understanding of multiculturalism but will also experience their community as a major influence in their lives. Involving the community in teaching is known as social action-based teaching.

Opportunities for social action-based teaching are created through an active link with the community. Community leaders can help with suggestions of possible experiences appropriate for young children. For example, taking action to clean the yard of an elderly person, working in the garden of a person with a disability, preparing crafts to give as welcome gifts to children moving into the neighborhood, or painting a park fence are some of the activities that provide concrete ways to demonstrate that we care about others in our diverse community.

Establishing contacts with community-based organizations is a way to gain access to unlimited ideas and experiences for your classroom. A note or a call to learn what services are offered will open the door to a world of resources right in your community.

WHAT LIES AHEAD?

Working with the families of children in your classroom is an experience that offers endless possibilities. Linking families and schools to work and respect each other is a way to gain equity

The dream of a multicultural classroom is a reality that we can make happen in our schools.

Wadsworth/Cengage Learning

for all, an important goal of multicultural education. If our classroom doors are truly open, the futures of children will be brighter. Building positive relationships with parents and families takes time. So, be patient and work toward productive relations with your partners in educating the children in your classroom.

Involving the community in the classroom requires that early childhood educators reach out and sometimes go out of their comfort zone. It is important to note that communities are very appreciative of such efforts as they are seen through the lens of friendship and acceptance. The bonds that the educators create with the community are lasting investments in the future of young children as well as significant contributions to the educators' professional expertise.

WHAT WE HAVE LEARNED—CHAPTER SUMMARY

This chapter emphasizes the importance of collaborating with parents and the community in helping young children. Parental involvement in a diverse classroom is very special. It presents unique challenges that educators must overcome. One of the most important things teachers must learn is how to work with adults from different cultures. This requires effort, tolerance, and sensitivity. Parents must be made to be allies in the process of positive development of the children. It is also important to meet the parents and other significant family members halfway. A comprehensive collaboration also includes the community and its resources. Teachers need to step out of the classroom to learn about the nature of the child's community and what it has to offer. Again, this means stepping out of the teacher's comfort zone and being proactive in exploring resources that will benefit the child. Profiling the community where the children live is essential in creating partnerships and collaborative efforts. There are also many professional organizations and publications that offer creative and innovative ideas about how to help the child and facilitate positive development. It is highly recommended that educators become members of professional organizations and keep up with the latest literature and research in the field of multicultural education for young children.

MAKING CONNECTIONS . . .

1. What do you think are some of the main problems faced by families today? Write a brief paper about what you believe are the most urgent issues.

2. We learn about others when we interact. Create a ten-item questionnaire and interview two families from different social and ethnic backgrounds. Ask them about their views concerning children. Compare their responses and find how similar and different they are.

4. We all have different perspectives of appropriate family/parent involvement in schools. Ask five of your colleagues about their views. Then ask five parents and compare their responses.

5. Explore the Internet and find three successful community programs. Create a PowerPoint presentation that includes the best attributes of all three programs.

6. Every classroom is different. Based on the nature of your own school and classroom, prepare a list of 10 possible ways to involve the families. Share the list with a colleague.

RECOMMENDED INTERNET RESOURCES

- The Comer School Development Program for parent involvement, from the Yale Child Study Center
  www.med.yale.edu/comer/

- "Communicating with Families," from the U.S. Department of Health and Human Services
  http://eclkc.ohs.acf.hhs.gov/hslc/Family%20 and%20Community%20Partnerships/Family%20 Partnerships/Communicating%20with%20Families

- The National Network of Partnership Schools' Center on School, Family, and Community Partnerships
  www.csos.jhu.edu/p2000/center.htm

- Promoting Responsible Fatherhood, from the U.S. Department of Health and Human Services
  http://fatherhood.hhs.gov/Research/index.shtml

YOUR STANDARDS PORTFOLIO

naeyc **Standard 2:** Building Family and Community Relationships

InTASC Standard 10: Leadership and Collaboration

Learning more about families is essential for building successful collaborations with the early childhood classroom. The following activities will help you in developing skills and knowledge for working with families of young children.

- Prepare a visual definition representing the diversity of families. Follow the diversity elements present in your own community and classroom.
- Create an inventory of agencies in your community that provide services to families and their children.

Decide on an appropriate way to make the inventory available to families in your community. Consider the needs of families who are English language learners. Share your inventory in class.
- Plan an informal meeting with families to share information about their children's progress. Specify the goals of the meeting and describe how you would ensure positive communication. Write a sample letter inviting the parents/family members to the meeting.

REFERENCES

Barrera, J., & Warner, L. (2006). Involving families in school events. *Kappa Delta PI Record, 42*(2), 72–75.

Berger, E. (2004). *Parents as partners in education: Families and schools working together* (6th ed.). Englewood Cliffs, NJ: Merrill.

Berger, E. (2007). *Parents as partners in education: Families and schools working together* (7th ed.). Englewood Cliffs, NJ: Prentice Hall.

Boyer, E. (1994). *Ready to learn: A mandate for the nation.* Princeton, NJ: The Carnegie Foundation for the Advancement of Teaching.

Broussard, C. A. (2003). Facilitating home-school partnerships for multiethnic families: School social workers collaborating for success. *Children & Schools, 25*(4), 211–222.

Children's Defense Fund. (2010). *The state of America's children*: 2010. Washington, DC: Author.

Coleman, J. (1991). *Planning for parent participation in schools for young children.* Bloomington, IL: ERIC Digest.

Couchenour, D., & Chrisman, K. (2004). *Families, schools, and communities: Together for young children.* Clifton Park, NY: Thomson Delmar Learning.

Eliason, C., & Jenkins, L. (2007). *A practical guide to early childhood education curriculum* (8th ed.). New York: Merrill.

Epstein, J. L., Sanders, M. G., Simon B. S., & Salina, K. C. (2002). *School, family, and community partnerships: Your handbook for action* (2nd ed.). Thousand Oaks, CA: Corwin.

Federal Interagency Forum on Child and Family Statistics. (2005). *America's children: Key national indicators of well-being.* Retrieved September 15, 2008, from http://www.childstats.gov/pdf/ac2005/ac_05.pdf.

Garbarino, J., Galambos, N., Plantz, M., & Kostelny, K. (1992). The territory of childhood. In J. Garbarino, *Children and families in the social environment* (2nd ed., pp. 202–228). New York: Aldine de Gruyter.

Garbarino, J., & Garbarino, A. (1992). In conclusion: The issue is human quality. In J. Garbarino, *Children and families and the social environment* (2nd ed., pp. 304–327). New York: Aldine de Gruyter.

Harry, B. (1997). *Cultural diversity, families, and the special education system: Communication and empowerment.* New York: Teachers College Press.

Henderson, A. T., & Mapp, K. L. (2002). *A new wave of evidence: The impact of school, family, and community connections on student achievement.* Austin, Texas: National Center for Family and Community Connections with Schools.

Jung-Sook, L., & Bowen, N. (2006). Parent involvement, cultural capital, and the achievement gap among elementary school children. *American Educational Research Journal, 43*(2), 93–204, 205, 209–218.

Kagan, S., & Rivera, A. (1991). Collaboration in early care and education: What can and should we expect? *Young Children, 47*(1), 51–56.

Lee, F. (1995). Asian parents as partners. *Young Children 50*(3), 4–9.

Lynch, E. W., & Hanson, M. J. (2004). *Developing cross-cultural competence: A guide for working with young children and their families* (3rd ed.). Baltimore, MD: Paul Brooks.

Moles, O. (Ed.). (1996). *Reaching all families: Creating family friendly schools* (Publication No. OAS 96-6005). Washington, DC: Office of Educational Research and Improvement.

National Association for the Education of Young Children. (2005). *Code of ethical conduct and statement of commitment* (Revised April 2005). Retrieved from http://www.naeyc.org/about/positions/PSETH05.asp.

National Commission on Children. (1991). *Beyond rhetoric: A new American agenda for children and families. Final Report of the National Commission on Children.* Washington, DC: Author.

Olivos, E. M. (2006). *The power of parents: A critical perspective of bicultural parent involvement in public schools.* New York: Peter Lang Publishing.

Pelletier, J., & Brent, J. (2002). Parent participation in children's school readiness: The effects of parental self-efficacy, cultural diversity, and teacher strategies. *International Journal of Early Childhood, 34*(1), 45–60.

Robles de Meléndez, W. (September 2006). Working with families. Paper presented at the Annual Conference of the Early Childhood Association of Florida. Orlando, FL.

Saville-Troike, M. (1978). *Guide to Culture in the Classroom.* Arlington, VA: National Clearinghouse for Bilingual Education.

Swick, K. (2004). *Empowering parents, families, schools, and communities during the early childhood years.* Champagne, IL: Stipes Publishing.

Turnbull, A., & Turnbull, H. R. (2004). *Exceptional lives: Special education in today's schools* (4th ed.). New York: Prentice Hall.

United Nations. (1994). Changing family structure. *1994 International Year of the Family.* New York: U. N. Department of Public Information.

U.S. Government. (2001). *A blueprint for new beginnings.* Washington, DC: U.S. Government Printing Office.

APPENDIX A

Recommended List of Selected Multicultural Children's Books

ETHNIC DIVERSITY

African

Chamberlain, M. (2006). *Mama Panya's pancakes: A village tale from Kenya*. Cambridge, MA: Barefoot Books.

Cleveland, R. (2006). *The clever monkey: A folktale from West Africa*. New York: August House.

Cunnane, K. (2006). *For you are a Kenyan child*. New York: Atheneum.

Diakite, P. (2006). *I lost my tooth in Africa*. New York: Scholastic.

Edmonds, L., & Wilson, A. (2004). *An African princess*. Cambridge, MA: Candlewick Press.

Johnson, T., & Jenkins, L. (2003). *A Kenya Christmas*. New York: Holiday House.

Krebs, L. (2004). *We all went on safari: A counting journey through Tanzania*. Cambridge, MA: Barefoot Books.

McBriar, P., & Lohstoeter, L. (2001). *Beatrice's goat*. New York: Atheneum.

Mendela, N. (2007). *Nelson Mendela's favorite African folktales*. Johannesburg, South Africa: W. W. Nelson.

Uche, G. (2006). *African folktales: Exotic stories from Africa for children around the world*. Bloomington, IN: Authorshouse.

African American

Barnwell, Y., & Saint James, S. (2005). *No mirror in my Nana's house*. New York: Voyager.

Dillon, L., & Dillon, D. (2002). *Rap a tap tap*. New York: Blue Sky Press.

Duncan, A. F. (2005). *Honey, baby, sugar, child*. New York: Simon & Schuster.

Hubell, P., & Tate, D. (2003). *Black all around!* New York: Lee & Low Books.

Hudson, C. W. (2010). *My friend Maya loves to dance*. New York: Abrams Books for Young Children.

Katz, K. (2003). *My first Kwanzaa*. New York: Henry Holt.

Smith, P., & Boyd, A. (2003). *Janna and the kings*. New York: Lee & Low Books.

Tarpley, N. A. (2001). *I love my hair*. New York: Little Brown Books.

Perry, R. (2004). *JATS holiday classics: It's beginning to look a lot like Kwanzaa!* New York: Hyperion Book.

Alaska Natives

Bania, M. (2004). *Kumac'a fish: A tale from the Far North*. Anchorage, AK: Alaska Northwest Books.

Damjan, M. (2002). *Atuk: A story*. Zurich, Switzerland: Nord-Sud Verlag.

Devine, M. (2002). *Carry me Mama*. New York: Stoddart Kids.

Edwardson, D. D. (2003). *Whale snow*. Watertown, MA: Charlesbridge Publishing.

George, J. C. (2001). *Nutik and Amroq play ball*. New York: Harper Collins.

George, J. C. (2001). *Nutik, the wolf pup*. New York: Harper Collins.

Harden, P. (2003). *Snow bear*. New York: Dutton Juvenile.

Kimmel, E. A. (2006). *The frog princess: A Tlingit Legend from Alaska*. New York: Holiday House. Straus and Giroux.

Sloat, T. (Illustrator), & Huffman, B. (2004). *Berry magic*. Anchorage, AK: Alaska Northwest Books.

Vanessa, Deb. (2006). *Totem tale: A tall story from Alaska*. Seattle, WA: Sasquatch Books.

Chinese Americans

Bins, T. B. (2002). *Chinese Americans*. New York: Heinemann Library.

Bridges, S. Y. (2002). *Ruby's wish*. San Francisco: Chronicle Books.

Chan, A. (2004). *Awakening the dragon*. Portland, OR: Tundra Books.

Cheng, A. (2003). *Grandfather counts*. New York: Lee & Low Books.

Katz, K. (2005). *My first Chinese new year*. New York: Henry Holt.

Lin, G. (2010). *Bringing in the New Year*. New York: Dragonfly Books.

Louie, A. L., & Young, E. (1996). *Yeh-Shen: A Cinderella story from China*. New York: Putnam.

Simmons, N., Swartz, L. & The Children's Museum of Boston. (2002). *Moonbeams, dumplings & dragon boats: A treasury of Chinese holiday tales, activities & recipes*. New York: Harcourt Children's Books.

Thong, R. (2001). *Red is a dragon: A book of colors*. San Francisco: Chronicle Books.

Thomas, E. (2004). *The red blanket*. New York: Scholastic.

Wu, F. (2010). *Chinese and English nursery rhymes: Share and sing in two languages*. Clarendon, VT: Tuttle Publishing.

Yip, M. (2005). *Chinese children's favorite stories*. Clarendon, VT: Tuttle Publishing.

Filipino Americans

Ferreol, Y. (2006). *Haluhalo espesyal*. Quezon City, Phillipines: Adarna House.

Lazo Gilmore, D. K. (2009). *Cora cooks pancit*. Walnut Creek, CA: Shen's Books.

Robles, A. D. (2003). *Lakas and the Manilatown fish/ Se lakas at ang isdang Manilatown*. Thousand Oaks, CA: Children's Book Press.

Romulo, L. E., & de Leon, J. (2000). *Filipino children's favorite stories*. Hong Kong, China: Periplus Editions.

Romulo, L. E., & Dandan-Albno, C. (2006). *Filipino friends*. Clarendon, VT: Tuttle Publishing.

Indian and Pakistani Americans

Arnet, R. (2003). *Finders keepers*. New York: Atman Press.

Babeaux, M. B. (2002). *Anklet for a princess*. New York: Shen's Books.

Cleveland, R. (2006). *The drum: Folktale from India*. New York: August House.

Das, P. (2004). *I is for India*. New York: Frances Lincoln.

Heydlauff, L. (2005). *Going to school in India*. Watertown, MA: Charlesbridge Publishing.

Hosell, K. P. (2004). *Pakistani Americans*. New York: Heineman Library.

Jeyaveeran, R. (2004). *The road to Mumbai*. New York: Houghton Mifflin.

Krishaswami, U., & Sitaraman, S. (2003). *Chachajis's cup*. Thousand Oaks, CA: Children's Book Press.

Novesky, A., & Wedman, B. K. (2004). *Elephant prince: The story of Ganesh*. San Francisco: Mandala Publishing.

Patel, S. (2006). *The little book for Hindu Deities: From goddess of wealth to sacred cow*. New York: Plume.

Smith, J. (2003). *Lily's garden of India*. New York: Gingham Dog Press.

Somjah, R., & Somajah, R. (2006). *Indian children's favourite stories*. Clarendon, VT: Tuttle Publishing.

Zucker, J. (2004). *Lighting the lamp*. New York: Barron's Educational Series.

Japanese Americans

Coerr, E. (2002). *Sadako and the thousand paper cranes*. New York: Putnam's Sons.

Falwell, C. (2003). *Butterflies for Kiri*. New York: Lee and Low Books.

French, J. (2007). *Too many pears*. Long Island City, NY: Star Bright Books.

Iwamura, K., & Carle, E. (2003). *Where are you going? To see my friend*. New York: Orchard Books.

Lee, M. (2002). *Nim and the war effort*. New York: Farrar, Straus and Giroux.

Myers, T. J. (2004). *Basho and the river stones*. New York: Marshall Cavendish, Children's Books.

Parker, L. K. (2003). *Why Japanese immigrants came to America*. New York: Power Kids Press.

Reynolds, B. (2006). *Japanese celebrations: Cherry blossoms, lanterns and stars!* Clarendon, VT: Tuttle Publishing.

Sakade, F. (2008). *Peach boy and other Japanese favorite stories.* Clarendon, VT: Tuttle Publishing.

Tran, T., & Phong, A. (2003). *Going home, coming home.* Thousand Oaks, CA: Children's Book Press.

Uchida, Y. (2004). *Journey to Topaz: A story of the Japanese-American evacuation.* New York: Heyday Books.

Uegaki, C. (2005). *Suki's kimono.* Toronto, Canada: Kids Can Press.

Korean Americans

Cheung, H. (2008). *K is for Korea.* London: Francis Lincoln Children's Books.

Heo, Y. (2004). *The green frogs: A Korean folktale.* New York: Sandpiper.

Ho, M. (2000). *Hush! A Thai lullaby.* New York: Scholastic.

Laiz, F. (2007). *Elephants of the tsunami.* (2nd ed.). Anacortes, WA: Earthbound Books.

Park, L. S. (2004). *The firekeeper's son.* New York: Clarion Books.

Recorvits, H., & Swiatkowska, G. (2005). *My name is Yoon.* New York: Farrar, Straus and Giroux.

So-Un, K. & Kyoung-Sim, J. (2004). *Korean children's favorite stories.* Clarendon, VT: Tuttle Publishing.

Turhan, S. (2005). *Milet mini picture dictionary: English-Korean.* London: Milet Publishing.

Thai Americans

Bridges, S. (2008). *The umbrella queen.* New York: Greenwillow Books.

Hosell, K. P. (2004). *Thai Americans.* New York: Heinemann Library.

Vietnamese Americans and Hmong

Cleveland, R. (2007). *How the tiger got his stripes.* New York: August House.

Frost, H. (2000). *A look at Vietnam.* Mancato, MN: Capstone Press.

Lin, G. (2003). *Dim sum for everyone.* New York: Dragonfly Books.

McKay, L., Lee, D., & Lee, K. (2000). *Journey home.* New York: Lee & Low Books.

Shea Deitz, P., Weill, C., Trang N., Viet-Dinh, P., Trang, N., & Pham, V. I. (2003). *Ten mice for Tet!* San Francisco: Chronicle Books.

Tran, T. (2003). *Going home, coming home/ve nha, tham que huong.* New York: Children's Press.

Caribbean

Gershator, P., & Meade, H. (2005). *Rata-pata-scata-fata: A Caribbean story.* New York: Starbright Books.

Goddard, A., & Wen, G. (2000). *Mama, across the sea.* New York: Henry Holt.

Isadora, R. (2002). *Caribbean dream.* New York: Puffin.

Lee, S. A. (2002). *My island and I: The nature of the Caribbean.* Nashville, TN: Pangaea.

Patten, H., & Clemenson. J. (1999). *Clever Anansi and boastful bullfrog: A Caribbean tale.* New York: Starbright Books.

Picayo, M. (2007). *Caribbean journey from A-Y.* Baldwin Park, CA: Campanita Books.

San Souci, R., & Pinkney, B. (2002). *Cendrillon: A Caribbean Cinderella.* New York: Simon and Schuster.

Hispanic Americans

Bernard Gonzales, D. (2004). *My pal, Victor/Mi amigo, Victor (Bilingual).* Green Bay, WI: Raven Tree Press.

Dorros, A. (1997). *Abuela.* New York: Puffin.

Filipe, J. (2001). *Calling the doves/El canto de las palomas (Bilingual).* Thousand Oaks, CA: Children's Book Press.

Garza Lomas, C. (1989). *Family pictures/Cuadros de familia.* Thousand Oaks, CA: Children's Book Press.

Geslin, C. (2004). *Elena's serenade.* New York: Atheneum Anne Schwartz Books.

Johnson, T. (2009). *Mi abuelita.* New York: Harcourt Children's Books.

Montes, M. (2003). *A crazy mixed-up Spanglish day.* New York: Scholastic.

Mora, P. (2009). *Book fiesta!: Celebrate, children's day: Celebramos el dia de los ninos/El dia de los libros.* New York: Rayo.

Soto, G. (1998). *The old man and his door.* New York: Putnam.

Tofolla, C. (2009). *What can you do with paletas?* Berkeley, CA : Tricycle Press.

Jewish Americans

Gross, J. (2005). *Celebrate: A book of Jewish holidays.* New York: Grosett & Dunlap.

Jules, H. (2008). *Good night Sh'ma.* Rockville, MD: Kar-Ben Publishing.

Manushkin, F. (2007). *Latkes and applesauce: A Hanukkah story.* New York: Scholastic.

Newman, L. (2007). *Runaway dreidel!* New York: Macmillan.

Polacco, P. (2001). *The Keeping Quilt.* New York: Aladdin.

Seidman, L. (2007). *What makes someone a Jew?* Woodstock, VT: Jewish Lights Publishing.

Middle Eastern and Arabic

Cleveland, R. (2006). *The magic apple: A folktale from the Middle East.* New York: August House.

Climo, S. (2001). *The Persian Cinderella.* New York: Harper.

Hickox, R., & Hillenbrand, W. (1999). *The golden sandal: A Middle Eastern Cinderella story.* New York: Holiday House.

Kyuchukov, H. (2004). *My name was Hussein.* Boston: Boyd Mills Press.

Matz Sidhom, C., & Farnsworth, B. (2002). *The stars in my Geddoh's sky.* Chicago: Albert Whitman.

Zucker, J. (2004). *Fasting and dates: A Ramadan and eid-ul Fitr.* New York: Barron's Educational Series.

Native Americans

Boucharad, D., & Sapp, A. (2003). *The song within my heart.* New York: Raincoast Books.

Boyden, L. (2003). *The blue roses.* New York: Lee & Low Books.

Bruchac, J., & Locker, T. (1999). *Between Earth and sky: Legends of Native American sacred places.* New York: Voyager Books.

Bruchac, J., & Voytech, A. (1998). *The first strawberries: A Cherokee story.* New York: Puffin Books.

Cohlene, T., & Reasoner, C. (2004). *Little firefly.* New York: Scholastic Books.

Lavarde, A., & Dwyer, M. (2000). *Three little Alaskan pigs.* Seattle, WA: Sasquatch Books.

Oughton, J. (2004). *How the stars fell out of the sky: A Navajo legend.* New York: Houghton Mifflin.

Thompson, L., & Savage, S. (2004). *A polar bear night.* New York: Scholastic.

Wakim Dennis, Y., Hirschfelder, A. B., & Ajmera, M. (2003). *Children of Native America.* Watertown, MA: Charlesbridge Press.

GAY AND LESBIAN

Clark, C. N. (2010). *My family! A multi-cultural holiday coloring book for children of gay and lesbian parents.* Maple Grove, MN: Dodi Press.

Considine, T. K. (2005). *Emma and Meesha my boy: A two mom story.* Twomomsbooks.com.

Newman, L. (2009). *Mommy, momma and me.* New York: Tricycle Press.

Newman, L. (2000). *Heather has two mommies.* New York: Alyson Books.

Parr, T. (2003). *The family book.* New York: Little, Brown Young Readers.

Valentine, J. (2004). *One dad, two dads, brown dad, blue dad.* New York: Prometheus.

SPECIAL NEEDS

Heelan, R. J. (2000). *Tolling along: The story of Taylor and his wheelchair.* Atlanta, GA: Peachtree Publishing.

Janover, C. (2004). *Josh: A boy with dyslexia.* Burlington, VT: Waterfront Books.

Lears, L. (2003). *Ian's walk: A story about autism.* Chicago: Albert Whitman.

Lesley, H., & Thomas, P. (2002). *Don't call me special: A first look at disability.* New York: Barron's Juveniles.

Maguire, A. (2000). *Special people, special ways*. Arlington, TX: Future Horizons.

Ochiai, M. & Manayamoto, S. (2005). *Different croaks for different folks: All about children with special needs*. Philadelphia, PA: Jessica Kingsley Publishers.

Shriver, M. (2001). *What's wrong with Timmy?* New York: Little, Brown.

Thomas, P. (2005). *Don't call me special: A first look at disability*. New York: Barron's Education Series.

Whitehouse Peterson, J. (1999). *I have a sister, my sister is deaf*. New York: HarperCollins.

GENDER

Brown, J. (1996). *Flat Stanley*. New York: HarperCollins.

Foberry, J. (2008). *My name is not Isabella*. Union City, CA: Monkey Barrel Press.

Lovell, P. (2001). *Stand tall, Molly Lou Melon*. New York: G. P. Putnam's Sons.

Munsch, R. (1992). *The paper bag princess*. Toronto: Annick Press.

Zolotow, C. (1985). William's doll.

AGE/INTERGENERATIONAL

Ackerman, K. (2003). *Song and dance man*. New York: Knopf Books for Young Readers.

Bowen, A. (2004). *When you visit grandma and grandpa*. Minneapolis, MN: Carolhoda Books.

Cheng, A. (2003). *Grandfather counts*. Lee & Lowe Books.

Hamanaka, S. (2003). *Grandparents' song*. New York: HarperCollins.

Katz, K. (2003). *Daddy and me*. New York: Little Simon & Schuster.

Lord, J. (2005). *Here comes grandma!* New York: Henry Holt.

Numeroff, L. (2004). *What aunts do best/What uncles do best*. New York: Simon & Shuster.

GENERAL MULTICULTURAL THEMES

Adolf, A. (2004). *Black is brown is tan* (Reprint ed.). New York: Amistad.

Ajmera, M., Ivanko, J., & Rogers, F. (2004). *Be my neighbor*. Watertown, MA: Charlesbridge Publishing.

DK Publishing. (2005). *A life like mine*. New York: DK Children.

Jordan, S. (2004). *Celebrate the human race*. New York: Sara Jordan Publishing.

Kalman, B. (2009). *What is culture?* New York: Crabtree Publishing.

Kalman, B. (2009). *How are we the same and different?* New York: Crabtree Publishing.

Kuklin, S. (2003). *How my family lives in America*. New York: Sagebrush.

Lester, J. (2005). *Let's talk about race*. New York: Amistad.

Parr, T. (2004). *It's OK to be different*. New York: Little, Brown Young Readers.

Scillian, D. (2003). *P is for passport: A world alphabet*. Detroit, MI: Thompson Gale.

Tyler, M. (2005). *The skin you live in*. Chicago: Chicago Children's Museum.

Weber, R. (2004). *Understanding differences*. New York: Compass Point Books.

Zurakowski, M. (2004). *Evening meals around the world*. New York: Picture Window Books.

Organizations That Support Multiculturalism and Diversity

Association for Childhood Education International
Website: http://acei.org
The goal of ACEI is to advocate and promote for quality education and developmental opportunities for children in the global community.

The Division of Early Childhood
27 Fort Missoula Road
Suite 2
Missoula, MT 59804
Website: www.dec-sped.org
An international professional organization aimed at advocating for appropriate services an education for children with disabilities.

National Association for Bilingual Education (NABE)
1220 L Street, NW
Suite 605
Washington, DC 20005
Website: www.@nabe.org
A professional association founded in 1975, NABE addresses the educational needs of language-minority students. It hosts an annual conference and publishes the Language Learner and the Bilingual Research Journal.

National Association for the Education of Young Children
1313 L Street, NW
Suite 500
Washington, DC 20005-4101
Website: www.naeyc.org

NAEYC is a professional organization serving the early childhood community. It provides resources and advocacy materials for teachers, families, and community members.

National Association for Multicultural Education (NAME)
733 15th Street, NW
Suite 4
Washington, DC 20005
202-628-NAME
Website: www.nameorg.org
NAME advocates multicultural education and educational equity. The organization provides resources including lesson plans, goals and objectives, and bibliographies.

National Black Child Development Institute
1313 L Street, NW
Suite 110
Washington, DC 20005-4110
Website: www.nbcdi.org
A national organization aimed at enhancing and improving the lives of African American children and their families.

National Clearinghouse for English Language Acquisition (NCELA)
The George Washington University Graduate School of Education and Human Development
2121 K Street, NW
Suite 260
Washington, DC 20037
Website: www.ncela.gwu.edu

NCELA provides information and resources about second-language acquisition and educational services and programs available in the United States and offers special resources for teachers and parents.

National Council of la Raza
Raul Yzaguirre Building
1126 16th Street, NW
Suite 600
Washington, DC 20036
Website: www.nclr.org
NCLR is a national civil rights and advocacy organization working to serve and empower Hispanic Americans including children and their families.

Teaching Tolerance
400 Washington Ave
Montgomery, AL 36104
Website: http://splcenter.org
A publication of the Southern Poverty Law Center, Teaching Tolerance is a semiannual magazine mailed at no charge that provides classroom strategies and curriculum ideas for teachers that focus on diversity and tolerance. The project has also developed a number of teaching resources, including videos and curriculum guides, on the civil rights movement and intolerance in U.S. history.

U.S. Committee for UNICEF
Education Department
333 East 38th Street
New York, NY 10016
Website: www.unicef.org/education
This center publishes a wealth of information concerning world development, including books, audiovisual materials, lesson plans, and other resources with an international perspective. Most resources are available for the price of postage, and videos are provided on loan for free.

World of Difference Institute
Anti-Defamation League
1100 Connecticut Avenue, NW
No. 1020
Washington, DC 20036
Website: www.adl.org
The institute provides professional development and curricular resources with an anti-bias focus.

APPENDIX C

Developing Multicultural Awareness: Sample Activities

WORKSHOP ACTIVITY: A YEAR TO CELEBRATE CULTURAL DIVERSITY

Background

Have you ever thought about the many festivities that are probably taking place around the world? Probably, right now, somewhere on our planet, a group of people are celebrating their culture. You and your students can join in their celebration if you decide to adopt the transformational curricular approach (Banks & Banks, 1993).[1] In multicultural education, a transformational approach (T-approach) for curriculum development implies a significant change in the structure and nature of the content area. A thorough revision of the scope, goals, and materials of a program is done to have students experience the concepts and topics from the point of view of different cultural groups (Hernández, 2000).[2] The result is a realistic, more current curriculum that will empower children with an honest vision of the essence of the society they live in.

Suggestions for Action

Concerted efforts must be taken by schools to follow the transformational approach. However, early childhood educators can initiate this approach by examining the holidays that are observed by the school. Holiday activities are fundamentally ways to manifest cultural values and ideas. Because of the very nature of celebrations, they serve to motivate and interest children. They also open the door to a more culturally responsive curriculum. During this workshop session, you will apply some of the principles of the T-approach using the holidays the main focus.

[1] Banks, J., & Banks, C. (2006). *Multicultural education: Issues and perspectives* (6th ed.). Needham Heights, MA: Allyn & Bacon.
[2] Hernandez, H. (2000). *Multicultural education: A teacher's guide to content and process* (2nd ed.). New York: Prentice Hall.

Into Action . . .

1. Begin by listing the cultures present in your classroom. Include also those found in the school and community. Keep this list handy to help you balance the focus of activities.

    My classroom has the following ethnicities/cultures: _____

    _____

    _____

2. Review the list of official/observed school holidays. Check whether they reflect the ethnic makeup of your children and of the community.

    The following are the official holidays observed at my school: _____

    _____

    _____

3. Now, ask people from different cultures what their main celebrations are. Also, check in the encyclopedia or ask the librarian. Select those that represent activities of cultural groups in your class. Add any not listed above.

    Celebrations Chosen:

    Celebrations Added:

4. Enter the cultural festivities into your calendar. Select a month of your choice and design a plan to incorporate these celebrations as part of that month's activities.

LET'S COOK, LET'S THINK! A DAP EXPERIENCE IN DIVERSITY FOR AGES 4–6: THE MANY WAYS OF . . . PASTA![3]

Introduction

Who isn't attracted to food? Almost no one, which is why cooking and food experiences are an excellent resource in the classroom. Besides allowing the obvious integration of academic areas, cooking can become a tool for multicultural education. In this example, you will use pasta to guide children in discovering how one object can hold a variety of forms and yet maintain the same identity.

Goal: To help children see that people can have a variety of characteristics while being all the same

Concepts: differences, similarities, people

[3]Adapted from an idea in the unit "Apples, Apples" in King, E. W., Chipman, M., and Cruz-Janzen, M. (1994). *Educating Young Children in a Diverse Society.* Boston: Allyn & Bacon.

Developmental areas targeted:

1. Cognitive—observing, predicting, comparing, evaluating
2. Language—describing, acquiring vocabulary, listening
3. Motor—pouring, stirring, sorting
4. Social—working in groups, waiting for turn, sharing utensils

Academic areas: Social studies, math, health

Materials:

- Different types of pasta (macaroni, ziti, lasagna, linguini, rotini, etc.); if possible, select those with different colors
- Paper plates
- Pot (to boil pasta)
- Sauce or sour cream (to prepare salad)

Suggested activities:

1. Have children sit in a circle. Place all the pasta in a box or any other container and have children guess what it is. Use some of these clues to guide them:

   - *What I have here are different sizes, shapes, and colors.*
   - *Although they can be placed in groups according to their shapes and sizes, they all belong to one group.*
   - *You can find them dressed differently.*
   - *They can have many purposes.*
   - *They are all made of the same things.*

   After they have guessed/attempted to guess, have one child open the box and show it to the class. Review the clues and discuss each idea with the group. Clarify any of the concepts presented through the clues.

2. Give each child a paper plate and pass around the pasta. Have each child take a handful. Invite children to observe and feel the pasta. Have them talk about it. Discuss how the types of pasta can be similar (texture, materials they are made of) and different (shapes, sizes, color).

3. Have children discuss how the types of pasta are used and say which ones they have tried.

4. Discuss the names assigned to pasta. Have labels to identify the different types. Introduce the relationship to people who, like pasta, also have different names. Have children select the ones they like best. Emphasize resemblance with people (there are some people we prefer to be with).

5. Establish the relationship between the pasta and people. Use the different characteristics they listed (color, size, shape, names) to define how people whom we find in the community may, like pasta, look different, and still be wonderful to be with.

6. Cook the pasta. Have children observe how it looks after cooking. Give each child a piece to smell, touch, and taste. Highlight once again the concept of people (still the same despite the changes).

7. Mix the pasta with sauce or sour cream and have the class enjoy it. Have a great diversity pasta snack!

Extensions:

- Place uncooked pasta in the art center for children to make art designs.
- Have some pasta boxes in the housekeeping area.
- Paste pasta samples on cardboard and place them in the writing corner. (Who knows what children will have to say about it!)
- Create a poster about the "pasta family." Ask children to describe and discuss what they did.

GLOSSARY

A

antibias an instructional approach to early childhood curriculum that centers on principles of equality and equity and strives to change existing social inequalities.

approach a set of instructional guidelines that defines an overall method used to attain a specific learning goal.

attitudes dispositions people have toward others and/or circumstances that guide their overt and covert behaviors.

awareness cognizance that allows the child to become familiar and/or to apprise the existence of ideas, concepts, issues, or physical objects.

B

behaviors actions exhibited by individuals in response to certain situations or stimuli.

bias any attitude, belief, or feeling that results in and helps to justify unfair treatment of an individual because of his or her identity.

C

checklist an assessment instrument, usually consisting of "go" or "no go" choices used in an educational setting to collect factual data objectively observed in the classroom about student behaviors, physical arrangements, use of materials and activities, and student achievement, among others.

child development process of biological, cognitive, and socio-emotional changes common to all children that occurs from conception to adolescence.

Civil Rights movement (1954–1968) organized political and social actions undertaken by African Americans to reform social practices and erase legal racial discrimination. The movement led to the Civil Rights Act of 1964, which recognized the civil rights of all American citizens and officially ended legal racial segregation in the United States. Dr. Martin Luther King, Jr., was the most prominent leader of the movement.

classroom environment the overall result of the arrangement and disposition of materials and equipment within a given learning setting. Designed to promote the physical, cognitive, and social-emotional development of young learners, the classroom environment is the sum of all the parts that comprise a teaching/learning setting. It includes the space, the social and emotional atmosphere, the cognitive opportunities, and the creative opportunities.

collaborative efforts actions and initiatives done by a variety of individuals or groups working together toward a common goal.

community resources services, organizations, individuals, and cultural objects create appreciation of the community's heritage and diversity.

content the topics, concepts, and themes selected for children to experience in the classroom.

creativity a special ability to see things in unusual or unconventional ways.

cultural contributions culturally rooted deeds, events, or actions that either made lasting changes and/or dramatically affected a culture.

cultural diversity contrasts, variations, or divergences from the ways of the mainstream or majority culture that, either singly or interactively, exert influence on individuals and on society.

cultural identity numerous cultural elements of a group that influence a person's individuality and identity.

cultural pluralism a social state based on the premise that all newcomers have a right to maintain their languages and cultures while combining with others to form a new society reflective of differences.

cultural schemas   the social conventions establishing the acceptable ways to behave in a culture or society. Information in schemes represents the way the particular cultural group interprets reality.

cultural values   a group's common beliefs in essential principles of life, rooted in a specific culture.

culture   the way of life of a social group, including all of its materials and nonmaterial products that are transmitted from one generation to the next.

curriculum   practically all "that happens" at school that lays out the paths of knowledge teachers and young children will take during the learning journey.

development   process of continuous change observed over time and experienced by all human beings.

developmental milestones   significant events children will exhibit at different periods of life. They describe typical characteristics of a child at a certain time during childhood, such as the onset of talking, walking, and reading.

developmentally appropriate practice (DAP)   a concept that defines quality in early childhood practices based on cultural and developmental elements.

diversity   a social concept and a frame of reference that acknowledges and celebrates a variety of characteristics such as culture, language, religion, ethnicity, nationality, social class, exceptionality, gender, age, and sexual orientation, among others.

early childhood curriculum   the formal and informal experiences through which young children are empowered to continue the process of knowledge acquisition and development.

early intervention   programs and services provided to young children (birth to age 5) with at-risk characteristics and their families, aimed at enhancing and promoting the children's developmental potential.

eclectic   a combination of two or more ideas or approaches to produce a new vision, solve a problem, achieve a goal, or define a position.

educational equity   access to the same educational resources and opportunities for all children, despite their diverse characteristics.

English language learners (ELL)   individuals who are learning English as a second language.

environment   the social and emotional tone, physical arrangement, and cognitive opportunities of the learning setting that influence the nature of experiences taking place.

equality   equal treatment under the law for all individuals in a society.

equity   equal distribution and access to resources and services for all regardless of their differences.

ethnic group   a social unit that shares a common culture and history.

exploration   the unstructured process of learning filled with random experiences and directed by the child.

family   a basic unit of society in traditional and nontraditional configurations responsible for the welfare and the raising of the child.

family configurations   the variety of combinations of individuals found in a family unit.

family involvement   activities and programs planned for the purpose of establishing effective ways to encourage the participation of all the family members involved in the education and appropriate development of the child.

family rituals   practices depicting rites and ceremonies performed by families across cultures with the intent to signify and mark a particular event.

family structure   the composition and associated roles of family members.

first language   refers to the language that is first learned by an individual; also called *home language*.

goal   a statement that defines the intent and aspirations of a program or of an activity.

goals and objectives   actions and purposes of the education process aimed at knowledge acquisition and appropriate development of the young child.

heritage language   the ancestral language first learned and spoken by an individual or a group.

immigrants   individuals from a country or a nation who settle in another country for various reasons, such as political differences, economic need, or family needs.

immigration   process experienced by those who leave their country and come to live in another one.

inquiry   a process of examination and appraisal whereby the child begins to consider his or her own beliefs while comparing them to the beliefs of others.

instructional experiences   activities developed around goals and specific objectives, usually organized around a specific developmental area or topic and intended to promote acquisition of concepts and skills.

instructional materials   broad categories of objects ranging from commercially produced resources to teacher-made classroom materials, real objects, objects on the walls and hanging from the ceiling, the costumes in the play chest, and any items that promote learning.

intervention   any special efforts done to assist the child who may not be performing to his or her potential.

involvement   collaborative participation of families, parents, the community, and the school in the development and education of the child.

learning encounter   activity especially designed to lead the child into the active self-discovery of a given set of ideas, skills, or knowledge.

M

material culture   those overt or tangible aspects of a culture that are easily observed. These include ways of decoration, what people eat, manners, and what they wear.

migrants   individuals who relocate to a different geographical region of one country or cross borders of other countries on a temporary but regular basis for a specific reason. (For example, farm workers move seasonally from one state to another to pick oranges.)

model   a conceptual framework of sequential stages and processes designed to meet a specific purpose or to complete a process.

multicultural content   the "what" of children's experience, which is defined by its significance, validity, interest, and usefulness.

multicultural curriculum   developmentally-based learning experiences developed with an embedded focus on diversity and cultural aspects.

multicultural early childhood educator   a teacher with a professional commitment to offer children from birth through 8 years of age specially designed developmental experiences, where both the child's immediate multicultural realities and those of the nation are considered and valued.

multicultural education   a comprehensive education process, inclusive of diversity elements, that is rooted in the principles of equality and equity for all children. It challenges racism and other forms of discrimination in schools and society and accepts and affirms the pluralism (ethnic, racial, linguistic, religious, economic, gender, and exceptionalities) that students, their communities, and teachers represent.

multicultural ethnic group   a group whose members claim to belong to more than one cultural, ethnic, or racial group.

multicultural literature   the collection of literature depicting ethnic groups and other elements of diversity.

multicultural society   a society where groups of many different ethnicities and extractions have come together to form a culturally diverse, pluralistic nation.

multiculturalism   a philosophical position and movement that assumes that the gender, ethnic, racial, and cultural diversity of a pluralistic society should be reflected in all the institutionalized structures of educational institutions, including the staff, the norms and values, the curriculum, and the student body.

multiple perspectives learning   the process of discovering reality through more than one point of view.

needs assessment an evaluation process used to determine the needs of a group or of an individual in which the results are used to develop culturally and developmentally appropriate activities and programs.

non-European Americans a broad category that includes all those who are not, or whose ancestors were not originally, from any part of Europe.

nonmaterial culture represents those things not overtly seen but discovered through interaction with people of a specific culture. Nonmaterial aspects include ideas, values, ethics, beliefs, and behaviors.

nontraditional family a family with a configuration different from the heterosexual two-parent model.

objective a statement that establishes the specific purposes for a learning activity or an exercise. It describes the nature and the level of knowledge the student will derive from the experience.

planning the process through which actions are taken and decisions are made to accomplish a chosen goal and the way the directions and procedures for implementation are selected and organized.

prejudice a social perspective and an attitude of negative nature not supported by facts or evidence and based on ideas and stereotypes about individuals and/or groups.

process ways and procedures used by teachers to deliver the curriculum content.

race the physical characteristics of a large group of people with somewhat similar genetic history.

racial awareness process of becoming cognizant of own racial characteristics and those of others. It emerges in early life and progresses accordingly with experiences. It is influenced by interactions in the environment and with adults.

second language acquisition a process consisting of stages for acquiring a new language. Many children acquire a second language while learning their first language.

socialization the process through which individuals learn the accepted patterns of behavior and interactions in the context of the society to which they belong. During the process, adults pass on to the young the group's social concepts that will mold them in consonance with their patterns.

stereotype an oversimplified generalization about a particular group, race, or sex, which usually carries derogatory implication.

survey an oral or written assessment instrument designed to get specific answers from a designated constituency. Similar to a questionnaire, a survey usually consists of a list of open- or close-ended statements designed to elicit information about targeted points or issues.

traditional family a basic societal unit typically represented by a heterosexual, legally married two-parent family.

tolerance an attitude of open-mindedness and understanding of diverse individuals and groups that promotes socially acceptable interactions.

utilization activities and opportunities offered to help the child apply what has been learned.

BEFORE WE END, A WORD TO THE READER

Caminante, no hay camino. Se hace camino al andar. [Traveler, there is no road. You blaze it as you go.]

Antonio Machado (1875–1939)

We could not conclude this work without saying to our readers: "Congratulations on your determination to explore how to create multicultural classrooms for young children!" Now that you are familiar with the basic knowledge about multiculturalism and have the working tools for teaching about diversity, the rest of the challenge is up to you. This is your opportunity to become a change agent for educational reform on behalf of young children. You can now put into practice your own ideas regarding diversity and education. This is, in fact, your best opportunity to demonstrate your personal and professional commitment to equality for young children.

We believe that one of the traits that best defines early childhood educators is the fact that they are people with strong beliefs. First, they believe in children; second, they believe they can make a difference in the lives of children. They also believe in the special talents and potential for success every child brings to the classroom. Early childhood educators are also dreamers. They dream all children will develop and flourish to give our society a hope for a future of continued progress. Such people are committed to equality as their fundamental ideal. Early childhood educators also realize that equality is still not fully evident in many young children's programs and services in the United States and in other countries around the world. Although considerable progress has been achieved, much still remains to be done, not only in our country but in the countries around the world, and early childhood educators believe that some of the most important victories for equal rights are won in young children's classrooms. Understanding humankind's quest for equality will help early childhood educators gain a better appreciation for the efforts of multicultural educators around the world.

The future is dependent on the ability of today's children to successfully face tomorrow's challenges. Education is the tool society provides to accomplish that mission. All efforts to guarantee and support equality and equity in education are an investment in our survival as a strong, advanced global society. Implementing an effective multicultural education system will facilitate the successful management of the diverse environments in which all of us live. Quality multicultural education for all children must be a global mandate for the twenty-first century.

Multicultural early childhood teaching is still unfolding. Although there are examples and ideas that tell us how it should be done, additional efforts are still required to give this kind of teaching its definitive shape. The challenge sometimes seems insurmountable. However, the beliefs that brought you here and your determination to provide an empowering environment for young children will let you conquer the obstacles. We have faith in your ability to create culturally empowering environments and classrooms for all our children. We know you will succeed because early childhood educators are people who have the courage to dare because they believe in children. That's why we believe in you.

> *Never doubt that a small group of thoughtful, committed people can change the world. Indeed, it's the only thing that ever has.*
>
> Margaret Mead (1901–1978)

INDEX